Arthur Frommer's

BRANSON!

by Arthur Frommer

MACMILLAN • USA

MACMILLAN TRAVEL
A Prentice Hall Macmillan Company
15 Columbus Circle
New York, NY 10023

ISBN 0-028-60256-0
LC 94-73809

Design by George McKeon
Maps by Ortelius Design

SPECIAL SALES

Bulk purchases (10+ copies) of Frommer's Travel Guides are available to corporations at special discounts. The Special Sales Department can produce custom editions to be used as premiums and/or for sales promotion to suit individual needs. Existing editions can be produced with custom cover imprints such as corporate logos. For more information write to: Special Sales, Macmillan, 15 Columbus Circle, New York, NY 10023.

Manufactured in the United States of America

10 9 8 7 6 5 4 3 2 1

To

Roberta

with deepest love

About the Author

ARTHUR FROMMER is America's foremost travel writer. Author of the famous *Europe on $5 a Day,* which launched the Frommer Travel Guide series, he has written scores of best-selling travel guides. He has been featured as a travel expert on the NBC Today Show, the Oprah Winfrey Show, and Regis and Kathy Lee. In addition to hosting his own popular nationwide radio call-in show, he also contributes to such leading publications as *Travel Holiday Magazine* and *Consumers Digest.* A graduate of Yale University Law School, he served with U. S. Army Intelligence during the Korean War, and later practiced law with the firm of the late Adlai Stevenson. He now devotes his full time to travel. As a keen observer of travel trends, Arthur Frommer was one of the first travel professionals to discover the phenomenon called Branson.

Contents

Maps

Preface: The Ozarks and Me

Although I didn't know it at the time, I visited an area near Branson when I was 10 and 11 years old. We lived then, my family and I, in Jefferson City, Missouri, over the quarters of a Mrs. Raithel, whose elderly father had relatives in the Ozarks. On several weekends, he took me in his car to visit them, and I spent a part of those joyful holidays listening to what were then called "hillbillies," as they played their fiddles and sang country songs.

It was the depths of the Depression, in 1939 and 1940. The poverty-stricken people of the Ozarks (this was a region closer to the Lake of the Ozarks, north of Branson) were very different from what many of them are today. Their homes were more like shacks. On the walls of their one-room abodes were, invariably, pictures of Democrat Franklin D. Roosevelt torn from a newspaper.

They were populists. They believed that a prime function of government was to assist the underprivileged. They disliked large corporations intensely and had a similar disregard for the wealthy. They had no interest in show business celebrities, and wouldn't dream of standing in a line for autographs. They had a personal dignity to them.

They wore their religion lightly, making no public show of it. Their patriotism was in their hearts and not on garish display. They worshiped in their own way and respected the right of others to do the same. Their preachers were poor, same as them, and they would have been flabbergasted to hear that a minister had become a mega-millionaire, like Pat Robertson, or engaged actively in partisan politics, like Jerry Falwell, or wore expensive jewelry or custom-tailored suits, as used to be the vogue before the downfall of Tammy and Jim Bakker.

They were, in sum, about as far as you can get from the movement today known as the "religious right." They would never have been the political allies of the rich. They would have hated the idea of performers amassing giant personal fortunes from publicly displayed patriotism, or immense trust funds, mansions, and investments from religious production numbers. Indeed, they would have been astonished to see performers charging admission at all to gospel-singing, let alone the gospel performed with scenery, costumes, and laser lights.

I am convinced that a majority of the present-day residents of Branson continue to share those basic values of their Depression-era grandparents; that they agree, with me, that some show business interests in their community have gone over the line into vulgarity. While proud of the impressive entertainment achievements that have made their city into a massive tourist destination, they would prefer, I think, for some of the Branson theaters to step back from right-wing excess and leave political and religious proselytizing to others. And I believe, therefore, that they will welcome this book, which attempts to distinguish between what I regard as the many attractive aspects of Branson and its fewer ugly ones. Certainly, if Branson is to grow, it must extend its appeal to a broader number of Americans who do not share right-wing ideologies; it has gone about as far as it can go with its present audience, and must certainly reach out to more.

In the hope that those goals will be understood, I present this book about an immensely entertaining American city—Branson, Missouri—with its remarkable theaters devoted to country music and other popular performing arts.

An Author's Note

Our readers will, of course, want to keep in mind theaters change, schedules change, and in Branson one or two theaters change their headliners in the course of a year. Although every effort was made to obtain accurate information for 1995-96, we obviously cannot be responsible for such changes, and suggest that you always phone ahead before relying on a particular date, price, time of performance, or performer.

An Additional Note

Please be advised that travel information is subject to change at any time—and this is especially true of prices. We therefore suggest that you write or call ahead for confirmation when making your travel plans. The authors, editors, and publisher cannot be held responsible for the experiences of readers while traveling. Your safety is important to us, however, so we encourage you to stay alert and be aware of your surroundings. Keep a close eye on cameras, purses, and wallets, all favorite targets of thieves and pickpockets.

1

An Introduction to the New "Broadway" of the Ozarks

Why 6 Million Americans Now Travel to Branson

You are about to begin an odyssey to a place of which you have probably never heard. Branson, Missouri, is—to date—a regional phenomenon of America's "southern Midwest." But it is so massively popular in that region, so heavily visited by millions from that area, so breathtaking in its growth, that there is no doubt at all about its eventual emergence onto the national scene. To the ranks of Las Vegas and Orlando, Branson is about to be added, with visitor numbers only slightly less than theirs.

It is a classic boomtown marked by construction cranes and the steel girders of massive new hotels and theaters. On the outskirts, trailer camps erupt to house thousands of job-seeking migrants from less favored places. Everywhere, feverish would-be entrepreneurs rush from one "for rent" sign to another, anxious to add their own brand of t-shirts and towels to a mountain of Branson souvenirs.

The Sound of Music

The phenomenon of Branson is based, essentially, on a cultural yearning almost identical to the urge that draws millions of people each year to Broadway theaters, and once drew multitudes of ancient Greeks to the stages of Athens and Epidaurus. It is the desire to enjoy performance art in a group setting, as large as possible, among kindred people, by the thousands. In this instance, it is a love for folk music—"country music"—presented not in small taverns, as is usually the case in Nashville, but in thousand- and two-thousand-seat theaters featuring lavish stage settings, and choruses, and near-mythical idols of the art, about whom the shows (or at least most of them) are focused. Celebrity theaters—of which there are now 32 in town, with more coming—are the main attractions of Branson, and periodically throughout the year, most of the great names associated with the past 60-year history of country are featured on their marquees.

"Country" Triumphant

Roy Clark and Box Car Willie, Johnny Cash and Jim Stafford, Loretta Lynn and Kenny Rogers, the Osmond Brothers and Anita Bryant, Barbara Mandrell and Dolly Parton, Glen Campbell and Charley Pride, dozens more, all present themselves for runs of at least a month, and some of them now appear on nearly every night of the year—as hard to believe as that may seem. Country stars now make their homes in Branson, and regard a once-a-night appearance here as much easier than a long road tour taking them to a different town every night.

In Branson, the demand for country is so powerful that some theaters present it throughout the day, as if they were whetting their guests' appetites for the glittering, smash performance of the evening. On a gradually ascending level of quality, they begin at 8am with the Lennon Brothers (not the sisters! at the Stage Door Canteen restaurant of the Lawrence Welk Champagne Theater), continue at 9am with low-priced shows of lesser names (Buck Trent's Breakfast Theater, "Waltzing Waters," with John and Paul Cody), reopen at 10am with more acts (*Jennifer in the Morning* at the Roy Clark Theater, the Brumley Show at the 76 Music Hall, Jimmy Travis's *Morning Mania*), offer matinees at 2pm (Mickey Gilley, Bobby Vinton, the Osmond Family, Berosini & Van Burch), and tea-time performers at 4pm (*Texas Gold Miners*) and 5pm (Yakov Smirnoff at the Osmond Family Theater). The result is as many as 50 or 60 daily performances throughout the Branson area, confronting the visitor with a dizzying problem of choice. It's scarcely surprising that Nashville, with its single Grand Ole Opry on the outskirts of town, and scattered downtown tavern performers, should now have been overtaken in its performance venues by the vaster scope of Branson (although Nashville remains the center of the country music recording industry and the preferred location for the younger, modern stars of country music).

Add: The Music of Nostalgia

But what began as a single-minded showplace for country music has now grown to include a much broader range of musical entertainment. Though country is the hard core of Branson and accounts for most of the shows, it has now been supplemented by theaters headlining popular songs of the '40s and '50s, and other classic American compositions unrelated to pure country. A bevy of celebrated ex-TV stars has descended in recent years on Branson and revolutionized its theater scene. Andy Williams at his Moon River Theater, Bobby Vinton at his Blue Velvet Theater (also housing the Glenn Miller Orchestra), Pat Boone in the *Will Rogers Follies,* John Davidson at the John Davidson Theater, Tony Orlando at Tony Orlando's Yellow Ribbon Theater, and more, have all proved amazing draws, still potent in their appeal to middle America. As you read this guidebook, one group has just resurrected Lawrence Welk and has begun operating a proudly sentimental Champagne Theater to feature the melodies and approach of the long-dead bandleader.

The music of nostalgia has thus joined the tunes of country and created an even broader audience for the celebrity theaters.

Enter: A Daily Carnival

And in the wake of these more "modern" noncountry attractions have come a flood of mini-theme parks (Heartland America, Sportopia, Mutton Hollow), magical illusion shows (done with all the color and scope of major Las Vegas acts), go-carts and family fun parks, giant Imax theaters *(Sinking of the* Titanic, *Grand Canyon),* scenic railroads, animal acts, mammoth outdoor historical pageants ("Shepherd of the Hills") and water parks, paddle-wheel boat rides *(Showboat Branson Belle)* and fishing trips, and upward of a dozen major shopping malls and arcades with manufacturers' discount outlets.

Everything Except . . .

What doesn't Branson have? To answer that question requires that, for a moment, we jump ahead of our story. It forces us to trespass a bit into our next chapter dealing with the history and growth of Branson, the events that caused it to develop a distinctive audience that is only now broadening to include a greater cross-section of the American public. But briefly, while most other places of entertainment in America have evolved with the times, have become increasingly open-minded, daring, explicit, and sophisticated, Branson hasn't. It is stubbornly mainstream and proper, immune to the sexual revolution, proudly old-fashioned. In Branson (at least for the time being), people don't swear or dress scantily, drink to excess, or doubt the old-time verities. And thus one finds everything in Branson except casinos; every form of music except rock, disco, heavy metal, and rap; every kind of squeaky clean distraction. The common element here is nostalgia and escape: a return to a simpler time, the America that once was, the idealization of a once-dominant majority culture, religion, and unquestioning patriotism. Branson is a family attraction to dwarf all others; it is the nirvana of the senior citizen as well; it is a heaven for people of quiet lives who yearn, just once, to be part of the glittering world of celebrities; and it is an undeniable capital of entertainment that expects to receive upward of 9 million visitors a year in a very short time from now.

We'll have a great deal to say—both pro and con—about the themes of entertainment in Branson, about its atmosphere, about what parts of it will appeal to you and what parts offend. Some Americans come here because the culture of Branson is their own. Others are bemused observers. An increasing number come here to view a strange "foreign" culture, almost as if they were sociologists visiting an isolated South Pacific island. Some come to scoff, but are then surprised to find pleasure in country ways, country music, country cuisine. Others are attracted by the newer aspects of Branson, and especially its recent experiments with popular American music of the '40s and '50s. In time, as a more representative group of Americans begins to mix with the area's traditional tourists, Branson will change (indeed, the process has already begun).

To explore how that change is coming about is the goal of our next chapter, dealing with the development of Branson. I think your enjoyment of this emerging entertainment capital will be enhanced if you know a bit of its history.

2

Branson: How It Got That Way

The Strange 90-Year History of America's Newest Entertainment Capital

It all began with a book, *The Shepherd of the Hills,* by a minister-turned-novelist named Harold Bell Wright. In 1907, his rhapsodic description of an earthly paradise in the hills of the Ozarks sold over a million copies in hardcover to become an American best-seller on the order of *Uncle Tom's Cabin*. In the following years, it sold millions more, as did other inspirational novels of Harold Bell Wright.

That book was about Branson. It told of a world-weary minister from Chicago (obviously, Wright) who had fled from personal tragedy and urban stress (as Wright had) to live with the simple, mountain people of a place called Mutton Hollow, in the southernmost portion of Missouri, near the Arkansas border. Mutton Hollow is a valley that sits just outside today's Branson. In dramatic plot twists and breathless descriptions of mountain violence, betrayal, vengeance, and redemption, Wright created a page-turner, a mystery that you couldn't put down, a whale of a story (we'll summarize its plot when we get to the nightly *Shepherd of the Hills* pageant on a vast outdoor stage near Branson, in our theater chapter). But more important than his fast-moving story line and its surprise ending was Wright's depiction of many of the so-called hillbillies of southwestern Missouri as the kindest and gentlest of people, a generally wise people, drawn by Wright with such sympathy, affection, and admiration that all of America fell in love with them. People idealized such Ozark characters (based, in some instances, on real people) as Wright's Uncle Matt and Aunt Mollie, the wise Samantha (Sammy) Lane, her father Daddy Jim Lane, the giant Young Matt, and Poor Pete, the shepherd himself. And they not only bought the book—they resolved to visit the area where these personages had supposedly lived.

What occurred, starting around 1908, was a tourist movement of sorts, a pilgrimage by thousands of Americans seeking to view the site and the characters of *The Shepherd of the Hills*. Using rail lines that had just been completed (Wright mentions the coming of those railroads in his final chapters), they came to the depot at Hollister, then the main rail hub in these parts, but made their way to Branson. Several residents of Branson in the ensuing years, people who *were* the models for Harold Bell Wright's characters, graciously received their out-of-state admirers and spun yarns for them from their rocking chairs on their porches. Other Branson residents began turning their homes into guest houses, and as you wander the streets of downtown Branson today, you will see some of the old structures that became inns of a sort because of Wright's book. It is clear that in those early years was laid the necessary foundation—in the form of a hospitality structure—for Branson's touristic explosion—and success—in future times.

They Stay to Fish

But though they came to view scenes of the shepherd and his gentle, admirable Ozark characters, the tourists stayed to fish and enjoy the nature of the Ozarks. In 1913, the completion of Ozark Beach Dam on the White River created a major recreational lake—Bull Shoals—to the east of Branson. The tourist figures increased, and more and more vacationers came to stay in the tourist homes and lodges of Branson and its vicinity. Others came to Branson to visit a famous nearby cave—Marvel Cave—whose owners had perfected the means of touring its dark chambers by mule. Gradually, the visitor figures mounted.

And then, starting in the late 1950s, the convergence of three phenomena—additional dams, better cave visits, and shoestring shows of country music—suddenly began to build the touristic figures into substantial ones, laying a foundation for the later celebrity theaters.

The dams were built by the federal government, that institution so hated by Branson's culture today. To bring electricity into the region, the Army Corps of Engineers constructed an enormous

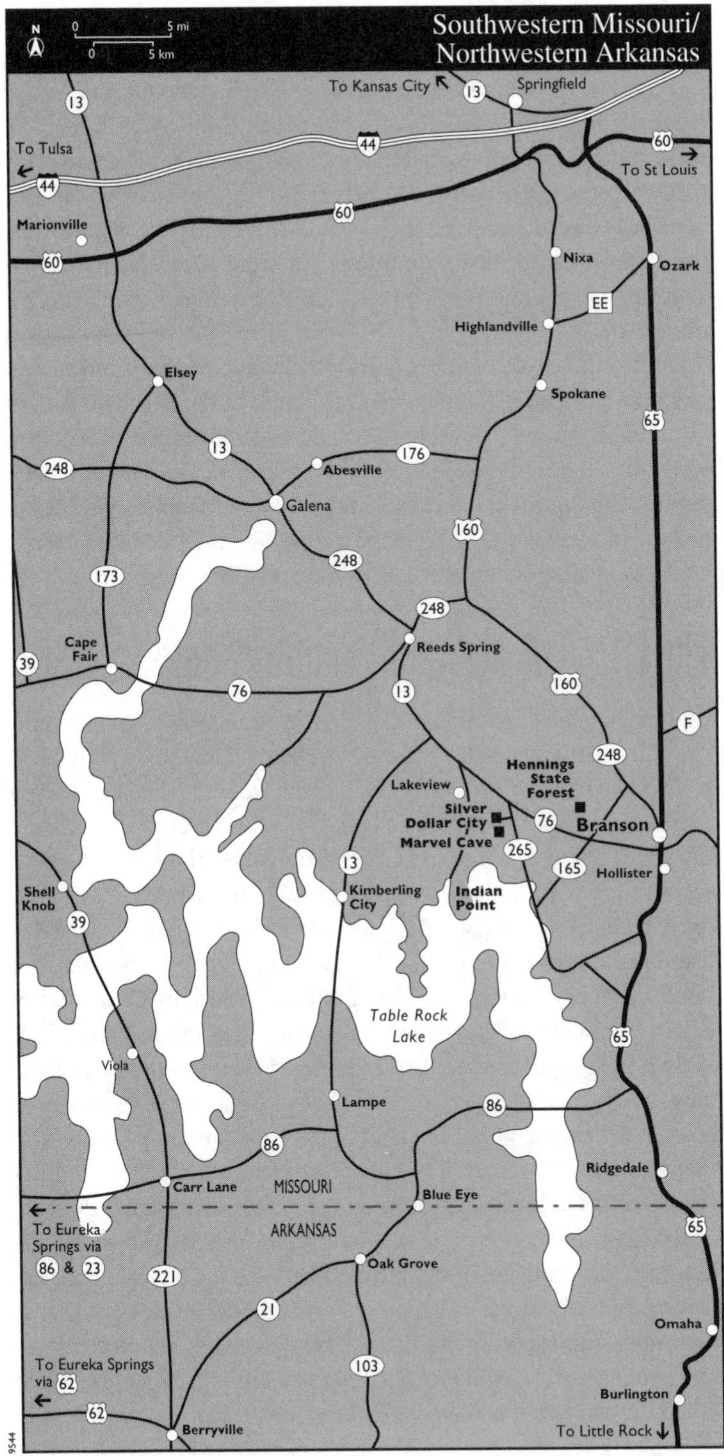
Southwestern Missouri/
Northwestern Arkansas
N
0 5 mi
0 5 km
To Kansas City
Springfield
To Tulsa
To St Louis
Marionville
Nixa
Ozark
Highlandville
Elsey
Spokane
Abesville
Galena
Cape Fair
Reeds Spring
Hennings State Forest
Lakeview
Silver Dollar City
Marvel Cave
Branson
Hollister
Shell Knob
Kimberling City
Indian Point
Table Rock Lake
Viola
Lampe
Ridgedale
Carr Lane
MISSOURI
Blue Eye
ARKANSAS
To Eureka Springs via 86 & 23
Oak Grove
Omaha
To Eureka Springs via 62
Burlington
Berryville
To Little Rock
9544

dam at the other end of the White River, just a few miles from downtown Branson. Behind the thick concrete barrier, Table Rock Lake arose, with hundreds of miles of shoreline that in time would attract homesites and resort developments. More and more midwesterners resolved to vacation around the new lake. The two dams that now occupied both ends of the White River converted that waterway into Lake Taneycomo, and the frigid temperatures of the latter created ideal conditions for trout—and trout fishing. Thus additional numbers came to the Branson area, this time for trout fishing.

Around the same time, a Chicago family (the Herschends) that had bought Marvel Cave decided to improve conditions for visiting it by installing a cog railway inside. More visitors to Branson were attracted, some 50,000 a year by 1957. As a means of further publicizing the cave, the Herschends decided to build a simulated, turn-of-the-century Ozark village called Silver Dollar City alongside the opening to that cave. Still more visitors came.

The First Two Makeshift Country Shows

Building on that continuously developing foundation—a small-but-lively touristic presence that could trace its heritage directly back to *The Shepherd of the Hills*—a Branson family called the Mabes decided, in 1960, "to put on a show," an evening of Ozarks music. They rehearsed at home with their banjos and fiddles, rented the second floor of the modest town hall for the weekends, installed folding chairs, sent their wives out with sandwich boards to advertise the show to fishermen at the lake, and called themselves the "Baldknobbers," after a real-life group of notorious 19th-century Branson vigilantes, who had also been depicted in the Harold Bell Wright novel. Though the Mabes at first held on to their day jobs, they were soon to make Baldknobbers into a lucrative full-time business. Several years later, another Branson-area family, the Presleys (no relation to Elvis), set up a modest stage on a quiet road—West Highway 76—occupying a ridge outside the little town of Branson. There they, too, played country music. And soon visitors began arriving not only for Silver Dollar City, the cave, and the fishing, but for the area's evening shows. A few motels opened, at first modest, preserving the surrounding greenery and forest. Visitors could see deer, could feel themselves still in the country, while lodged in modern rooms.

Enter the Celebrity Theaters

The rest is history—show biz-style. In 1968, Baldknobbers moved out to the same West Highway 76, built a proper theater there. In the early to mid-1970s, two or three others—the Foggy River Boys, the Plummer Family—joined them on the same stretch of road. And then in 1983, the breakthrough: Roy Clark of "Hee Haw" TV fame, a recognized name, a truly national figure, built a theater that bore his name on the same West Highway 76, and the rush was on. From all over America, country performers honed in on Branson and scrambled to line up bankers who would build them a celebrity theater on the about-to-be-famous "Strip."

The "Stars" Who Came to Branson

From the start, and down to the present day, the performers who opened theaters in Branson, or signed on for lengthy appearances of several weeks or more, were not the younger practitioners of country or the slender, youthful stars in black jeans, whose country music has acquired a contemporary flavor. Especially today, the Branson performers are not the ones whose records get played heavily on radio or are heard by a vast young audience. In fact, many of the older names who did appear in Branson, and appear there today, are no longer played on radio at all, and some of the Branson stars have bitterly complained about being frozen out of the modern country music industry. Later, in our theater chapter, we'll tell you about a song performed by country great Glen Campbell at his Branson theater. The lyrics tell of a graying country singer who's "too old for videos," too removed from the current tastes, and not wanted anymore. So what does he do? "He's building a mansion . . . in Branson," sings Campbell, triumphantly.

Except for a rare fleeting appearance by one or two of them, current country stars like Garth Brooks, Travis Tritt, Wynonna Judd, Joe Diffie, George Jones, Tanya Tucker, Tim McGraw, Carlene Carter, John Michael Montgomery, Holly Dunn, Brother Phelps, and Trisha Yearwood seldom appear in Branson. Their country sound is too modern, their lyrics too advanced and controversial, their appearance often too youthful. Their headquarters is Nashville; some of them occasionally refer to Branson as "Jurassic Park."

Rather, the performers of Branson are those who deliver the pure country sound of the past, the older classics of country, the country unaffected by modern attitudes and musical experiments, the country that isn't combined with or influenced by other recent musical approaches. Though such performers aren't currently hired by the record companies, for whom Nashville is headquarters, they flourish in Branson, and make Branson into a species of museum, a "Hall of Fame" if you'd like. And the reason has much to do with the kind of early Branson audience that reacted to the opening of the celebrity theaters there. That audience—a fixed and finite one that may now have reached its demographic limits—craved the music of their youth; the last thing they sought was experimentation with the pure sounds of country.

Branson's Early Audience

The people who came to hear the Presleys, Baldknobbers, Roy Clark, and other early Branson pioneers were from the nearby Midwest, not from afar. They were conservative folk looking for wholesome family entertainment. They came for what was familiar rather than innovative. The performers in these Ozark hills had a strong appeal to people who were put off by almost everything that seemed to rush at them from the late 1960s on: the feminist movement preaching the equality of women, the civil rights movement seeking equality for blacks, the advocates of greater sexual freedoms, the composers of rock 'n' roll music and rap, the increasing violence on TV and in movies, the growing youth culture.

To the early Branson audiences, America was getting out of hand, and it was time to restore an earlier, easier way of life. Branson was to be a haven for the right way of thinking and performing, the antithesis to Hollywood, Las Vegas, and Miami Beach. And the Branson country performers quickly complied. They immediately saw that they had only to play to their audience's sentiments and sense of nostalgia and they would be successful beyond their wildest dreams. Out the window went any further evolution of their country music, any experimentation, any attempt to deal with contemporary life in their lyrics. Nostalgia was the thing, the familiar classics that Branson audiences had heard in their youth. Into every show went flag-waving and gospel, and such has remained the formula to this day. The gap between Branson's country music and that performed in Nashville or on records or over the radio continued to grow. Every single country performer of Branson—Box Car Willie, Roy Clark, Moe Bandy, the charismatic young Japanese violinist Shoji Tabuchi, Mel Tillis, and others—designed their shows to be more like historical retrospectives than showcases for new songs and novel musical approaches. This is not to say that their shows are not enormously satisfying, affecting, in some respects enchanting; they very definitely are—and I, for one, take enormous delight in hearing the skillful renditions of old country numbers in Branson.

The Arrival of a Second Musical Style

The discovery that nostalgia could attract vast throngs to Branson was soon put to use by musicians of a noncountry background. In an amazing development that has greatly broadened the musical appeal of Branson, Andy Williams—the singer of popular romantic ballads, the vocalist for fox-trots—came onto the scene with his own Branson theater in 1991, followed by the Osmond Brothers, Bobby Vinton, and John Davidson in 1992, Tony Orlando, Pat Boone (in the *Will Rogers Follies*), and Broadway's *Pump Boys and Dinettes* in 1993, the Lennon Sisters in a theater named for Lawrence Welk in 1994—not a country singer among them. But they, too, quickly learned how to satisfy a Branson audience. When Pat Boone's *Will Rogers Follies* first opened, letters appeared in the Branson newspaper complaining about the show's dialogue and costumes. The musical's language apparently included one or two hells and damns. The showgirls revealed too much flesh. But Boone quickly squelched the controversy in his own letter to the paper. The language would be cleaned up. Will Rogers's father, as played in the show, would no longer exclaim, "What the hell, Will," but rather, "What the hey, Will." And the showgirls, Boone explained, were now wearing nude-colored bodystockings to protect their modesty.

And Boone's show, having only a tenuous connection with country music, continues to play to large Branson audiences. All over the Strip, and in new theaters on adjoining roads, the romantic ballads of the '40s and '50s have joined the repertoire beloved by fans of the Grand Ole Opry.

From all over, one hears of still further departures from country music themes that are currently planned for Branson. In mid-1994, great excitement was stirred with the announcement that the Radio City Music Hall Rockettes would start regular appearances in Branson for some six weeks each fall, leading up to their annual Christmas show in New York. For 1995, Dolly Parton plans to open a dinner theater of rodeo acts and Civil War pageantry containing no real country music. From several Broadway producers, one hears of additional Broadway musicals—without a country content—that may soon be moved to Branson. Clearly, the regional attraction known as Branson is on its way to becoming a national entertainment center of enormous appeal.

Branson Today

I've tried not only to tell the dramatic story of Branson's growth, but also the history of its special approach to entertainment. I've indicated, too, how other forms of music and entertainment have recently joined the country shows. All this is by way of preparing you for Branson, and for the choices you will soon have to make among its dizzying array of entertainments and attractions.

The story of Branson's physical growth is a more obvious one. With the advent of more and more shows, of an ever broader appeal, the touristic "plant" of Branson (its hotels, restaurants, roads, shops, recreations) has expanded more rapidly than any other American resort city. You have only to look around when you first arrive, at the frantic activity, construction, and movement, to grasp the magnitude of that development—and of its accompanying problems. The traffic, the crowds, the daunting variety of choice among lodgings and food, the alternatives for reaching the city and then negotiating its routes to theaters and other attractions, all require that we deal with certain basics of geography and transportation, before we turn to more exciting matters, like the never-ending round of entertainment that Branson provides.

3

Getting There and Getting Around

Transportation to and Within Regions and a Bit About the Region's Natural Features

Your destination is in the heart of the Ozarks, about 40 miles south of Springfield, Missouri, the largest nearby town. Springfield itself is 220 miles almost due south of Kansas City, and 250 miles southwest of St. Louis.

And what are the Ozarks? They're a 30,000-square-mile area of forested, low mountains that cover, among other places, much of southwestern Missouri and northwestern Arkansas. They are the only major elevation in terrain to be found between the Appalachian Mountain chain in the eastern part of the United States and the Rocky Mountain range in the West.

Yet these are really more like rounded hills than mountains, rarely more than a modest 1,600 feet high. Nevertheless, they are so very hilly and thickly wooded that they were difficult to penetrate before the extensive building of railroads and roads around the turn of the century. The people living here were virtually isolated from most of the commerce and communication of the rest of the nation, and developed a reputation in the late 19th century as unworldly, unlettered hillbillies. Harold Bell Wright did much to change that critical image with his 1907 novel, *The Shepherd of the Hills,* but TV shows like the "Beverly Hillbillies" tended to resurrect the caricature in more recent years.

Using modern roads and air routes, it's no longer difficult at all to explore the Ozarks, and the options are many, from every part of the United States.

Springfield Is the Key

The overwhelming bulk of the visitors to Branson come here by car or bus along broad federal highways; in almost every instance, their destination is busy Springfield, Missouri (population: 130,000), an easy 40 miles from Branson. From Springfield, one simply drives south on U.S. Highway 65 to Branson. The only motoring tourists who don't head into Springfield first are those living in that part of the deep south of the United States, directly underneath Branson, who come via Little Rock, Arkansas, instead.

From Springfield, the drive south to Branson, once you're on Highway 65, is an hour long, on a decent highway that is gradually being widened to four lanes; it's already that broad in scattered sections.

But keep in mind that reaching Highway 65 from the Springfield airport, or from other highways going to the sprawling city of Springfield, is often a matter of 20 minutes or more, and that additional time should be included in your planning, especially if you're to make air connections in Springfield on the return trip. From Springfield Airport, you drive east for 15 minutes or so on Interstate Highway 44 to reach its intersection with Highway 65 (at exit 82 on Highway 44), and then drive south on Highway 65 to Branson. To reach Springfield Airport from Branson, you drive north on Highway 65 to its intersection with Highway 44 (wait until you actually see a turnoff for 44, and avoid all temptations to drive off earlier, for example, at Kearny Road), and then head west on 44 to reach the airport in 15 minutes more.

By Car or Bus, All the Way

Springfield itself is reached on excellent highways from the 10 major cities surrounding it.

From **Chicago,** you reach Springfield and then Branson by taking U.S. Highway 55 (a four-lane interstate) south to St. Louis, and then the equally speedy U.S. Highway 44 in a southwesterly direction to Springfield; from Springfield, you drive south to Branson on U.S. Highway 65, a distance of 40 miles. The total drive from Chicago, one-way, is 539 miles.

From **Des Moines,** you reach Springfield and Branson by driving south on U.S. Highway 35 (another big interstate) to Kansas City, then on Highway 13 south to Springfield, then on Highway 65 south to Branson. Total distance: 414 miles.

From **St. Louis,** you reach Springfield and Branson by taking U.S. Highway 44 in a southwesterly direction to Springfield, and then U.S. Highway 65 south to Branson: a total of 250 miles.

From **Kansas City,** you drive east for a short distance on U.S. Highway 70 to Highway 13, then south on 13 to Springfield, and on U.S. Highway 65 farther south to Branson: a total of around 220 miles.

From **Topeka, Kansas,** you first take U.S. Interstate 70 east to Kansas City, and then follow Kansas City instructions (above) south to Springfield and then Branson. Total trip: 281 miles.

From **Wichita, Kansas,** you drive north on U.S. Interstate 35 to Kansas City, then east on Highway 70 and south on Highway 13 to Springfield, and from there south on Highway 65 to Branson. Total distance: 307 miles.

From **Oklahoma City,** you drive on U.S. Interstate 44 in a northeasterly direction to and through Tulsa to Springfield, and then turn south to Branson on Highway 65. Total mileage: 302 miles.

From **Tulsa,** you drive northeast on U.S. Highway 44 to Springfield, then south to Branson on Highway 65. Total mileage: only 183 miles.

From **Little Rock, Arkansas,** you simply go north on Highway 65 to Branson, a distance of only 177 miles.

From **Nashville,** you drive due west on Highway 60 to Springfield, and then due south from Springfield to Branson on Highway 65. Total distance: 486 miles.

Planning to drive to Branson from more remote cities? The mileages are as follows: from New York (1,290), Cleveland (811), Dallas (440), Denver (831), Indianapolis (494), Los Angeles (1,641), Memphis (292), Milwaukee (626), Minneapolis (662), Omaha (407), Orlando (1,072).*

And always remember that Springfield has a Greyhound bus depot and receives a great many interstate buses each day. Thus, some tourists let others do the driving for that first segment of their trip, and then rent a car in Springfield for the shorter leg south to Branson.

By Air to Springfield, Then by Car to Branson

Other visitors fly into Springfield Regional Airport, and then rent a car for the trip to Branson. While Springfield is no Chicago or Dallas, it is nevertheless a valid destination by air and enjoys frequent service on Northwest, TWA, American Airlines, United Airlines, and USAir, among others, to and from other larger airline hubs.

Planes fly nonstop and directly to Springfield from St. Louis, Kansas City, Chicago, Denver, Nashville, Memphis, and Dallas.

From **St. Louis,** you can fly on TWA to Springfield, and then drive the short route south to Branson.

From **Kansas City,** you can fly on USAir Express to Springfield, and then go by rental car to Branson.

From **Chicago,** you can fly to Springfield on either American Airlines or its commuter service, American Eagle.

From **Dallas,** you can fly to Springfield on American Airlines, American Eagle, or Delta Connection.

From **Denver,** you reach Springfield on United Airlines.

From **Memphis,** you can fly to Springfield on Northwest Airlink.

From **Nashville,** you can fly to Springfield on American Airlines or American Eagle.

*I'm indebted to the Ozarks Marketing Council for these instructive figures.

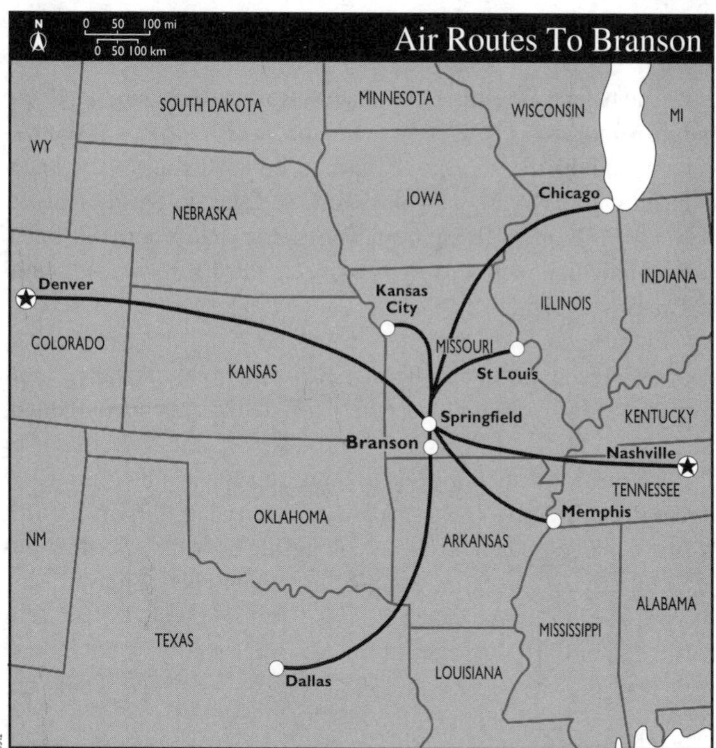

N
0 50 100 mi
0 50 100 km
Air Routes To Branson
SOUTH DAKOTA
MINNESOTA
WISCONSIN
MI
WY
NEBRASKA
IOWA
Chicago
INDIANA
Denver
Kansas City
ILLINOIS
COLORADO
MISSOURI
KANSAS
St Louis
Springfield
KENTUCKY
Branson
Nashville
TENNESSEE
OKLAHOMA
Memphis
NM
ARKANSAS
ALABAMA
MISSISSIPPI
TEXAS
Dallas
LOUISIANA
9542

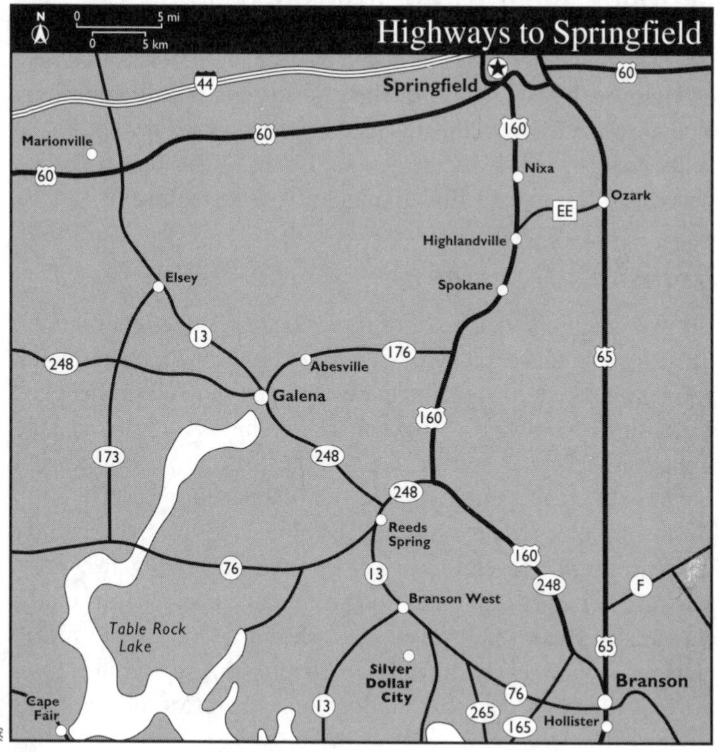

N
0 5 mi
0 5 km
Highways to Springfield
44
Springfield
60
Marionville
160
Nixa
Ozark
EE
Highlandville
Elsey
Spokane
13
248
176
Abesville
65
Galena
160
173
248
Reeds Spring
76
160
F
Branson West
Table Rock Lake
Silver Dollar City
Branson
Cape Fair
265
165
Hollister
9543

And from New York, Los Angeles, Boston, Philadelphia, Pittsburgh, Minneapolis/St. Paul, Washington, D.C., Baltimore, Atlanta, Miami, and others, you can fly into St. Louis or Kansas City, and connect with TWA flights going from St. Louis to Springfield, or with USAir Express flying from Kansas City to Springfield. Once in Springfield, of course, you drive by car the 40 or so miles south to Branson, on Highway 65.

Eight nationwide car rental companies—all the well-known names—are found at or near Springfield Airport, and generally you'll pay about $160 for a week's rental of a mid-size car, with unlimited mileage.

It is probable that in years to come, companies will be flying directly into Branson's own small M. Graham Clark Airport (owned by the College of the Ozarks and alongside it), which is currently used by private planes. A group calling themselves Branson Airlines did so for a time (from Kansas City, St. Louis, Dallas, and Nashville) in 1993, then interrupted their service in 1994, but claims they may resume service in 1995. You can reach the would-be Branson airline by dialing toll free 800/422-4247.

Getting Around Within Branson

About an hour after you have begun the ride south from Springfield on Highway 65 you will reach the Branson area; you'll know it by a pickup in activity, billboards, and buildings of every type (especially your first celebrity theater, Pat Boone's *Will Rogers Follies,* which you'll spot on a hill looking down at the highway).

Branson's Downtown

But you are in the real heart of things only when, going south on 65, you come to the junction with West Highway 76. At this point, you can either turn right (and west) to the famous theater- and motel-lined Strip (more about that later) or—if you're an avid sightseer—left (and east) to the "original" Branson. I'd turn left and head downhill; and if you do, you'll notice that West Highway 76 soon becomes Main Street. You are now in historic, pre-country music Branson, a several square-block area of charming, two-story, early 20th-century buildings along a riverlike lake that make up a classic American small town. Though they're of a more recent vintage than the scaled-down Main Street U.S.A. shops and stores of Walt Disney's Magic Kingdom (and therefore not quite as attractive as Disney's idealized late 19th-century town), they are a touching sight for Americans from large industrial cities, and some visitors have their very first encounter with an old-fashioned American small town when they first enter downtown Branson. It's an attraction in itself, and well repays a decision, later, to stroll about its quiet commercial streets.

The fact that the original downtown of Branson has been maintained, refurbished, preserved, and protected from modern incursions (all the buildings here are period structures); the fact that every storefront is occupied by a going concern, that none is shuttered up, but all are vital and active; the discovery that residents, not simply tourists, stroll up and down here and patronize these old-fashioned restaurants and cafes, maintaining a community life; the fact that the area contains an authentic five-and-dime (Dick's 5&10) of 1920s vintage, barber shops and cafes whose interiors haven't changed in 60 years, as well as fishing docks along the narrow "lake" at the bottom of Main Street—is all a great achievement of Branson's downtown merchants and community. It didn't happen without action and struggle, and it serves as an inspiring example for other American communities of the benefits that can be brought to a city from strong policies of historical preservation.

We've described several restaurants, lodgings, and shops of downtown Branson in later chapters of this book, as well as the fishing and boat facilities that can be rented at the docks found near the bottom of Main Street, which runs into Lake Taneycomo (the former White River, now dammed at either end and made into a lake resembling a river). Whether or not you plan to use those downtown facilities, you ought to set aside a few morning hours in the course of your Branson stay to stroll the streets of this remarkable, small town area, where residents still enjoy a sense of community and pleasant, restful aesthetics.

On to the Strip

Now turn around in your car and go uphill on Main Street, which soon becomes West Highway 76 again (Highway 76 on the other side of Lake Taneycomo is East Highway 76); it changes that designation (from Main Street to "76") in just a few hundred yards, as it ascends in altitude and proceeds upward to a long ridge atop one of those low, rounded mountains of the Ozarks. Here, for about the next 4 miles, always on West Highway 76, you encounter the famous (or infamous, according to your tastes) *Strip* of Branson, the scene of its soaring commercial explosion and triumphs, its main theaters, restaurants, malls, go-cart tracks and mini-golf courses, bungee jumps, souvenir and t-shirt shops, 7-Elevens, and screaming neon signs.

The Strip—West Highway 76, also called Country Music Boulevard—is a joyous place to some, an ecological disaster to others. Many years after Branson's counterpart city of Orlando had begun correcting the unsightly conditions of its own Strip known as International Drive, a full two decades after wiser minds took drastic steps to preserve the greenery and nature-based appearance of numerous other incipient "strips" in other American cities, the municipal and business interests of Branson unapologetically built or failed to check the growth of a full-scale, rip-roaring, billboard-and-neon-crammed Strip, at least 4 miles long, lining the sides of West Highway 76 with blacktopping, pavements, discordant buildings, gasoline stations and malls, but hardly any sidewalks, and even fewer trees. Directly on the Strip (West Highway 76) or near it are at least 20 of the 30 or so large celebrity theaters of Branson. A single one of the Strip theaters—that of Jim Stafford—places plants and flowers in front, to recapture some of the area's bygone beauty, and Andy Williams's Moon River Theater and the Grand Palace have an element of landscaping, but they're off the Strip. Scarcely anyone else even tries.

The recent trend in Branson's continued expansion is to build along roads and highways *away* from the Strip. Some of the more attractive theaters with lawns and the like (Shoji Tabuchi's, Charley Pride's, Pat Boone's, Lawrence Welk's, Tony Orlando's) are going up on Shepherd of the Hills Expressway, or on Highways 65, 165, and 248, in still other sections of town 10 or so minutes from the Strip. But the inescapable fact of life for tourists is that, for at least part of their theatergoing, meals, and shopping, they must learn how to negotiate the Strip.

Traffic Along the Strip

And it's a problem, a big one. Through all the era of massive growth, West Highway 76 has remained two lanes with a center turn lane. Emphasize that word *turn* for the center lane—it's for turning off the road, not for passing or gaining a jump on the bumper-to-bumper traffic (which incurs a heavy fine). Before the matinees, before the evening performances, and especially after them, when many thousands of visitors return simultaneously to their motels, you often

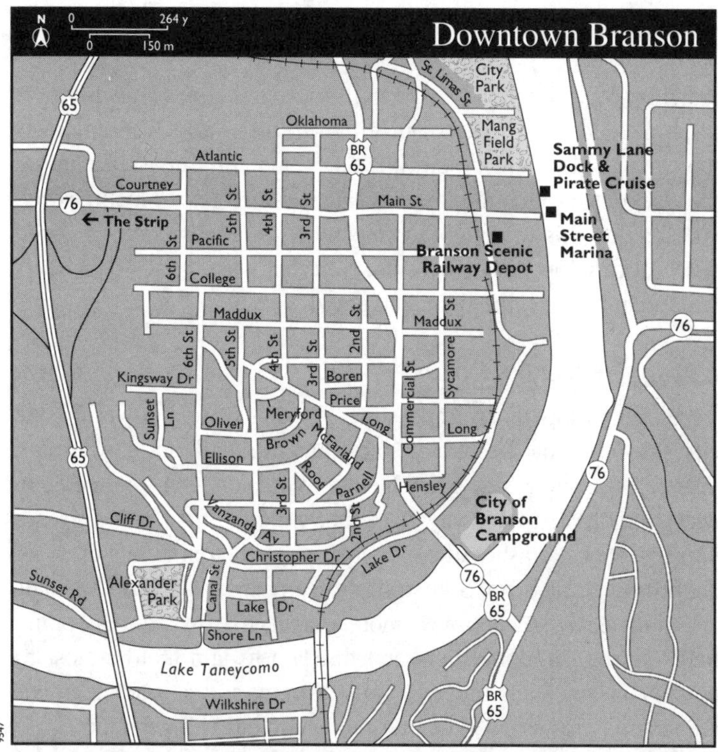
Downtown Branson
N
0 264 y
0 150 m
City Park
St. Limas St
Mang Field Park
Oklahoma
BR 65
Atlantic
Sammy Lane Dock & Pirate Cruise
Courtney
Main St
Main Street Marina
76
← The Strip
6th St
5th St
4th St
3rd St
Pacific
Branson Scenic Railway Depot
College
Maddux
Maddux
2nd St
Sycamore St
Commercial St
76
Kingsway Dr
6th St
5th St
4th St
3rd St
Boren
Price
Sunset Ln
Oliver
Meryford
Long
Long
Brown
McFarland
Ellison
Roof
Parnell
Hensley
76
65
Cliff Dr
Vanzandt Av
3rd St
2nd St
City of Branson Campground
Christopher Dr
Lake Dr
Sunset Rd
Alexander Park
Canal St
Lake Dr
76
BR 65
Shore Ln
Lake Taneycomo
Wilkshire Dr
BR 65
9547

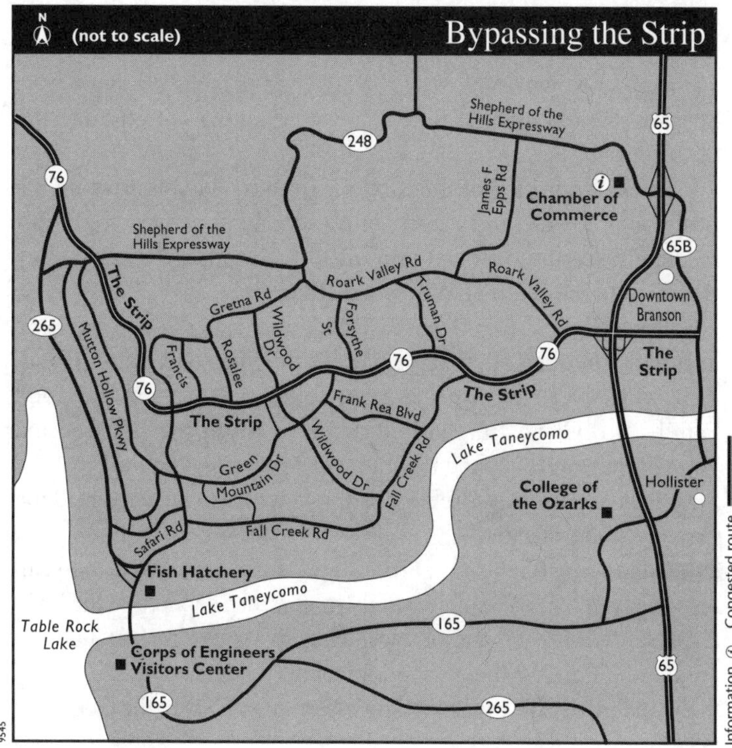
Bypassing the Strip
N
(not to scale)
Shepherd of the Hills Expressway
248
65
76
James F Epps Rd
Chamber of Commerce
Shepherd of the Hills Expressway
65B
Roark Valley Rd
Roark Valley Rd
Downtown Branson
The Strip
Gretna Rd
Wildwood Dr
Forsythe St
Truman Dr
265
Mutton Hollow Pkwy
Francis
Rosalee
76
76
The Strip
76
The Strip
Frank Rea Blvd
The Strip
Lake Taneycomo
Green Mountain Dr
Wildwood Dr
Fall Creek Rd
Hollister
College of the Ozarks
Safari Rd
Fall Creek Rd
Fish Hatchery
Lake Taneycomo
Table Rock Lake
165
Corps of Engineers Visitors Center
65
165
265
Information
Congested route
9545

crawl on West Highway 76; a half-hour, and sometimes more, is often needed to extricate yourself from the gridlock. Sometimes the worst jams occur on the weekends and conditions ease up on the weekdays; sometimes the exact opposite occurs. Sometimes you speed along this thoroughfare supercharged with neon and paved with parking lots, and you think, well that wasn't bad. Two hours later, you try the same route and crawl.

Enter the Relief Roads

Because it is apparently impossible to widen West Highway 76, the city's response has been to cut more and more relief roads through the verdant countryside a few hundred yards or even a half-mile to each side of West Highway 76, roughly paralleling the main road; you'll see these slashes of concrete through the remaining green of the hills near the Strip. Sometimes it seems that as fast as the roads are built, new theaters, new motels, and new discount shopping malls spring up along them and threaten to jam them almost as quickly as they open. Indeed, condominiums and retirement homes are reaching to where the motels and neon haven't yet gone.

Nevertheless, the new roads do bring a considerable degree of the relief they promise—especially for the experienced resident of Branson who knows how to use them, and to the tourist who spends a few minutes with a map. Nowadays, the persons driving *on* the Strip are mainly the first-time visitors unfamiliar with the alternative routes.

Look at our map of those by-pass roads. As you drive up the Strip from downtown Branson in a westerly direction, you'll immediately see that you can turn off to the north at **Roark Valley Road**, or to the south at **Wildwood Road**.

Turning off at Roark Valley Road, you can continue on along **Truman Road**, and then drive back to the Strip on **Gretna Road**. This will bring you close to a whole host of theaters (Osmond Family, Roy Clark, Jim Stafford, John Davidson, the Jubilee), and you will have reached them without encountering the traffic of the Strip itself. Alongside Gretna Road, you will also have reached the Charley Pride Theater.

Continuing on this relief road to the north of the Strip, you can also easily get onto the increasingly important Shepherd of the Hills Expressway, site of numerous new theaters, motels, restaurants, and attractions (among them, Shoji Tabuchi, the Imax, the Five Star, the wonderfully inexpensive Ozark Mountain Buffet, the Civil War

Museum), and you will have reached them all in quick order without having once ventured onto the Strip, and especially without having had to go first to the far west end of the Strip for the purpose of turning onto Shepherd of the Hills Expressway from there.

Alternatively, you can turn south of the Strip on **Fall Creek Road**, and reach a number of important theaters, restaurants, malls, and the like from their *rear* entrances and parking lots. Proceeding first on Fall Creek Road, you can turn back to the Strip at **Wildwood Drive**, and voila! you'll find yourself at the back of the Andy Williams Theater, the Grand Palace, the Grand Village, Bobby Vinton's, Baldknobbers, and Moe Bandy's. In some cases you'll have reached these places without having ventured onto the Strip at all, or at worst by simply driving a few hundred yards on the Strip.

Or, instead of continuing on Wildwood Drive all the way back to the Strip, you can turn left onto **Green Mountain Drive**, which almost perfectly parallels the Strip until it crosses Highway 165. By then turning back to the Strip on Highway 165, you'll find yourself in the midst of no fewer than 11 theaters (Jim Stafford, John Davidson, Boxcar Willie, Cristy Lane, Roy Clark, Mickey Gilley, among others) and the liquid amusement park known as White Water. Again, you will have reached those attractions without having first had to crawl for a couple of miles along the Strip, or at worst by driving only 200 or 300 yards along the Strip. It may sound confusing in prose, but the map we've provided should make the situation clear at a glance.

In 1992, in an effort to be of even greater assistance, the Branson Chamber of Commerce created a color-coded "Time-Saver Map" that used three basic hues to outline the major by-pass routes. It created a "blue route," a "red route," and a "yellow route," designated as such by signs and arrows along the Strip. Because that map will be republished in 1995, and widely distributed (a black-and-white version appears in this chapter), you'll want to briefly familiarize yourself with the colors and the roads to which they apply. The "red route" is north of the Strip and takes you roughly parallel to it by using Highway 248 and Shepherd of the Hills Expressway; various cutoffs permit you to rejoin the Strip. The "blue route" also goes north of and parallel to the Strip, on Forsyth Street and Gretna Road. The "yellow route" is found south of the Strip, along Fall Creek Road, Wildwood Drive, and Green Mountain Drive, and enables you—via turnoffs—to approach several of the main theaters, malls, and restaurants from their rear, avoiding the traffic of the Strip. Though we've referred to the same roads in our text on avoiding Strip traffic, the colors are a convenient way to keep those routes in mind, and various signs and arrows along the Strip (West Highway 76) virtually beseech you to turn off when you see those colors and take the easier way.

The Remaining Geography You'll Need to Know

It's both important and gratifying that a great many of the newer theaters, restaurants, and motels aren't located anywhere near the Strip and can be reached on relatively untrafficked roads, quickly and pleasantly.

The *Will Rogers Follies* and Glen Campbell's Good Time Theater are both alongside Highway 65, and you pass them both as you first enter Branson (from Springfield). Mell Tillis's Theater is near the junction of Highway 248 and Shepherd of the Hills Expressway. The new Lawrence Welk Theater is well south of the Strip off Highway 165, on the way to Table Rock Lake. Pump Boys and Dinettes, and Buck Trent's Breakfast Theater, are also on 165, closer to the Strip (but most easily reached by proceeding along Green Mountain Drive). And, of course, more and more theaters and other establishments—attracted by the success of the Shoji Tabuchi Theater—are placing themselves on Shepherd of the Hills Expressway, which thus far has retained the landscaping and greenery so markedly absent from the Strip.

You reach Shepherd of the Hills Expressway either by driving all the way to the west end of the Strip and turning right from there, or, better yet, by entering Shepherd of the Hills Expressway from Highway 248, and thus avoiding the Strip. Just once, in the course of your visit, you may want to traverse the entire length of the Strip for sightseeing purposes, but once is enough.

Shepherd of the Hills and Silver Dollar City

Shepherd of the Hills Expressway should not be confused with Shepherd of the Hills amphitheater, homestead, and tower complex, about 2 miles past the end of the strip, still on West Highway 76 as you drive along it in a westerly direction. The important Silver Dollar City theme park is also found by driving even farther out (to the west) on West Highway 76, a mile or so beyond the Shepherd of the Hills amphitheater. You should drive along this scenic

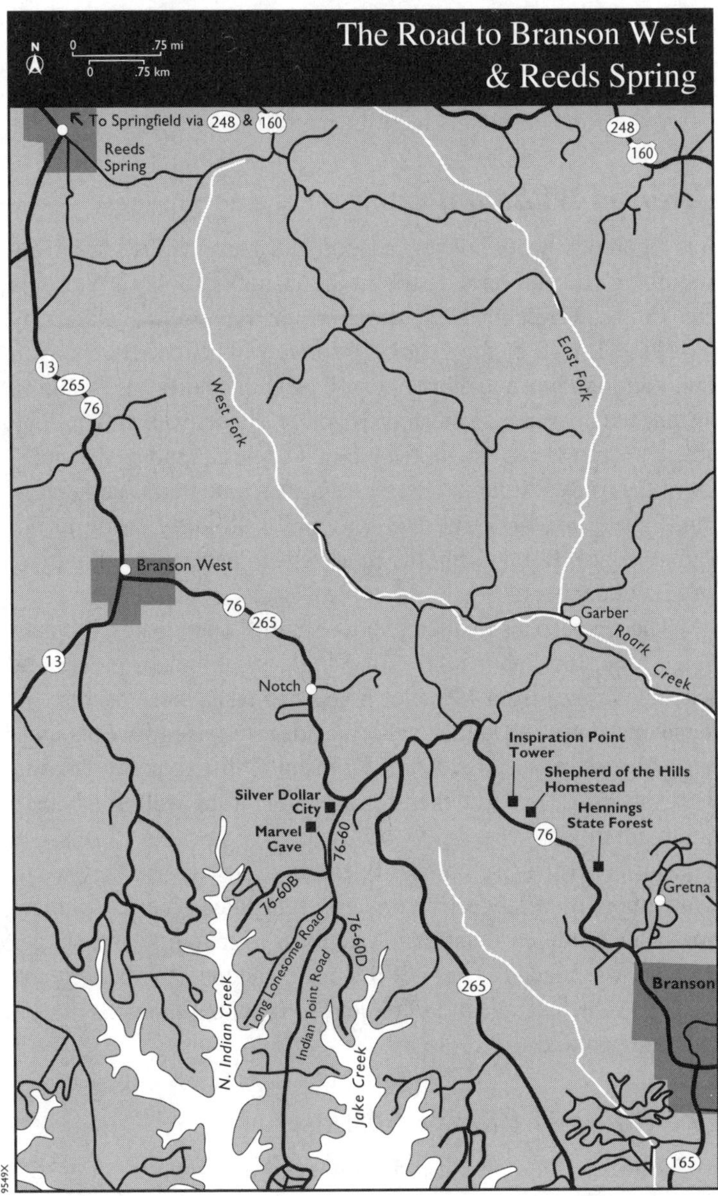
The Road to Branson West & Reeds Spring
N
0 .75 mi
0 .75 km
To Springfield via 248 & 160
Reeds Spring
248
160
13
265
76
West Fork
East Fork
Branson West
76
265
13
Garber
Roark Creek
Notch
Inspiration Point Tower
Shepherd of the Hills Homestead
Silver Dollar City
Marvel Cave
Hennings State Forest
76
76-60
76-60B
Gretna
Long Lonesome Road
Indian Point Road
76-60D
265
Branson
N. Indian Creek
Jake Creek
165
9549X

route even if you're not planning to visit the two theme parks (although both are close to being indispensable attractions of Branson), because the setting is a classic Ozark vista, much as Branson looked before its great development of the past 10 years.

Branson Without a Car?

It is theoretically possible to vacation in Branson without a car. By stationing yourself on the Strip in the vicinity of John Davidson's and Jim Stafford's theaters (which means staying in such nearby motels as Lodge of the Ozarks, Caprice Motor Inn, Blue Bayou Inn, Victorian Inn, and others), you'll be within fairly easy walking distance of at least nine theaters. If you're a better walker, you'll be able to reach at least two more on foot. Or you can stay in the vicinity of the Andy Williams Theater (at the Crowne Plaza, large Days Inn, Palace Inn, Melody Lane Inn) and walk fairly easily to the Grand Palace, Bobby Vinton's Blue Velvet Theater, Moe Bandy's, and Baldknobbers.

There is also a so-called "Show Shuttle" operated by Branson Stage Line, Inc. (phone 417/334-5463), which makes pickups at scheduled times from 19 major hotels and takes those passengers to major shows or shopping malls; the price is $4 one way, $6 round-trip. And there is, of course, Branson Cab Company (phone 417/334-5678), to be booked for individual trips well in advance of curtain time.

But none of those courses is entirely satisfactory; they leave you without modestly priced or easily scheduled access to numerous other scattered theaters, attractions, restaurants, and shops. Branson was made for the self-drive car, and the car—either your own or a vehicle rented in Springfield—is your best possible means of getting around.

The Route to Eureka Springs

A side trip to the unusual Arkansas town of Eureka Springs, 50 miles from Branson, is often made by visitors to Branson at the end of their stay; see our separate chapter on Eureka Springs near the end of this book for a description of its almost perfectly preserved Victorian old town, with its charming bed-and-breakfasts, high-level restaurants, and historic hotels. The trip there is an unusually scenic one that can be made on either of two routes, both of them similar in distance and time.

From Branson, you can drive south on Highway 65 until you come to Highway 86, then turn west on 86 and drive to the route called "P"; at the Missouri/Arkansas border, "P" becomes Highway 23, and leads you straight into Eureka Springs. As an alternate route, you can drive south on Highway 65 into Arkansas, and then turn west on Highway 62 going to Eureka Springs. Either way, you ought to make the trip to historic Eureka Springs, which was once a major spa resort of the United States, and has a great deal to teach us today.

4

Is There Anything Not to Like About Branson?

A Few Cautions Before You Come

We've completed the historical and geographical prelude to Branson; we're about to turn to weightier matters—hotels, restaurants, theaters, sights, and shops; but first we must answer the question: Are there warnings to be made about Branson, or must the author of a travel guide write only in breathless style about the warm and comfy aspects of a destination, and not about its negatives as well? Unlike political writers who criticize, and restaurant and movie and book reviewers who criticize, is a travel writer required to remain oblivious to problems and write with a never-fading, dumbly-vapid smile on his face?

I've never believed that. In a lifetime of writing about travel, and in radio and TV appearances from coast to coast, I've railed against certain aspects and excesses of Las Vegas, while never ceasing to talk about the fun of a trip there. I've severely criticized practices and antitourist attitudes in my own New York, without ever abandoning my love for that city. I've warned about the high costs of Scandinavia, the impossible traffic gridlock of Bangkok, the authoritarian pall over life in Istanbul, while still recommending that readers travel to Europe, Thailand, and Turkey.

A Balanced Picture of Branson

What's needed is journalistic honesty, a fair-minded assessment, as in a movie review that touts the film but points out its shortcomings. And that's why I must first repeat that I enjoy vacationing in Branson. I find it fun, as well as unusually inexpensive. I find its culture utterly different from the one by which I'm usually surrounded, and a trip there—for me—has much of the flavor of going overseas, to areas where everything—attitude, cuisine, ways of speaking—is refreshingly different from life at home. I enthusiastically believe that more Americans should spend a few days in Branson, and taste the distinctive culture of the Ozarks.

I also love country music, and have since I was a child living in Missouri and occasionally traveling to the Ozarks. Later, as a young man, I listened to country for hours as it emerged from the radio speaker of a fellow G.I. in the next bunk, in an army barracks located in what was then Camp Gordon, Georgia. I also like gospel music, which is an essential part of country music. Long before hearing about Branson, I've bought tickets to presentations of gospel on Broadway, by several different African-American groups. I vastly enjoy seeing and hearing the great Branson names in country music, for the low ticket prices—sometimes only $15—that prevail in Branson. And I like the prospect of attending such shows in bulk, every evening, and at several matinees—and after enjoying one of those salty Southern-style meals costing under $10.

But if I were to fail to point out that some of those shows—not all, but some—are marked by a strong element of religious and political proselytizing, I would not be fulfilling my obligations to you. If I were to overlook the domination of certain elements of the Branson scene—again, not all, but some—by the religious right, I would not be a travel writer you can trust. If I were not to mention the wholesale destruction of the ecology by certain Branson developers, the ugly racism that—to my eye at least—is so painfully evident in the casting of most Branson shows, the overly vulgar commercialization of some (not all, but some) Branson theaters, the violent jingoism of certain Branson performers who themselves have never served in the military, I'd be writing a puff sheet, not a travel guide.

Why Criticism Can Aid a Destination

There are reasons why a travel guide should deal with the bad as well as the good.

First, to enable the visitor to make intelligent use of his or her time at the destination; no one can go to 32 celebrity theaters in the average five or six days of a Branson vacation, or patronize scores and scores of hotels and restaurants; one must pick and choose among a dizzying array of options. Unless travel writers express their own honest judgments, on what else is the visitor to base a decision? This is a particular problem in Branson, where local newspaper and tourist broadsheets describe nearly every attraction in rave terms, and in effect criticize nothing. Branson simply has not yet developed a press that honestly appraises country shows, tells who's talented and who isn't, who's an entertainer and who is off the wall. Again, the outside travel writer asks: If not us, who?

The second reason has to do with improving the quality of the touristic product. Imagine what the character of American movies, plays, and books would be if there were no such things as book reviewers, movie and theater critics, observers of performance art. Valid criticism from an outsider keeps the creative juices stirring, compels an artist, writer, actor, producer, or performer to constantly review the merits of what they have done, jolts them out of complacency, shatters their isolation, removes them from the stifling atmosphere of the sycophants, and directs their attention to matters of which they might otherwise never have thought.

And the third reason has to do with the self-interest of Branson. If Branson is to reach a national audience—a goal that you frequently hear expressed by leading citizens—it obviously cannot continue following an exclusionary policy of limiting its appeal to a small number of unworldly fundamentalists, of one race, background, and outlook. If Branson is to fill the hotels and theaters sprouting from every hillside, it must cease giving political or religious offense to giant segments of the American public.

Enveloped by a stifling atmosphere of conformity, serviced by local media of only one political outlook, many Bransonites are unaware of how exclusionary many of their policies are, and of the offense they give to millions of potential visitors. It is therefore in the interests of Branson, and to its benefit, that I list some of its less attractive features.

Unadvertised Preaching

You pay at the box office for a pleasant, heartwarming evening of country music and suddenly find yourself in the equivalent of a revival tent. Not in all Branson shows, but in a significant minority of them. And the problem is, there is no way to know this in advance.

Almost as if it were a regulation of the Branson City Council, nearly every one of the country music shows sooner or later presents a religious segment, usually of one or two gospel numbers. No one, of course, can have any real objection to those gospel numbers. Gospel is a vital part of the country music tradition, and most performers here present it in a wholly natural fashion, in a seamless evolution of their country classics.

Others, however, go well beyond, and enter the world of religious proselytizing. Without giving the slightest advance notice to their visitors, the Osmond Brothers—as one example—devote an entire, lengthy, multimedia production number—the virtual climax of their show—to preaching a sectarian, religious message. Cast upon a giant motion picture screen behind them are graphic portraits of New Testament scenes of the sort found in the visitor centers of proselytizing religions, including depictions of Jesus as handsomer than any movie star. The music swells to ear-splitting levels, the message is shouted to the members of the audience by the Osmonds, and many of them respond by bursting into thundering, approving applause, often standing, in fact, in a sustained ovation. To one who does not share this approach to religion, the impact is like a physical assault.

In other shows, the gospel segment is preceded by an audible change of mood, lighting, and sound. The performers, who have hitherto worn a mix of costumes, reappear in white, the women in long lace dresses up to their chins. Even in some of the noncountry musical shows, like that of Andy Williams, lyrics are sung that are a proud profession of a fundamentalist, sectarian faith. Unprepared, the visitor is bemused at least, but often stunned and offended.

It is not that these shows have no right to proselytize; all of us, surely, would vehemently defend their constitutional, artistic, and moral right to do so. It is a matter of advance disclosure. When people go to a theater for music and entertainment, aren't they entitled to know that certain shows are heavily devoted to preaching? Shouldn't the Osmonds, in a further example, disclose that their show has a heavy sectarian component, even if such disclosure would hurt their box office receipts? If a Branson resident were to purchase tickets on Broadway for a light-hearted show like *Crazy for You*, wouldn't that person have a valid complaint if a major production number, unrelated to its well-advertised story line, suddenly ran a movie of the Pope and bishops, lauding the organization of the Catholic Church? Or if Jewish members of the cast suddenly interrupted the proceedings and sang of the Jewish faith as the only true religion, with music booming to a climax?

For years, rumors have circulated in the musical community that country shows will not be tolerated in Branson unless they include a proselytizing religious component; that without this component, necessary permits will be denied, or performers will be run out of town, or producers' lives will be made uncomfortable. Those reports have acquired greater substance from a statement recently made by country great Merle Haggard, and reported in the "Arts and Leisure" section of the *New York Times* (Sunday, August 21, 1994, page 28). "Branson and me just don't mix," said Haggard. "If you're not a born-again Christian, ready to stand up and tell them that, they won't even loan you money to build a place. If you don't believe as they do, then you're just out."

Again it's for Branson to decide. If performers are determined to exclude large sections of the population from enjoyment of their shows, as they have every right to do, let them at least notify potential audiences of their show's heavy sectarian content. Until they do, this broader-than-gospel element of many (not all) shows remains a strong negative about Branson, offensive not simply to other religions but to that broad swath of Americans who do not believe in mixing commercial entertainment and money-making with religion.

Unadvertised Politics

A very small minority of Branson's musical shows go overboard in the unadvertised preaching of right-wing political messages. Again, they have every right to do so, but shouldn't theatergoers know in advance—as they know in every other theater capital of the world—that politics will be a part of the show? When Glen Campbell sprinkles his show with remarks critical of President Clinton, when other performers do the same, when the Osmond Brothers place a large color photograph of Nancy and Ronald Reagan at one of the two indoor entranceways to their theater, and a similar color portrait of Barbara and George Bush at the other, supplemented by similar framed portraits of Charlton Heston and like-minded conservatives elsewhere, are they not saying, in effect, that their show is meant to advance right-wing policies (something you discover for the first time only after you have purchased tickets to it)? (Former President Jimmy Carter and Rosalyn Carter are conspicuously missing from the Osmond Brothers' display of presidents, although the

Carters are as fervently religious as many others).* If a Broadway theater were to be festooned with photos celebrating major figures of the Democratic party, and no one else, wouldn't it be felt that this theater was practicing a somewhat exclusionary policy? And aren't exclusionary policies the last thing that sincere promoters of Branson should applaud?

Obligatory Patriotism

And then there's the tub-thumping, flag-waving number. Almost by rote, in lock-step and unison, some of the country music shows also include patriotic production numbers as the closing segment of their performances. Country singers put on costumes imprinted with the stars and stripes, in-theater fireworks go off in one show, people march, the music swells magnificently, performers proclaim that this is the greatest, single nation on earth, eyes fill with tears, the audience rises and joins in "The Star Spangled Banner." With the prominent exception of the show of Box Car Willie (who, unlike most other Branson performers, actually served in the armed forces), and several others, the near-obligatory patriotism number is heard over and over in the course of one's visit, almost as if a municipal regulation required it. A private emotion about one's country that should stem voluntarily from one's own principles and beliefs becomes an element of money making. A quiet pride in our freedoms of speech and religion, our diversity and our democratic traditions becomes a tool to frighten dissenters. The nation that is shocked by eruptions of violent nationalism in other countries is suddenly portrayed by these affluent Branson performers as equally nationalistic, a place whose citizens are expected to follow unquestioned orders regardless of conscience—"my country, right or wrong."

Make no mistake about it—in a few of the Branson shows, the obligatory patriotism number has been preceded by a song about the threat of the flag burners (as if that infinitesimally small

*When I first saw the portraits of Presidents Reagan and Bush hanging over the two entrances to the Osmonds' auditorium, I immediately complained volubly to an official of the Osmonds' theater who was standing nearby, and the next day to an official of the Branson Convention and Visitors' Board. When, after writing the above text, I later returned to Branson, the two portraits had been taken down and replaced with photos of country music stars, apparently in response to my complaints. I am nevertheless leaving the above text unchanged as a dramatic lesson that visits to Branson by outsiders and a more varied Branson audience can bring about healthy changes in that community. When the Branson performers learn that mixing of right-wing politics with entertainment can cost them money, they apparently quickly change their ways.

number of exhibitionists posed any real threat!), and comic country performers like the Baldknobbers, hitherto slouching about on stage, suddenly stand erect, military-like and grim, and punch out their hatred of these types who refuse to march in step. My country, right or wrong! As someone who grew up, as I did, when Americans reserved their open displays of patriotism for one day—July 4—but loyally served the country and went into the military when the times required it, I resent the mixing of patriotism with commercial money-making in some Branson shows; the activity is like the last refuge, as Samuel Johnson reminded us, of scoundrels.

Racial Casting

The ugliest blemish in Branson's makeup is what I regard as the undeniable racism of many of its promoters. As I write this guidebook, whole casts of shows—large bands, large dance troupes—contain not a single black, even when the performers on the stage are playing blacks. Shoji Tabuchi presents a major production number set in the black Caribbean, but uses not a single black in it. Andy Williams and others put gospel choirs on stage, and sometimes have them sing and act out the hand-clapping, fast-rhythm, bouncy spirituals of a black church, but do not use a single black in that choir, or a single black in an individual part or as an individual character. Among the scores and scores of soloists, both vocalists and instrumentalists, magicians, jugglers, ventriloquists, comics, and others that are recruited from all over the nation to appear in Branson, there is scarcely a minority among them. Except for four black members of a single band playing in the Tony Orlando show, one black dancer at the Lawrence Welk Theater, the recent hiring of a black superstar, Charley Pride, to head his own theater, and an occasional Sunday night appearance by Bill Cosby, one searches hard for anything other than a fleeting glimpse of a minority performer. It is as if the clock has been turned back to the time when this nation was racially segregated; but even the television and motion picture industry of the '40s made more use of minority actors and performers than Branson does, although almost wholly in roles of servants and the like. None of the gains in casting that the national media have achieved since then seem to have affected the celebrity producers of Branson, though some of them—like Andy Williams and Bobby Vinton—come from that broader national background.

When you confront a thoughtful resident with questions of racism here, they seem embarrassed and reach uneasily for defensive arguments, like referring to the fact that open auditions are held in Branson for many shows, and black performers fail to appear for them. In the almost wholly white setting and atmosphere of Branson, one wonders what blacks would be so foolish as to make that trip, or where they would live—what housing would be available to them in this nearly all-white city—if they were to land a part. Obviously, at least some auditions for a theater industry as large as Branson's should be scheduled for large cities, and encouragements offered for help in finding housing if a role is secured. For the purpose of obtaining the best possible performers, summer stock and regional theaters all over the nation hold auditions in such cities as New York and Chicago, and the analogy to the seasonal theater of Branson is an apt one.

By making the racial composition of casts in Branson as different as one could imagine from the makeup of nationally done films, TV shows, plays, and musicals, the wealthy country stars of Branson are surely pandering to their audiences. They feed the mood of nostalgia and escapism that their present audience likes; they attempt to re-create for them an easier time, when that sort of audience held the upper hand, and minorities suffered in silence, a calm achieved at a terrible human cost. They—the producers—have also cut themselves off from a large potential audience. In a stay of several days in Branson, you will see only an occasional minority family attending the country shows.

The Stench of Humbug

For entertainers to have made such an accommodation with bigotry, and then to sing gospels from the stage, is to me the essence of hypocrisy. It is more shameful still for some of these millionaire performers from Hollywood, Palm Springs, and Nashville—a world not unknown for its hard drinking, drug taking, profane womanizers—to stand on stage and deliver pious teachings of virtue to the rest of us. In one show, a country music star makes critical jokes that cast aspersions on the past private life of President Clinton. That performer has himself been married four times, and in between two of the marriages, carried on a boozy, brawling affair with a female country singer that made headlines around the world. *He* is teaching *us* virtue? And when a country music superstar adds to his fortune in pious Branson, I can't forget the day when, coming off pills, he systematically smashed up the footlights of the Grand Ole Opry, scattering glass over the audience. To their credit, the more recently famous country performers rarely turn to sermonizing when they appear in Nashville, or make profitable use of their own private religious beliefs. Couldn't the established stars of Branson learn something from the younger ones' modesty?

And finally, it is distasteful to watch the patriotic, flag-waving production numbers of performers who have never served in the armed forces of this country, despite having been of military age when their services were needed. I am not referring to those persons who sought deferments because they questioned participation in past wars, but rather to those who applauded those wars, but failed to volunteer for them (which I assume was the position of some Branson performers). With the honorable exceptions of Boxcar Willie and Bobby Vinton, one has to search to find even a few other Branson performers who went into the armed forces of the nation they shout is the greatest on earth. One of them actually paints his theater in red, white, and blue, and wears a costume of stars and stripes in one number. At the time of the Vietnam War, when he was of military age, he was establishing himself on the country music scene and never served in the military. Another, who is 50 years of age today, and was of military age during the time of Vietnam, never served—which does not stop him from continually proclaiming his admiration for veterans as part of his moneymaking career. To encounter such hypocrisy in commercial entertainment attractions in Branson is not only unpleasant but not in the long-term interests of Branson.

A Summation for Now

With those sentiments off my chest, and (I hope) received in the positive manner in which they were intended, let's turn to the immensely pleasurable and attractive features of Branson that more than warrant a trip here. Starting on the next pages: the best of Branson's highly acclaimed entertainers and shows, the best of its lodgings, restaurants, shops, and amusements.

5

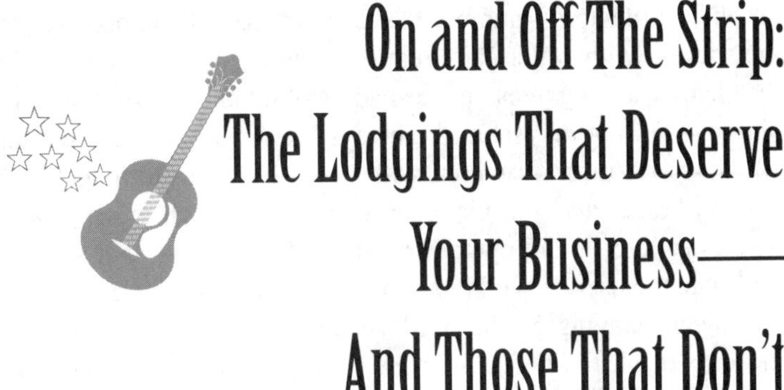

On and Off The Strip: The Lodgings That Deserve Your Business—And Those That Don't

63 Choices from a Field of 180

Branson, as you'll recall, is a boomtown, and like all such places suffers from hasty and ill-considered hotel-building, at least in the earliest stages of its growth. A great many of the current lodgings in Branson were thrown up by investors of neither conscience nor taste, in a plain and unabashed effort to get-rich-quick. Some of them are barely able to comply with building codes or easily receive certificates of occupancy. Most are standard highway motels of cookie-cutter design, full of neon and kitsch, and utterly without relevance to the local landscape, culture, or history of the Ozarks. Inside is worse, and most visitors get placed in guest rooms of unimaginative—if adequate—furnishings, and crushing boredom.

But note that we referred to "a great many" of Branson's lodgings. A blessed minority of others have done better, and those are the lodgings featured in this chapter. From the more than 180 hotels, motels, rustic resorts, residence halls, campsites, condos, and tiny B&Bs of Branson, I've chosen 63 that provide pleasant and reasonably aesthetic surroundings (there are, of course, more than that number). And I've described a few others that I don't particularly admire, but are nonetheless tolerable lodgings—"last resorts"—for those occasions when certain areas in Branson are packed, and you need an immediate alternative in the vicinity.

How Were They Selected?

My criteria for selecting these 63 properties are intensely personal ones with which you may very much disagree. They are not based on physical factors—number of elevators, size of rooms—but on the success with which they reinforce the experience of living in the Ozarks, among trees, in the shadow of mountains, by a lake, in nature—and not on asphalt highways lined with cars and cheap, cookie-cutter motels covered with neon. I like rustic lodges and country homes and inns that bear the personal touch of the people who both live in and operate them. I admire hotels that seek to associate themselves with the history and culture of the area, and if that means staying on the outskirts and driving for five minutes more to reach the theaters, so be it. I also enjoy the charming, bygone, small-town feeling of downtown Branson, whose preservation and vitality is one of the most encouraging features of the entire area; and I've recommended several hotels there, away from the Strip.

At the same time, I haven't eliminated all the hotels and motels on the Strip or near it; I've chosen and described several, especially those from which one can walk—not drive—to a cluster of nearby theaters. I like the ones designed not simply for short-term greed, but with the interests of people in mind. I admire those owners of even the most commercial properties who have taken steps to humanize their hotels, with decent art on the walls, separate bed lamps for each person, large and thick towels, closets instead of hanging clothes racks, a pot of coffee always on hand. And I also applaud the properties that maintain a reasonable price level, even when the town is packed.

In the years ahead, as this guidebook goes through revised editions, your own hotel comments will be of great assistance to our readers. Please tell me how you've fared and how they've treated you (by writing to the address appearing earlier in this book), and we'll include those statements, intact, in editions to come.

And How Were These Lodgings Grouped?

Our choices are set forth in *ascending* order of price, starting with the very cheapest of Branson's most suitable motels (double rooms for under $40), and proceeding upward from there to the large or upscale hotel/resorts that charge slightly more than $100 a night (a high price for Branson). Those groupings are based on *high-season* (usually defined as mid-April through October) rates, though I've also attempted to indicate what off-season prices will be at the same establishments. Here they are, in all their variety:

Double Rooms for Under $40 a Night

Allendale Resort and Sharp's Resort (jointly managed)
411 North Commercial Street in downtown Branson, phone 417/334-3327

Location: Both line the banks of Lake (it looks more like a river) Taneycomo. Consists of separate units scattered about rustic grounds at least five acres in size. Some are log cabins, others little bungalows of 1920s and 1930s construction.

Rates: 44 units, renting year-round for $30 to $32 for two persons, and to parties of four to six persons (in two or three beds) for never higher than $48. Weekly rates are even better, and start at $168 for a double-bedded unit, increasing to never more than $310 for seven nights in a multi-bedded cottage for four or six persons. MC, V.

Oldest of the old-style fishing resorts, old-fashioned in both appearance and rates, and built right into the original and well-preserved downtown of Branson; you can still go on a fishing trip from a lakefront dock at the foot of the combined resorts whose grounds slope right down to the lake. Five of the units are actual log cabins dating from the 1920s, but even they have the same air conditioning, heating, and carpeting of the more modern facilities built from sawn planks, not logs. Furniture is basic but comfortable; dishes and cooking utensils are supplied, as are linens; and every room has color cable television. Added amenities: outdoor swimming pool, coin laundry, barbecue pit. But don't look for style, other than the refreshing simplicity of a woodsy bungalow colony.

About the Symbol

The ★ you'll periodically see at the start of a listing indicates that the lodging in question is outstanding and of particular value in its price category.

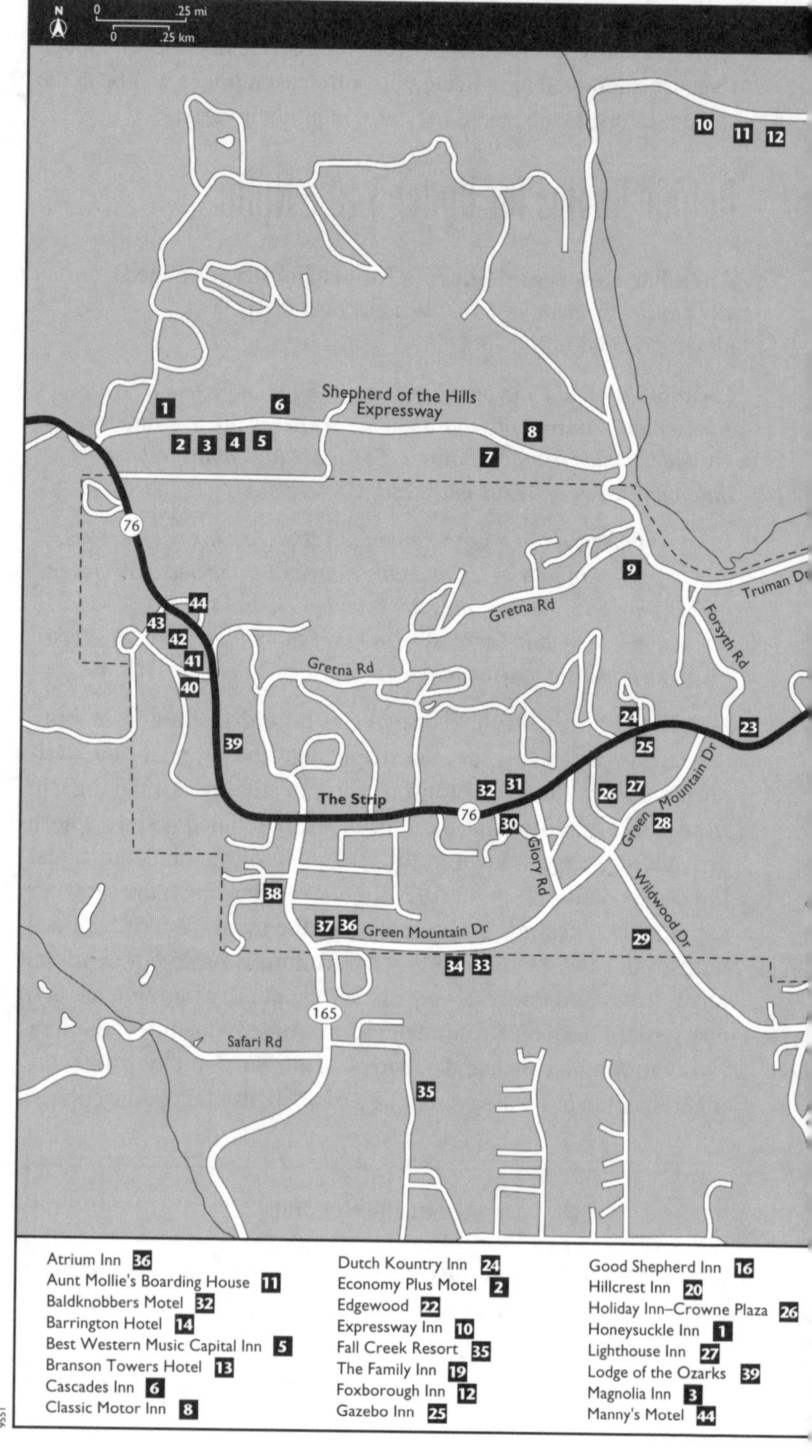
N
0 .25 mi
0 .25 km
Shepherd of the Hills Expressway
76
Gretna Rd
Gretna Rd
Truman Dr
Forsyth Rd
Green Mountain Dr
The Strip
76
Glory Rd
Wildwood Dr
Green Mountain Dr
165
Safari Rd
Atrium Inn 36
Aunt Mollie's Boarding House 11
Baldknobbers Motel 32
Barrington Hotel 14
Best Western Music Capital Inn 5
Branson Towers Hotel 13
Cascades Inn 6
Classic Motor Inn 8
Dutch Kountry Inn 24
Economy Plus Motel 2
Edgewood 22
Expressway Inn 10
Fall Creek Resort 35
The Family Inn 19
Foxborough Inn 12
Gazebo Inn 25
Good Shepherd Inn 16
Hillcrest Inn 20
Holiday Inn–Crowne Plaza 26
Honeysuckle Inn 1
Lighthouse Inn 27
Lodge of the Ozarks 39
Magnolia Inn 3
Manny's Motel 44

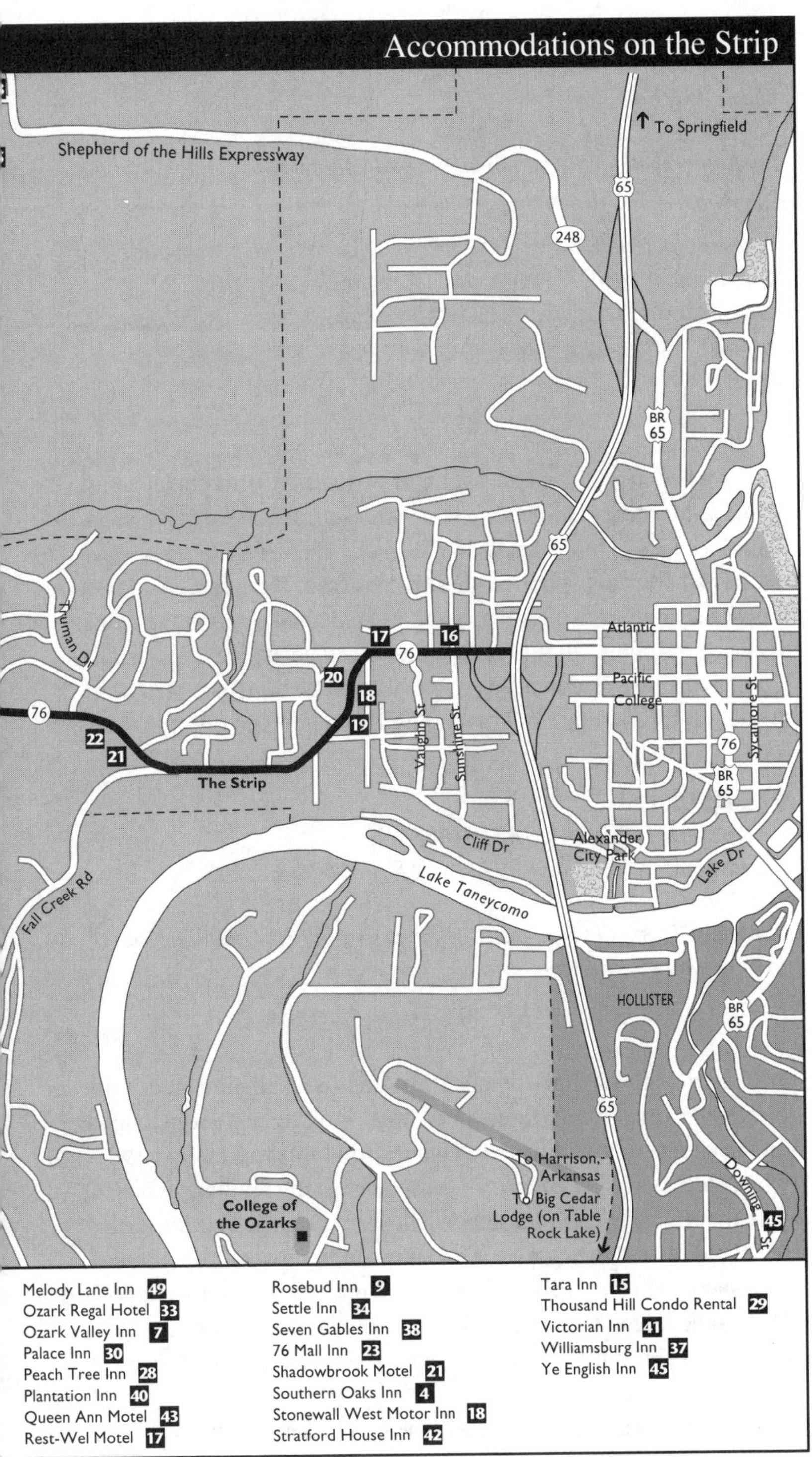
Accommodations on the Strip
To Springfield
Shepherd of the Hills Expressway
65
248
BR 65
65
Truman Dr
17
16
76
Atlantic
20
18
Pacific
College
76
19
Vaughn St
Sunshine St
22
21
The Strip
76
BR 65
Sycamore St
Cliff Dr
Alexander City Park
Lake Dr
Fall Creek Rd
Lake Taneycomo
HOLLISTER
BR 65
65
To Harrison, Arkansas
To Big Cedar Lodge (on Table Rock Lake)
Downing St
45
College of the Ozarks
Melody Lane Inn 49
Ozark Regal Hotel 33
Ozark Valley Inn 7
Palace Inn 30
Peach Tree Inn 28
Plantation Inn 40
Queen Ann Motel 43
Rest-Wel Motel 17
Rosebud Inn 9
Settle Inn 34
Seven Gables Inn 38
76 Mall Inn 23
Shadowbrook Motel 21
Southern Oaks Inn 4
Stonewall West Motor Inn 18
Stratford House Inn 42
Tara Inn 15
Thousand Hill Condo Rental 29
Victorian Inn 41
Williamsburg Inn 37
Ye English Inn 45

Stonewall West Motor Inn
1040 West Highway 76 (the Strip),
phone 417/334-5173

Location: Just north of the junction with Highway 65, and thus at the very start of the Strip as you drive uphill from downtown Branson.

Rates: 26 units renting at $38 for a double room even during the June through October high season, $32 for same in May, $28 in November and December, $22 in April. In past years, closed January through March, but is now considering year-round operation. AE, D, DC, MC, V.

★ Though its rock-paneled and shingled appearance is that of a rather basic motel, it pursues a bit of distinction with botanical art in the guest rooms (something you won't see elsewhere in Branson, with its supply-store approach to decor), ornamental lattices separating the sleeping space of guest rooms from their vanity areas, a tiny heat lamp in bathrooms, and coffee available round the clock in the tiny lobby. Rooms have either two queen-size beds or one king, and all were redone early in 1994. Single drawback: only one bed lamp for reading. Still, a top buy in the low end of motels.

Ye English Inn
28 Downing Street, Hollister, MO 65672,
phone 800/554-7188 or 417/334-4142, fax 417/337-5548

Location: In the historic small(er) town just across Lake Taneycomo from downtown Branson.

Rates: Double rooms for $35 throughout the year. MC, V.

★ Amazingly enough for the Ozarks, this is a half-timbered, half-plastered, Tudor-style, three-story hotel looking as if it belonged on the streets of a Yorkshire village in Britain. It was built in 1909, when Hollister—not Branson—was the important railway junction hereabouts, and the proud settlers chose an English Tudor look for the city's main thoroughfare, Downing Street (now on the National Register of Historic Places—you'll definitely want to drive across Lake Taneycomo, less than 10 minutes from downtown Branson, to see the charming town, so touching in its aspirations, even if you're not staying there).

The progressive Hollister was the first in Taney County to have an iron bridge, a paved street, electric lights, a movie theater, and

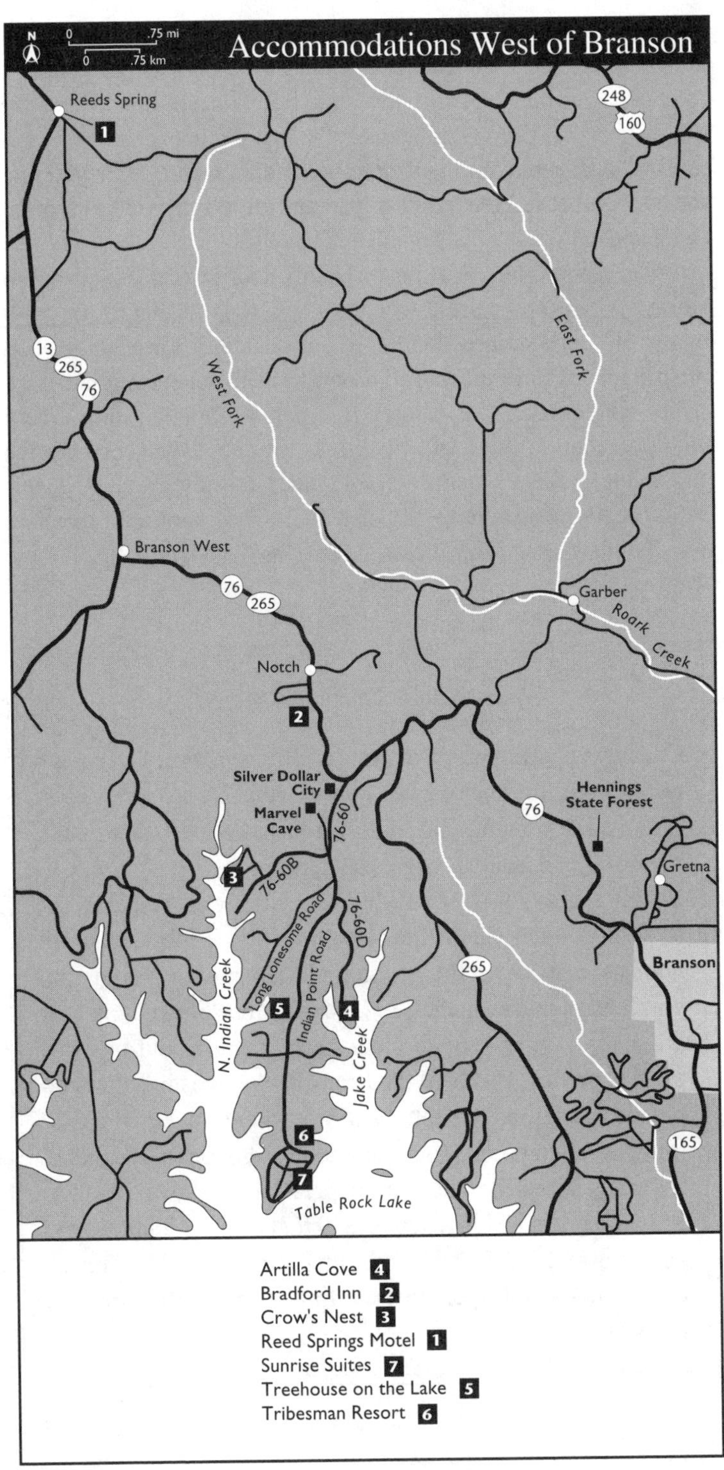
Accommodations West of Branson
N
0 .75 mi
0 .75 km
Reeds Spring
1
248
160
13
265
76
West Fork
East Fork
Branson West
76
265
Garber
Roark Creek
Notch
2
Silver Dollar City
Marvel Cave
76-60
3
76-60B
Long Lonesome Road
76-60D
Indian Point Road
Hennings State Forest
76
Gretna
Branson
265
N. Indian Creek
5
4
Jake Creek
165
6
7
Table Rock Lake
Artilla Cove 4
Bradford Inn 2
Crow's Nest 3
Reed Springs Motel 1
Sunrise Suites 7
Treehouse on the Lake 5
Tribesman Resort 6

steam-heated hotel (Ye English Inn). While some of the rooms here are at the level of a low-end motel of the '70s, anyone lucky enough to choose Ye Inn—and who loves old hotels—will quickly realize the miles-apart difference between rooms like these in a lovingly preserved structure and the same in a 1970s motel. Here you feel the history that sets the lodging apart and know that you're at something special.

The stone lobby, with open beams and a fireplace, rises two stories. Most rooms seem to have been done in the 1920s, with heavy old dark-stained doors, old commercial brown knobs, and miscellaneous furniture, but all rooms have TV, phone, digital clock radio, coffeemaker (along with free danish supplied daily), bath with porcelain tub/shower, and either two double beds or a double and a single; there's a considerable mix, and suites are also available. Finally, guests have use of a swimming pool, and there's a coin laundry down the block. A best buy, budget-style, for the Branson area.

How About Those $24 Signs?

Occasionally, as you drive through Branson, you'll see temporary signs in front of modest motels that seem to offer rates of only $24 a night—far less than the $40 level with which my own hotel analysis begins. When you stop to inquire, you are invariably told—somewhat uneasily by an embarrassed desk clerk—that $24 is the price for a *single* room, and that doubles cost $39. Often, as in a classic case of a come-on, you'll learn that even the $39 is for only one or two units that are already rented. Such tactics are practiced during slow periods or slow cycles of the Branson high season (prices do plunge further in the depth of winter). In any event, the only time these temporary signs can be relied upon in your hotel search is when they add the expression "for two" to their come-on price. A sign reading "$39 for two" is a double room, and is a real value; a sign reading simply "$24" is for an occasional single person traveling through Branson. Be forewarned.

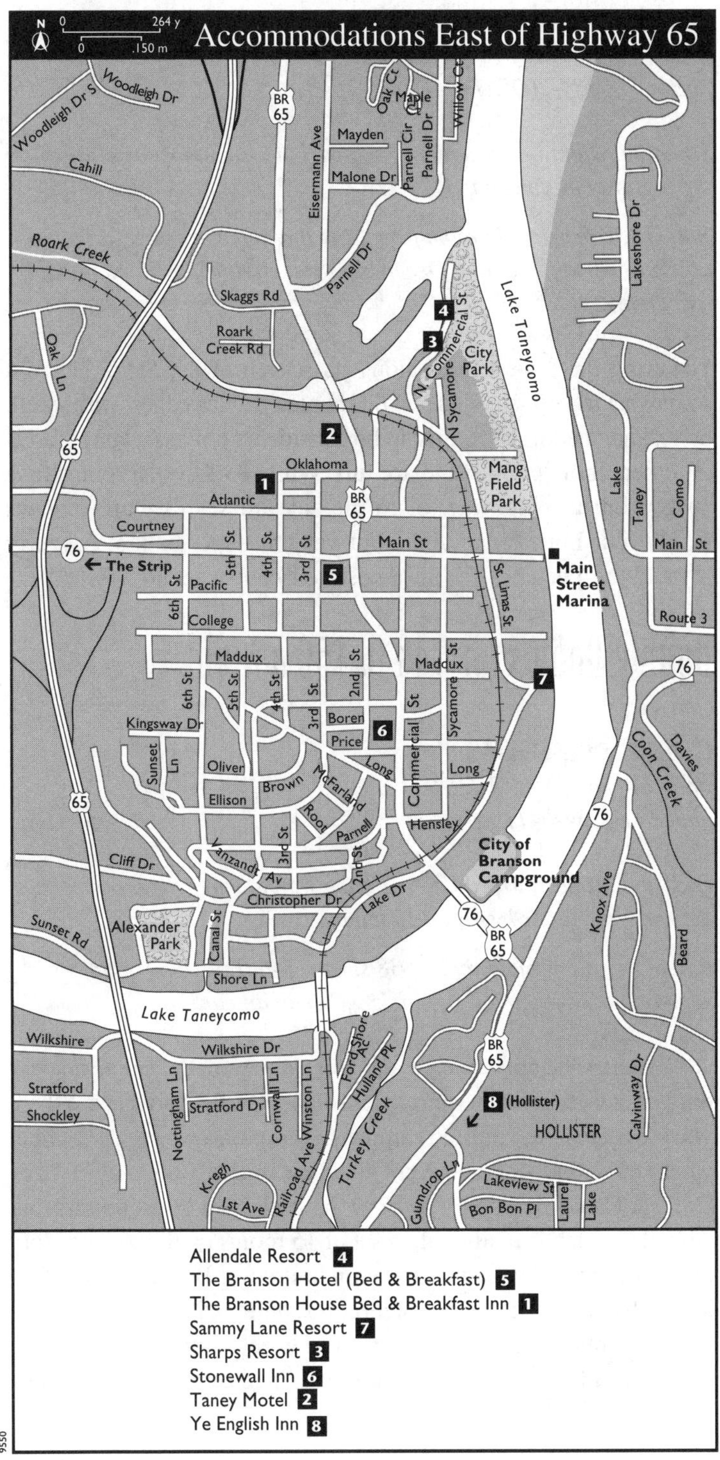
Accommodations East of Highway 65
N
0 264 y
0 .150 m
Woodleigh Dr S
Woodleigh Dr
Cahill
Roark Creek
Skaggs Rd
Roark Creek Rd
Oak Ln
Eisermann Ave
Mayden
Malone Dr
Oak Ct
Maple
Parnell Cir Ct
Parnell Dr
Willow Ct
Lakeshore Dr
Lake Taneycomo
N. Commercial St
City Park
N Sycamore St
Oklahoma
Atlantic
Courtney
Mang Field Park
Main St
The Strip
Pacific
College
6th St
5th St
4th St
3rd St
2nd St
Maddux
Main Street Marina
St. Limas St
Lake
Taney
Como
Route 3
Kingsway Dr
Sunset Ln
Boren
Price
Long
Oliver
Brown
McFarland
Ellison
Root
Parnell
Commercial St
Sycamore St
Hensley
Coon Creek
Davies
City of Branson Campground
Cliff Dr
Vanzandt Av
3rd St
Christopher Dr
Lake Dr
Knox Ave
Beard
Sunset Rd
Alexander Park
Canal St
Shore Ln
Lake Taneycomo
Wilkshire
Wilkshire Dr
Stratford
Shockley
Stratford Dr
Nottingham Ln
Cornwall Ln
Winston Ln
Ford Shore Ac
Hulland Pk
Turkey Creek
Railroad Ave
Kregh
1st Ave
Gumdrop Ln
Lakeview St
Bon Bon Pl
Laurel
Lake
(Hollister)
HOLLISTER
Calvinway Dr
Allendale Resort 4
The Branson Hotel (Bed & Breakfast) 5
The Branson House Bed & Breakfast Inn 1
Sammy Lane Resort 7
Sharps Resort 3
Stonewall Inn 6
Taney Motel 2
Ye English Inn 8
9550

Hillcrest Inn
1109 West Highway 76 (the Strip),
phone 417/334-2095, fax 417/335-2618

Location: Right in the center of things, but also almost as close to the highway as you can get.

Rates: $37 per double room from May through November, a remarkable $19 per double from December through April. Swimming pool. AE, D, MC, V.

Featuring the lowest rates along its stretch of the Strip, here's a somewhat frayed selection, a little splintered at the edges, with small, boxy, and unadorned rooms, to be considered only as a last resort if all others in its price range are full. While 8 of the 16 rooms face away from the highway, or to the side, they still won't always fulfill your hopes for quiet. And yet this super-budget property is totally respectable, for ultra-cost-conscious vacationers.

Double Rooms for $40 to $50 a Night

College of the Ozarks
Point Lookout, MO 65726,
phone 417/334-6411

Location: Almost directly across Lake Taneycomo from downtown Branson, the latter less than 10 minutes away.

Rates: $42 per double room, $38 single, $46 triple, $50 quad, year-round. No alcohol, no smoking, no credit cards.

★ Unquestionably one of the top values of the area, heavily booked, and therefore requiring reservations well in advance. Where you are is the lovely hilltop campus of this pioneering Ozark school where all 1,600 students work for their tuition (they call it "The College That Works"). So some of the students work at this 15-unit "motel," which is really only a set of 15 rooms on the second story of one of the college administration buildings. But rooms here are larger than most standard motel rooms, quiet, with large windows, pleasant grassy views, two queen beds in each, two reading lamps, a phone, bathroom heat lamp, firm beds, and ceramic tub/showers, just like in better motels everywhere. While guests do not have use of college recreational facilities, they're of course admitted to the outstanding, college-affiliated Ralph Foster Museum ("Smithsonian of the Ozarks"), which also offers some of the best gift items in all the Branson area. And meals at the nearby, ultra-inexpensive Rose O'Neill Friendship House (see the opening selection of our restaurant chapter) are bountiful and affordable.

(About the college's location: it's a short, several-minute drive from downtown Branson, which is itself about 15 to 20 minutes from most of the shows on the Strip, under usual driving conditions. Since you'll almost always need a car to reach the celebrity theaters [a single exception is discussed near the start of this chapter], the choice of the college's accommodations adds but the slightest additional time to your trip.)

The Family Inn
208 Old County Road,
phone 800/798-2213 or 417/334-2113

Location: A quiet half-block off Highway 76, close by Engler's Block (a distinguished shopping emporium discussed later on), and therefore near the very start of the Strip as you approach it from downtown Branson. The hotel is also close to where Roark Valley Road intersects with Highway 76, and Roark is one of the back roads that parallel the Strip, enabling you to avoid the heavy traffic as you drive to one of the theaters.

Rates: Double rooms are $44 from May through October, closer to $20 in April and November; closed December through March; two-bedroom units for four are $65 a night in all months of operation. D, MC, V.

A rather ordinary and unmemorable place, but affordable and clean, with 25 units (of which 9 have full kitchenettes) dating from the 1970s, all since remodeled by Larry and Jan Sloan, who took over in 1983. These are typical motel spaces with sculpted carpets, basic contract furniture, two queen-size beds per room. Guests enjoy free morning coffee, a small pool, and a relatively peaceful setting. Good value for what's available in the low-end category of Branson accommodations.

Good Shepherd Inn
100 West Main Street,
phone 800/324-3457 or 417/334-1695

Location: Near the Highway 65 interchange with Highway 76, and thus near the beginning of the Strip, but not yet on it.

Rates: Open year-round, the inn charges $46 per double room from mid-May to Christmas, $37 from mid-April to mid-May, $26 all other times. Swimming pool. AE, D, DC, MC, V.

A rather basic, 63-unit motel two stories high, clean and fairly well maintained, and operated by Ray and Helena Hunter who fled Ontario's cold winters in 1977 to take over the property. Ray is an articulate observer of today's Branson, and he and Helena are usually at the front desk and accessible to you. Rooms are all with two double beds, a single reading lamp, bedcovers that don't match but are color-coordinated with curtains. Decent value.

Reed Springs Motel
HCR-1, Box 10, Reed Springs, MO 65737,
phone 417/272-3833

Location: In a town of 411 inhabitants, some 7 to 8 miles north of Silver Dollar City, 4 miles north of Branson West, about 15 miles from Branson itself.

Rates: $40 per double room in the peak summer season (plus an extra $1.50 if you're paying with credit card), $28.50 in mid-season, $20 in January and February (same credit card surcharge).

Thanks to a talented mayor (Dr. Jane Fitzgerald, ornithologist, who heads the Ozark Center for Wildlife Research), a caring population, a main street made pretty with flower beds and attractive signage, and weekend musical presentations, Reed Springs is beginning to make a name for itself, which keeps its 12-room, one-story motel busier than you'd expect. Units are arrayed in a long row just off the road, far enough away to be quiet, and though they're rather basic, they have some character. Five have bedrooms separate from a living room, and tub-showers; others are one large room with stall showers only. All, nonetheless, are priced the same. And while each has a television set, none has a phone.

Rest-Wel Motel
1033 West Highway 76,
phone 417/334-2323

Location: At the relatively quiet start of the Strip, where Roark Valley Road cuts off to provide an alternative back road to many of the theaters on the Strip.

Rates: As high as $48.50 per double room in the peak May-through-October high season, with members of AAA or AARP getting $4 off; the same rooms are as low as $22 from January through mid-April. D, MC, V.

A 15-unit mom-and-pop with good, low rates. What you get is a basic motel room with tired-looking (though clean) sculptured carpet, well-used gold fabric upholstery, and furniture matched in what must once have been a popular antique look. But the beds are super firm, and two queen-size varieties occupy each room. All rooms also have at least three chairs, four pieces of art, and EuroBath liquid soap in both the bathroom and alongside the lavatory outside the bathroom. So although the rooms have a yesteryear aspect, they're as complete as motel rooms costing at least $20 a night more. Guests also have use of a little front pool and receive free morning coffee.

Stonewall Inn (not to be confused with Stonewall West Motor Inn, see above)
511 S. Commercial Street in downtown Branson,
phone 417/334-3416

Rates: $40 to $46 per double room (depending on size) from June through October; $32 in May, November, and December; $22 in April; closed second week of December through March. AE, D, MC, V.

Back in the 1960s, when Baldknobbers, the Presleys, and Silver Dollar City were the only entertainments in or near Branson, the owners lived in a frontier-style colonial house that still stands in the very midst of their 17-unit "inn" consisting of two separate sections (the one in back is quieter). Today, rooms here are about as close as you'll find to tacky, but they're clean and reasonably well maintained, brown and beige, with lots of vinyl, veneer paneling, and almost shaggy (just shy of that) carpeting. But the beds are firm, the bathrooms adequate, and you can't beat the price for lodgings within easy walking distance of anything in the downtown area of Branson.

Manny's Motel
3515 West Highway 76 (the Strip),
phone 417/334-2815

Rates: $42.50 per double room in high season, $38.50 single; $17.50 single or double in lowest season, with various intermediate price levels. D, MC, V.

Another "last resort" in this low-priced category. These 12 upstairs rooms that are part of Branson's standout Mexican restaurant are rather small; and you might want to ask in advance to make sure that the light/heater in the little bathroom isn't as noisy as a rattletrap bus. Furniture is two softish double beds, two cushioned captain's chairs, chenille bedcovers, pseudo-open beams, a block wall, another wall of vinyl-synthetic paneling, a third wall of textured covering. Somehow, it's so basic, so without pretense, that it's almost as romantic as those small Mexican hotels where you might have stayed as a youth while traveling through the provinces of Guerrero or Yucatan. But there's a TV set and phone in each.

Double Rooms for $50 to $65 a Night

Fall Creek Resort
1 Fall Creek Drive,
phone 800/56-CONDO or 417/334-6404

Location: 2½ miles south of the Strip along Highway 165, on the way to Table Rock Dam (Table Rock State Park is less than 10 minutes away), in the country.

Rates: Standard units (sleeping two, king bed) are $59 a night, and are often discounted by 10% and more to AAA or AARP members. Studios that sleep four and include kitchenettes are $72. One-bedroom units sleeping up to four, with full kitchen, are $84. Two-bedroom condos that sleep six, $109. All subject, again, to those AAA or AARP discounts. Open all year. AE, D, MC, V.

★ Just when you think you've seen the best, you come across Fall Creek Resort. This condo-rental community is so far ahead of most other lodgings in Branson that you'll ask: Why stay elsewhere? (provided you can find a vacancy). At least 600 units of every description will be available here in 1995—everything from rustic cabins to super-deluxe two-bedroom apartments in the most upscale of the resort's divisions. You'll pay less for a fully equipped unit with kitchen than you will for a distinctly inferior motel room on certain stretches of the Strip.

You are among trees, you can hear birds. Some units are directly on Lake Taneycomo, just about a mile below Table Rock Dam. Fishing is the best. Stay here, and at night, after a show and with the use of a good map, you'll find yourself on one of the back roads of Branson leading here—whoosh!—out of the traffic. How did all this come to be? Because of the decision of most condo owners here to put their units into a rental pool; this way they earn income during those months when they themselves are not in residence. The units themselves? All furnished in modern, comfy-contemporary style; all in buildings of from two to three stories, with no elevators. Get into the more luxurious units and you find exceptional facilities—better than most of us enjoy at home: double lavatories in bedrooms, single and double Jacuzzi tubs, nearby golf course or waterfront facilities, wood fireplaces with wood supplied. All units are serviced daily; all possess color cable TV and dial phones with free local calls; and all but the standard units have at least some kind of kitchen facility with dishwasher. Add: a central fitness center, four swimming pools (one indoor-out), mini-golf, complimentary continental breakfast, clubhouse, tennis courts, shuffleboard, and full-service marina (though, of course, with charges for boat rentals).

Artilla Cove
Off Indian Point Road in Branson,
phone 417/338-2346

Rates: High-season (June through August) rates of $51 per double for duplex, nonkitchen units, $63 for stand-alone A-frame, $64 for up to four persons in one-bedroom duplex, $95 for up to six persons in two-bedroom, stand-alone unit. Low season (March, April, November, and December) rates are $15 to $45 less, and still further reduced for four-night stays. A "shoulder season" of May and September is priced between high and low season levels. Closed in January and February. D, MC, V.

With its knock-your-socks-off view as you drive down the side road from Indian Point Road (Artilla is the last of some six resorts on this country lane), its big picture windows, its cook-out areas, this 10-unit property is the value pick of the Indian Point resorts. Units—a woody mix of trapezoid A-frames (alpine in feeling, with sharply peaked roofs and loft sleeping quarters) and freestanding and duplex cabins—are some 30 years old, but beautifully maintained, light in tone, and with lots of wood paneling and textured ceilings. All the homelike units (far better than your usual fishing camp lodging) have kitchens equipped with coffee pot, toaster, and either microwave or conventional oven; country art on the walls; and queen or king beds. And finally, guests have use of an outdoor pool, coin laundry, grills, and picnic tables.

Crow's Nest
HCR 1, Box 792, Branson 65616,
phone 417/338-2524

Location: Like Artilla Cove (see immediately above), this is as close to the lake as resorts can get, though west off Indian Rock Road, not east, and the view down isn't quite as striking.

Rates: In season, from $54 per double for a one-bedroom unit to $72 and $75 for two-bedroom units for up to four persons. April rates are two-thirds of on-season levels, rates for May, September, and October are about three-quarters those levels. Closed November through March. MC, V.

Another of the smaller, rustic resorts on giant Table Rock Lake, dating from the mid-1960s, with 15 units in one- and two-bedroom wood-paneled cottages, both stand-alones and duplexes, each with fully equipped kitchen and deck. An advantage of these older resorts is their superior landscaping, their well-developed flower beds, their natural colors more consistent with nature's surroundings, less decorator-styled. Guests barbecuing meals at the outdoor grills feel removed not simply from cities, but from suburbs. They have use of a large pool, a game room, a playground; and here, as at Artilla Cove (see above) and Tribesman Resort (see below), they can rent boats and hire guides at the resort marinas for lake fishing.

Tribesman Resort
Rt. 1, Box 1032,
phone 800/447-3327 or 417/338-2616

Location: On an extension of Highway 76; the Indian Point cutoff road is 9 miles from the western edge of the Branson build-up, 3 miles south of Silver Dollar City.

Rates: In high season rates average about $56 for two persons, and go up to $136 for a four-bedroom lodge with eight beds; they then drop by $10 to $20 in less pressured months. Open all year. AE, D, MC, V.

Spread over some 25 rustic acres, Tribesman is one of the largest, and among the best, of the approximately 30 resorts that line Table Rock Lake along Indian Point. And though the stretch of Highway 76 that brings you here is decidedly hilly, curvy, and difficult, many visitors to the area prefer to lodge in this somewhat remote lakeside area and then make the 15-mile drive to town in the evening for the shows, preferring the superb bass fishing by day, and the quiet late at night. Lodgings at Tribesman are of many kinds, from one-bedroom apartments to two-story houses that sleep up to eight. All units are carpeted, have portable barbecues, phones, AC/heat, color cable TV, clothes washers and dryers, parking spaces right at the door, comfortable furnishings (upholstered sofa and chairs, dining room tables with chairs), firm double beds, some scenic art in living rooms, and access to two pools, a marina with rental boats, and sundries shop; and, although you don't get housekeeping, you do receive fresh towels daily. Most important, there's a busy summer program of activities for children (treasure hunts, fishing tournaments, storytelling), and the resort's only drawback, to my mind, is that not all units have lake views; inquire about that when you book.

(Incidentally, these resorts along Table Rock Lake are not of the same quality as the posh hotels lining the Lake of the Ozarks north of here. For one thing, they're in occasional danger of being flooded from increased water levels at Table Rock, and therefore aren't the subject of heavy investment. For another, the generally low regard in the Branson area for government-enforced zoning and construction regulation means some of the resorts look tacky or cluttered.)

Sammy Lane Resort
320 E. Main Street,
phone 417/334-3253

Location: In the heart of downtown Branson, along Lake Taneycomo.

Rates: Individual cabins are $55 a night for up to four persons, $65 for units in the multi-unit lodge housing up to six persons apiece. Closed November through February. No credit cards accepted, no phones in any of the units.

Sammy Lane, in case you're wondering, is Samantha Lane, the spirited and beautiful heroine of *Shepherd of the Hills*, that massively bestselling novel of 1907 that first unleashed tourism on Branson; the Sammy Lane Resort was opened in 1924, and has had only three owners (the current ones are Mike and Claudia Brown) in all the ensuing years. A resort (a collection of cabins and little hut-like bungalows) on several acres surrounding the largest privately owned swimming pool in Missouri, this is a very plain, but exciting, camp-like facility at the very foot of downtown Branson on the lake.

What's most compelling about Sammy Lane's is its ability to house families affordably. Its $55 units take four persons easily, six on occasion, and have kitchens (some with microwaves), gliders on the porch, and fireplaces inside; everyone has access to a barbecue grill near the water, and washing machines for laundry. Some units are actual log cabins (with logs both inside and out), sans carpeting; others, more recently built, have screened porches, board paneling, and carpets. Best units ($65 a night) are those that are not freestanding: six of them, in what's called "the lodge." These have two bedrooms each, carpeted sleeping suites with cathedral-ceiling living rooms, and again the fireplaces and full kitchen. Sofas, upholstered chairs, beautiful plank tables, fireplaces built into high rock walls, make them swank, even though rustic.

Honeysuckle Inn
3598 Shepherd of the Hills Expressway,
phone 800/942-3553 or 417/335-2030

Location: Near the intersection with Highway 76 (and that's at the very end of the Strip, away from downtown Branson).

Rates: A pleasing $64.95 for double-, queen-, or king-bedded rooms from April through October; $57.95 November and December, $39.95 from January through March. Seniors get a $4 per room discount. Add: an outdoor pool and spa, coin laundry with two washers and dryers, free coffee, free continental breakfast.

Two hundred and fifteen rooms in two two-story wings are of attractive, yellow clapboard construction with white trim. About the only thing wrong with the property is its immense blacktop parking area between the wings (you can instantly imagine how differently—and how much better—it could have been laid out). But all is redeemed inside through the distinctive furnishing and decoration of rooms. In fact, Honeysuckle Inn alerts you to how even a boxy, basic motel room can be furnished with enough style to leave you feeling the place is special. They do that here in several ways.

Furniture is oak and substantial; headboards have country embossing. A slight darkness is effected, which is to say, something good, a sense of stage management, creating a mood. You glimpse a pair of upholstered chairs in a pleasing curved back pattern and graceful legs; you have digital clock radio, two lamps for the two beds, lace instead of routine curtains, a pair of botanical prints on the wall, vanity lights to the rear lavatory area, bedcovers of vivid, abstract patterns, leaf-like, flame-like, burgundy carpets, pink-tinted walls (in all but the west wing); the tinting is barely that, but the pink is just enough that these rooms glow. You sense the burgundy rising, a palette gently carried from intensity through to reflection, a room encompassing a range of emotions, more than just a place for sleeping. The stage is set. A couple in these rooms might work something out.

Ozark Valley Inn
2693 Shepherd of the Hills Expressway, phone 800/947-4666 or 417/336-4666

Rates: Double rooms for $59.95 from May through mid-December, $45 in late April, $35 in March and early April, $25 from mid-December through February, always with free continental breakfast included. Other amenities: an outdoor pool, hot tub, game room with pool table, coin laundry.

An attractive, independently owned, 66-unit motel that's kept super-clean, has a friendly desk staff of family owners, and offers several subtle distinctions, such as brick-styled balconies around its exterior corridors. Two stories up front, the motel changes to three stories out back, where rooms to the rear look out onto what was a dense forest before Charley Pride built his theater there and they put in a big power line. Early risers, though, can still see deer forage. Best of all, there's no sea of blacktop out front. You'll like the spaciousness of the rooms, their two reading lamps for two beds, their scattered floral art, their firm mattresses (curtains, however, don't well match the attractive quilted bedcovers, and bathroom doors are thin).

Expressway Inn
691 Shepherd of the Hills Expressway,
phone 800/688-3682 or 417/334-1700

Rates: $52 per double room from May through October, $40 in November and December (with free continental breakfast thrown in year-round), closed January and February. D, MC, V.

A relatively new (built from 1991 to 1993), family-run, 106-unit motel of several buildings, whose chief distinction is its quiet location, rustic-style furniture, cleanliness, and good rates; among the better values in Branson. The motel is of two and three stories, and has no elevator, but is so laid out that you needn't walk more than one flight up to reach your room. Outdoor pool, coin laundry, and good sheltering canopy out front.

Taney Motel
311 Highway 65 Business North,
phone 800/334-3193 or 417/334-3143

Location: On the north side of downtown Branson, where Highway 65 crosses Roark Creek.

Rates: $52.75 per double room from mid-April through October, $38.75 the rest of the year (and the Taney is open year-round). Rooms with microwave oven and large refrigerator cost $82.75 high season, $52.75 all other times. AE, D, MC, V.

This ordinary-looking 28-unit roadside motel will surprise you with features that many far more expensive properties don't possess. Rooms have at least a small fridge, heat lamps in bathrooms, twin reading lamps, art on the walls, two queen-size beds or a king; and some rooms have two sinks. Wonder of wonders, the Taney takes pets without charge (though if the pet damages the room, you pay). And there's a swimming pool and free coffee in the lobby. It certainly isn't the cheapest in town, but one of the better.

Stratford House Inn
3502 West Highway 76 (the Strip),
phone 417/334-3700

Rates: A uniform $62 per double room from May through October. All other months, is open weekends only, but may go into year-round operation if more theaters adopt an all-year policy. AE, D, DC, MC, V, and AARP reduction of 10%.

A better value than the Victorian Inn next door, though both are under common ownership. Both hotels are themed (faintly Tudor), but unlike the Victorian, the Stratford carries that colorful approach into guest rooms, and the difference is rewarding. Each has a separate desk with its own chair, an armchair, upholstered luggage rack, separate vanity area, separate toilet and shower/tub compartments, lamps with either two separately switched bulbs or, in the king rooms, two lamps, textured ceiling, better color-coordinated bedspreads and curtains. There are nonsmoking rooms, handicapped-accessible rooms, and an outdoor pool.

Rosebud Inn
2400 Roark Valley Road,
phone 417/336-4000

Rates: Double rooms for $64 from June through October; $54 in May; $45 in April, November, and December; $39 from January through March. AE, MC, V, and $5 per room discount for AARP members.

A new (November 1993), 65-unit, three-story motel with swimming pool that's best chosen for its quiet and convenient location atop a hill near the Charley Pride Theater, and on one of those valuable bypass roads that lets you reach theaters on the Strip without actually driving on the Strip. Rooms are larger than most, beautifully new, but with nothing more to show for their newness and upscale rates than at any other basic and cheaper motel: only a single reading lamp per room, no wall art, bright green carpets, open hanging racks—you know the rest. There's also a high canopy out front that's not so embracing as to assure dryness if you face a driving rain.

Gazebo Inn
2424 West Highway 76 (the Strip),
phone 800/873-7990 or 417/335-3826

Rates: $63 double nightly throughout the year, except in October when the rate advances to $73. You can save $3 a night by booking in advance or with an AARP card. Entire property is nonsmoking, and there's one handicapped-accessible room. AE, D, MC, V.

What distinguishes this new (early '90s) three-story lodging is its decision to add a bed-and-breakfast flavor to what is otherwise a fairly standard, 73-unit motel (set back far enough from the highway to be quiet). It's achieved through styling. You come in and you say, "Ah, different," which translates to "Ah, better." And you're reacting, essentially, to the dust-ruffle bedcovers in a blowsy floral matched by curtains, to the solid oak (but contract) furniture, the vanity lights over the wash area. Rooms either have two queens or a king with loveseat that isn't convertible to a sleeper. And there are nice picket touches to the exterior facades, including pretty porches.

Southern Oaks Inn
3295 Shepherd of the Hills Expressway,
phone 800/324-8752 or 417/335-8108

Location: On that easier-to-drive, winding thoroughfare that now houses the Shoji Tabuchi Theater and several good restaurants.

Rates: Open all year; $61.95 for double rooms from May through October, $51.95 in November and December, $46.95 in April, $43.95 in March, $39.95 in January and February. Indoor and heated outdoor pools, coin laundry, free coffee, large blocks of nonsmoking rooms, spacious two-story lobby with separate seating sections. D, MC, V.

A 150-unit motel for people who like large, uncluttered rooms. These, as characterized to me by a desk clerk, are "Texas-sized" rooms designed to be that way by their Lone Star State owner, and corner rooms are larger still; they also have recessed closets rather than simple hanging clothes racks. Otherwise, sad to say, Southern Oaks is motel city, the usual: you'll find twin bed lamps but no art in rooms, a choice of either two queen beds or king, the usual molded baths with outside vanities beneath fluorescent bulbs, burgundy and burgundy-mottled green color schemes.

Aunt Mollie's Boarding House

633 Shepherd of the Hills Expressway,
phone 417/334-0366

Rates: Double rooms for a favorable $52 from May through October, $45 in November and December, $35 in April, always with continental breakfast included; closed January and February. D, MC, V.

This 62-unit, two- and three-story motel is named for a favorite character in Harold Bell Wright's turn-of-the-century novel about the Branson area, *The Shepherd of the Hills*, as was another motel down the road, Uncle Matt's (Aunt Mollie's husband). Both were built by the same person (Gary Snadon), and both are identical (Uncle Matt's is at 3306 Shepherd of the Hills Expressway, phone 417/334-0031). Indeed, the two were the first lodgings to appear (1987) on the Expressway, from the same blueprints, each facing an almost identical hill on the other side of the road. Gary Snadon is one of the wheels in Branson, who at one time owned most of the land on both sides of the Expressway, and who has built many of the better motels along here (Foxborough, Expressway, among them).

For the rates set forth above, you get a basic motel room made a bit different by two rocking chairs and turned bedsteads. Mattresses are as good as they get, but these beds are only doubles (extra long at that), not queens. (Some will be converted to the wider variety next year). Guests have use of a pool and coin laundry, they're fed a continental breakfast, and coffee is kept hot (if not fresh) in the little lobby, just big enough for a rack of Branson t-shirts and brochures (is there a lobby in Branson that doesn't tout the shows?). Friendly people at the desk, well informed about the town. Good, deep canopy out front. But pool sits plop in the middle of the blacktop. Uninviting. Price is what makes this a good value.

Magnolia Inn
3311 Shepherd of the Hills Expressway, phone 800/222-7239 or 417/334-2300

Rates: Double rooms rent for $62 from May through October, $54 in November and December, $45 in April, $35 January through March. D, MC, V.

Just when you think you've seen it all, along comes this 153-unit motel built in 1991, where the color scheme throughout is bright purple, apparently in an effort to pursue a "colonial" theme, for reasons that escape me. (Elsewhere are Tara-suggestive columns that hold up the big driveway marquee.) In large units with double queens or kings, you actually find purple carpets, bedcovers in purple, mauve, and blue, chairs in rose, and walls papered in a motley of purple and other colors. (Contrary Mary's Restaurant, across the street, affiliated with the inn, is also in purple.) And what does the title "Magnolia Inn" refer to? Nothing. Like so much in Branson, it's simply a name. Guests have use of an outdoor pool and hot tub, a gift shop, coin laundry, beauty salon off the lobby, and a coffeemaker at work around the clock in a tiny room off the lobby. Decaf is one of the options.

76 Mall Inn
76 Country Music Boulevard (another name for West Highway 76, the Strip), phone 800/356-4336 or 417/335-3535

Rates: From $54 to $67 per double room throughout the year. AE, D, MC, V.

A big one, 330 units in size, smack dab in the center of a colorful, family-owned shopping mall that has the largest-volume Bonanza Steak House in all of America, and also presents country music shows almost continuously from 10am to 10pm, daily. If you're into indoor mini-golf, 3-D movies, video game arcades, or simply having the reassurance of nearby mall shopping, you'll love it. Actually, the motel is clean and well run, a notch above the routine in Branson; rooms are larger than mini, beds are firm, the AC/heat works well, the mirrors are large, and twin reading lamps make reading in bed easier for two, and there's free coffee for guests all the time. To be sure, there's not an ounce of greenery in sight.

Seven Gables Inn
305 Highway 165 South,
phone 800/280-7077 or 417/334-7077

Location: Next to the pleasing Sugar Hill Farm Restaurant.

Rates: $60 a night takes care of up to four in a room (that's in peak season, April 20 through October), $50 from November through mid-December, $35 from March to April 19, $30 December 18 through February. D, MC, V.

A 78-unit motel, about to become 130 units in the year ahead. Typical of Branson, you get an interesting exterior of multiple gables and dormers—think of what "Seven Gables" evokes—but inside everything is bland and generic, the exact opposite of the raging, varied themes—love, honor, and conflict—of country music. Rooms have two queens or a king, two chairs—you know the rest. Beds are semi-firm, there's a piece of wall art, and local calls are free. Don't you wish that the exciting promise of the facade could have been carried through inside?

Peach Tree Inn
2450 Green Mountain Drive,
phone 417/335-5900

Rates: Double rooms are $64 from June through mid-September, $69 mid-September through October, $54 mid-April through May, $45 November through mid-April; will probably be closed in January and February. AAA, AARP, and anybody else who makes a case gets $3 off per night. AE, D, DC, MC, V.

One more basic motel, except that it has an elevator (rare in this sort of establishment) to service the topmost of its three stories. There's a heated outdoor pool plus a hot tub, and a coin laundry with two washers, two dryers. Otherwise, you know the rest: two queen beds (super-firm), molded bath, two reading lamps, vanity lights, a bit of art.

Foxborough Inn
589 Shepherd of the Hills Expressway,
phone 800/335-4369 or 417/335-4369

Location: Just down the hill from the former Wayne Newton Theater, now renamed the Shenandoah South Theater.

Rates: $59 double in season (May through October), $42 off-season, 10% discount for seniors. Extra amenities include free continental breakfast, coffee around the clock, a swimming pool, some nonsmoking and handicapped-accessible rooms. AE, D, MC, V.

A relatively new (1992), sparkling clean, 177-unit, green-and-white-colored motel with a stylish colonial look to its rooms; each of them has two queen beds, a side table, two upholstered side chairs, a molded bathroom with washbasin outside the toilet/tub/shower compartment, with open hanging clothes rack, TV, phone, no charge for local calls or for ice, elevator servicing all four floors of the building. Competently run.

Friendship Inn
3015 Green Mountain Drive,
phone 800/324-8749 or 417/335-4248

Location: On a hillside, about a half mile behind the Grand Palace Theater.

Rates: $62.95 for a double room from April through October, $49.95 from November through March, always including free continental breakfast served in the pine-floored lobby. AE, D, MC, V.

This time, a 99-unit, two- and three-story motel built and furnished to formula, and a fairly tired formula at that (two beds, two chairs, hanging rack, molded tub/shower), but with one or two distinctive elements that make it a tiny bit special. To create a much-lived-in colonial look, the contract furniture has been stained mahogany, the headboards have split pediments, there's a hunt club scene on guestroom walls, and paisley bedcovers on the two queen beds in most rooms match the curtains. At least it's different. Regrettably, the rooms need two or three prints instead of one, but balancing out those disappointments are free local and credit-card long distance calls and a large, attractive hothouse-like, heated indoor swimming pool. A good value.

Victorian Inn
3500 W. Highway 76 (the Strip),
phone 417/334-1711

Rates: Double rooms range from $56 to $64 from May to mid-December, average $35 to $40 in March and April. Closed mid-December through February. 10% discount for AARP members. AE, D, DC, MC, V.

The exterior theme is Victorian, with much gingerbread, and you find a few Victorian-like gifts on sale in the lobby, but otherwise this is simply a basic lower-end motel along the highway, with 39 standard rooms containing two doubles or a king bed; most face the back in a two-story wing, and are therefore quiet. Contract furniture, only a single bed lamp in rooms with two beds, open hanging clothes rack. Outdoor pool, free coffee any time in the lobby, no charges for local calls.

Baldknobbers Motel
2845 Highway 76 West (the Strip),
phone 417/334-7948

Location: In the very midst of the Strip, an easy walk to as many as nine celebrity theaters.

Rates: From $58.85 to $69.85 for double rooms, May through October; from $47.85 to $58.85 in March, April, and from November to December 10. The motel closes from December 11 to March 1. AARP discount of $2. AE, D, MC, V.

Two stories, with a pool, and right next door to the Baldknobbers Hillbilly Jamboree Show featuring those millionaire hillbilly make-believes (Droopy Drawers, Stub) who started the Branson entertainment scene more than 35 years ago. You are in one of the most action-packed, neon-lit, people-heavy segments of the Strip. What the motel supplies is just that—basic motel. Rooms are clean and have firm beds (two double beds or a king-size one with Jacuzzi), though you may get a chair that wants re-upholstering. Curtains and bedcovers don't necessarily match, and there's only one reading lamp for the two of you. But if you've come here with the main intention of catching the Baldknobbers show, you'll be oblivious to those slight defects.

Dutch Kountry Inn

2425 West Highway 76 (the Strip),
phone 800/541-5660 or 417/335-2100

Rates: Double rooms for $50 and $60 from March 25 through December, $40 from January 1 to March 25, but the real values are duplex lofts or adjoining rooms for families of four to six persons renting for $85 from March 25 through December, and for $60 from January 1 to March 24.

As a general rule, it's best in my experience to avoid places that deliberately misspell their names; they're trying to draw attention by tricks when, typically, what they offer doesn't rate attention by itself. The three-story, 292-unit Dutch Kountry Inn goes further with a big replica of a paddlewheel mill outside. Its owners are mainly in the business of what they call "outdoor recreation"—mini-golf and go-carts in a mini-amusement park for kids just outside the motel. That said, Dutch Kountry still offers something worthwhile.

Although most of the units are ordinary motel-style, furnished with basic stock out of the contract warehouse, an unusual group features downstairs and upstairs loft units, good for two couples traveling together who want their privacy, or equally, of course, for a family with two or more kids. Downstairs is a bedroom with king bed and full bath; upstairs—up the circular stairs—a second bedroom with queen bed and half bath (no shower). Beds are semi-firm to soft. Other family units include adjoining rooms that can be set up with as many as four double beds for sleeping as many as eight. How would I rate this lodging vis-á-vis other family hotels? It's a notch below the Queen Anne—about the level of the Victorian, but not as good a value. It is only the loft units that recommend the property at all.

Economy Plus Motel

Shepherd of the Hills Expressway,
phone 800/335-7221 or 417/334-8890

Location: Near the Shoji Tabuchi Theater.

Rates: Off-season, they can drop as low as $21 for two. High-season, they can go up to $62. Swimming pool. No discounts. MC, V.

This 91-unit motel provides the poorest aesthetic quality of any lodging in its vicinity. It makes a big thing out of being the cheapest (with an immense sign on the road), and it's true that it gets that way in low season, when prices can drop to $21 and less, for two. Yet during the peak, its room rates can soar as high as $62, and you can clearly do better than that in a great many nearby properties. I suspect that readers will share my own dismay over a place that promotes itself as cheap, and then occasionally tries to get a higher rate than better properties in the area. Moreover, the look of the place is hardly winning. Construction resembles the cheap curtainwall buildings of mid-century—it puts you in mind of industrial construction where protection from the elements is the sole goal. The paved parking lot is also twice as big as you'd expect, because next door, without any wall, is an RV park run by the same people.

Rooms are ordinary, with no embellishments; no art, the TV flush on the dresser, two bed lamps beside either two queen beds or a queen and a double. Morning coffee provided; no lobby at all, just a check-in desk. I'd make this a last resort along Shepherd of the Hills Expressway, and mention the motel only by way of supplying an impassioned, opinionated warning about it.

Double Rooms for $65 to $75 a Night

Lighthouse Inn
2375 Green Mountain Drive,
phone 800/237-LIGHT or 417/336-6161

Rates: Double rooms for $67.50 to $77.50 from April through October, $59.50 to $69.50 in November and December, closed from January through mid-March. Nonsmoking and handicapped rooms; small discounts for AAA and AARP members.

★ A 91-room winner! A Branson breakthrough! Indoor corridors, spacious rooms, all at the same rates that elsewhere get you less. In addition, a bit of a hotel feeling. No cramped lobby, but one two stories high, and an atrium-like, high-windowed terrace beyond the lobby, where guests can socialize a bit over their free continental breakfast of bagels and hot cider in addition to the standard items.

Guests also enjoy in-room coffee with free refills, on-site coin laundry, a heated outdoor pool and hot tub, free local calls, a game room, and two queen-size beds in every room, each with firm mattresses. Why the title of "Lighthouse"? A pure gimmick, like the title of Peach Tree Inn for the motel down the street, which has nothing to do with peach trees or Atlanta. Nevertheless, a winner; it doesn't transform Branson, but it does establish that better is always possible.

Shadowbrook
1610 West Highway 76,
phone 800/641-4600 or 417/334-4173

Location: Despite the address, just outside downtown Branson, away from the garish neon section known as the Strip, in 27 acres of private park.

Rates: Double rooms for $65 to $72 from May to mid-September, $74 to $78 from mid-September through October, $58 to $62 in November and December, $48 to $52 in April. Closed from January 1 to March 31.

★ An outstanding value, and the top selection in its price category. Shadowbrook is the companion lodging to Edgewood (a somewhat costlier resort discussed below), but it's the older and the far more desirable of the two hotels that face each other across a green expanse where deer and albino squirrels can be sighted as the property backs away from the deathly highway. Shadowbrook is a delightful, three-story structure in which every room looks out onto nature; each unit has an attractive green canopy that not only enhances the look of the overall property, but also provides privacy for guests not wanting to close their curtains. Rooms have the best kind of age: Their beds are oak-framed with a bit of carved detailing, they are topped with attractive, quilted bedcovers, and other oak pieces include a small desk, a chair, and dresser. Beds are firm, baths have heat lamps built into the ceiling, a dehumidifier is elsewhere in the room, and the value begins in a large, almost lodge-like lobby with several seating areas looking out onto the woody landscaping. An on-site swimming pool is a pleasant final touch.

Treehouse on the Lake
HCR 1, Box 1163-12, Branson 65616,
phone 417/338-5199

Location: Near Indian Point (Indian Point being that lakefront peninsula just below Silver Dollar City).

Rates: Studios (with partition arch between bed and cooking areas), sleeping up to four persons, rent for $65 a night. Two-bedroom, two-bath units, housing up to six, rent for $115. Closed for a month after Christmas. MC, V.

In addition to resorts, the Indian Point area has a number of condo communities with units for rent. Best is this semi-rustic, woody, hillside development begun in 1988, where every unit has an excellent view of the lake. The value is undeniable, and the area is close enough to be convenient for the theaters, yet away from any traffic-jammed, through road; it's the sleeper of Branson. So far, 26 units are in the rental program, all varying in decor (because each is separately owned). Yet basic to all is a distinctively styled, rustic wood exterior, with interiors contemporary in their furnishings, fully carpeted, and with art on the walls. Colors tend to be pastel, there's much upholstered furniture, the closets are walk-ins, the kitchens are fully supplied and have dishwashers, and there's a swimming pool and laundry room on the grounds. Elevator in the four-story wings, none in the two-story kind.

Ozark Regal Hotel
3010 Green Mountain Drive,
phone 417/336-2200

Rates: Doubles for $69 a night in May, June, September, and October; $59 in July and August; $49 November through April. 10% discount for seniors in May, June, September, and October. D, DC, MC, V.

Though this is, technically, simply a two-story lodging with 100 units, it's elevator equipped, and has a sense of solidity and avoidance of common motel features. The manager and people at the desk are quiet in demeanor, and all rooms are accessed from the interior, which means that the bathroom isn't at the far end of the room as in most motels; here, you don't enter looking down to an oh-so-dreary sink against the back wall and inevitable hanging clothes rack. Standard rooms offer either two queen-size beds or a king, with standard table and two chairs; suites (costing $20 a night more) have seating areas with two deep-cushioned armchairs and unusually large bathroom/vanity areas with exceptional storage space, two sinks, and a full-length mirror.

Barrington Hotel

263 Shepherd of the Hills Expressway,
phone 800/760-8866 or 417/334-8866

Rates: Start at $44 in low season (November through April), and hit a maximum of $66 from May through October, though rooms with king-size beds cost $6 to $19 more, depending on time of year. All rates include a free continental breakfast. AE, D, MC, V.

Another solid hotel—four stories with a grand stone facade—charging far less than for equivalent rooms at, say, the Crowne Plaza (see below). While you might wish that they had three-way bulbs or recessed closets, you don't have quite the supply warehouse look of, say, the Branson Towers (see below), and you also get luggage racks, vanities, and good, metallic-threaded bedcovers. Add: two elevators, coin laundry, pool, hot tub, and an immense lobby fireplace (so far, blessedly left without a gas log) with three antlered deer heads alongside.

Settle Inn

3050 Green Mountain Drive
phone 800/677-6906 or 417/335-4700

Rates: Double room rates vary, essentially, by the month and by midweek or weekend (the latter Thursday through Saturday). Lowest weekend rate is $39 (January), and highest $73 (October). April through mid-December weekday rates are $65 to $69. Fanciful, themed suites (see below): $100 on weekends year-round, $80 midweek, with pets accepted for a nominal one-time charge of $3. Amenities include two indoor pools, hot tubs, and a game room. And continental breakfast, as well as complimentary coffee at all hours, is included in all room or suite charges. AE, D, MC, V.

A big, sprawling, 320-unit, hillside hotel in a series of three large buildings (the third completed in 1994) styled in a kind of Cape-Cod-in-the-Ozarks manner. Design features include false dormers and trapezoidal roof lines with lighthouse towers atop limestone-clad turrets. It's all a bit much, to which you add medieval statuary and a grandly arched stone column that evokes castle architecture. (Somehow, though, the excess is moderated at night when the roofline is festively outlined in white lights.) It's very definitely a hotel, not a motel, and increasingly popular in Branson, with its features of valet parking and bell staff. Even the staircases are thoughtfully carpeted.

Standard rooms? They're quite comfortable, with two firm, queen-size beds in most rooms (or one such bed in others, with a recliner), a desk, adequate mirrors (though none full length), well-placed lamps (though only one bed lamp in a room with a single queen bed), complementary colors on bedcovers and drapes, and at least one reproduction of a scenic painting per room. But most popular are the 28, whirlpool-equipped, "theme suites." One variety is called "Jewel of the Nile," and has a king bed with lion-head footposts, elephant trunk handles on an urn, murals of Cleopatra, Memphis-style footlockers. Another, "Observatory," has space murals and simulated comet trails, all in sky blue. Still other irresistibles are named "Outback," "Sherwood Forest," and "Moonshine Hollow"—the latter rather tame (to my mind), with a single mural of a copper still watched by attending hillbillies; it also has a gingham love seat, quilted king bedcover, old wagon wheels, and farm implements. Guests are obviously drawn, as well, to the theme rooms' double whirlpool.

Tara Inn

245 Shepherd of the Hills Expressway,
phone 800/525-TARA or 417/334-TARA

Rates: Double rooms $70 from May through October, only $40 off-season (and the hotel is closed in January and February), but management is presently struggling with whether to raise off-season rates in the year ahead. Outdoor pool; indoor boutique; free continental breakfast; coffee available all day. AE, MC, V.

Family-run, elevator equipped, and newly built (in 1993), this is a competently laid-out, competently managed, three-story lodging designed to look like a Southern colonial mansion, in what some will regard as a highly desirable part of town: as close as you can get to what was formerly Wayne Newton's Theater (now Shenandoah South, presenting changing country stars) and close to

Pat Boone and the *Will Rogers Follies.* With its attractive lobby, draperies, and bedcovers, it has a dressed-up hotel look, less like a motel, and rooms are well-furnished with twin reading lamps, two chairs, better-than-ordinary shower heads, Eurobath soap dispensers, and a piece of pop movie art showing Gable and Leigh on the screen in a drive-in.

Branson Towers Hotel
236 Shepherd of the Hills Expressway,
phone 417/336-4500

Rates: Double room rates range from a mid-December to mid-April low of $42 to a spring-summer high of $68 and an autumn $76. These are for walk-in guests; motorcoach groups, who will find the hotel outstanding, receive substantial discounts. An indoor pool, restaurant, games area, and gift shop round out the amenities. Major credit cards accepted.

This large, 211-unit, three-story property was opened in 1993 with a keen appreciation of the way that Branson would increasingly be marketed: year-round to bus tours. Its location is close to the newest, most elaborate performance halls, those of Mel Tillis, Wayne Newton (now the Shenandoah South), Pat Boone, Glen Campbell, and—via the relatively traffic-free Shepherd of the Hills Expressway—to the theaters of Charley Pride and Shoji Tabuchi. Chief characteristic of the hotel is surface charm and an absence of back-up detail. It reminds me of Harris Rosen's mass-volume operations in Orlando.

The hotel is done in a vinyl version of the architecture beloved of the region, a pioneer clapboard—kind of an Ozark colonial—with dormers atop the peaked roof, and an enormous columned entry marquee that easily accommodates the largest tour buses. The lobby is immense, with three-story-high ceiling, best to absorb the sound of several tour busloads.

Throughout, the emphasis is on essentials rather than detail. The thought is that large groups of guests are least likely to regard their lodging as something special; it's really only a place to get ready for the next excursion out, and a spot to plop at night. Hence, in complete contrast to the way in which bed-and-breakfast lodgings are designed, the idea is to put nothing in the guest rooms that might be vulnerable to inattention. The rooms may be large, the beds comfortable, and the bathrooms spacious enough, with all the essentials. But lamps are totally inadequate for two persons reading at the same time (there's only one between two queen beds), nor are lamps positioned at the desk or close to tables. Electrical outlets are few, and definitely not in work spaces. Bath towels are as thin as music hall sentiment. All furniture is contract, and so are the pictures on the wall. Even in suites—which are immense—the place feels like a ballfield in off-season. And for rooms as large as these are, with space easily available for a closet, there is only a motel-like hanging clothes rack. No interior designer has done any really creative work here; was an interior designer even used?

Atrium Inn
3005 Green Mountain Drive,
phone 800/656-5555 or 417/336-6000

Rates: For a standard room in high season (and including a quite remarkable free breakfast; see below), you'll pay $69 for two, $56 in November and December, $47 the first two weeks of April, and $39 if you come in March, when Branson's weather can still dip below freezing. Closed in January and February, when owners Frank Taber and Kathy Kuykendall go traveling to warmer climes. $4 off for AAA and AARP members in high season. MC, V.

Reasonably good value at this rather new, two-story, candy-colored pink-and-green motel in two separate wings that date from 1992 and 1993. The chief bonus here is a so-called "fresh-start" breakfast that includes fruit, dry cereal, bagels with cream cheese, juice, and coffee, tea, or milk. But there's also an exercise room and tanning salon in the hotel (the latter, $5 per 20-minute session), plus a guest laundry and a policy of free local phone calls. Rooms—of which 70% are nonsmoking—are a little larger than standard (12 by 26, not the usual 12 by 24), and they all have a couple of pieces of art, tasteful wallpaper, textured ceilings, and bright vanity lights over the washbasin area. Contract furniture, but the twin queen beds are exceptionally firm—and the towels will at least wrap around the waist of a full-bodied person. And there's a little deli and ice cream parlor in the lobby.

Classic Motor Inn
2384 Shepherd of the Hills Expressway,
phone 800/334-6991 or 417/334-6991

Location: Close by the Roark Road cutoff, close by Charley Pride's new theater, and near to where the Osmond Brothers are planning to open their mega-complex of theaters, motels, restaurants, par-3 golf course, and amusements.

Rates: Between $38 and $68, low season to high, for which you also get a swimming pool and free continental breakfast; closed January through March. AE, D, MC, V.

This mid-scale, 62-unit, motel is typical of several others currently opening along the bypass roads that roughly parallel the Strip (West Highway 76); most feature vinyl versions of clapboard, with sharply contrasting colors (here, white with green doors), in a city of copycat hotel developers. Look along Shepherd of the Hills Expressway, and you'll see many properties with this look. Trying to place some distance between itself and the others, this one fills its lobby with a giant Cadillac convertible from 1951, a virtual boat; though what that does for guests, heaven knows. Guest rooms are on two floors, and they're larger than standard, with twin reading lamps, three-way bulbs, and a piece of peacock art that, at least so far, you won't find anyplace else.

Edgewood
1700 West Highway 76,
phone 800/641-4106 or 417/334-1000

Location: On the Strip, but away from its more crowded, neon-lit segments.

Rates: From January 2 to April 6: $35 standard, $40 king or queen "leisure," $50 queen "deluxe" (two queens and a loveseat sleeper). April 7 to April 30, and in November and December: $47/$52/$62. May 1 to mid-September: $66/$71/$81. Mid-September to October 31: $73/$78/$88. Swimming pool, coin laundry, immediately adjacent Home Cannery Restaurant (under similar ownership), nonsmoking and handicapped-accessible rooms.

Well-located just east of all the shows on the Strip, these 298 units in three-, four-, and six-story buildings offer good, middle-of-the-road motel-style accommodations at reasonable prices. The three- and four-story units are accessed from the outside; the six-story units, all with deluxe queen-size beds, have elevators and interior corridors. Rooms are basic, with two upholstered side chairs, round table, two reading lamps in all units, hanging clothes racks, and decent vanity lights above the tiny washbasin, which is outside the tub/shower/toilet compartment. There's no art, and bathrooms are small. Best rooms are the "king leisures," which feature a loveseat sleeper, and most rooms extend well back from the road, and are therefore quiet. Best feature of this property is its location alongside a 27-acre private park.

Melody Lane Inn
2821 West Highway 76,
phone 800/338-8598 or 417/334-8598

Rates: Double rooms for $71.54 from late May through October; $54.06 in November, December, and the first three weeks of May; $43.69 in March and April; closed January and February. King-bedded rooms for $3 to $6 more, depending on time of year. No discounts. AE, MC, V.

A once-exciting, wonderfully authentic, ceramic shop called Mama Bear's, well out into the western hills of Branson, has been transformed through the magic of tourism into an ordinary, 140-unit, yellow-and-brick-surfaced motel. What remains are the old stone pillars of the original house, now worked into the two-story lobby, by far the most interesting part of the property. Rooms are utterly standard, though the the bedcovers and curtains do match. Otherwise, along with two pieces of floral wall art, you've seen it before (right down to the single reading lamp for the two queen beds). Features that might recommend it: a heated swimming pool, hot tub, coin laundry, coffee shop where guests can have a continental breakfast that's not included in the rate, and the fact that it's close to the Bobby Vinton, Andy Williams, and Grand Palace theaters.

Queen Anne I Motel
3510 West Highway 76 (the Strip),
phone 800/229-3170 or 417/335-8100

Rates: Double rooms for $68 from June through October, $57 from mid-April through May, $45 from April 1 to April 14, $40 in November and December, $32.50 from January through March. Add $5 a *night for a king-size bed if you want one, in all periods other than November and December when the surcharge is only $2, or from January through March when there's none. Suites (larger spaces with sitting area and small fridge, but no extra room) are $15 to $17.50 extra. 5% discount to AARP members. Outdoor heated pool and free coffee in the lobby. AE, D, MC, V.*

The name is Queen Anne and the exterior has fish-scale shingles and gingerbread bracketing, but here too, as at the Victorian Inn, the theming in the rooms disappoints. About as far as it gets is two-poster beds and inverted tulip lamps over the vanity. At a newer (1991 as against 1988) and larger (40 rooms here, 88 rooms there) sister hotel called the Queen Anne II, two blocks off the highway, the architectural theming is more ambitious, with cupola and extra dormers, but again stops short of the rooms themselves. (Queen Anne II does offer two queen beds per room, as contrasted with Queen Anne I's two doubles.) Otherwise you've seen it all too many times before: open, hanging clothes rack in the vanity area, molded tub/shower/toilet compartment, no art on the walls, single lamp between beds, mahogany-stained contract furniture. Ranks ahead of the Victorian Inn, behind the Stratford.

Plantation Inn
3460 West Highway 76,
phone 800/324-8748 or 417/334-3600

Location: In the heart of things, within walking distance of at least 10 theaters.

Rates: Double rooms for $69 from April 15 through August, $64 in September and October, $50 in November and December, and again from March through mid-April. Currently closes in January and February, but that policy is subject to change. No discounts, no elevator; but there's a swimming pool, complimentary coffee, free local phone calls, and several sofas for conversation and relaxation in the lobby.

A rather basic, mid-range motel with 78 units that opened in 1993. Units are entered from outdoors; nice color combinations in rooms; digital radio alarm clocks; twin reading lamps; and the rest standard, a couple of botanical prints on the walls. Beds are either double doubles or double queens. Particularly suitable for visitors who'd prefer to walk to the theaters; you're very near here to the Roy

Clark Theater and, as noted above, within walking distance of 10 more, with the White Water amusement park across the highway. Good, too, about this motel is that it's well recessed behind a companion restaurant, so that it's quiet. But there's not a trace of greenery (you're surrounded by parking lots), and to the immediate rear is the immense, sprawling Days Inn.

Double Rooms for $75 to $85 a Night

Bradford Inn

Highway 265, Branson 65616 (HCR 9, Box 1276-10), phone 417/338-5555

Location: On dogwood-pretty Compton Ridge with wonderful views of hills and valleys; Highway 265 runs from Highway 76 west of Branson down to Table Rock Dam, and along the way offers some of the best scenery in the Branson area.

Rates: Double rooms for $69 to $99, including a full but uncooked breakfast in an adjoining grocery. Off-season, the inn adjusts its rates to whatever the market demands. May stay open all year. MC, V.

★ You'll be happily surprised by this exceptional, people-friendly lodging of Gene and Diane Nelson and of Bob and Lucyanna Westfall. Though it's in a breathtaking rural setting, it's still only 10 to 15 minutes by car from the center of the entertainment action of the Strip. The inn has 15 guest units on four floors, in a building that is colonial in facade and shape but utterly contemporary in decor. Keen imaginations are at work here, about as far as you can get from the imitative, cookie-cutter approaches of much of Branson's hotel industry. Rooms and suites—some with fireplaces stocked with wood—are boldly geometric, with eaves and dormers; lamp bases circle their way up, tables may be beveled or show the exposed ends of leaves set for expansion; fabrics are brilliant florals in some rooms, paisleys and plaids in others; exceptional wall art includes photography; crown wallpaper descends from ceilings in an effect you've never seen before; colors are the softest nonpastels; furniture and accessories are chosen for comfort and beauty; a wicker rocker and a wing chair with footstool attest to the thoughtfulness of the people who organized these spaces for guests. One room called "Wisteria" seems almost to float between the bedcover and walls; another room is hunt-inspired, with a brass and oak king bed; still another contains unpainted, butcher-block furniture that creates a state-of-the-art setting, clean and fresh.

The inn, in sum, is like an expanded B&B, with no two units even remotely alike. Yet the rooms aren't precious, or frilly, or intensely detailed in the way B&Bs tend to be. There are no antiques in these spaces, but rather an imaginative selection of what are, after all, reproductions. You are reminded that even relatively affordable lodgings can be done well.

I'd like to encourage visitors to Branson to stay at a lodging like this. It trains us to know what's better, and over time, through our choices, it may train the lodging industry to supply more of such thoughtfulness and quality. Highest recommendation in the Branson area.

Branson Suites
3706 West Highway 76,
phone 417/335-3233

Location: At the far west end of Highway 76 just before tinsel town fades into countryside. Despite the name, some units here are standard motel rooms with beds described as "double doubles"; all others are suites.

Rates: In high season, $75 per standard double room, $85 for suites, $105 "king Jacuzzi" suites; off-season, all units are $10 lower, and all rates are for up to four persons in a room. Free continental breakfast, free local phone calls, use of a coin laundry.

★ If you're at all interested in aesthetic advances in the hotel industry, you'll want to know about this 40-unit property, one of the few in Branson to have given a major role to its designing architect. Despite its small size, it has the flavor of a resort, its units descending a slope behind the spacious lobby area. The building is strikingly geometric, copper flashed, beautifully textured; its rooflines rise dramatically into skylight peaks, its partly carpeted, partly tiled exterior corridors are alone an innovation. Even the standard rooms have generous, 12-foot-high ceilings; are oddly but intriguingly laid out, with vanities, clothes racks, and bathroom doors lying behind a succession of baffles; and you have art inside that you haven't seen anywhere else. You also have twin reading lamps, though only twin double beds in the standard, $75-a-night rooms.

Best units at Branson Suites are the exceptional "king Jacuzzis" (sleeping up to six for $115 in high season), perhaps the best of their kind in the area. These are virtual homes, one king bedroom behind a living room, kitchenette to the side, the other king bedroom in an upstairs loft. Spaces feature dramatic openings: an overlook from the loft bedroom to the living room area with its gas-log fireplace in a stone-faced wall, and with a skylight that on clear days pours sunshine through a triangular space. Living rooms have sofas, a recliner, other upholstered chairs, and fabrics are beautiful flame patterns and camellias flowered in greens and rose. Kitchenettes are equipped with small fridge and microwave oven, but otherwise have no other cooking facility. And, of course, there's a Jacuzzi in the loft.

Firmest beds in all rooms. Very special. Highly recommended.

Branson House Bed & Breakfast Inn
120 4th Street, in downtown Branson,
phone 417/334-0959

Location: On a side street in that central area near Lake Taneycomo.

Rates: $85 per room per night, except for one room that rents for only $65. No credit cards; no smoking; house phone for guest use.

This grandly yellow, old three-story house is my preferred bed-and-breakfast in town. It is owned and operated by Opal Kelly, her daughter Teri, and Teri's husband, who moved here from California to help revive the historic downtown, even as the Strip was turning into Vegas East. This seven-room guesthouse was a banker's home when it was built in the 1920s, and its period is still Eastlake. You'll see that in the graceful wood trim that frames the spacious and comfortable parlor, the china cabinets, and the custom-made high-backed chairs that surround the dining table. Typical of its homey antique furnishings are three living room lamps: one of brass, another of floral porcelain, and a third with two inverted craftsman glass lamps hung from an art nouveau base. Alongside is a foot-pump organ looking vaguely Bavarian.

Opal has taken the one third-story room of the house for her own, so that guests now have the use of six, which include two on the first floor, the others up one flight of stairs; and all but one have their own private bath. All are delightfully furnished in an assortment of styles: in one, a cherry-wood old bookcase with its original wavy glass, in another French double doors leading to a private balcony; in several, wing-backed chairs, several burgundy sofas, other chairs so soft that you sink into them with a sigh of indulgence. And French linens—handsomely striped in blue and white—are beneath the bedcovers. Other treats of the establishment: a free, full breakfast, wonderful collections of old Missouri postcards, and the joys of that parlor.

Branson Hotel (Bed and Breakfast)
214 W. Main Street,
phone 417/335-6104

Location: In the center of downtown Branson.

Rates: Double rooms for $75 and $95, including full American breakfast for everyone. No smoking on the premises, no credit cards accepted, but free local phone calls encouraged.

Stone-columned, yellow clapboard with white trim, picket-fenced, picket-porched, in frontier-Federal style, this nine-room B&B lends authenticity to downtown Branson, the very opposite of the Strip. And to keep even less of the blighting impact from her sanctum, owner Teri Murgia rebuilt the hotel in 1991 for quiet. You would not believe, sitting in the parlor beside busy Main Street, that the windows had not been double glazed. The hotel dates back to 1903, when it was built in anticipation of the St. Louis Iron Mountain & Southern Railroad arriving in town (it got here two years later). The entryway recalls Ozark chronicler Harold Bell Wright with a photo of his stay here in 1905, and with a flyer from a later movie version of his *The Shepherd of the Hills*. Though the hotel continued to take guests throughout the century, it was badly run down when Teri acquired and restored it.

Generally speaking, the rooms are only okay to good. They are not like those showplace B&Bs, with their mounds of lace and ribbon, that get photographed to appear in elegant magazines. The rooms are not large, though two of them have king-size beds, and all are with private baths. But they are interestingly themed to become "English garden," "Victorian," or "rose-like" in style. One room called the Fox's Den is a lair of fox paraphernalia, from a beautiful large print over the bed to knick-knackery on the tables. Another called the Duck Club has decoys and duck lamp bases. The Wicker Room is as you'd expect. All have TV. And beds are variously cannonball, sleighbed, canopied, or high-backed oak—on thickly carpeted floors. Best of all, guests enjoy a full cooked breakfast each morning of daily-changing ingredients: maybe eggs Benedict, maybe oven-baked French toast, always with potatoes, fresh fruits, juices, home-baked breads or muffins, coffee. After you've visited endless motels in Branson, as I have, this B&B becomes a welcome change of pace.

Emory House Bed & Breakfast
143 Arizona Drive, Branson 65616,
phone 800/484-9469 or 417/334-3805

Location: 4½ miles north of downtown.

Rates: Double rooms for $75 to $95 a night in high season, $5 less for single occupancy, $5 less for third, fourth, or fifth night; as yet unspecified discounts for off-season stays. All rates include a full American breakfast. Open all year. D, MC, V.

For vacationers unfamiliar with the bed-and-breakfast concept, Emory House—a 12- to 15-minute drive north of Branson—is an excellent way to experience this more personal style of overnighting. Its appeal lies in the modern comforts that have been integrated into this Victorian-style house which, you'll be surprised to learn, is brand new, built in 1993. It occupies 7½ acres of woodlands, fronting down the slope on Emory Creek. Yet the house is only a few hundred feet up from Highway 65. Thanks to its siting and construction, it admits none of the nearby highway noise. Modern conveniences include private baths with each of the seven guest rooms, large Jacuzzi tubs in each, bathrobes, slippers, digital clock radios, good lighting, plenty of electrical outlets, TV (of course), AC/heat in each room, and excellent insulating which keeps each of the guest rooms quiet and private.

Though rooms are not equipped with individual phones, guests have use of a dedicated line and a phone in one of the parlors, and a portable phone is available. (There is no charge for local calls or for credit-card long-distance calls.) Decor? It is all brilliantly Victorian, in both guest and public rooms, and features such antiques of the mid-1800s as Araby-fringed lamps, grandly carved beds, old horse prints, upright Chickering pianos, marvelous gothic desks, bottles and hurricane lamps, among many other thoughtfully chosen touches, like an impressive library of classics. And a grand staircase rises to the open second story from the main salon of the house.

Cascades Inn
3226 Shepherd of the Hills Expressway, phone 800/588-8424 or 417/335-8424

Rates: From $50 (off-season) to $80 (high season) for standard rooms with two queen-size beds, always including a free continental breakfast. Rooms with king beds are $5 more; larger kings with Jacuzzis in a larger bath and an easy chair with ottoman, $15 more. Open all year. AE, D, DC, MC, V.

Four stories and 159 units, serviced by elevators, on a hillside near the Shoji Tabuchi Theater, with a sizable lobby, enclosed heated pool and hot tub area, sauna, steam room, exercise room, game room, guest laundry, and sundries shop. Like the hotels it most closely resembles (Branson Towers, Palace Inn, Ozark Valley, and Lighthouse), this is like a cross between a motel and a hotel despite its interior corridors, and bathrooms placed next to the doorway, not at the far end of the room. Like the others, what makes it akin to a motel is the ordinary nature of the furniture and decor: no historical aspect, nothing drawing your attention to Ozark heritage or anything about Missouri, no molded wall features, no books or details serve to soften the commercial room-for-the-night impression.

Obviously, many hotels and motels hereabouts think their success depends completely on the draw of the country music halls, and aren't interested in diverting their guests from anything but showtime; the hotel itself needn't be exciting. On the plus side: Rooms have blond furniture, teal carpets, a couple of tropical art prints, twin reading lamps, and night tables. Bathrooms supply shampoo and mouth wash; towels are better in weight and length than what most motels supply. The rest you know. Ultimately, the location and certain hotel features prevail to make this an attractive buy. (If I were to rank the Cascades Inn among the other hotels I've just mentioned, I'd rate it ahead of the Branson Towers and the Palace Inn, but behind the Ozark Mountain Valley Inn and the Lighthouse.)

Best Western Music Capital Inn
3527 Shepherd of the Hills Expressway, phone 800/528-1234 or 417/334-8378

Rates: Double rooms for $79 May through most of August, $72 late August, $80 September and October, $61 November and December,

$66 April, $58 March, always including free continental breakfast; closed January and February. Surcharges for holiday weekends of between $2 and $10; 10% discounts for AARP members. AE, D, DC, MC, V.

Directly across the street from the super-popular Shoji Tabuchi's, you can believe that this new 93-unit hotel-like motel is in high demand. More substantial than any motel, it is four stories with elevator, with interior-access rooms, and its features include an indoor pool, spa, sauna, sun deck, exercise room, cable TV with free HBO, guest laundry, game room, and small gift/sundries shop. As if rising to the challenge of Shoji's multi-million-dollar showplace across the street, it mounts a substantial brick facade, a three-story-high lobby with several seating areas.

Standard rooms have character, and a lot to distinguish them from motel rooms. Though no larger than most motel units, they feature good recesses, one for the hanging clothes rack, the other for a second lavatory that is directly outside the bathroom; there's even a bit of a foyer as you first enter. Floral prints under glass above most headboards; a single bed lamp but with two bulbs that operate on separate switches; two washbasins in the bathroom, one in a separate compartment outside the otherwise complete bathroom; heat lamp; full-length mirror; an excellent showerhead that offers options in water flow; and a packet of free shampoo. The rate seems warranted for what you get.

Palace Inn
2820 West Highway 76,
phone 800/PALACE-N or 417/334-ROOM

Location: In the very heart of the Strip, alongside the Grand Palace Theater, where such superstars as Barbara Mandrell appear.

Rates: Double rooms for $80 from the last week of May through October, $65 the first three weeks of May, $52 from November through December, $49 from January through April. "King rooms" (all with fridge and recliner) are an additional $3 to $10 depending on time of year. Continental breakfast not included in rate; no discounts. AE, MC, V.

You are paying a premium to stay here for public features that aren't, in my opinion, really related to a good night's sleep. What this 166-unit hotel (five floors, three elevators) offers is an upscale look. A big-pillared marquee, balconies, large lobby. But all this isn't necessarily followed through with something you can make use of. Consider the rooms. Those in the hotel do have balconies, though rooms in a motel wing, behind Buckingham's, the dining room, do not. Rooms themselves, to my eye, seem rather plain. Tote up the pluses and minuses: wall-mounted hairdryer in the bath along with toiletries supplied, an additional row of vanity lights outside the bath above a mirror. Yet only a single reading lamp, contract furniture, one of the thinnest hanging clothes racks you'll ever see. Other features of the property: heated indoor/outdoor pool, indoor and outdoor Jacuzzis, sauna, beauty shop, massage service, boutique, coin laundry. Bellhop service.

Double Rooms for $85 to $100 a Night

The Crowne Plaza
126 South Wildwood Drive,
phone 800/428-3386 or 417/335-5767

Location: A few hundred yards off the Strip, yet in the heart of things.

Rates: Double rooms for $102 high season, as low as $65 in deep off-season periods; probe for the lowest rate you can get.

Who would ever have thought I would wax rhapsodic over a hotel operated by Holiday Inn? Yet in Branson, this immense place is a winner. Its 500 units, built onto a sloping hillside next to the Andy Williams Theater, are the pick of the town, new since 1994. For little more than you'd pay at ordinary places, here you can get that slick styling, that sense of interior illusionist at work, that characterizes the better upscale places anywhere. It is resort-style in its ambitions, if not in the fullness of its amenities.

First things first. Big lobby, deeply carpeted, marble-like black granite pillars, real interior greenery (virtually unheard of in Branson), plush furniture in attractive seating areas, including a sunken section with a baby grand piano. Four elevators lead to guest rooms, which are essentially "double doubles" (two double beds) and kings. Rooms are sizable, but especially corner rooms, thanks to their dog-leg entry and a wall of windows plus another window on the wraparound corner. And rooms have extras only occasionally found in other Branson hotels: acoustical tile ceilings, thick towels, multi-force showerheads, hairdryers, designer toiletries, full-length mirrors, soundproofing making for quiet, self-making coffee devices with free coffee packet refills. After all that, it's a disappointment to find open hanging clothes racks instead of closets.

Other features: a workout room, an art gallery (mediocre), hair salon, indoor/outdoor pool, hot tub and sauna, gift shop, and bell service. Finally, the estimable McGuffey's chain has a restaurant and separate lounge on the lower level. For once, it's a pleasure to recommend an upgraded Holiday Inn.

Lodge of the Ozarks
3431 West Highway 76 (the Strip),
phone 417/334-7535

Location: Situated among four big showcases: Roy Clark, Mickey Gilley, Boxcar Willie, Jim Stafford, all either next door or across the street.

Rates: $80 per double room from April through December, $95 for rooms with Jacuzzi tubs, $55 to $65 from January through March. No-smoking and handicapped rooms. AE, D, MC, V.

One of the better upscale lodgings in Branson, but not top drawer. True, the dimensions are grand: four stories with two elevators, 191 rooms, a three-story-high lobby whose roof slopes in back to a huge indoor swimming area (which also has two pool tables). There are three restaurants, cocktail lounge, various gift shops and game arcades, a beauty parlor, and tiny spa; yet there are aspects of a motel here—like the fact that you can look up from the lobby and see the indoor corridors and doors of the upper three stories—which detract from the sense of luxury, and were obviously dictated by cost and investment factors. And the entryways to guest rooms, along with the more functional parts of rooms—bathroom, open hanging clothes rack, built-in desk—are all vinyl-like and motel related (though the bathrooms do have a couple of attractive, paisley-papered panels).

Bedroom areas themselves are more attractive, luxurious with large sofa, queen bed, two wingback chairs, all done in burgundy and blue. The feeling is solid, traditional, hotel-like, comfortable. Some rooms have two queen-size beds, no sofa. Go for the rooms with the sofa, and if you need to stay where four people can sleep together in two beds, try the multi-person loft units of the nearby Dutch Kountry Inn (see above).

Double Rooms for $100 and Higher

Big Cedar Lodge
612 Devil's Pool Road, Ridgedale 65739,
phone 417/335-2777

Location: On an arm of Table Rock Lake.

Rates: Standard double rooms in multi-unit lodges for $125 high season (generally, May through October), $79 low season, deluxe double rooms (fireplace, Jacuzzi) in lodges for $199 high season, $169 low season; one-bedroom cabins for $139 in high season, $99 low season, two-bedroom cabins for $349 in high season, $229 low season. Pool, highly rated restaurant, lake marina, trails, mini-golf. Open year-round. AE, D, MC, V.

★ The difference between Big Cedar Lodge and any other lodge, inn, motel, or hotel in the Branson area is that you go to the latter establishments for the purpose of attending country music shows; you go to Big Cedar Lodge for itself. Since 1921, people have been coming to Big Cedar who had never heard of Branson. Big Cedar is its own destination, its own outdoor recreational resort spread over 250 acres of Ozark hills and lakes. It's big and it's brawny, and yet it fits easily into its region with a sense of history and shape that's grown directly from the soil, from the trees. It is also festooned with the heads and entire bodies of wildlife, for this has been, historically, a hunting and fishing lodge, although current-day visitors often come for neither of those activities.

The accommodations are in several multi-unit lodges, and in separate cabins, for a total capacity of about 250 persons. But it is the cabins that stand out. They combine a heritage look with exceptional comfort. To begin with, these are virtual houses, as small as they may initially seem. They offer complete electric kitchens with dishwashers, stone fireplaces supplied with ample cut logs, large bathroom suites with separate Jacuzzis and shower stalls outfitted with four shower heads that hit you with water from both sides and up and down; you get thick, long towels, quality soaps and toiletries. A king bed, a sofa living room area, a fully equipped kitchen/dining area (with starter units of coffee, tea, decaf), and a balcony overlooking the lake, fill the available space, but still leave you with some room for walking around. Each cabin, by the way, is slightly different. As for their heritage look, they are each constructed of logs and show that appealing rusticity throughout their interiors: stone fireplace, knotty plank ceiling, log beams. Embellishments include an antler chandelier, another of iron, chairs framed of branches, backed with straw. Floors are plank, but with hook rugs in all the right places. Art all around shows fishing, hunting, and other long-ago recreational pursuits on the rivers and lakes of the Ozarks. Altogether an outstanding resort, one of America's best.

Sunrise Suites
Indian Point, Branson,
phone 417/338-5170

Location: On the lakefront peninsula just below Silver Dollar City, about a 15- to 20-minute drive west of Country Music Boulevard (the Strip, West Highway 76).

Rates: A terrific value for what you pay: $109 for as many as four persons occupying a house by the night, only $395 for a total of four nights; and you can negotiate for less in off-season. Credit cards are not accepted.

Freestanding houses, not part of a resort. Quite a number of vacationers these days seem to want a vacation house all to themselves, the farther removed from others, the better. Yet in a place like Branson, with its sky-high land costs and the need to pack 'em in, these are increasingly rare, which makes the two houses of Sunrise Suites particularly appealing. One of them, known as Sunrise Bed & Bath, is a pretty little board-and-block house with nothing immediately around and with glorious back porch views of Table Rock Lake in the distance. The house is completely furnished, carpeted, and supplied with art on the walls, and provides two bedrooms, two baths (master bath with Jacuzzi for two), screened porch, barbecue grill, and carport. The other, simply referred to as "the Lake house," is almost shoreside on the lake, and from its broad porch offers grand sunset viewing, and similar amenities.

Thousand Hills Condo Rental
2700 Green Mountain Road,
phone 800/864-4145 or 417/336-5873

Location: Not far from the Strip but utterly removed from the atmosphere and appearance of the latter.

Rates: In high season (April through October): $139 a night for a 1,220-square-foot, two-bedroom, two-bath condo housing four persons, of which there are six to a building block, $119 in November and December, $99 from January through March; and you can rent for as little as one night. AE, MC, V.

These are attractive little "homes" (apartments) only minutes away from the action, but quiet and dignified, and with extraordinary housekeeping; the one I most recently visited had been in the rental pool for more than a year, and its white carpet was pristine, as was everything else. Kitchens are large enough to include clothes washer and dryer, dishwasher, vacuum, iron and board, all kitchenware; master baths have large, separate vanity areas with handy built-in drawers, carpeted walk-in closets, large and thick towels. In bedrooms: two reading lamps with three-way bulbs, digital clock radios, modern art throughout. Living rooms have a good combination of sofas and upholstered chairs, a breakfast bar with three large upholstered seats, and a dining room table. And there are plenty of closets throughout. Outdoors: a pool and clubhouse. An alternative condo development: Foothills, just a minute's drive away, with condos 1,336-square-feet big, indoor and outdoor pool, sauna, hot tub, and workout room. As Branson develops further, expect to see more of these modern developments designed for semi-permanent residents but available, via a rental pool, to transients like us.

6

Dining Out, Ozarks-Style

From Collard Greens to Haute Cuisine, 32 Choices

Chicken-fried steaks—if placed end-to-end, they would reach the moon. Buttermilk biscuits, tens of thousands of them each day.

String beans in a bacon-flavored stock. Fried catfish and fried shrimp. Barbecued and smoked pork ribs swimming in a flour-based gravy. Mashed potatoes with more gravy. Mushy broccoli and cauliflower flowerettes gooped in a cream sauce or sausage gravy. Everything heavily salted and breaded. And for dessert: Jell-O with a thick, marshmallow topping. Canned fruit salad in heavy syrup. Hot strawberry cobblers. Bread pudding.

Such is the dominant cuisine of Branson. If you like the Midwestern approach to Southern-style cooking and specialties—*and I do*—you'll be in heaven.

But what if you don't? What if you'd prefer avoiding a heart attack before age 40? Or maintaining—not gaining—weight through proper diet? Suppose you're a green-and-yellow vegetable lover? Or even a vegetarian? Is there anything for you in Branson?

I've tried to deal with all types of meals in this restaurant chapter. From that overwhelming percentage of Branson restaurants that practice the Southern approach, I've chosen several that I consider to be the best in town, and several others that are clearly the cheapest for acceptable meals. But I've also tried hard to find restaurants offering a healthy dining alternative in Branson, the few places that include broiled or baked dishes, healthy pasta, fresh vegetables, seafood. Sometimes this involves simply navigating one's way through a menu that stresses the greasy and the caloric in search of an occasional wholesome dish. You'll note such an effort in the discussion that follows.

Finding Your Kind of Place

I've organized our restaurant discussion by geographical location. Because most visitors will want to dine in an area close to a particular celebrity theater—the places to which they have tickets for a matinee or evening performance—we've grouped some of our selections according to the theaters they're near. Thus, a typical heading will read: "Country Music Boulevard (Highway 76), Near Moe Bandy's, the Presleys, the Osmond Family Theater." Another will be for eating places "Close to the Shoji Tabuchi Theater, on Shepherd of the Hills Expressway." The purpose is to reduce the driving time from your restaurant to the theater you've booked; in too many areas of Branson as many as 40 minutes are required to remove your car from the parking lot, drive through gridlocked traffic to the theater, and then park again. Hopefully, a wise choice of restaurants according to location will cut that time in half.

Within each geographical section, restaurants are listed in *ascending* order of cost, starting with the *cheapest* and moving *up* from there. And although we take great pains to set forth the exact price of each major menu item, and the average price for a three-course meal at each restaurant, we also include a general shorthand description of the restaurant's price category right next to the initial listing of the restaurant's name and address. Those categories are five in number, and they are, in ascending order of price: (1) CHEAP, (2) INEXPENSIVE, (3) MODERATE, (4) PRICEY, and (5) EXPENSIVE. We also place a large star ★ next to restaurants that are a particular value within their price category.

Please note as well, that we indicate the credit cards accepted at each establishment: AE for American Express, D for Discover, DC for Diners Club, MC for MasterCard, V for Visa. Those are especially important listings in Branson, as a great many restaurants accept only some of those cards.

Though you may have mixed reactions to the food that Branson serves, you won't complain about its prices for meals—they are among the lowest in the nation. You'll have a sense of that when you dine for $7.35, totally all-inclusive, in the very proper setting of our first selection.

At the end of this chapter you'll find menus for all the restaurants I discuss, in alphabetical order.

In Downtown Branson

Alongside College of the Ozarks, relatively near to the Glen Campbell, Mel Tillis, and Pat Boone Theaters

We start in the charming, original Branson, several square blocks of well-preserved, one- and two-story shops off the banks of Lake Taneycomo, away from the Strip of celebrity theaters, but easily accessible to them. The campus of the College of the Ozarks is across Lake Taneycomo from here (via a bridge to the west of downtown, and then a couple of miles inland), and also nearby are the simple middle-class homes of the small population that lived here before the era of the highway theaters and enormous expansion of Branson began.

Rose O'Neill Friendship House
Exit 3341, at the entrance to the campus of the College of the Ozarks, phone 417/334-6411

Location: Across Lake Taneycomo from downtown Branson.

Open: Daily throughout the year for all three meals, except closed early (3pm) on Sunday, Thanksgiving, and Christmas. INEXPENSIVE

★ Named for the creator of the Kewpie doll, who grew up in Branson and contributed heavily to its college, this is a large (300 seats), help-yourself, all-you-can-eat buffet restaurant in a dignified peak-roofed and shingled building of great charm, with roomy tables and captains' chairs. Because rolls, muffins, dessert, and beverage are included in an unlimited lunch or dinner costing a flat $7.35, I count it a great value. You'll pass a soup and salad bar just inside the door, then a table of hot vegetables, alongside a heavily stacked board of multiple entrees (fried chicken, Italian sausage stew, cheese tortellini, barbecue brisket, among them).The $7.35 price gets you everything, or you can limit the meal to soup and salad (with drink and dessert) for only $5. Downstairs is a fine gift shop of student-made crafts (ceramics, woven items)—surpassed,

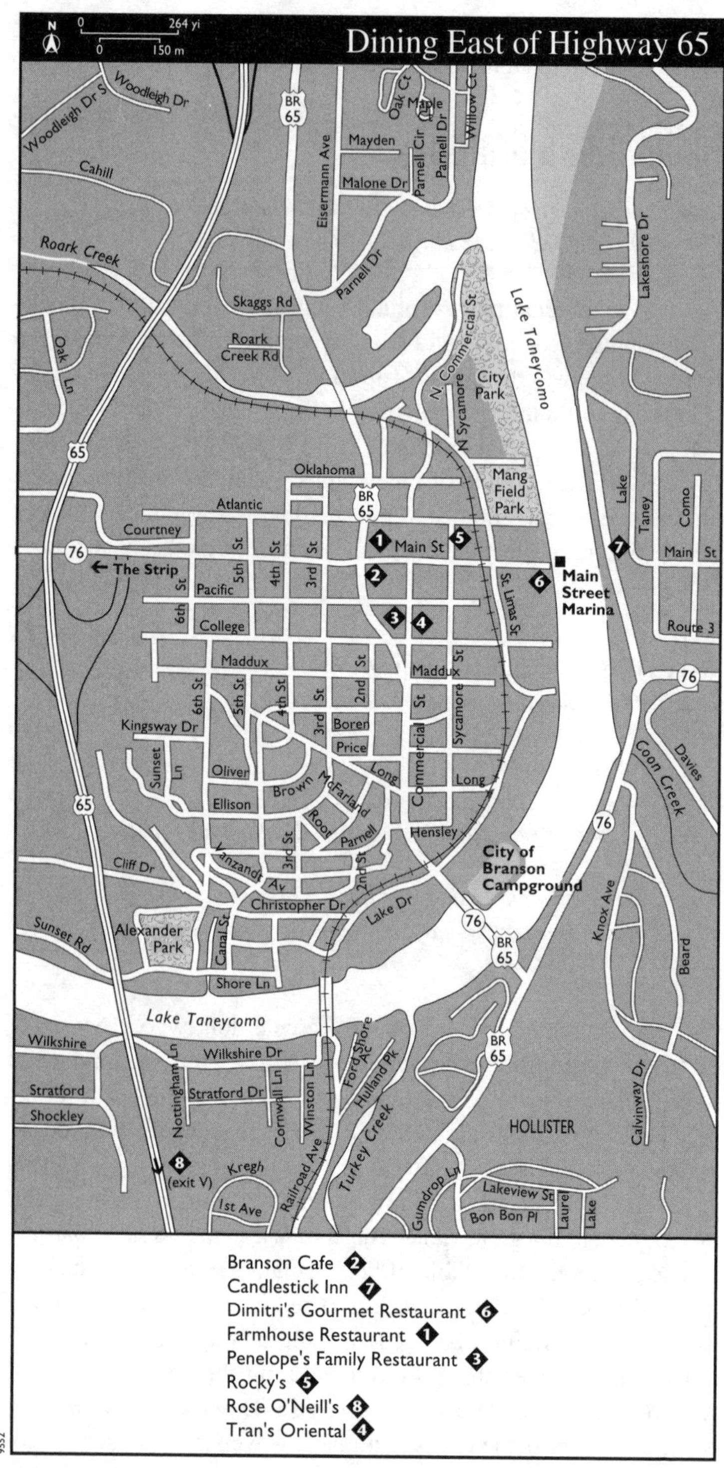
Dining East of Highway 65
Branson Cafe 2
Candlestick Inn 7
Dimitri's Gourmet Restaurant 6
Farmhouse Restaurant 1
Penelope's Family Restaurant 3
Rocky's 5
Rose O'Neill's 8
Tran's Oriental 4
Lake Taneycomo
City Park
Mang Field Park
Main Street Marina
City of Branson Campground
Alexander Park
HOLLISTER
The Strip
Roark Creek
Turkey Creek

9552

to my mind, only by Engler's Block on Highway 76 as the best gift outlet in Taney County; and everywhere, as you'd guess, are sketches of Kewpie dolls.

Tran's Oriental

114 S. Commercial Street, in the heart of downtown Branson, phone 417/334-0815

Open: Daily except Thanksgiving and Christmas for both lunch and dinner. INEXPENSIVE

A tiny Chinese restaurant on one of the main streets of downtown Branson. Though its menu is standard bland Cantonese—cashew chicken, moo goo gai pan, sweet and sour pork, 30 other rather uninventive plates—its great merit is that it enables you to eat healthily in a city otherwise known for its fried, breaded, salted, and barbecued meats dripping with fat, doused with gravies. And its rates are extraordinary: $3.19 to $3.49 for most large luncheon (11am to 3pm) dishes served with large mounds of steamed rice (green pepper steak, chicken chow mein, beef and broccoli, among them), $5.29 to $5.99 for most dinner plates (served with rice, hot tea, and a fortune cookie). Thus, $5.29 brings you a filling Hawaiian chicken (accompanied by Asian vegetables and pineapple chunks), and only the seafood platters (again with rice, tea, and cookie) go up to $6.99 and $7.49 (shrimp and crabmeat in lobster sauce is one). Add wonton or egg drop soup for a dollar, and it's still hard to spend as much as $5 at lunch, as much as $9 (or even $8) at dinner. (In a recent development, four scattered dishes are prepared hot and spicy). Hard, molded plastic booths for seating, but a pleasant and dedicated staff.

With the recent demise of the much lamented Koi Garden Oriental Restaurant on West Highway 76, slated to be replaced by an office building, Tran's becomes the only Asian restaurant in Branson, though hopefully that may change in coming years.

Branson Cafe

120 Main Street, heart of downtown, phone 417/334-3021

Open: Daily except Sunday, and year-round except for two or three weeks after Christmas. INEXPENSIVE

Unlike those plastic chain operations carefully designed to look aging and quaint, this is an authentic bit of Americana dating from 1910, which was just shortly after the time of Harold Bell Wright (when the railroad came to Branson). It has been in continuous operation ever since, a straightforward dining place for the common folk of the Ozarks, with a row of booths along each side and a simple row of tables in between; farm implements and dried corn cobs still hang from the eaves, along with old packaging from the days of Gold Dust Washing Powder and Argo Laundry Starch. If all this leads you to believe that the food is standard unadorned American, you're right; but the prices are also right. A Blue Plate Special, which changes daily (chicken-fried steak on my most recent visit), is $5.49, including potatoes, salad, vegetable, roll and butter. Otherwise, the choices are other varieties of steak, chopped steak, chicken, shrimp, catfish, trout, and a few salads, all priced at under $7 and $8. For dessert, a bowl of cobbler is only $1.25, and coffee only 45¢ and bottomless—the waitresses, some straight from a TV sitcom, go dashing up and down the aisle to refill your cup as soon as you set it down. Don't miss the Branson Cafe when you're downtown, although equally good is Penelope's (even though not as historical).

Farmhouse Restaurant
119 W. Main Street, heart of downtown,
phone 417/334-9701

Open: For breakfast, lunch, and dinner every day of the year except Thanksgiving and Christmas. INEXPENSIVE

Across the street from the Branson Cafe, this is yet another in-town, down-home informal and affordable local hangout, dating from the 1930s, and catering today in almost equal portions to residents talking about Taney County politics and tourists asking "Where's the Strip?" (the latter starts in just about 2 miles, going uphill along Main Street, which then becomes West Highway 76). Country music plays continually in the background; country artifacts (bough wreaths, lacy heartsakes, Ozark dolls) line the walls. And the food? No surprises: chicken, chicken-fried steak, chicken livers, spaghetti, ribeye steak, shrimp, fried catfish, roast beef, all of it done and served in plain-Jane fashion and priced variously at $7, $8, and $9 per platter, garnished with veg-and-potatoes, small salad, roll and butter.

Rocky's
118 North Sycamore (a side street off Main Street), in downtown Branson, phone 417/335-4765

Open: Daily except Sunday for lunch and dinner, closed Thanksgiving, Christmas, and New Year's Day. Features a live jazz/blues trio Wednesday through Saturday evenings. MODERATE

Branson's best Italian restaurant, not because its food is superior to its two rivals, Spaghettata and the Olive Garden (see below; actually, all three do a reasonable job of preparing their classic specialties), but because Rocky's gets far more locals than do the tourist-oriented Spaghettata and Olive Garden; has a lively, convivial bar; and is in a historic downtown setting, a block from Main Street. Its plain dark building dates from early in the century, and you can see original rock walls near where the dart board hangs.

Once seated in its high cushioned booths, surrounded by country art and antiques (including a copper still), you can start with an appetizer of peel-and-eat shrimp for $4.95, and then move on to copious pasta dishes ranging from linguine with meatballs or sausage for $6.75, lasagna or fettucine Alfredo for $7.50, canneloni or spaghetti carbonara for $8.50, linguine with clam sauce for $8.75, or any number of chicken dishes for $8.95. Only the steak or veal (piccata or marsala) goes up to $10.50 and $11.25; and most everything comes down in price by nearly half at lunchtime. From around noon to 2, you pay only $3.50 for spaghetti with tomato sauce, $4.50 for the same with meatballs and sausage, $5.25 for tortellini with cream sauce. And half orders of the pasta are always available for children.

Warning: Rocky's faces the least attractive block in all of downtown Branson, a semi-industrial space atypical of the charming downtown, and may initially appear gloomy inside; but when you see the owner's book of recipes displayed for sale at the cashier's counter, you'll know that the restaurant has aspirations to higher things.

Dimitri's Gourmet Restaurant
500 Main Street in downtown Branson, phone 417/334-0888

Location: In a barnlike building atop a barge on the water, at the foot of Main Street, just outside the Sammy Lane Resort.

Open: Continuous operation in Branson since the mid-1970s; open every day. PRICEY

Branson is badly in need of a few outstanding upscale restaurants, but this isn't one of them, despite its high price level (by the standards of Branson), its 250 seats, and the enthusiastic way in which it is often touted by well-meaning residents. (To me, the similarly priced Paradise Grill is better, and the costlier Candlestick is, of course, the foremost restaurant in town.) While Dimitri's Greek dishes are competently prepared, they're just a bit off; and the menu is only barely Greek: 6 out of 14 appetizers (Greek meatballs, spanakopita, feta cheese and olives, stuffed grape leaves, charcoal-broiled octopus, each $5.99, except for the $6.99 octopus), perhaps 3 out of 22 seafood and meat entrees (Dimitri's spaghetti, $14.99, Grecian-style lamb chops, $19.99, shish kebab, $19.99). Apart from those, you have a good selection of standard meat plates (prime rib, duck à l'orange, filet mignon), most at $16.99 to $19.99; a wide variety of fish selections (catfish, trout, orange roughy, others) for $14.99 to $15.99; and desserts serving two persons (bananas flambé, cherries jubilee, strawberries Romanoff; you get the picture) for $12.99.

What I don't like about Dimitri's is a certain lack of sharpness in the operation: disappointing dishes on my last two visits, including a steak doused in a funny-tasting oil, perhaps a bit rancid; barnlike dining areas, spaces too open, chairs too supply-store issue (and less comfortable than the ones at the entrance), artificial flowers, a building that looks like a plastered warehouse with a nondescript entrance ramp. Twice I've entered the anteroom to find no one in attendance there. Some redeeming features: industrious and well-meaning waiters in tuxedoed splendor; they aren't backed up by the kitchen operation or, for that matter, by the overall management. And I do not care for the imprint at the bottom of the menu that, "Gratuities for waiter are not added to check, 15% is expected. Above 15% your waiter would be most appreciative." I suspect the waiters would be appreciative of better pay by Dimitri.

Candlestick Inn
East Highway 76,
phone 417/334-3633

Location: Atop Mt. Branson just east of little Hollister (take the bridge that crosses Lake Taneycomo).

Open: Daily for dinner only, but closed Christmas Eve, Christmas Day, and the first two weeks of January. Full bar; 130 seats; reservations advised. EXPENSIVE

★ A grand and traditional, old-line restaurant of dignity and elegance, where you are served by attentive waiters as you gaze out onto the finest view in Branson. The Candlestick Inn, here since 1960, sits atop Mt. Branson, the high bluff across Lake Taneycomo from town. From a window table—where you'll want to sit—you look across the waterway down below, lined by cabins of the Sammy Lane Resort. Beyond lies the railroad track that first brought tourists to Branson, and Branson itself, looking like a toy-scaled, two-story complex of neatly squared-off blocks, its hills quite junior to Mt. Branson.

Because the Candlestick makes no rustic pretense, it is different from almost all other places to eat in Branson. The dining rooms (smoking and nonsmoking, divided by a bar) are upscale, the nonsmoking room long, open-beamed, mauve and tan, set with mate chairs, paisley table covers; the other dining room a bit more upholstered, more square, slightly smaller—in a word, more sophisticated.

You'll spend about $30 per person for a three-course meal without wine, which is more expensive than either the Devil's Pool at Big Cedar Lodge or Paradise Grill, two other standout restaurants of the area. Obviously, you can spend slightly less through careful ordering. But many visitors to Branson for more than a couple of days will find dinner here worth the price. The Candlestick thinks of itself as a seafood restaurant (though it serves a broad array of meat dishes, too). It features the usual shrimp and scallops ($13.95 to $14.95), but also daily specials that might include snapper, salmon, swordfish (daily changing market prices). It also claims these items are flown in fresh on ice, not frozen, but you can imagine the time that must elapse to bring a portion of salmon from Norway to Branson, so that even if not frozen, the fish you eat here is simply not going to be as fresh as along the coasts. Still, it's quite fine indeed. Most of the costlier meat entrees range from $15.95 to $18.95 per main dish (prime rib, steak au poivre, strip sirloin, filet mignon, tournedos of beef), but several other lower-priced and local specialties (the menu calls them "Ozark Traditions") top out at a maximum of $14.95: fresh trout fillets, trout stuffed with crabmeat dressing, farm-raised Channel Catfish fillets, smoked Ozark mountain pork chop—center cut, several veal dishes, and a few pastas.

Appetizers (oysters on the half shell, escargots bordelaises, stuffed mushrooms, Ozark mountain smoked trout) average $4.95 to $6.95; French onion soup au gratin, simmered in sherry wine broth, is $4.50; and all entrees are served with salad and hot baked bread. But you'll have to spend $2.25 extra for each side dish: baked potato, stuffed sweet potato, Candlestick fries, seasoned rice, vegetable du jour, sautéed mushrooms. Most everything that's brought to the table has, in my experience, been done with skill and care.

Slightly North of Downtown

Near the Mel Tillis, Pat Boone, and Glen Campbell Theaters

McGuffey's Diner
225 Violyn Drive,
phone 417/336-4331

Location: Close to the newest hotels and theaters near the north end of Shepherd of the Hills Expressway.

Open: It's advertised to be open every day but Thanksgiving and Christmas until 2:30am, and is therefore the premier late-night restaurant of Branson. But warning: this McGuffey's, unlike the others, has been known to close temporarily during slow seasons (like after October 15). AE, D, MC, V. MODERATE

Strictly a chain operation (one of five McGuffey's in Branson), and the kind you'd never single out in larger cities, it is nevertheless highly regarded by a great many residents, possibly because its more modern cuisine and style differ somewhat from the more traditional, countrylike Branson buffets and restaurants. And keep in mind that this McGuffey's, unlike the others, is theoretically a "diner" (but of vast, 289-seat proportions) with a menu that's a tiny bit more limited than at the others, and with more of the dishes you'd find in a roadside eatery. It serves a dozen different hot entrees, and they range over a broad spectrum of prices: from a remarkable $3.99 for sausage, buttermilk biscuit, and country gravy to $4.99 for a vegetable platter of homemade mashed potatoes, coleslaw, a green vegetable, and a biscuit; from $6.99 for "Mile High Meatloaf" with mashed potatoes, fresh vegetables, and a biscuit to $7.99 for country-fried steak with country gravy, mashed potatoes, fresh vegetables, and a biscuit; to $8.99 (at lunch; $9.99 at dinner) for pot roast cooked overnight until unusually tender and served with potatoes, fresh vegetables, and a biscuit; to $8.99 for Southern-fried catfish with spiral fries, coleslaw, and a biscuit; to $8.99 for barbecue pork ribs (half a rack of them) cooked for six to eight hours and served with spiral fries, coleslaw, and a biscuit; to the same for grilled pork chops served with mashed potatoes, country gravy, fresh vegetables, and a biscuit. Sandwiches, soups, and salads are listed in abundance for lighter eaters. But of all these offerings, nostalgia is the biggest, as captured in a decor of chrome, vinyl, and neon set off by '50s music, punctuated by photographs everywhere of Elvis, Marilyn Monroe, and (don't ask me why) Paul Newman. And there are particularly interesting framed photos of Missouri diners from that less complicated time of 40 years ago.

On West Highway 76

Between U.S. Highway 65 and the start of the Strip as you approach it from downtown Branson, near the 76 Music Hall, Memory Land, and Foggy River Boys, and relatively near the Grand Palace and Theaters of Andy Williams and Bobby Vinton

Subway
1314 West Highway 76,
phone 417/334-SUBS

Open: Every day of the year except Thanksgiving, Christmas, and New Year's Day. No credit cards. CHEAP

And now, don't laugh. I've mentioned this familiar, bright yellow, hole-in-the-wall (part of an 8,000-branch chain around the world) only because it's one of several havens in Branson for our vegetarian readers. It was suggested to me by herbalist Kan Rainier, of Nature's Sunshine Healthfoods in the Branson Heights Shopping Center (West Highway 76, phone 417/335-HERB). She advises that one of her own choices for enjoying a satisfying-but-sane quick meal is the foot-long vegetable sandwich on whole-wheat roll at Subway. It's a mix of shredded head lettuce, black olives, pickle, green pepper, tomatoes, onions, with a squirt of mixed olive and vegetable oil—to which you can add American cheese and various dressings if you're so inclined, all for a total price of $2.69 ($1.59

for a roll only six inches long). While you may miss some dark green leafy vegetables, something dark orange, you'll nevertheless want to give thanks for small blessings. Apart from its veggie sandwich, Subway specializes in standard subs, burgers, various cold cuts, and soups, brownies, cookies, and coffee. And you may want to know that there's another Subway on Highway 248, a new one about to open on Highway 65, both with those tasty and cheap vegetable sandwiches.

Bonanza Steak House

In the extensive 76 Mall on West Highway 76 (the Strip), phone 417/335-2434

Location: More or less across from the Bungee Jumping Attraction near the Outback Restaurant.

Open: Every day all year, since 1986, from 6:30am to 9pm, Sunday through Thursday, until 10pm on Friday and Saturday. AE, D, MC, V. CHEAP

This is the WalMart of the fast-food industry (non-hamburger division), a must for budget travelers, the largest volume Bonanza Steak House in America, with 500 seats in three main dining areas. How have they grown so big? Through price: they serve a complete breakfast buffet for $2.99, a lunch buffet for $5.19, a dinner buffet for $6.19 (although on Saturday and Sunday, the lunch and dinner rates are a uniform $6.19 all day), and both buffets are taken from a 10-item salad bar, a 10-item hot food bar (two soups and eight entrees, like Salisbury steak, baked chicken, Swedish meatballs, spaghetti and lasagna, ham, catfish on Friday), a 4-item dessert bar (two cobblers, brownies, bread pudding). Beverages are extra, with coffee priced at 89¢ with free refills, soft drinks and iced tea at 99¢ with free refills. (Total prices are almost identical to those of the Ozark Mountain Buffet described later in this chapter, which includes beverages in its all-you-can-eat rates.) And why is it called the Bonanza *Steak* House? Because steaks costing only $6.79 for a "petit, 5-oz. filet" and $8.99 for a 16-oz. porterhouse are the featured highlight of the operation, and purchasing them at those prices entitles you to the all-you-can-eat buffet at no extra charge; in other words, you pay the steak price ($6.79 or $8.99) and get the buffet free. You also receive, I should add, that friendly, gracious Branson service, despite the ultra-low prices.

Home Cannery
1810 West Highway 76,
phone 417/334-6965

Open: Closed Christmas and during January and February. Otherwise, open daily. AE, MC, V. MODERATE

One of the city's several self-service, all-you-can-eat buffet restaurants (though it offers menu service, too), this one is a country barn type of a place looking two stories high, but only one story in reality; it charges $6.50 per person at lunch, $9 at dinner, for its all-you-can-eat repast taken from a line of beef dishes, catfish, ham, salads, almost always accompanied by mashed potatoes with gravy, a few hardly-to-be-noticed vegetables, and a luscious bread pudding for dessert. Main courses are usually four in number (hand-carved roast beef, fried chicken, catfish, roast pork); beverages are always extra, and run under $1 for coffee or various soft drinks. Truth to tell, I'm impressed more with the value and variety of several other buffet-restaurants in the Branson area, and described in this chapter; Home Cannery seems excessively angled toward motorcoach groups and their preference for get-'em-in get-'em-out buffets; and the restaurant has, in fact, been named by a trade organization as one of America's five best for the serving of group tours. Average à la carte main courses: $7.

Wayne's Gravel Bar Restaurant
1335 West Highway 76 in Engler's Block (see our shopping chapter),
phone 417/334-5482

Open: Daily except Christmas and New Year's Day, throughout the year, for lunch and dinner. Full bar. D, MC, V. MODERATE

You likely won't see its sign from the road, because Wayne's is inside and to the back of the impressive Engler's Block, one of Branson's outstanding, multi-craftsman, shopping emporiums, a key sightseeing attraction even if you don't plan to buy a thing. Wood from top to bottom, and decorated with old canvas tents, camping cots, feed sacks, skillets, and bamboo fishing rods, it captures an authentic aspect of the Ozarks better than any other place in town. And its view is one of the best around. Unlike most other Branson restaurants that are either fully enclosed or look onto parking lots or adjacent motels, here the long back wall is all windows, and the vista is an Ozark landscape of atypical calm in Branson. You look onto a lowland with only a few peaked roofs in the near distance that fit the mood of time past. Get here soon, because even those pristine meadows and woods will probably soon be asphalted-over for additional, cookie-cutter motels.

The menu here is standard American fare, a bit better than competent in its preparation, a nice value. At lunch, big sandwiches average $4.25, and a few hot plates include chicken livers with "broasted" potato and coleslaw for $5.50, catfish with fries and coleslaw for $6.25, hamburger steak with grilled onions and peppers for $5.75. The dinner menu, however, is far more ambitious (and dinner is when bus groups tend to show up less): a local, specialty appetizer of steamed crawfish to be dipped into cajun tomato sauce, for $5.75; fish platters all from local catches (fried catfish, blackened catfish, trout amandine, baked hokie, frogs legs, for $11.25 to $12.75); various chicken preparations (including cornish game hen) for $12.75; top sirloin, hickory-smoked ham steak, pork medallions, or beef short ribs, for $12.75. And all dinners are served with a choice of soup or salad, vegetable, and choice of baked potato, baked sweet potato, rice pilaf, or french fries, adding to the value. All in all, this 100-seat restaurant, with space for another 100 on the open deck, is a fine choice for your evening dining, and is characterized by gracious service.

(I can't resist mentioning that though the restaurant itself is new since 1994, the family of the late Wayne Hargis—the "Wayne" of the title—has operated restaurants locally for almost 30 years. This one is named for the high ground that forms in the region's rivers, where a boatsman can usually safely camp overnight, away from mosquitos and snakes).

Outback Steak and Oyster Bar

1914 West Highway 76, opposite the 76 Mall, behind the Bungee Jump and down the hill from the side of the road, phone 417/334-6306

Open: Every day of the year. AE, D, MC, V. MODERATE

If you ever doubted that Branson would someday broaden its appeal to an open-minded, more youthful, more worldly audience, you have only to visit the funky Outback, with its distinctly different clientele, looking like the "in" restaurant crowd of a

Ft. Lauderdale or Denver. They're a lively and talkative set, sophisticated in the best sense, lighthearted and looking for fun. The theme is "down under"; the building is a large, rustic barn of a place (with space for 270 diners, of whom 100 sit outdoors on an encircling wooden balcony that can be heated and protected from the winds by a roll-down canvas in poor weather); and the interior is fully detailed Aussie designer chic, with a monster Australian flag draped from the rafters. An attractive pub with fireplace adjoins the dining spaces, and you can accompany your draft Fosters beer there with a plate of raw Apalachicola oysters (half dozen for $5.95); I recently did, and was surprised, in this city so far from the sea, to find them as obviously fresh and tasty as they were.

The setting and the conviviality can sometimes overwhelm the food, but the management wisely restricts itself, mainly, to plain grilled items, done in an open kitchen area fully in sight; who can ruin a good piece of meat cooked in that manner? Biggest sellers are grilled steaks (half-pound top sirloins for $10.95, one-third-pound filets for $12.95, three-quarter-pound strip steaks for $13.95), lamb chops for $12.95, 10-oz. prime rib for $12.95, half-slab of barbecued ribs for $11.95, various beef, shrimp, or combo kebabs (on skewers, with grilled garden vegetables). Keep in mind, as you assess those prices, that each entree is accompanied by your choice of an outback dinner salad, spinach salad, or soup of the day, and a choice of rice, Aussie fries, baked or au gratin potatoes, and fresh baked bread, thus making a full meal. For lighter eaters, there are seafood or chicken Caesar salads for $9.95; and for vegetarians, there's the option of simply requesting that those salads come without seafood or chicken but with all the vegetables stored in the larder for the same $9.95. A person at the next table recently did just that, and received a plate both humongous and nutritious.

In the Heart of the Strip

West Highway 76 (Country Music Boulevard), near the Theaters for Moe Bandy, The Presleys, Roy Clark, Jim Stafford, Box Car Willy, Mickey Gilley, and many more

Carmen's Authentic Mexican Food
3515 West Highway 76,
phone 417/334-2815 or 417/335-2042

Location: On the same side of the highway as the White Water Amusement Park, across the highway from Cristy Lane's Theater.

Open: Daily from March through October, closed November through February. D, MC, V. INEXPENSIVE

★ Carmen and Manuel Solis are owners of this absolutely first-class, affordable cantina of sane eating. Everything here is fresh, served hot (unless it's meant to be cold, like guacamole), clean, un-greasy. Old Mexican travelers leave the little 22-table restaurant exclaiming how they haven't tasted dishes like this since last they were south of the border. The secret is a caring family in the kitchen and on the floor. It's their own reputation at stake, and they've been caring for it, in Branson, since 1979. Southern Missouri isn't that far from the Mexican border that Mexicans haven't found their way here, so that today Branson can boast maybe a half-dozen Mexican restaurants, though nothing better than this.

The menu is a large one that features some two dozen Mexican entrees. In addition to the usual chile rellenos, the quesadillas, chimichangas, and such, Carmen and Manny serve a creamy potato taco with Mexican spiced rice and refried beans for $5.95, an unusually tasty, fresh vegetable stew with rice that they call "Vegetable Caldo," accompanied by three dry but supple corn tortillas for a total of $5.95, and a full enchilada dinner (cheese enchiladas served with Mexican rice and refried beans) for $6.95. The top-priced house specialty is half an order of guacamole salad with one beef taco and one cheese enchilada served with Mexican rice and beans, for $8.25; and ultra-cost-conscious sorts can have an enormous, filling, chicken stew with Mexican rice and 3 corn torillas, for $5.95. On the menu, little Mexican Hat symbols mark the dishes that have no meat. And Mexican beers ("Limit 3 per person") cost $2.50 per bottle of Corona, Dos XX, Carta Blanca, and Tecate, all of them in stock. Obviously, the restaurant is totally authentic, and its setting equally exciting: walls of brick, open beams, small iron chandeliers with amber lamps, all quite cozy, and tables set with fringed blue cloths under glass. Don't miss it.

Penelope's Family Restaurant
3015 West Highway 76 (otherwise known as the Strip, or Country Music Boulevard),
phone 417/334-3335

Location: Close to the west end of Highway 76 near the Roy Clark, John Davidson, Boxcar Willie, and Jim Stafford theaters, and toward Mutton Hollow.

Open: Every day of the year. MC, V. INEXPENSIVE

Good for a quick meal in this theater-packed portion of the Strip, Penelope's is a little 85-seat restaurant with country styling, a bit of lattice, a few country crafts, a light and airy look, and menu items (all under $10 per entree) that should cause the area to be renamed "Cardiac Gulch": ribeye steak, strip steak, fried breaded shrimp, fried catfish nuggets. You'll love the advisory at the *bottom* of the menu. You reach it after you've read through a brimful listing of burgers topped with smoked bacon and served with piping hot fries, patty melts, fried shrimp platters, cream of broccoli or bacon-vegetable soups, pork chops, Reuben sandwiches, roast beef Italian sandwiches with mozzarella cheese and creamy Italian dressing.

The advisory reads: "We cook in cholesterol-free shortening."

Homemade cobbler at $1.95 rates a rave; coffee is only 75¢; soup and salad bar only $3.95; and from the latter, you can find an uncreamed broccoli. Another Penelope's is located in downtown Branson.

Peppercorns Restaurant and Bakery
2421 West Highway 76,
phone 417/335-6699

Open: Every day but Christmas from March through December; closed January and February. MC, V. INEXPENSIVE

A superlative modern setting (immense bay windows, high ceilings, comfortable booths and tables) that attempts to evoke the appearance of a Southern garden; some less superlative work in the kitchen on their self-service buffet items, better on the à la carte dishes, especially the salads. True, the buffets are big and affordable: a breakfast buffet for $4.49, with fruit bar, homemade cinnamon rolls, hot apple butter, biscuits and gravy, hash-browns, scrambled eggs, all sorts of breakfast meats, pancakes with hot syrup and strawberries, hot muffins. The lunch buffet is only $5.99, but offers far less than the number of items (on my recent visit) served that day at the Ozark Mountain Buffet (see below), and the dishes I most recently tasted were mainly overcooked, tough, stringy, and

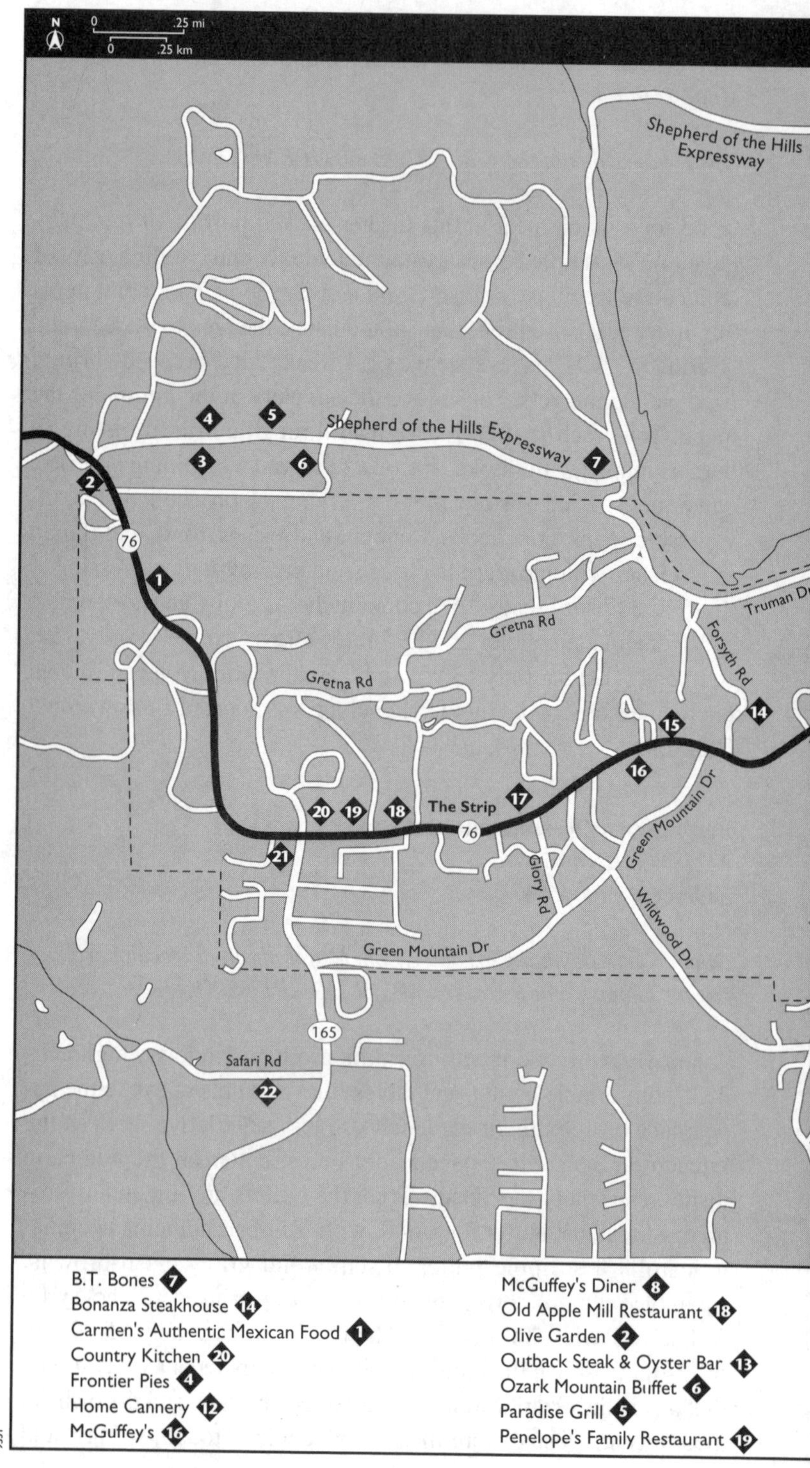
N
0 .25 mi
0 .25 km
Shepherd of the Hills Expressway
Shepherd of the Hills Expressway
Truman Dr
Gretna Rd
Gretna Rd
Forsyth Rd
The Strip
76
76
Green Mountain Dr
Glory Rd
Wildwood Dr
Green Mountain Dr
165
Safari Rd
B.T. Bones 7
Bonanza Steakhouse 14
Carmen's Authentic Mexican Food 1
Country Kitchen 20
Frontier Pies 4
Home Cannery 12
McGuffey's 16
McGuffey's Diner 8
Old Apple Mill Restaurant 18
Olive Garden 2
Outback Steak & Oyster Bar 13
Ozark Mountain Buffet 6
Paradise Grill 5
Penelope's Family Restaurant 19

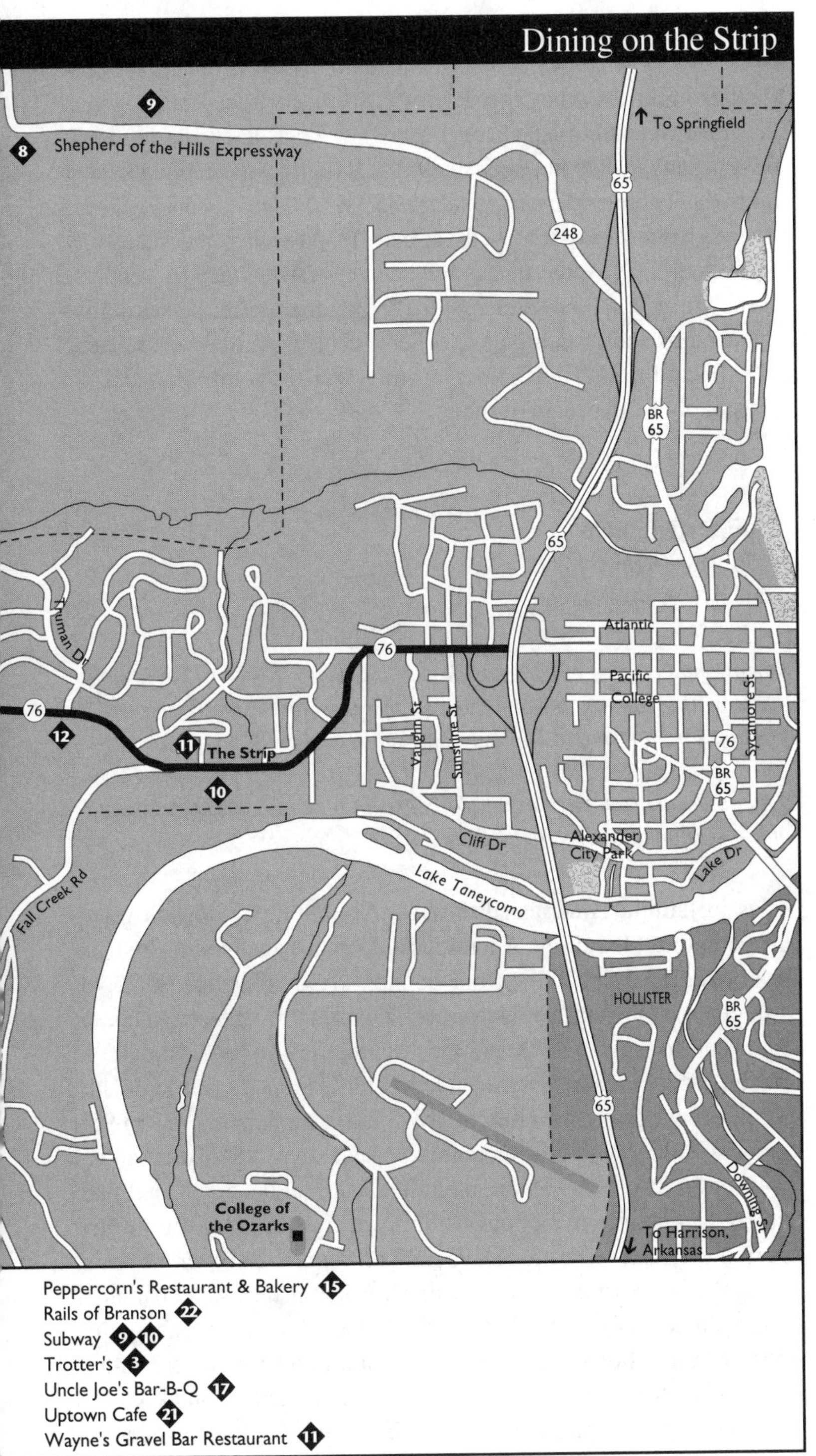
Dining on the Strip
To Springfield
Shepherd of the Hills Expressway
248
65
BR 65
76
Truman Dr
The Strip
Vaughn St
Sunshine St
Atlantic
Pacific
College
Sycamore St
Alexander City Park
Cliff Dr
Lake Dr
Lake Taneycomo
Fall Creek Rd
HOLLISTER
Downing St
College of the Ozarks
To Harrison, Arkansas
Peppercorn's Restaurant & Bakery 15
Rails of Branson 22
Subway 9 10
Trotter's 3
Uncle Joe's Bar-B-Q 17
Uptown Cafe 21
Wayne's Gravel Bar Restaurant 11

generally tasteless. The dinner buffet is $8.99, and like the lunchtime variety, includes soups, meat main courses, one fish item (breaded and dry), hot cobbler for dessert, even ice cream (with beverages an additional charge). Yet while I was lately staring morosely at my less-than-adequate buffet, Roberta was reveling in her individually ordered chef's salad for $5.49, wonderfully put together (there's a big selection of well-garnished sandwiches and salads for $4.99 to $5.49). What makes the uneven performance of Peppercorns' kitchen all the sadder is that the quite enchanting setting is matched by the restaurant's excellent service. Waitresses are caring, friendly, and quick, performing well beyond what could reasonably be expected of them.

Country Kitchen
3225 West Highway 76,
phone 417/334-2766

Location: Just east of where Highway 165 cuts off toward Table Rock Dam, within 10 minutes of numerous theaters, and directly across the road from Osmond Brothers and Yakov Smirnoff.

Open: Until 11pm each night, daily except for eight weeks beginning mid-December. MC, V. INEXPENSIVE

Classic, familiar American dishes for an extremely reasonable price in a comfortable setting. A jam-packed, eight-page menu here lists every regional specialty from country-fried steak for $6.75 to "smothered chicken" (boneless breast overlaid with melted cheese and sautéed fresh onions and mushrooms) for $6.95. There are a dozen different entrees for even less (old-fashioned meat loaf with thick brown gravy, two side dishes, and a dinner roll for $5.95; country turkey with gravy, cranberry sauce, two side dishes, and a roll for $6.25); an $8.75 dinner buffet (without beverage, and just so-so) served from 4:30pm to 9pm in high season; big multi-ingredient sandwiches for $4.95; and senior citizen (over 60 years of age) dinners (main courses with two side dishes, salad bar, and warm dinner roll) for $4.45 to $4.95. You can't complain about the costs of this Midwestern chain restaurant, in its attractive country setting of stone-surfaced columns, light pine tables, plank walls, and country-style paned windows. There's often a line outside.

Uncle Joe's Bar-B-Q
2819 West Highway 76,
phone 417/334-4548

Location: Across the road from the Palace Inn and diagonally opposite the Grand Palace Theater, in the very center of the Strip.

Open: Until 9pm, daily except from the third week of December until mid-February, when it is closed. D, MC, V. INEXPENSIVE

★ Here, now, is the city's barbecue king, and since people hereabouts are consummate connoisseurs of barbecue, the quality is, arguably, among the best in all the state. One of the oldest restaurants in Branson, here since 1956, it serves nothing other than various barbecued meats doused in a remarkable, homemade sauce, and the end product compares with all the famous names in barbecueing, bar none (even Arthur Bryant's of Kansas City is no better, in my view). The restaurant is also refreshingly cheap if you order the smaller portions of everything, which themselves are more than anyone other than a trencherman could possibly consume.

An example is the classic lunchtime selection of a quarter-pound barbecue sandwich (your choice of either pork shoulder, ham, or beef brisket), which arrives in the form of a large soft roll overflowing with razor-thin slices (but piled up high) of the hickory-smoked juicy meats swimming in that tangy barbecue nectar, and hardly to be eaten except with fork and knife. That sandwich costs $5.50, and you'll need to take the uneaten portion home to your hotel room for later that day. (I can't even imagine who could finish the costlier, $6.50, half-pound version of the same thing.) And yet, both the $5.50 and $6.50 sandwiches also come with a side dish of either corn on the cob, wedge fries, barbecue beans, or soup at no extra charge. Evenings, you can have a third of a slab (almost a pound) of pork spareribs in barbecue sauce (accompanied by soup and salad bar, hot roll and butter, and one side dish of corn on the cob, wedge fries, or baked potato) for $10.75—no one could possibly complete it. But better yet, you and your companion might consider ordering one "sliced meat dinner" of pork shoulder, beef brisket, or ham (over half a pound), with all the accompaniments, for the two of you, costing $10.95 (although, to be fair to Uncle Joe's, another smaller dish should also be ordered). And as a final bonus, the several small dining rooms in which you'll gamely attempt to finish these meals are pleasantly wood-paneled (especially the attractive

Atrium Room), filled with hanging plants, and redolent with the faint odor of slow, hickory-smoked preparations and barbecue bastings. Draft beer ("bush draw"): $2.

The Old Apple Mill Restaurant
3009 West Highway 76,
phone 417/334-6090

Location: Set back behind the Hall of Fame Motel.

Open: Closed from Christmas through March; otherwise open daily for all three meals. AE, D, MC, V. MODERATE

Another moderately priced, standard American restaurant where nearly every entree other than expensive steaks and seafoods is priced at from $7.75 to $9.95, and those reasonable rates also include house salad, and your choice of potato, corn on the cob, "dirty rice," or ham and beans. A special "family feast" supplies an entire family with complimentary fresh baked breads, apple muffins, and cinnamon rolls, a large bowl of fresh salad, mashed potatoes and gravy, corn on the cob, ham and beans, and a family-size platter of fried chicken, barbecue ribs, and roast beef—all for only $8.95 per adult, $4.95 per child 7 to 12, $1 per child 6 and under. It's a world wonder.

Still other main dishes are grouped under the headings of "red and delicious" (steaks, roast beef), "poultry and pork," and "from the wharf." On first seeing the Old Apple Mill Restaurant, you'd swear it was one of a chain with its water wheel and rustic styling that seems just right for replicating all over the nation. But no, it's a one-of-a-kind built in 1984, originally almost entirely for tour groups. It's so popular that you can come in at 6pm and face a line of patient people, and by 7:15 find the place empty, as everyone has been assembled for the bus ride onward to that evening's show.

Inside, the old-timey look gets worked out in pressed tin ceiling inserts, plank surrounds, country flower wallpapers, and—best of all—an ingenious system of pulley-driven ceiling fans, worth the wait. Some guests sit at a row of plank booths to the back of the main dining room or on separate wooden seats at tables (least cushioned of any restaurant in Branson, but that's the price you pay for charm). And beer, wine, or mixed drinks are also served.

McGuffey's
3600 West Highway 76,
phone 417/336-3600

Location: Alongside the Andy Williams Theater, which means near Bobby Vinton's as well, not to mention the Grand Palace, a short walk farther on.

Open: Closed Thanksgiving and Christmas. AE, D, MC, V.
MODERATE

When you ask well-informed residents of Branson to name the restaurants they consider to be among the area's best—and I've put that question to a great many—they frequently include McGuffey's in their answer, and they are referring to this full-service McGuffey's, not to McGuffey's Diner (described earlier in this chapter). I've often felt they make that choice because McGuffey's cuisine is so different from the traditional country dishes that dominate the list at many other Branson restaurants. Here, at McGuffey's, you could imagine yourself in Boston or Philadelphia; the crowd is youthful and/or sophisticated; the menu carries not a single reference to country-fried steak or catfish or bread pudding. By Branson standards, it's positively effete in this trendy, woodsy interior (a large, labyrinthine space) that tries to reflect the schoolhouse atmosphere of that era when schoolchildren everywhere were taught with McGuffey's reader. (The restaurant seeks to establish its connection with something authentic, and it succeeds; if only others on the Strip attempted to reflect the culture of the Ozarks!)

And the menu—the menu actually features the low-fat dishes of a nutritious cuisine. There is honey-mustard chicken with green onions and white wine ($9.99), a blackened chicken sans its skin, served over rice pilaf with fresh vegetables ($9.99), a blackened tuna steak with fresh lime, rice, and sautéed vegetables ($9.99), a penne pasta marinated with broiled tuna chunks, olive oil, and asparagus tips ($8.99). Giant bowls of salad—themselves a full meal—are $4.99 without meat, $6.99 with. And meals are accompanied by a loaf of homemade dark bread, and sometimes finished with a low-fat yogurt dessert ($1.99). Is Branson being invaded by Liberals? Highly recommended.

Near the Shoji Tabuchi Theater

Either at the very end of the Strip, or on Shepherd of the Hills Expressway

Ozark Mountain Buffet
Shepherd of the Hills Expressway (toward the west end just east of the Cascades Inn),
phone 800/365-6742 or 417/335-5811

Open: Daily except from the third week of December until the second week of March, when it is closed. Family owned and operated. MC, V. CHEAP (lunch) to INEXPENSIVE (dinner)

★ A value matched only by the Rose O'Neill Friendship House (see above), this is Branson's most remarkable self-service, all-you-can-eat Western-style chuckwagon buffet, costing $5.95 at lunch (11am to 2pm), $7.95 at dinner (4 to 7:30pm), including dessert and unlimited nonalcoholic beverages. It's conveniently located about 200 yards from the Shoji Tabuchi Theater on Shepherd of the Hills Expressway (with Branson's Civil War Museum almost next door). A plain and unpretentious warehouse of a building, both inside and out, this is a 40-yard-long, 350-seat dining room of plastic-topped tables and metal chairs surrounding a long, metal buffet server crammed with as many as 40 items, and supplemented by another table of daily-changing, sweet-and-juicy cobblers (usually peach) for dessert, the cubed-up pies topped with soft ice cream that you draw yourself. Self-service Coke, Sprite, Fanta, Dr Pepper, and apple juice or lemonade punch spigots permit you to pour as much of these soft drinks as you crave.

Unlike other buffets in town, whose lunchtime offerings are occasionally skimpy and ill-prepared, overcooked and dry (see Peppercorns as a possible example, hopefully improved as you read this), here the standard of preparation is at its Southern best, and the fried chicken—in particular—is moist and only slightly breaded. At lunchtime, you start with 12 salad items, including celery, peppers, and black olives—as many as you wish. You go on to macaroni, coleslaw, Jell-O, potato salad, and slices or chunks from a two-foot-high (literally) mound of cheddar cheese. You select vegetables cooked with butter or bacon, ranging from mashed potatoes with either brown or white country gravy, stringbeans, carrots, corn on the cob, peas, and tasty turkey stuffing. And then you select from 4 entrees at lunch (among them, pork ribs in rich, brown "leavings" and "Masterpiece BBQ Sauce," large slices of sweet country ham, fried chicken, au gratin potatoes with ham chunks in cheese sauce) and 9 entrees at dinnertime (all the above plus shrimp stir fry, fried catfish, and others). There's dessert (the above-described cobblers with ice cream and others), coffee, juices, and soft drinks, and the entire total cost—I need to repeat it again, to properly express my sense of wonderment—is $5.95 at lunch and $7.95 at dinner. But watch those early evening closing hours. A budget find!

Frontier Pies

3562 Shepherd of the Hills Expressway in the IMAX Theater Mall, phone 417/336-4680

Open: Daily except Christmas for all three meals. AE, D, MC, V.
INEXPENSIVE

The Branson branch of a western restaurant chain (mainly in Utah, Montana, Idaho, Arizona), whose gimmick is a selection of no fewer than 32 different pies made fresh on the premises each day (apple, cherry, raspberry, boysenberry, triple berries, strawberry rhubarb, peach, pumpkin, pecan, walnut, banana cream, coconut cream, chocolate cream, peanut butter and chocolate, cherry chocolate, tropical cream, lemon meringue, to name a few), and selling for $2.29 (fruit pies) or $2.49 (cream pies) a slice. Those are for dessert, of course.

Earlier, you have chosen from dozens of rather surprising plates a bit different from the standard Branson variety, and really to be characterized as "eclectic" (the manager, disagreeing with me, claims that "mother's home cooking" should be the descriptive term). But mother never made Navajo tacos ($4.99), quiche lorraine ($4.89), chicken fajita salads ($6.59), steamed veggie platters ($4.99), baked lasagna ($6.79), and a half-dozen other state-of-the-art, contemporary California-style dishes that offer a welcome change of pace from the classic main courses of Branson. Biggest seller, according to the same manager, are those aforementioned Navajo tacos (they come with Indian fry bread swamped in chili and topped with a mix of cheeses, tomatoes, lettuce, onions, olives, and sour cream), with chicken pot pie ($5.99) and vegetable stir fries mixed with shrimp or chicken ($6.79) coming in second and third. The restaurant's home-baked cornbread is free with every dish ordered. And about the only concession made to local tastes is a chicken-fried steak smothered in country gravy served with potatoes and soup or salad ($7.89), one of Frontier Pies' highest-priced items.

As you can see, this is a menu that you could easily have encountered in trendy, sophisticated sections of San Francisco, Seattle, or Santa Fe, utterly unlike what Branson is mainly known for. Special, smaller-portion meals for senior citizens, accompanied by a cup of soup, are a welcome, final touch at $4.99 for baked meat loaf with potatoes, $6.49 for fillet of cod with rice pilaf, tartar sauce, and lemon.

Trotter's
3559 Shepherd of the Hills Expressway,
phone 417/336-3415

Location: Across from the Country Tonight Theater, diagonally across from the IMAX Theater.

Open: Daily except Christmas, closed January and February. AE, D, DC, MC, V. Full bar. INEXPENSIVE (breakfast), MODERATE (lunch or dinner)

To me, this is Branson's best breakfast restaurant, even though it serves all three meals, and despite the fact that its $5.49 price (with coffee) for unlimited breakfast choices is higher than at the Bonanza Steak House in the 76 Mall (described above). But Trotter's selection is bigger, its 250-seat setting more attractive, and its location on a more pleasant, lightly traveled boulevard just down the hill from where the road drops away from the end of the Strip. The breakfast bar is divided into three sections. One features fresh citrus chunks, pitted prunes in their juice, a bowl of luscious strawberries in season (nothing pulpy about these), a big bowl of canned fruit in heavy syrup (some people actually prefer it that way), and an equally big bowl of fresh and frozen fruit. Another section has all the classic breakfast meats (brisket hash, sausages, and bacon), pancakes and waffles, grits and hot oatmeal, scrambled eggs, and the fixings for a dozen omelets (green pepper, mushrooms, ham, swiss cheese, ripe olives, bacon, turkey), french toast, biscuits and gravy, potatoes. The third has four kinds of dry cereals in large jars, three varieties of fat-free yogurt including one sugarless, four kinds of toppings, three or four different pastries including home-baked cinnamon rolls and one sugarless, and bagels and cream cheese.

Someone is obviously at work thinking about what might delight guests, in addition to giving them a few healthful, nutritious choices among the rest.

While Trotter's also serves lunch and dinner, those meals are mainly rather standard grills (ribs, chicken several ways, steaks) costing about $19 per complete meal. (Although if you wanted something lighter, you could choose from a big salad bar, soup, breads, and dessert for only $7.50.)

Paradise Grill
Shepherd of the Hills Expressway,
phone 417/337-7444

Location: Next door to the Shoji Tabuchi Theater.

Open: Daily for lunch and dinner, except on Thanksgiving and Christmas. AE, D, MC, V. PRICEY

★ Vies with Candlestick Inn as Branson's best restaurant; its arrival here may presage a new stage in Branson's development. This is hip Branson, colorful as a rainbow inside, full of whimsy and playful neon-and-patterned-glass dividers, always full of guests and chatter. And its fanciful American menu is different as can be. Yes, there is country-fried Ozark mountain chicken ($11.99), yes, there are Texas tenderloins ($11.99) and Georgia-style "Macon bacon melts" (sandwiches of thick-slab bacon and tomatoes) with french fries. But there are also Iowa lamb chops coated in mustard and bread crumbs, sautéed and served with white beans, sun-dried tomatoes, prosciutto, spinach, and arugula ($18.99). There's an oven-roasted white-water salmon fillet with white beans, tomatoes, artichoke hearts, and salamata olives beneath a balsamic butter sauce ($14.99). There's also an exceptionally well-done wok stir fry with a garlic soy ginger sauce served over linguine and topped with coconut and shaved almonds (only $9.99). It's savory, appetite arousing. About the only disappointment I've ever had with Paradise Grill has been the focaccia (pasty white bread with only a trace of cracked pepper, strictly from nowhere).

But all is redeemed by the hot, fresh, mushroom soup ($2.99), the root beer floats ($2.25) for dessert, or "Crisp of the Day" (fresh seasonal fruits baked with a thick brown sugar topping and served with ice cream) ($2.95). Staff, you'll be interested to know, wear Ralph Lauren Polo white shirts with string ties above long white aprons. In Branson! The look is tailored and smart, the service attentive, the servers informed about their menu. Highly recommended for both food and setting.

Olive Garden

3790 West Highway 76, a block from where Shepherd of the Hills Expressway intersects, near the extreme end of the Strip miles away from downtown Branson,
phone 417/337-5811

Open: Daily except Thanksgiving and Christmas, throughout the year. AE, D, MC, V. MODERATE

The third of Branson's Italian restaurants. One of the newest in town (open since summer of 1994), colorful, slick, and modern, if a little plastic (it's one of a nationwide chain), it is a U.S. vision of what Italy looks like, and lists every familiar Italian dish from pasta e fagioli (ground beef, beans, and pasta for $2.65, with complimentary refills) to fettucine crab Alfredo (pasta covered with snow crabmeat in an Alfredo cream sauce for $10.75), competently but not brilliantly done. Straight, filling pasta dishes mainly range from $6.65 to $8.25 and you can order them with your choice of six sauces: meat, marinara, Sicilian, tomato, Alfredo, and pesto cream. Many patrons choose the "Tastes of Italy" platters, sampling three famous dishes at once: "Tour of Italy" for $11.75 (chicken parmigiana, lasagna classico, and fettucine Alfredo, with one side dish of either sautéed spinach or other green vegetables), "Northern Italian" for $11.75 (veal piccata, Venetian grilled chicken, and fettucine Alfredo, with a side dish), or "Southern Italian" for $11.50 (veal parmigiana, lasagna classico, and manicotti al forno, along with a side dish). Stays open until 10pm on weekdays, until 11pm on weekends, and can often be used for after-theater dining if you've chosen a show with an early (7pm) curtain time.

B. T. Bones Steakhouse

Shepherd of the Hills Expressway near Gretna Road, a couple of miles away from where Shepherd of the Hills starts at its intersection with the Strip,
phone 417/335-2002

Open: Daily throughout the year (except for Christmas), from 11am to 1am (last serving at 12:30am) Monday through Saturday, from noon to midnight on Sunday. AE, MC, V. MODERATE

Branson's largest steakhouse seating 300 persons, and open until very late at night, a good point to remember. It's part of a Texas chain, decorated in Texas roadhouse-style with ads for oil companies upon its pine-paneled walls; and yet the steak you get is like that from a good, independently owned steakhouse and not at all like a chain product. Provided you limit yourself to the 8-oz. or 6-oz. sizes, you rarely pay more than $11.95 or $12.50 for your steak (always from Iowa beef), $12.95 for prime rib, which comes with house salad or soup, potatoes, vegetable of the day, and bread. For the potatoes, try the "Texas Taters," which are like chunky french fries, wonderfully mushy inside.

In the Vicinity of Green Mountain Drive and Highway 165

Near the Theaters for Pump Boys and Dinettes, Lawrence Welk, Cristy Lane, Tony Orlando, the Osmonds, and others.

The Rails of Branson
On Safari Road just west of Highway 165, phone 417/336-3401

Open: For dinner only, 4:30 to 8pm, seven days a week, but closed from mid-December into early March. MC, V. INEXPENSIVE

The price is exactly $9.95 for Branson's best, all-you-can-eat *seafood* buffet, which comes as a considerable surprise. But beverages—like coffee or soft drinks—are 75¢ extra, with free refills. All this is served cafeteria-style, in a rather plain, 250-seat, barn-like building next door to an RV lot, and considering the fact that everything has to be shipped in frozen, from a long distance away, the quality isn't bad (though it isn't thrilling, either).

Here you get all you can eat of baked cajun-spicy catfish fillets, boiled shrimp, fried catfish, fried shrimp, clam strips, or a seafood gumbo, plus vegetables cooked in butter and vegetables steamed, baked potato, two different types of dinner rolls, a very uninspired lettuce and tomato salad. Desserts are also included, and feature a choice of several cobblers and a nondairy ice cream substitute that, agreeably, is only mildly sweet.

Uptown Cafe
185 Highway 165, a short walk from where Highway 165 intersects with West Highway 76, near the Osmond Brothers and Jubilee theaters,
phone 417/336-3535

Open: Daily in season, open daily except Monday at all other times; closed (probably) January and February. D, MC, V. MODERATE

A brand-new (1994), slick reproduction of a '50s diner, but with extensive floor space and not in narrow, diner-like design; big band music plays in the background. Broad range of American dishes, served fairly fast; its key advantage, to my mind, is that it stays open until midnight during most months of the year, and gives you a place to dine after you've gone to the theater. Limited dinner menu offers five entrees: baked catfish or chicken (both done in butter sauce) for $8.95; country-fried steak, $9.95; brisket of beef, $9.75; prime rib, $12.50, all with rolls, vegetable, salad. Coffee is 65¢ extra; sandwiches and snacks, cakes, pastries, and soda fountain sundaes and the like, round out the list. No surprises. Although the food is competently prepared, and the decor is quite impressive, this doesn't rise to the imaginative food levels of Paradise Grill, though it also doesn't approach the latter's price level, either. A reliable standby for casual meals.

Sugar Hill Farms (Restaurant and Cannery)
405 South Highway 165,
phone 417/335-3608

Open: Daily including holidays, but closed late December to mid-March; may change that policy to a year-round operation, depending on whether more theaters do the same. D, MC, V.

An impressive and friendly little operation of 192 seats, but with a rather formal atmosphere, befitting a special dining occasion; live music is played most evenings by a solo performer of many instruments; and much art is displayed on the walls. This isn't rustic country. Nearly all main courses (which come with soup or salad, choice of saffron rice, mashed or baked potato, and fresh bakery roll) are priced at only $8.95 or $9.95, and the popular specialty of the house is pot roast for $9.95—cooked ever so slowly throughout the day in a beef stock and vegetables; it's then served with the items we've listed above, accompanied by much gravy. Runners-up: chicken-fried steak and country gravy for $8.95, various chicken dishes for $8.95 and $9.95, pasta of the day for $8.95. Desserts are chosen from a tray of delicate pastries prepared daily.

The restaurant's most attractive feature—apart from its pastiche of a facade evoking second-empire France and you name it—is that there is a real Sugar Hill Farm just south over the border in Lead Hill, Arkansas. From there—where many of the restaurant's employees help out—Branson's Sugar Hill Farm gets almost all the fresh vegetables and fruits served here—peaches, strawberries, grapes, apples, onions, corn, and tomatoes. The restaurant also operates its own cannery and bakery, and offers a good variety of vegetables in glass jars to take home (and cookies to munch on after the meal). They serve three meals a day, and expect within the immediate future to have a beer and wine license, and perhaps full drink service, though without a sit-down bar. Though you aren't required to dress up for your meal here, it tends—as we hinted before—to be a rather dressy restaurant, despite its moderate costs. Be warned.

Shorty Small's Great American Restaurant
3270 Yellow Ribbon Road, off Highway 165 at the Tony Orlando Theater,
phone 417/334-8797

Open: Every day of the year for lunch and dinner. AE, D, DC, MC.
MODERATE

Dining as entertainment, and more to be valued for its showiness than for its food. Convenient to Tony Orlando's Yellow Ribbon Theater, to Table Rock Dam, and generally to the western end of the Strip, though a mile south of it on Highway 165. The building is a large, wooden, rustic-styled barn of a place sporting old Coke, soda, and cigar signs. Inside, strung from the open-raftered ceiling, are every manner of vintage items from the Gold Rush era, from early bicycles to mining paraphernalia. The look is intensely busy (there are 400 seats inside and out), and the restaurant is popular among youthful singles as a good-times scene.

Food, however, is a somewhat standard mix of burgers, chicken, ribs, brisket, steaks, catfish, shrimp, a few salads, soup, a few sandwiches, and the usual cobbler of the day. Almost all main items are slightly under $10, though the steak entrees can run from $14 to $17. It's not entirely cheap, and the same items, in my experience, can be had elsewhere in town for several dollars less. You pay for atmosphere.

Dondie's Riverboat Restaurant
3100 Green Mountain Drive, an area somewhat more upscale than the Strip,
phone 417/335-4345

Open: Daily except Thanksgiving and Christmas, closed January and February. AE, D, DC, MC, V. MODERATE

A large, 550-seat restaurant designed to accommodate the busloads, it's in the shape of a riverboat, smokestacks and all, and is again one of those personality restaurants that you visit more for the setting than the food. The menu is typical of the area, but with some surprises, like mesquite chicken grilled with vegetables on a rice pilaf, and several dinner salads, several pasta dishes. The chicken and pasta entrees are mostly under $10, salads under $8; but other main courses, like porterhouse T-bone, can go to $15 and $17. Most visitors stay with the house specials: prime rib (8 ounces) with burgundy mushrooms and traditional or Caesar salad, for $12.95; Danish baby back ribs with "Daddy's BBQ Sauce," slaw, and curly fries for $12.95; Southern-fried catfish with curly fries and Daddy's slaw for only $9.95. And chocolate lovers will want to check out the Hershey's Bar Cake, a homemade chocolate cake made from Hershey's chocolate bars, along with premium vanilla ice cream and hot fudge. Believe it or not, there are people who eat such concoctions.

Spaghettata
2805 Green Mountain Drive,
phone 417/336-3376

Open: Daily in season; otherwise, closed Monday and Tuesday, closed Christmas, and closed January and February. AE, MC, V. MODERATE

A decent-quality Italian restaurant of Branson, in a fresh and imaginative setting that needs a few years to mature and become less plastic. You enter into an attractive, bright courtyard with a cart full of flowers, and then into a choice of five dining rooms scattered in different directions so that the 550-seat restaurant (ever ready for busloads) never seems overwhelmingly barn-like. Indeed, one of the rooms opens only evenings, and features tablecloths and nightly guitar music.

The menu is of all the standard Italian specialties, with no surprises, but prices vary sharply from lunch to dinner. At lunchtime, Caesar salads in appetizer portions are $4.95, soups (like minestrone) $2.75, and pasta dishes (spaghetti marinara, linguine with clam sauce, ravioli, fettucine Alfredo, pasta primavera) range from $4.95 to $5.95. Evenings, while soups and appetizers remain unchanged in price, pasta dishes ascend to from $6.95 to $10.95 (the latter for various tortellini dishes and linguine with clam sauce). Meat plates in evening range from $10.95 to $11.95 for various preparations of chicken (parmigiana, cacciatore, marsala), $13.95 for fish (tuna steak, mahi mahi, swordfish, and salmon), $13.95 to $16.95 for various forms of hard-shelled seafood (shrimp, seafood diablo), and to $15.95 to $17.95 for steaks. Children's plates (10 and under) run $3.95. Again, these are standard Italian dishes cooked by non-Italians (Wisconsin restaurateur Morrie Wakefield is the owner), and can't reach the levels they do in large cities with a tradition of fine Italian dining, but are reasonably well-prepared for Branson.

A NOTE ABOUT THE MENUS STARTING ON THE NEXT PAGE

The menus appearing on the pages that follow—taken from the actual, recent menus of the restaurants discussed in this chapter—are included as a service to our readers, enabling them to know in advance the full dining options and prices of those restaurants.

They are not advertisements, and no restaurant paid for their inclusion here, nor did any restaurant know that its menu was being reproduced in this book.

Menus appear in alphabetical order.

Branson Cafe

The Best Hamburger in Town

Ken's Burger **$4.25**
Double meat, double cheese and chips

Jumbo Hamburger **$2.60**
1/3 pound of ground chuck on a toasted bun

Super Cheeseburger **$2.70**
Charbroiled with cheese on a toasted bun

Ye Olde English Burger **$4.25**
A jumbo burger served with a rasher of bacon and cheese on a toasted bun

Chili Size **$4.25**
A jumbo burger served open faced and smothered with our homemade chili, topped with cheese

Burger Basket **$4.25**
Hamburger on a toasted bun, french fries and cole slaw

The Lighter Side

The Thin Liner **$4.35**
Broiled ground beef patty or fried cod filet with cottage cheese, fruit, hard-boiled egg and tomato garnish

Vegetable Plate **$3.75**
Potatoes and gravy, vegetable of the day, and choice of salad with toast

Lo-Cal **$4.35**
Chicken breast, charbroiled with cottage cheese, fruit, side salad and toast

Chef's Supreme Salad
small **$2.25**
medium **$3.65**
large **$5.35**
Crisp mixed greens, topped with ham, turkey, and cheese with egg and tomato garnish

Garden Salad Bowl
small .... **95¢**
large **$1.55**
With choice of dressing

Homestyle Dinners

Chicken Fried Steak Dinner **$7.50**
Chopped Sirloin **$7.50**
Ham Steak, Hawaiian Style **$7.50**
Center Cut Pork Chops **$7.50**
Golden Fried Chicken
quarter **$5.35**
half **$6.85**

Fish and Chips **$7.50**
Channel Catfish **$8.75**
Rainbow Trout **$8.75**
Jumbo Fantail Shrimp **$8.75**
Boneless New York
Strip Steak **$8.95**
Rib Eye Steak **$8.95**

Above entrees are accompanied by: Choice of french fries, mashed or fried potatoes, or baked potato, and homemade soup, vegetable of the day, or tomato juice, and homemade rolls and butter

Today's "Blue Plate" Special

Changes daily

1/4 Fried Chicken $3.99
Our own famous batter, mashed potatoes, vegetable, choice of salad, rolls and butter

Children's Selection

(10 and under, please)

Peanut Butter and Jelly and Tater Tots $2.89

4 oz. Hamburger Steak $2.89
French fries, vegetable, and roll

Fish and Chips $2.89
Vegetable and roll

Hot Dog on Bun $2.89
With side salad

Country Style Breakfasts

Two Eggs with 8 oz. Chop Sirloin $5.35

Two Eggs with choice of Bacon or Sausage $3.50

One Egg with Ham $3.80

Two Eggs with Ham $4.25

Two Eggs (any style) $2.60

One Egg any style $1.95

The above prepared with country fresh eggs and served with toast or biscuits and jelly

From the Griddle

Sugar-cured Ham $1.95

Order of Bacon $1.65

Sausage Patties $1.65

Old-fashioned Buttermilk

Hot Cakes (3) $3.25

Short Stack (2) $2.65

Pecan Pancakes (2) $3.50

Golden French Toast $3.25

Waffle $2.65

Served with butter and hot syrup

Omelets

Ham or Sausage Omelet $4.75

Cheese Omelet $3.95

Western Omelet $4.75

Ham and Cheese Omelet $4.75

B. T. Bones Steakhouse

Starters

Bone Bits $4.95
Tender cuts of beef, marinated then fried or grilled

Texas Bullets $4.95
Cheese stuffed, deep fried jalapeño peppers

Lone Star Wings $3.95

Peel 'n Eat Shrimp $8.95

Shrimp Cocktail $6.95

Texas Chili
- **cup** $1.95
- **bowl** $2.75

Soup of the Day
- **cup** $1.75
- **bowl** $2.25

Tater Skins $3.50

Onion Rings $2.75

Fried Mushrooms $3.50

Grilled Mushrooms $2.95

Cheese Stix $3.95

Curly Q's $2.95

Fried Veggie Basket $3.95

Ultimate Nachos $5.95

Corn Nuggets $3.95

Dinner Entrees

All entrees include house salad or soup, potato, vegetable of the day and bread. Potato with "the works," add $1.00

24 oz. Sirloin $17.25

12 oz. Sirloin $13.50

8 oz. Top Sirloin $11.95

Chopped Sirloin $8.50

12 oz. Rib Eye $13.95

10 oz. Filet $16.50

8 oz. Filet $14.50

6 oz. Filet $12.50

14 oz. Kansas City Strip $15.95

10 oz. Kansas City Strip $12.95

18 oz. T-Bone $17.25

8 oz. Prime Rib $12.95

16 oz. Prime Rib $16.95

Beef K-Bob $11.50

Fins & Feathers

8 oz. Chicken Breast $9.95

Luckenbach Chicken $13.50
Grilled breast topped with grilled mushrooms, onions, cheddar & jack cheese and honey mustard

Southwest Chicken $13.50
Grilled breast topped with cheddar and jack cheese, salsa, bacon, and green onions

Chicken K-Bob $9.95
Chicken, onions, peppers, and tomatoes on a bed of rice

Quail $11.95
2 semi-boneless breasts on a bed of wild rice

Trout $9.50

Fried Catfish $9.95

Mahi Mahi $10.50

Pacific Salmon $10.50

Fried Shrimp $13.95

8 oz. Lobster Tail .... market price

Twin Tails .... market price

Snow Crab Cluster $11.95

Shrimp K-Bob $12.95

Shrimp Scampi $13.95
Served with rice pilaf

Combos

Filet & Shrimp **$16.95**
Filet & Lobster Tail .... **market price**
Filet & Crab **$16.95**

Wine list available

Children's Menu

Chopped Sirloin **$3.95**
Fried Fish **$3.25**
Fried Shrimp **$4.95**
Chicken Breast **$4.95**
Fried Chicken Fingers **$4.25**
Lil' Tex Burger **$4.25**

Candlestick Inn

Restaurant and Lounge

Appetizers

Oysters on the Half Shell **$5.95**
Oysters Mt. Branson **$6.95**
Shrimp Cocktail **$6.95**
Ozark Mountain BBQ Trout **$6.50**
Stuffed Mushrooms **$4.95**
Escargot Bordelaise **$6.95**
Toasted Ravioli **$4.50**
Breaded Cheese Stix **$4.50**
Breaded Mushrooms **$4.50**
Chef's Appetizer Basket **$7.50**

Soup and Salad

French Onion Soup au gratin **$4.50**
Cioppino Stew **$5.50**
Chef's Choice Soup du jour **$3.95**
House Salad à la carte **$2.95**

Seafaring Delights

Selected seafood entrees prepared fresh daily, served with crisp house salad, one à la carte selection, and hot bread

Breaded Shrimp **$13.95**
Breaded Scallops **$14.95**
Frog Legs Provençal **$15.95**
Charbroiled Swordfish Steak **$16.95**
Fisherman's Treasure Chest **$17.95**
Broiled Treasure Chest **$24.95**
Broiled Lobster Tail **$29.95**
Alaskan King Crab Legs **$24.95**
Seafood Specialties .... **market price**

House Specialties

All entrees served with crisp house salad, one à la carte selection, and hot baked bread

Prime Rib of Beef au jus **$15.95**
Slow roasted and served with a yorkshire puff

Kansas City Strip Sirloin **$17.95**

Filet Mignon **$17.95**

Delmonico Ribeye Steak **$15.95**

Tournedos of Beef **$17.95**
Two tenderloin medaillions topped with tomato crown and burgundy mushroom sauce

Steak au Poivre **$18.95**
Peppered ribeye steak and burgundy mushroom sauce

Filet of Pork Tenderloin **$15.95**
Bacon wrapped filets, a pork lover's treat

Steak and Shrimp Combo **$22.50**
Filet mignon and lightly breaded shrimp

Steak and Lobster **$35.95**
Filet mignon and lobster tail with drawn butter

Lighter Gourmet Fare

Charbroiled Breast of Chicken **$11.95**

Orange Roughy **$14.95**

Petite Filet Mignon **$14.50**

Ozark Traditions

Fresh Trout Fillets **$12.50**

Stuffed Ozark Trout **$13.95**

Fried Catfish Fillets **$12.50**

Smoked Ozark Mountain Pork Chop **$13.95**

Ozark Fried Breast of Chicken **$12.50**

Continental Delicacies

Veal Parmigiana **$14.95**
Breaded veal cutlets, fettuccini noodles topped with provolone cheese and sauce Italiano

Veal Oscar **$16.95**
Tender veal cutlet, crabmeat, and asparagus spears topped with sauce bearnaise

Breast of Chicken Oscar **$15.95**
Broiled breast of chicken, crabmeat, and asparagus spears topped with sauce bearnaise

Chicken Piccata **$13.50**
Sliced chicken breast sauteed in lemon butter sauce, with seasoned rice

Fettuccini Alfredo con Broccoli **$10.95**
Egg noodles, broccoli flowerettes and mushrooms in a rich butter cream sauce

Scallops Fettuccini Gourmet **$14.95**
Tender scallops in cream sauce with mushrooms and shallots, topped with provolone cheese over fettuccini

Seafood Stuffed Pasta **$14.95**
Jumbo shells filled with shrimps, scallops, crab and ricotta cheese topped with provolone cheese

À la Carte Selections

Baked Potato **$2.25**

Stuffed Sweet Potato **$2.25**

Candlestick Fries **$2.25**

Seasoned Rice **$2.25**

Vegetable du jour **$2.25**

Sauteed Mushrooms **$2.25**

A 15% gratuity will be added for all groups of 8 or more

Carmen's Authentic Mexican Food

Appetizers

Guacamole Salad $3.75
Nachos Con Queso $3.75
Nachos 'Ala Works' $5.75
Cheese Dip $3.00
Combination Salad $1.75
Quesadillas $3.95

Mexican Food

Please No Substitutions

Manny's Favorite Plate **$7.25**
2 chile relleños served with Mexican rice and refried beans

Chicken Tacos **$6.75**
2 crispy chicken tacos served with Mexican rice and refried beans.

Taco Salad **$6.95**
Garden lettuce, tomatoes, shredded cheese, and seasoned ground beef topped with sour cream

Quesadillas **$5.95**
3 flour tortillas with melted white cheese, served with Mexican rice and refried beans

Potato Tacos **$5.95**
3 potato tacos served with Mexican rice and refried beans

Chimichangas **$6.95**
2 fried 6" tortillas with beef, beans and cheese, served with Mexican rice and refried beans

Manny's Mexican Pizza **$6.95**
An 8" corn tortilla shell with beans, beef, lettuce, cheese, tomatoes, our own sauce and topped with guacamole

Beef Caldo **$5.95**
Beef stew served with Mexican rice and three corn tortillas

Chicken Caldo **$5.95**
Chicken stew served with Mexican rice and three corn tortillas

Vegetable Caldo **$5.95**
Vegetable stew served with Mexican rice and three corn tortillas.

House Specialty **$8.25**
½ order of guacamole salad, 1 beef taco, 1 cheese enchilada served with Mexican rice and refried beans

Tex-Mex Border Plate **$8.25**
1 beef tostada, 1 burrito and 1 beef enchilada served with Mexican rice and refried beans

Green Chile Burrito **$7.95**
1 burrito (cooked pork with green chiles) and 1 beef enchilada served with Mexican rice and refried beans

Mexican Chile Con Carne **$7.95**
Lean pork with our special sauce and green peppers served with Mexican rice and refried beans

Enchilada Dinner **$6.95**
2 cheese enchiladas served with Mexican rice and refried beans

Tamale Spread **$7.25**
3 tamales served with Mexican rice and refried beans

Taco Dinner **$6.50**
3 crispy tacos served with Mexican rice and refried beans

El Sanchote **$7.25**
A 10" tortilla with beef, beans, lettuce, tomatoes, and sour cream rolled and covered with melted cheese

Chicken Enchilada Dinner **$7.25**
Two chicken enchiladas covered in our green sauce and melted cheese served with Mexican rice and refried beans

Fajitas **$8.95**
Beef or chicken strips served with ½ an order of guacamole salad, Mexican rice, frijoles ala charra and an order of flour tortillas

Para Los Ninos

(for the children)

1 beef taco and 1 cheese enchilada served with Mexican rice or refried beans $3.95

1 burrito and 1 beef taco served with Mexican rice or refried beans $4.25

American Food

Chicken Fried Steak $5.95
Served with country gravy, french fries, dinner roll and salad

Rib Eye Steak $6.50
6-oz. steak served with french fries, dinner roll and salad

Chicken Fillet $5.95
Served with french fries, dinner roll, and salad

Chicken Sandwich $2.95
Fried chicken filet on a white bun served with lettuce, tomatoes and pickles

Taco Burger $2.75
Served on a white bun with lettuce, tomatoes and pickles

Hot Dog $1.50

French Fries $1.35

Desserts

Sopapillas $2.00
Specially made flour dough covered with honey

Apple Sticks $2.00
6 juicy apple filled desserts surrounded by a crust

A la Carte

Chorizo Burrito (Mexican Sausage) $2.50
Burrito $2.25
Green Chile Burrito $2.50
Tamale $1.65
Chile Relleno $2.25
Chimichanga $1.95
Cheese Enchilada $1.50
Beef Enchilada $1.80
Taco $1.50
Chicken Taco $1.80
Potato Taco $1.50
Soft Taco $1.80
Bean Tostada $1.50
with beef 25¢ extra
Order of Mexican rice $1.50
Order of Refried Beans $1.50
Order of 3 Flour Tortillas .... 65¢
Order of Jalapenos .... 50¢
Order of Chips .... 75¢
Order of Frijoles ala Charra $2.95

Country Kitchen

Appetizers

Chicken Fingers $4.25
Mozzarella Cheese Sticks $4.25
Potato Skins $4.25
Jalapeño Poppers $3.95
Country Onion Rings $2.95

Soups and Salads

Old-Fashioned Calico Bean Soup
cup $1.75
bowl $1.95
Soup of the Day
cup $1.75
bowl $1.95
Grilled Chicken Breast Salad $5.95
Taco Salad $5.75
Chicken Fajita Salad $5.75
Oriental Chicken Salad $5.75
Salad Bar $4.95
with Sandwich $2.50
All-American Hot
Sandwiches $4.75
Grilled Chicken Breast
Sandwich $5.25
Chicken Bacon Melt $5.45
San Francisco Melt $5.45
French Dip $5.25
Deluxe Clubhouse $5.65
Beef or Chicken Fajita
Hoagie $5.75
Deluxe BLT $4.75
Hot Ham & Cheese Hoagie $5.25
Soup & Sandwich $4.75
Burgers .... $4.75 to $5.25

Sandwiches and Burgers

All of our sandwiches and burgers are served with seasoned French fries and pickle

Chicken Bacon Melt $5.45
All American Hot Sandwiches ... $4.75
Beef or Chicken Fajita Hoagie .. $5.45
Deluxe Clubhouse $5.65
Country Boy $4.95
Classic Hamburger $4.75
Mushroom Cheeseburger $4.95
Patty Melt $4.95

Great Regional Entrees

Served from 11am to 11pm

All entrees come with soup and salad bar
Steak: We feature USDA Choice cuts of meat
Includes two side dishes of your choice and dinner roll

6 oz. Top Sirloin $7.25
8 oz. Rib Eye Steak $9.95
10 oz. Kansas City Strip $10.95
Country Fried Steak $6.75
Includes two side dishes and dinner roll

Old-fashioned Meat Loaf **$5.95**
2 generous slices. Includes two side dishes and dinner roll

Country Turkey **$6.25**
Sliced breast of turkey with moist stuffing topped with rich country gravy, served with cranberry sauce, choice of two side dishes, and dinner roll

Grilled Chicken **$6.65**
Includes two side dishes and dinner roll

Smothered Chicken **$6.95**
Grilled boneless breast smothered in a heavenly combination of sauteed fresh onion, mushrooms, and melted mozzarella cheese, served with two side dishes and dinner roll

Chicken Fingers **$6.95**
Served with BBQ or honey mustard sauce for dipping. Includes two side dishes and dinner roll

Chicken or Beef Stir-Fry **$6.25**
Tender strips of chicken or beef with a medley of oriental vegetables, served on a bed of steaming rice pilaf, with savory teriyaki sauce and a dinner roll

Breaded Shrimp **$6.95**
Deep fried jumbo shrimp served with tangy cocktail sauce for dipping and two side dishes and dinner roll

Rainbow Trout **$6.95**
Grilled and served with two side dishes

Baked Lasagna **$6.25**
Multi-layered combination of pasta, tomato sauce with sausage, and creamy ricotta cheese, served with parmesan cheese and garlic toast

Spaghetti with Meatballs **$5.95**
4 plump meatballs atop a plate of spaghetti smothered in zesty marinara sauce and served with garlic toast

Herb Grilled Chicken and fresh Tomato Pasta **$6.25**
Tender mostaccioli pasta topped with our marinara sauce and strips of chicken breast grilled with tomatoes and herbs and parmesan cheese, served with garlic toast

Pasta Alfredo **$6.75**
Mostaccioli pasta topped with a rich, creamy alfredo sauce and fresh shredded parmesan cheese, served with garlic bread
Add a charbroiled chicken breast **$6.75**

Dinner Buffet

From 4:30 p.m. until 9:00 p.m. daily

Our buffet will satisfy the heartiest appetite with soups, salads, roast beef, barbecued ribs, chicken, catfish, vegetables, whipped potatoes, gravy, fruit, puddings, and more!

Adults **$8.75**

Children (10 and under) **$4.25**

Breakfast

Pancakes Plus: Best Pancakes in Town .... **$4.25 to $5.25**
With your choice of bacon, ham or sausage

Skillet Breakfasts .... **$4.75 to $5.25**
featuring eggs, sausage, bacon, ground beef, cheese, biscuits, and hash browns

Omelets and egg combinations of your choice .... **$4.65 to $10.95**

Breakfast Buffet
adults **$4.85**
children (10 and under) **$2.45**

For Our Senior Guests

(60 and better)

Items that feature smaller portions, for a special guest. For "Dinners," each meal (except spaghetti) includes your choice of two side dishes, a warm dinner roll, and salad bar

Desserts

Our famous fruit pies, served hot $1.95
Irresistibly à la mode $2.45
Today's cream pie $1.95
Ice Cream Sundaes $2.25
Down-Home Apple Dumpling ... $2.25
The Country's Best Bread Pudding.................................... $2.25
Hot Fudge Cake $2.25
Pecan Pie $1.95

Kids' Meals

For kids under 10, we have special reduced portions. Each one includes choice of small juice, soft drink, or a special dessert

Dimitri's

Family Menu

Open 11 a.m. daily for carry out (417) 334-0888

Appetizers

Jalapeno Stuffed with Cream Cheese **$4.99**
Toasted Ravioli **$4.99**
Dolmades **$4.99**
Stuffed Grape Leaves **$5.99**
Feta Cheese and Olives **$4.99**
Greek Meat Balls **$4.99**
Spanakopita **$4.99**
Saganaki **$5.99**
Fresh Oysters on the Half Shell **$6.99**
Caesar Salad for Two **$12.99**

Burgers (Family Menu)

Served with french fries

Hamburger **$4.99**
Cheddar burger **$5.29**
Dimitri Burger with Feta Cheese **$5.29**
Rivermans Special **$5.29**
Ground chuck with cheddar cheese, chili, and onions, served open face

Sandwiches (Family Menu)

Gyro with Fries **$4.99**
Broiled Chicken with Fries **$4.99**
Reuben with Potato Salad **$5.99**
Greek Omelet **$5.99**

Dinners (Family Menu)

Spaghetti with Meat Sauce **$6.99**
Gyros Plate **$7.99**
Chicken Kabob over Rice **$7.99**
Moussaka **$7.99**
Baked eggplant, zucchini, potato, ground chuck with bechamel
Combination Dinner **$9.99**

Above served with salad

Seafood (Gourmet Menu)

Fresh-arriving daily

Channel Catfish (deep fried) ... **$14.99**
Trout Almondine (baked) **$14.99**
Fried Shrimp **$14.99**
Seafood Fettucini à la Dimitri . **$16.99**
Abalone Steaks (pan fried) **$21.99**
King Crab Legs .... **market price**
Lobster Tail .... **market price**
Catch of the Day .... **market price**

U.S.D.A. Prime Meats (Gourmet Menu)

Spaghetti and Meat Sauce $12.99
Dimitri's Spaghetti $14.99
Olive oil, feta and parmesan cheeses, Greek spices
Chicken Francaise $14.99
Pan fried with mushrooms and served over rice
Prime Rib Special $16.99

Duck à l'Orange........................ $16.99
Grecian Style Lamb Chops...... $19.99
Shish-Kabob $19.99
Pepperloin Steak (filet mignon) $19.99
Steak Diane for Two $59.99
Veal of the Day .... market price
Children's Spaghetti and Meat Sauce $4.99
Children's Prime Rib $7.99

Dinners are served with salad with Dimitri's gourmet dressing, and potato or spaghetti and meat sauce unless served with rice or pasta

Desserts

Banana Flambé (for two) $12.99
Cherries Jubilee (for two) $12.99

Strawberries Romanoff (for two) $12.99
Ambrosia Flambé (for two) $12.99

Gratuities for waiter are not added to check, 15% is expected. Above 15%, your waiter would be most appreciative.

A minimum charge of $10 per person in our (gourmet) dining room.

Dondie's Riverboat Restaurant

Est. 1989
"We Make the Difference"

Appetizers

Florentine Tostado $4.95
A crispy flour tortilla shell with creamed parmesan spinach, artichoke and jalapeno, topped with cheese tomatoes and scallions
With chicken add **$2.50**

Cheeze Fries $4.75
Curly fries with melted cheddar and Jack cheeses, topped with bacon and sour cream

Crispy Chicken Tenders $5.95
With a side of Daddy's BBQ sauce over curly fries

Toasted Cheeze Bread $2.95

Con Queso with Chips $3.95
Crispy tortilla chips with cheese or spinach Con Queso

B&B Nachos $6.95
Tortilla chips with chili, cheese, shredded lettuce, tomatoes, jalapenos and sour cream

Chips and Salsa $2.95

The Lighter Side

Housemade dressings: honey mustard, bleu cheese, thousand island, lite ranch, lemon basil vinaigrette & Caesar

Signature Salad $7.95
Half a fresh pineapple filled with Mom's chicken salad and fruit for nibbling

Grilled Chicken Salad $6.95
Our traditional salad topped with mesquite grilled chicken and vinaigrette dressing

Traditional House Salad $4.35
Crisp greens, sliced tomatoes, bacon

Caesar Salad $4.75
Romaine lettuce tossed in Caesar dressing with fresh grated parmesan cheese and croutons, with chicken add **$2.50**

Loaded Baked Potato and Traditional or Caesar Salad ... $6.50

Soup and Traditional or Caesar Salad $7.25

Broccoli and Cheese Soup or Today's Housemade Soup $2.95

Quiche of the Day $5.95
Served with cinnamon apples, with Traditional or Caesar salad add **$2.25**

Chicken and Pasta

With a traditional or Caesar salad, add $2.25

Barbeque Chicken $9.95
Served on rice pilaf with Daddy's BBQ sauce and slaw

Mesquite Lite Chicken $9.95
Seasonal vegetables, creamed parmesan spinach, on rice pilaf

Southwest Chicken $10.95
Bacon, melted Jack cheese, on rice pilaf with seasonal vegetables

Crispy Chicken Tenders Platter $8.95
With curly fries, Daddy's BBQ sauce and slaw

Chicken Pasta $8.95
Grilled chicken with fettucine alfredo and choice of traditional or Caesar salad

Seafood and Chicken Pasta $11.95
Grilled New Orleans jumbo shrimp and marinated chicken with fettucine alfredo and choice of traditional or Caesar salad

Pasta Primavera $7.95
Seasonal vegetables tossed with fettucine alfredo

House Specials

Slow Roasted Prime Rib
8 oz. $12.95
12 oz. $14.95
With burgundy mushrooms and traditional or Caesar salad

Danish Baby Back Ribs........... $12.95
Rack of ribs with Daddy's BBQ sauce and slaw with curly fries
With traditional or Caesar salad add **$2.25**

Catch of the Day—filleted in house, mesquite grilled, basted with seasoned butter
7 oz. Rice pilaf and sugar snap peas and traditional or Caesar salad .... **market price**
9 oz. Rice pilaf and sugar snap peas and traditional or Caesar salad .... **market price**

Southern Fried Catfish $9.95
Served with curly fries and Daddy's slaw

Steaks & Seafood

Served with your choice of traditional or Caesar salad

Porterhouse T-Bone $16.95
16 oz. mesquite grilled with loaded baked potato

Filet $14.95
8 oz. mesquite grilled with loaded baked potato. Our finest cut

New York Strip.......................... $13.95
12 oz. mesquite grilled with loaded baked potato

Ribeye Delmonico $11.95
10 oz. center cut, mesquite grilled with loaded baked potato

Fresh North Atlantic Salmon ... $14.95
9 oz. filleted in house, mesquite grilled, basted with seasoned butter served with rice pilaf and seasonal vegetables

New Orleans Jumbo Shrimp ... $13.95
Mesquite grilled, served on a bed of rice pilaf with seasonal vegetables

Sandwiches and Burgers

Monterey Chicken Sandwich..... $6.75
Melted Jack cheese and honey mustard on multi-grain bread

Chicken Club $5.95
Melted Jack cheese, bacon, mayonnaise, on a toasted multigrain bun

Branson Country Club $6.75
Turkey, ham, bacon, Colby and Jack cheese, with lettuce, tomato, mayonnaise on toasted multigrain bread

½ Branson Country Club and Soup $5.95

½ Branson Country Club and traditional or Caesar Salad $6.25

Southwest Burger Platter $6.25
With housemade chili and Wisconsin Cheddar cheese

American Cheeseburger Platter $5.45
With Wisconsin cheddar, red onion, lettuce, tomato and pickles

Bacon Burger Platter $5.95
With bacon, Swiss cheese, lettuce, tomato

Prime Rib Sandwich $7.95
On a sourdough hoagie with horseradish sauce and au jus

Desserts

Hershey's® Bar Cake $3.95
Housemade chocolate cake with Hershey's® chocolate bars, premium vanilla ice cream and hot fudge. We dare you to finish one!

Grand Marnier Cheesecake $3.95
Topped with fresh strawberries

Nuts n' Stuff $3.45
Premium vanilla ice cream, hot cinnamon apples and rum walnuts

Old Fashioned Shakes $2.45

Children's Menu

Served with a choice of soft drink. Ages 12 and under

Child Dog.................................... $2.95
Hot Dog and curly fries

Hamburger $2.95
¼ pound burger with curly fries

Crispy Chicken Tenders $2.95

Farmhouse Restaurant

Salad Bar

All You Can Eat $4.55
Your health is our concern. We serve Kraft fat free, cholesterol free dressings

Salad Bar with sandwich or meal $1.95

Our Specialties

2-Piece Chicken $6.35
Served with mashed potatoes, gravy, choice of vegetable and biscuit. (add 50¢ for all white)

Chicken Fried Steak $6.95
Served with mashed potatoes, gravy, choice of vegetable and biscuit. This item is so popular we have it on every evening

Rib Eye Steak 6 oz. $6.95
Cooked the way you like it. Served with choice of potato and vegetable and a biscuit

Whole Catfish 7 oz. $6.95
Delicious farm raised catfish served with choice of vegetable, and biscuit

Spaghetti Plate $5.45
Heaping plate of spaghetti, smothered in our rich meat sauce and served with Texas toast. Includes dinner salad

Chicken Livers $5.95
Tender chicken livers, browned to perfection, served on bread, mashed potatoes, gravy and choice of vegetable

Boneless Chicken Breast $7.45
Charbroiled to perfection with choice of potato, choice of vegetable and biscuit

Chicken Plate $5.25
Served with 4 chicken strips, french fries, BBQ sauce

Shrimp Plate $6.55
Generous amount of shrimp, french fries, small salad, choice of Kraft dressing and hush puppies

White Cape Fish $6.45
Generous portion of white filet served with mashed potatoes, gravy, choice of vegetable, and roll

Dinners

With salad bar

½ Chicken Dinner $7.95

All White $8.95

Country Ham Steak $8.95

Roast Beef Dinner $8.95
Generous portions of roast beef smothered with brown gravy, choice of potato, biscuit and salad bar

Barbecued Boneless Chicken Breasts $10.45
Charbroiled to perfection, smothered in BBQ sauce, served with choice of potato, biscuit and salad bar

Open Faced Beef $6.45
Generous portions of sliced beef, served on bread with mashed potatoes smothered in brown gravy, served with small salad

Seafood Dinners

With salad bar

White Cape (2 pieces) $11.95
Generous portion of white filet served with mashed potatoes, gravy, choice of vegetable, roll and salad bar

Catfish (11–13 oz.) $11.95
Farm raised catfish served with choice of potato, biscuit and salad bar

Rainbow Trout Filet $11.95
Served whole, with choice of potato, biscuit and salad bar

Shrimp Dinner $11.95
Generous portion of shrimp, fried golden brown, served with choice of potato, hush puppies and salad bar

Desserts

People drive for miles, just to have our blackberry cobbler. Try it for yourself.

Blackberry Cobbler $1.95
à la mode add .... 65¢
Apple Dumpling $1.95
with cinnamon ice cream add .... 65¢
Apple Pie $1.75
Cherry Pie $1.75
Pecan Pie $1.75
Cake of the Day $1.75
Vanilla Ice Cream $1.65
Cinnamon Ice Cream $1.65
Rainbow Sherbet $1.65

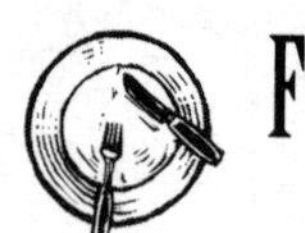

Frontier Pies Restaurant

Remember to save room for pie!

Frontier Specials

Navajo Taco

Reg. **$4.99**

Super **$5.99**

Indian Fry Bread or Corn Bread smothered in our own chili, topped with cheddar and mozzarella, tomatoes, lettuce, onions, olives & sour cream

Stir Fry **$6.79**

Fresh cut vegetables stir fried with our own rice recipe and your choice of chicken or shrimp, served with grilled French bread

Steamed Vegie Platter **$4.99**

Served with hot cornbread and honey butter

Pot Pie, Chicken or Beef **$5.99**

Tender chucks of chicken or beef and garden vegies in a delicious gravy, topped with a flaky pastry, served with hot cornbread

Quiche Lorraine **$4.89**

Our trailmaster's favorite, made with freshly fried bacon, ham, and plenty of cheese, served with hot cornbread

Fish and chips **$5.99**

Northern cod dipped in our own lemon batter and deep fried to a tender crunch, served with french fries and tartar sauce

Country Ham and Eggs **$4.79**

Soups, Chili, Salads

Cup/Bowl of Soup .... **$1.49/$2.99**

Made from scratch every day, served with hot cornbread

Soup 'n a Bun **$3.99**

We fill a loaf of french bread with your choice of our delicious homemade soup

Frontier Chili **$4.29**

Lean ground beef, beans, and just the right amount of south-of-the-border seasonings topped with cheese, chips, and onions

Taco Salad **$5.99**

Shredded beef, kidney beans, mixed greens, tomatoes, onions, olives and cheeses in a crispy flour tortilla

Chicken Fajita Salad **$6.59**

Atop salad greens and grated cheeses, with tortilla chips

Frontier Suppers

Chicken Fried Steak $7.89
Smothered in country gravy and served w/ your choice of potato. Includes soup or salad

Baked Lasagna $6.79
Made with lots of cheese and meat, served with garlic cheese bread

Chicken Supreme $8.39
Hand breaded for quality. Top it Malibu style or w/ our own BBQ sauce and cheese! Served with rice pilaf or potato

Orleans Red Snapper $8.99
Flaky red snapper seasoned with cajun spices and grilled to perfection. Served with rice pilaf or potato, soup or salad

10 oz. Choice Sirloin Steak $11.99
Broiled by our Grubmaster just the way you want it, served with your choice of potato and soup or salad

Baked Meatloaf $7.49
With beef gravy or BBQ sauce and cheeses!

Filet of Cod $7.00
Flaky cod, lightly doused in a choice blend of light herbs and spices, grilled to perfection

Broiled Chicken Hawaiian $8.79
Two boneless, skinless chicken breasts marinated in teriyaki and served with grilled pineapple and rice pilaf

Combo Special $5.99
A lunchtime favorite: half of any sandwich from our sandwich menu and a large bowl of hot, homemade soup

Breakfast

Omelets .... $4.99 to $5.69
Stack of Pancakes .... 2 for $2.50
3 for $2.99
French Toast $3.69
Pancake Combo
(with 2 eggs) $3.69
French Toast Combo
(with 2 eggs) $4.79
Country Ham and Eggs $4.79
Chicken Fried Steak and Eggs .. $5.89
Two Eggs (any style) $3.49
Hot Biscuit Breakfast $3.79
Hot or Cold Cereal $1.49

Home Cannery

Breakfast at the Home Cannery

Served 6:30 a.m. through 11 a.m. Buffet service also available

Egg combinations .... **$4.79 to $8.99**
Served with potatoes and choice of toast or homemade biscuits

Omelets **$5.89**
Specially prepared with 3 large grade-A eggs, served with potatoes and choice of toast or homemade biscuits

Pancakes and Waffles ... $4.69 to $5.69

French Toast with bacon **$5.69**

Large Homemade Cinnamon Roll (with juice) **$3.99**

Muffins: Blueberry, Bran or Banana (with juice) **$3.99**

Fruit Plate **$4.99**

Lunch at the Home Cannery

Sandwiches .... **$4.49 to $6.79**
With choice of fries, salad, baked beans or potato salad, garnished with tomato, lettuce, and pickle

Chicken Garden Salad **$7.99**

Shrimp Garden Salad **$7.99**

Shrimp Scampi with Pasta and Salad **$12.99**

Diet Plate **$7.99**

Blackened Chicken Breast with Pasta and Salad **$8.99**

Soup of the Day **$3.89**

Cajun French Fries **$2.69**

Dinner at the Home Cannery

Wine, beer or cocktails available

Served 4 p.m. to closing. Buffet service also available

Steaks

Sirloin for Two **$21.95**

New York Strip **$14.95**

Filet **$15.95**

Top Sirloin Steak **$9.95**

Steak and Shrimp **$16.95**

We at the Home Cannery recommend rare to medium for the best flavor. The Home Cannery's steaks are cut from the choicest corn-fed beef and aged for tenderness and flavor. We cannot guarantee tenderness of steaks cooked medium well and over

Seafood

Salmon Steak **$11.95**

Blackened Tuna Steak **$12.95**
Served with pasta and salad

Australian Roughy **$11.95**
A delicious mild white fish sautéed and served on a bed of rice

Fried Shrimp **$12.95**

Shrimp Scampi with Pasta and Salad **$13.95**
Sautéed in garlic lemon butter and fresh tomato

Blackened Scallops with Pasta and Salad **$12.95**

Whole Catfish **$10.95**
Grain fed, breaded and deep fried

Country Style

Country Fried Steak **$8.95**
A specialty of the Ozarks

Country Ham Steak **$8.95**
Center cut country steak

Char-broiled Chicken Breast **$8.95**

Char-broiled Pork Chops **$9.95**

The above entrees served with vegetable, choice of soup or salad, choice of baked potato, french fries or new red potatoes and homemade bread. No potato served with dinners served with pasta

Sandwiches

Charbroiled Chicken Breast **$6.29**

Pork Tenderloin **$6.29**

Fish Fillet **$5.99**

Jumbo All-Meat Hamburger **$6.29**

With Cheese **$6.49**

Tuna Melt **$5.79**

All sandwiches served with coleslaw and choice of baked potato or French fries

For the Lighter Eater

Ground Beef Steak **$7.49**
With mushroom gravy served with baked potato, vegetable of the day and coleslaw

Char-broiled Pork Chop **$6.49**
Served with mashed potatoes, vegetable and coleslaw

Quarter Chicken **$6.29**
Served with mashed potatoes, vegetable, and coleslaw

White Meat (2 Breasts) **$6.49**

Hot Roast Beef Sandwich **$6.49**
Served open-faced with mashed potatoes, gravy, and coleslaw

Hot Turkey Sandwich **$6.29**
Served open-faced with mashed potatoes, gravy, and coleslaw

All are served with a peach half and homemade bread

McGuffey's

Appetizers

Onion Rings **$3.99**
Chips and Salsa **$2.99**
Pretzel Sticks **$2.99**
McGuffey's Famous Fried Cheese **$4.99**
Ultimate Nachos **$6.99**
Buffalo Wings **$4.99**

Remember: Wednesday is "Wing Day" at McGuffey's with half-price wings all day in our bar/lounge area

Salads

Small Dinner Salad **$2.99**
House Salad **$4.99**
Caesar Salad **$4.99**
Grilled or Blackened Chicken Salad **$6.99**
Thai Chicken Salad **$6.99**

Burgers and Sandwiches

Basic Burger **$5.49**
Blackened Burger **$5.69**
Cheeseburger **$5.79**
Mushroom-Swiss Burger **$5.99**
Bacon Cheeseburger **$5.99**
McGuffey's Double-Decker Club Sandwich **$6.99**
Chicken Parmesan Sandwich **$6.99**
Ham Club Sandwich **$6.99**

Beef and Pork

Pot Roast **$10.99**
A dinner portion of our slow-cooked pot roast served with fresh vegetables and rice pilaf

Ribeye Steak **$12.99**
A 10-oz. center cut ribeye, charbroiled or blackened, served with baked potato and fresh vegetables

Porterhouse T-Bone **$16.99**
16-oz. king of steaks, charbroiled to order. Served with baked potato and fresh vegetables

Barbecue Ribs
full **$12.99**
half **$9.99**
A full or half rack of our famous babyback pork ribs, slow cooked for 8 hours, with fries and a fruit garnish

Chicken

Chicken Fingers $9.99
A house specialty served with french fries, barbecue sauce and honey-mustard dressing

Blackened Chicken Pasta $11.99
A double chicken breast tops a plateful of spicy pasta swirls with red peppers, green onions, and Cajun spices in our homemade alfredo sauce

Szechuan Stir Fry $10.99
Diced fresh breast of chicken and 7 fresh vegetables, plus cashews tossed in a mildly spicy sauce, served in a wok over rice pilaf

Seafood

Blackened Tuna Steak $10.99
A half lb. center-cut steak flame-seared with Cajun seasonings, with fresh lime, rice and sauteed vegetables

Szechuan stir fry with shrimp .. $11.99

Vegetarian

Pasta Primavera $9.99
Fresh vegetables and our fantastic alfredo sauce tossed with linguini

Szechuan stir fry with vegetables only $8.99

Pasta Alfredo $8.99
Our homemade pasta tossed in a rich, creamy sauce

Where the Stars Eat

McGuffey's has become the restaurant of choice of many of Branson's famous entertainers. The following selections include favorite dishes from Andy Williams and his wife, Debbie, and others who have perfected their favorite dishes in our kitchen

Andy's Moon River Pasta $12.99
With penne noodles sauteed in a pure olive oil sauce with asparagus tips

Debbie's Salad $5.99
Debbie showed us her favorite salad creation topped with homemade bleu cheese dressing

Andy's Moon River Vegetable Pasta $9.99
Marinated fresh vegetables, tossed with penne noodles, sauteed in a pure olive oil sauce

Pepper Steak Sandwich $7.99
Thinly sliced prime rib, sauteed in wine with mushrooms, onions, peppers, and topped with cheese in a hoagie roll

Seafood Delight $12.99
The #1 rated dish as taste tested by our guests. A blackened albacore tuna steak topped with creamy Cajun sauce with shrimp, peppers, and onions. Served over rice with vegetables

Chicken Miguel $10.99
A fresh chicken breast topped with sauce Miguel and served with rice and fresh vegetables

McGuffey's Diner

Appetizers

Pretzel Sticks **$2.99**
Chicken Finger Basket **$5.99**
Fried Cheese **$4.99**
Chili Fries .... **.99**

Hot Sandwiches

Philly Cheese Steak Sandwich ... **$5.99**
Prime Rib Sandwich **$6.99**
Classic Reuben **$4.99**
Grilled Ham and Swiss **$3.99**
Fried Catfish Sandwich **$4.99**

Soups and Salads

Grandma's Chicken Noodle Soup
cup **$1.99**
bowl **$2.99**

Soup of the Day
cup **$1.99**
bowl **$2.99**
Texas Chili and Beans **$3.99**

Homemade Dressings: Honey Mustard, Country Buttermilk, Ranch, 1000 Island, and Blue Cheese (Kraft lo-cal Italian also available).

Hot Lunch Entrees

Sausage Biscuit and Country Gravy **$3.99**

Vegetable Platter **$4.99**
Our homemade mashed potatoes, cole slaw, a generous portion of fresh vegetables and a biscuit

Country Fried Steak **$7.99**
Sirloin steak specially breaded and deep fried until golden, smothered in country gravy, served with mashed potatoes, fresh vegetables and a biscuit

Half Rack Barbeque Ribs **$8.99**
We cook our St. Louis style pork ribs overnight for 6–8 hours to get them just right (our apologies if they fall off the bone). Served with spiral fries, cole slaw and a biscuit

Hamburgers

All hamburgers are ½ lb. USDA choice grade chuck, fresh ground

Hamburger **$3.99**
Cheeseburger **$4.29**
Bacon Cheeseburger **$4.49**
Mushroom Swiss burger **$4.49**

Daily Blue Plate Dinners

Mile High Meatloaf **$6.99**
Served with mashed potatoes, fresh vegetables and a biscuit

Pot Roast **$9.99**
Cooked overnight 'til tender. Served with mashed potatoes, fresh vegetables and a biscuit

Grilled Pork Chops **$9.99**
A real southern treat! Two chargrilled, center cut pork chops, served with mashed potatoes, country gravy, fresh vegetables and a biscuit

Barbeque Pork Ribs
full rack **$11.99**
half rack **$8.99**
We cook St. Louis style pork ribs overnight for 6–8 hours to get them just right (our apologies if they fall off the bone); served with spiral fries and a biscuit

Chicken Finger Dinner **$8.99**
Tender strips of chicken breast lemon pepper battered and fried golden brown. Served with honey mustard and BBQ sauce, spiral fries, cole slaw and a biscuit

Pasta Dishes

Blackened Chicken Pasta **$10.99**
Spiral noodles in an alfredo sauce with cajun spices, topped with blackened chicken

Pasta Alfredo **$8.99**
Spiral noodles tossed in a creamy alfredo sauce

Pasta Primavera **$9.99**
Fresh vegetables and our fantastic alfredo sauce tossed with spiral noodles served with a garlic bread stick

Wayne Newton's Favorite **$9.99**
Angel hair pasta with a special marinara sauce

The Old Apple Mill Restaurant

Daily Lunch Special

Hot Beef (open face)	**$4.95**
Hot Turkey (open face)	**$4.95**
2 Piece Chicken Dinner	**$4.95**
House Salad	**$1.95**
Chef's Salad	**$4.95**
Open Face Prime Rib	**$5.95**
Filet of Fish	**$4.95**
1/3 lb. Hamburger	**$4.95**
Chicken Breast	**$4.95**
Smoked Turkey	**$4.95**

Entrees

The Family Feast

Adults **$8.95**
Children 7–12 .... **$4.95**
6 & under **$1**

Includes complimentary fresh baked breads, apple muffins, and cinnamon rolls, a large bowl of fresh salad, mashed potatoes and gravy, corn on the cob, ham and beans, and a family-size platter of fried chicken, BBQ ribs and roast beef

The Ultimate Feast

Adults **$11.95**
Children 7–12 .... **$7.95**
6 & under **$1**

Includes complimentary fresh baked bread, apple muffins, and cinnamon rolls, a large bowl of fresh salad, mashed potatoes and gravy, corn on the cob, ham and beans, and a family-size platter of prime rib, marinated teriyaki chicken, and seafood mornay

All entrees below are served with a house salad and choice of potato, corn on the cob, dirty rice or ham and beans

Red and Delicious

Roast Prime Rib, 10 oz. cut	**$11.95**
Chicken Fried Steak	**$7.95**
Kansas City Strip, 12 oz.	**$11.95**
Roast Beef, 8 oz.	**$7.95**
Filet Mignon, 8 oz.	**$11.95**
Teriyaki Steak	**$11.95**

Poultry and Pork

Millers Chicken **$8.95**
Boneless breast, breaded, fried, and topped with cashews, sunflower seeds and a special sauce

Country Fried Chicken **$7.95**
Breaded in our special flour mix

Teriyaki Chicken **$7.95**
Two marinated chicken breasts, grilled and topped with teriyaki sauce

Smoked Turkey Breast **$8.95**
Boneless turkey breast hickory smoked and slow roasted

Smokehouse Hamsteak **$9.95**
Country-cured ham sliced thick and grilled

Smoked Ribs **$9.95**
Hickory smoked pork ribs, in our soon-to-be-famous BBQ sauce

From the Wharf

Whole Catfish **$8.95**
Breaded in our special flour mix, then fried golden brown

Stuffed Red Snapper **$9.95**
Boneless whitefish with crab stuffing, baked then topped with crab sauce

Smoked Trout **$8.95**
A 10 oz. whole trout hickory smoked

Seafood Mornay **$11.95**
Shrimp, scallops and crab with mushrooms in a white wine, cream & cheese sauce

Butterflied Shrimp **$10.95**
Extra large shrimp butterflied and batter fried

Batter Fried Fish **$6.95**
Boneless fish filet dipped in batter and fried

Fisherman's Platter **$9.95**
Combination of fried shrimp and fish filet

Delightful Duos **$11.95**
All duos are served with a 6 oz. Kansas City strip or 6 oz. prime rib and your choice of smoked ribs, butterflied shrimp, or teriyaki chicken

Breakfast

All You Can Eat Breakfast
adults **$4.95**
children (8 and under) **$1.95**

The Olive Garden

Appetizers

Artichoke and Spinach Dip **$4.75**
Mozzarella and Zucchini **$3.85**
Pizza Americana **$4.45**
Calamari **$5.50**

Italian Sampler **$5.65**
Nachos Italiano **$4.65**
Stuffed Mushrooms **$3.95**

Tastes of Italy

Tour of Italy **$11.75**
Chicken parmigiana, lasagna classico and fettuccine alfredo. Choice of side

Northern Italian **$11.75**
Veal Piccata, Venetian Grilled Chicken and fettuccine alfredo, choice of side

Southern Italian **$11.50**
Veal parmigiana, lasagna classico, and manicotti al forno, choice of side

Specialty Pastas

Capellini Pomodoro **$6.65**
Angel hair pasta, fresh diced tomatoes, basil, and olive oil

Lasagna Classico **$7.95**
Fresh pasta, parmesan, ricotta, romano and mozzarella with meat sauce

Eggplant Parmigiana **$6.95**
Eggplant, mozzarella, parmesan and tomato sauce, served on spaghetti

Three Cheese Ravioli **$8.25**
Cheese ravioli, marinara or tomato sauce, mozzarella and parmesan

Penne alla Vodka **$7.50**
Tomatoes, parmesan, cream and Italian herbs, flavored with vodka

Manicotti al Forno **$8.75**
Pasta tubes with ricotta cheese and herbs with marinara and mozzarella

Penne con Zucchini **$7.35**
Grilled zucchini, black olives, and penne pasta in a Sicilian tomato sauce

Fettuccine Chicken Florentine .. **$9.35**
Spinach and egg fettuccine, sauteed chicken and spinach in a Fontina cheese sauce

Capellini Primavera **$8.25**
Fresh vegetables, sun-dried tomatoes, and herbs in a light broth

Straw and Hay Fettuccine **$9.45**
Spinach and egg fettuccine, ham, peas and mushrooms in a rich cream sauce

Chicken Primavera **$9.75**
Chicken, fresh vegetables, sun-dried tomatoes and herbs in a light broth

Pastas and Sauces

Choose your favorite sauce to complement any pasta

Pastas: Linguine, Spaghetti, Fettuccine, Penne, Angel Hair

Sauces:

Meat **$7.15**
Marinara **$6.65**
Sicilian **$7.15**
Tomato **$6.65**
Alfredo **$8.25**
Pesto Cream **$7.95**

Add meatballs or sausage to any entree for $1.00

Chicken, Veal, and Steak

Chicken Parmigiana **$9.65**
Chicken, mozzarella, parmesan, and tomato sauce on spaghetti

Chicken Marsala **$9.75**
Chicken, marsala wine, and mushrooms

Venetian Grilled Chicken **$8.95**
Grilled marinated chicken breasts served with marinara

Veal Parmigiana **$10.25**
Naturally raised veal, mozzarella, parmesan, and tomato sauce, on spaghetti

Steak Siciliano **$12.95**
Grilled 12 oz. center cut strip steak topped with Sicilian tomato sauce, with roasted potatoes and vegetables

Steak Tuscany **$12.95**
Grilled with olive oil, our center cut strip steak is served with roasted potatoes and vegetables

Veal Piccata **$13.50**
Naturally raised veal sauteed with lemons, mushrooms, and capers

Seafood

Shrimp Primavera **$11.50**
Sauteed shrimp, peppers, mushrooms, onions, and spicy tomato sauce over angel hair

Linguine with Clams **$8.95**
A classic with clams, garlic, wine, and Italian herbs

Fettuccine Crab Alfredo **$10.75**
Snow crab meat in alfredo sauce

Seafood Linguine **$9.75**
Shrimp, clams, crab, and mushrooms in a seafood cream sauce

Linguine alla Scampi **$11.50**
Shrimp sauteed in garlic butter

Garden Fillet **$10.50**
Orange roughy fillets baked and served with freshly chopped tomatoes, green onions, and mushrooms

Outback Steak and Oyster Bar

We proudly serve oysters hand-picked on the docks of Apalachicola, Florida, by our good friend Captain Jack Edwards. Apalachicola oysters are known throughout the world for their consistently superior quality

Aussie Teasers

½ dozen Oysters on the Half Shell $9.50
Oysters Kilpatrick $5.95
Cap't Jack's Oysters $5.95
Oysters Combo $5.95
Oysters Outback $5.95

Oysters Deep Fried $5.95
Peel and Eat Shrimp $5.95
Alligator Tail $5.95
Aussie Onion $5.95
Combo Aussie Teaser $9.95

Soups and Salads

Soup of the Day
bowl $2.75
cup $1.95
Seafood Chowder
bowl $2.95
cup $2.25

Seafood Salad $9.95
Chicken Caesar Salad $9.95
Pecan & Chicken Salad $9.95
Ham & Turkey Salad $9.95
Grilled Chicken Salad $9.95

House Specials

The Aussie Plate $12.95
In the tradition of the Australian Outback, a juicy lamb chop, 2 "snaggers" (large spicy sausages), tomato and white onion slices, and a fried egg. A great "down-under" treat

Melbourne Mixed Grill $15.95
This classic Australian plate combines emu, lamb tenderloin, and New Zealand red deer. Give it a burl!

Seafood and Chicken

Coconut Shrimp $13.95
Large gulf shrimp dipped in Outback batter, rolled in shredded coconut and fried in low-fat canola oil

Fried Oyster Dinner $12.95
12 plump and juicy oysters fried golden brown. If you prefer your oysters steamed, let us know

Outback Chicken Breast . $9.95/$11.95
1 or 2 6-oz. boneless breasts

One breast $9.95

BBQ Chicken Breast .... $9.95/$11.95
1 or 2 Outback's famous 6-oz. marinated chicken breasts, grilled and basted in our delicious sauce

Blackened Chicken Fettucine .. $12.95
Fettucine smothered in seasoned cream sauce and topped with strips of blackened chicken breast

Alligator Tail Dinner $12.95
By popular request, everyone's favorite Aussie teaser is now available as a dinner

Lobster Tail .... market price
Grilled, smoke-grilled, or steamed. Choose from a 1/4 lb. Australian tail or a 1/2 lb. Gulf tail

Grilled Fish $11.95
Choice of two selections daily

Koori Lemon Pepper Chicken .... $10.95/$12.95
1 or 2 of our classic marinated chicken breasts, seasoned with a unique blend of lemon and pepper. Spicy hot!

Ribs, Chops and Kabobs

Outback BBQ Ribs
sheilas' half slab $11.95
blokes' full slab $14.95
Baby, back slabs on the barbie, slow cooked and basted with our special sauce

Lamb Chops $12.95
Two sweet, tender and juicy chops. Find out why lamb is a favorite of the Aussies

Beef Kabob $12.95
Two skewers of marinated choice beef chunks grilled between fresh garden vegetables

Shrimp Kabob $12.95
Throw another shrimp on the barbie, mate! Two skewers of large gulf shrimp and fresh garden vegetables

Combo Kabob $12.95
A skewer of beef and a skewer of shrimp

Pork Chops $10.95
Two choice loin cut chops, hot off the barbie!

Beef

We recommend our steaks rare to medium for tenderness and flavor

Prime Rib
blokes' full pound $15.95
sheilas' 10 oz. $12.95

Strip Steaks
blokes' full pound $15.95
sheilas' 3/4 lb $13.95

Top Sirloins
blokes' full pound $12.95
sheilas' half pound $10.95

Filets
blokes' full pound $12.95
sheilas' 1/3 pound $12.95

T-Bone $16.95
A strip and a filet on opposite sides of the bone. Well over a pound.

Aussie Sirloin $11.95
Add a 1/4 lb. Australian tail or a 1/2 lb. Gulf tail to any entree for an additional $14.50

Outback Spiced Steak $1.00
Try your favorite with our Outback spices and basting

Sautéed Mushrooms and Onions $1.95
Added to any steak on the side

Toppers

Australian Mud Ball $3.95
Coffee ice cream rolled in cornflakes and brown sugar. Quick fried for a crispy shell and topped with hot fudge and whipped cream

Kiwi Tart $3.25
A graham cracker crust filled with kiwi mousse, topped with fresh kiwi slices and whipped cream

Pavlova $3.25
A traditional Aussie meringue cake topped with whipped cream and fresh fruit

Complete list of Aussie wines, from driest to sweetest, from famous Aussie vineyards. Aussie beer on draft and in cans

Specialty Drinks

Tasmanian Twister: An Aussie-Rita twisted with frozen sangria

Melbourne Mudslide: Frozen coffee liqueurs and ice cream

Down Under Daiquiris: Strawberry, peach, banana and raspberry

Over 64 ft. of good home cooking

Breakfast Buffet $3.95
Includes drink and fruit bar

Lunch Buffet $5.95
Includes drink, salad, and dessert bar

Dinner Buffet $7.95
Includes drink, salad, and dessert bar

Paradise Grill

Hot Sandwiches

All sandwiches served with french fries

Cheeseburger in Paradise $5.99

The Classy Patty $5.99
Freshly ground beef, sauteed onion and melted swiss cheese on rye bread

Sure Fire Chicken Sandwich $6.99
Charbroiled chicken breast with southwest seasonings

Downtown Club $6.99
Smoked turkey, Ozark ham, thick sliced bacon, monterey jack cheese, with tomato, avocado and ancho aioli, served on focaccia bread

The CBS $6.99
Grilled chicken breast, thick slab bacon, cheddar cheese, served on a fresh toasted bun

Grilled Flank Steak $6.99

The Tuna Melt $5.99

Cold Sandwiches

All sandwiches served with Art's chips

Talkin Turkey $5.79
Tender sliced turkey breast with avocado, monterey jack cheese, tomato and lettuce dressed with our special cilantro mayonnaise

Cafe Chicken Salad $5.79
Smoked breast of chicken blended with mayonnaise, Granny Smith apples, and candied pecans

Tablerock Tuna $5.79
Flaky albacore tuna tossed in smoked onion mayonnaise with egg, celery and secret house pickles

Macon Bacon BLT $5.99
Smoked, grilled thick slab southern style bacon, fresh lettuce, tomato, and mayonnaise, served on grilled focaccia bread

Soup and Sandwich $5.99
All the sandwiches above are available in half portions with your choice of house soup or soup of the day

Salad and Sandwich $6.99

All the sandwiches above are available in half portions with your choice of any small salad

Entrees

Served with salad or soup

Wok This Way $9.99
Fresh vegetables and your choice of beef or chicken sauteed, with a garlic soy ginger sauce, served over linguine noodles

Ozark Mountain Chicken $11.99
Fresh chicken breast stuffed with Ozark ham, and herbed cheeses lightly fried, then oven roasted, served with a creole mustard sauce, today's fresh vegetables and rice pilaf

Texas Tenderloins $11.99
half portion $8.99
Sauteed beef tenderloins tossed with mushrooms, bacon and sundried tomatoes, served over fettuccini with a brandy cream sauce

White Water Salmon $14.99
Oven roasted salmon filet with roasted baby red potatoes, roma tomatoes, artichoke hearts, and calamata olives topped with a balsamic butter sauce

Show-Me-Cat **$9.99**
Fresh sauteed Missouri farm raised catfish rolled in corn meal, topped with a citrus dijon mustard sauce, served with rice pilaf

Country Chicken-Not! **$11.99**
Boneless breast of chicken in a white wine sour cream shallot sauce, served with mashed potatoes and vegetable

The Big Easy **$16.99**
Seasoned beef tenderloin grilled to order topped with a roasted mushroom demi-glace, served with mashed potatoes

Coyote Ribs $13.99, half portion $9.99
Marinated smoked pork ribs topped with green onions, served smothered in spicy barbecue sauce with french fries

After 5:00pm Only

Rockhill Lamb Chops **$18.99**
Tender Iowa lamb chops coated in mustard and bread crumbs, sauteed and served with white beans, sundried tomatoes, prosciutto ham, spinach and arugula

KC Strip Cowboy Style **$18.99**
KC's finest aged beef, grilled to order, served with buttered, barbecued onions and fresh thyme

Salads

Spinach Salad
small **$3.50**
large (with grilled chicken) **$6.95**

Cobb Salad
small **$5.35**
large **$6.96**

Cory's Chicken Salad
small **$5.35**
large **$6.95**

Shanghai Chicken Salad
small **$5.35**
large **$6.95**

Euro Chicken Salad
small **$5.35**
large **$6.95**

Soup and Salad **$6.99**

Desserts

Shake It Up **$2.95**
Double thick hand-scooped and blended vanilla, chocolate or strawberry ice cream, plus anything else you can dream up

Root Bear Float **$2.25**
Start a new tradition!

Sundae, Sundae **$2.95**

Teensie Eensie .... **99¢**
Your choice of ice cream with freshly whipped cream, chopped nuts and topped with kahlua hot fudge sauce and a cherry

Crisp of the Day **$2.95**
With Ice Cream **$3.95**
Might be apples, may be raspberry, could be peaches. We will pick the best of fresh seasonal fruits and bake them with a thick brown sugar topping. Sure thing you'll love it

White Chocolate Cheesecake **$3.25**
Mere words don't do it justice!

Banana Split **$3.25**
Strawberry, vanilla bean, and chocolate ice cream with a trio of toppings, with a potassium-rich South American banana

Penelope's Family Restaurant

Charbroiled Burgers

A Fried Onions, Mustard, and Pickle
B Lettuce, Tomato, Mayonnaise, Onions, and Pickle

Burger **$3.95**
1/3 pound of fresh ground beef. Choose style A or B

Burger and Fries **$4.50**
Choose style A or B

Burger Platter **$4.99**
Fries and slaw or baked beans. Choose style A or B

Specialty Burgers

Bacon Cheeseburger and Fries **$4.99**
1/3 pound of fresh ground beef

Bacon Cheeseburger Platter **$5.50**
Fries and slaw or baked beans

Swiss and Mushroom Burger and Fries **$4.99**
1/3 pound of fresh ground beef

Swiss and Mushroom Burger Platter **$5.50**
Fries and slaw or baked beans

Patty Melt and Fries **$4.99**
1/3 pound of fresh ground beef with melted American cheese, fried onions, on toasted rye bread and a kosher pickle spear

The Penelope **$5.25**
For a special taste, try this 1/3 pound of ground beef smothered in sautéed mushrooms, melted Swiss cheese, and ranch dressing served open-faced with buttered Texas toast and golden fries

Extra Cheese .... **add 25¢**
Extra Burger Patty .... **add 99¢**

Kids' Corner

(Under age 12)

Burger and Fries **$2.25**
Grilled Cheese and Fries **$2.25**
Chicken Strips and Fries **$2.25**

Platters and Salads

Breaded Chicken Breast Strips Platter **$5.50**
Served with hot fries, Texas toast & cole slaw

21 pc. Shrimp Platter **$6.25**
Deep fried served with hot fries, Texas toast, & cole slaw

Catfish Strips Platter **$6.25**
Deep fried served with hot fries, Texas toast, and cole slaw

Soup and Salad Bar **$3.95**

Soup and Salad Bar
with purchase of sandwich **$1.99**

Sandwiches

Charbroiled Marinated Chicken Breast Sandwich
With bacon, swiss cheese, and tomato **$5.25**
With mayonaise, lettuce, and tomato only **$4.75**

Hot Roast Beef Sandwich $5.25
With mashed potatoes & gravy and a hot vegetable

Pork Tenderloin $4.85
With mayonnaise, lettuce, tomato, and a side of slaw

The Clubhouse $4.75
Thinly sliced turkey and smoked bacon with mayonnaise, lettuce and tomato

French Dip Supreme and Fries $5.39
Thinly sliced choice roast beef grilled with sautéed onions, green peppers and mushrooms, topped with melted Swiss cheese on a French bun served au jus with hot golden fries

French Dip and Fries $4.99
Thinly sliced hot choice roast beef on a toasted French bun, served au jus with hot golden fries

The Reuben $4.85
A generous portion of thinly sliced corned beef topped with sauerkraut and Swiss cheese grilled on pumpernickel with a kosher pickle spear

Hot Ham and Cheese $4.75
A mound of shaved smoked ham topped with American or Swiss cheese and a side of slaw

Turkey Deluxe $4.40
Thinly sliced cold turkey topped with mayonnaise, lettuce and tomato on light wheat bread

BBQ Beef and Fries $4.99
Thinly sliced hot choice roast beef served on a toasted French bun with hot golden fries

BLT $4.25
Smoked bacon, served on toast with lettuce, tomato, mayonnaise and a side of slaw

Grilled Cheese $3.95
Served with a side of slaw

Pasta of the Day

Served with soup and salad bar and bread $6.95

Dinners

Charbroiled Ribeye Steak
10 oz. $11.95
Charbroiled Strip Steak
10 oz. $11.95
Charbroiled Sirloin Tips $8.99
With sautéed green peppers and onions
Charbroiled Chopped Sirloin $7.99
Half pound of choice ground round
Pork Chop Dinner $8.50
2 juicy center-cut chops
Marinated Chicken Breast......... $7.99
Country Fried Steak $7.99
Lightly breaded; tender and juicy

Breaded Shrimp Dinner $9.50
8 jumbo shrimp
Breaded Cod Fillet...................... $7.99
8 oz. cooked golden brown
Catfish Strips Dinner $7.99
Fried Chicken Dinner
1/4 .... $7.99
1/2 .... $8.99
With all white meat, add:
1/4 .... 50¢
1/2 .... $1.00
Sauteed mushrooms and/or onions 69¢

Above dinners include soup and salad bar, potato, vegetable and roll

Desserts

Pecan Pie $2.25
Fruit Pie (apple or cherry)......... $1.80
Cream Pie $1.95
Homemade Cobbler $2.15
Specialty Cake............................ $2.75
Cheesecake $2.35
Hot Fudge Brownie Supreme $2.95

Sundaes
small $1.85
large $2.45
Hot fudge, real strawberry, hot caramel; topped with whipped cream and a cherry
Root Beer Float $1.99
Ice Cream $1.09

Shakes and Malts

Hand-dipped ice cream blended the old-fashioned way: topped with whipped cream and a cherry

Chocolate, Vanilla, Real Strawberry, and Hot Fudge

Regular $2.25
Large $2.59

Breakfast

Served until 11A.M.

Belgian Waffle combinations .... $3.15 to $4.15
French Toast .... $3.09 to $4.09
Pancakes .... $2.89 to $3.89
Biscuits and Sausage Gravy $2.25
Bagel with cream cheese and strawberry jam $1.65

Egg Combinations

Steak and Eggs, Hash Browns ... $5.95
Country Ham and Eggs, Hash Browns $4.25
2 Eggs, Sausage or Bacon, Hash Browns $4.10
2 Eggs, Sausage or Bacon $3.69
2 Eggs, 3 Pancakes, Sausage or Bacon $4.49
3-Egg Omelet combinations .... $3.45 to $4.25
Child's Breakfast (under age 12) $2.25
1 egg, 1 pancake, 2 strips of bacon, or 1 sausage patty

Side Orders

Ham $1.90
Bacon or Sausage $1.75
1 or 2 Eggs .... 85¢/$1.60
Hash Browns $1.30
Sweet Roll $1.55
Blueberry Muffin and Butter $1.29
Biscuits and Jelly $1.25
English Muffin and Jelly $1.19
Toast and Jelly $1.09
Bagel and Cream Cheese $1.65
Cold Cereal................................ $1.25
Oatmeal $1.29

Peppercorns Restaurant & Bakery

Peppercorns Breakfast Buffet

Buffet **$4.49**
Children (10 & under) **$2.29**

Fresh fruit bar, homemade cinnamon rolls, hot apple butter, biscuits and gravy, hash browns, scrambled eggs, bacon, ham, sausage, grits, pancakes (with hot syrup and strawberries) and hot muffins from our very own bakery

Breakfast to Order

Breakfast served from 7 am to 11am

Belgian Waffle **$3.99**
Belgian Waffle with Fruit **$4.49**
Belgian Waffle **$4.99**

With 3 strips of bacon or 2 sausage patties, add 50¢ per egg

All egg combinations come with hash browns or grits, toast or biscuits, and jelly

Ham, Bacon, or Sausage and Eggs **$5.25**
Ozark Omelet **$5.99**
Steak and Eggs **$5.99**

Peppercorns Lunch Buffet

Buffet **$5.99**
Children (10 & under) **$3.49**

A variety of Peppercorns' homemade entrees, hot vegetables and fresh-from-the-garden salad bar, homemade soup, freshly baked bread and delicious hot cobbler for dessert, plus ice cream!

Salads

Chef's Salad **$5.49**
Garden-fresh salad with shaved ham, shredded cheese, tomato and boiled egg topped with almonds and your favorite dressing. Try some of our fresh-baked bread

Chicken or Tuna Salad Plate **$5.49**
Served with cottage cheese, sliced tomato, pickle spear, boiled egg, olives, and our fresh-baked bread

Chicken or Blackened Chicken Salad **$5.99**
Our fresh house salad topped with charbroiled or blackened strips of chicken breast

Sandwiches

All sandwiches are served with pickle spear and potato chips

Bacon/Lettuce/Tomato $3.99
Served on toast

Tuna or Chicken Salad Sandwich $3.99

Tuna Melt on Rye $4.49
Tuna salad topped with grilled onions, melted cheese

Grilled Ham and Cheese $4.49
Piled high on grilled bread with Swiss and American cheese

Ham and Cheese $4.49
Cold shaved ham with Swiss and American cheese on white or wheat bread, onions, tomato, lettuce

Hamburger $4.49

Cheeseburger $4.79
With Swiss and American cheese, lettuce, tomato, onion

Bacon Cheeseburger $4.99
Charbroiled cheeseburger with bacon, lettuce, tomato, onion

Mushroom Cheeseburger $4.99
Charbroiled cheeseburger topped with American and Swiss cheese, sautéed mushrooms and onions

Patty Melt $4.99
Lean ground beef charbroiled and topped with American and Swiss cheese, smothered in sautéed onion, placed on grilled rye bread

Charbroiled Breast of Chicken $4.99
Charbroiled and topped with Swiss cheese and sautéed mushrooms

Charbroiled Chicken Melt on Rye $4.99
Charbroiled chicken breast served on grilled rye bread with melted cheese, tomato and sautéed onions

Barbecued Chicken Breast Sandwich $4.99
Boneless, skinless breast of chicken, charbroiled and barbecued to perfection, with onion and tomato on the side

Blackened Chicken Sandwich ... $5.25
Flame seared in a cast iron skillet with Cajun spices. Served with lettuce, tomato, onion

Peppercorns Chicken Sandwich $5.25
Boneless, skinless breast, lightly dusted with fresh cracked peppercorns and sautéed with onions, bell peppers, mushrooms

Peppercorns Club $5.25
Triple decker with shaved ham, bacon, lettuce, tomato, Swiss and American cheese

Philly Cheese $6.99
Sautéed onions and bell peppers on thinly sliced prime rib with Swiss cheese

Prime Rib $6.99
Tender corn-fed Iowa beef thinly sliced and piled high. Served au jus and with batter fries

The Rails of Branson

All You Can Eat Catfish & Seafood Buffet $9.95

All dinners include buffet and dessert bar

Fried Catfish Filets
Baked Cajun Filets
Boiled Shrimp
Fried Shrimp
Stuffed Crab
Seafood Gumbo
Clam Strips
BBQ Ribs
Buffalo Hot Wings
Chicken Strips
Grilled Chicken Breasts
Hushpuppies
Regular Fries
Cajun Fries
Onion Rings
Corn Nuggets
Corn on the Cob
Fried Okra
Baked Beans
Cole Slaw
Potato Salad
Green Salad
Baked Potatoes
Waldo Dinner Rolls
Homemade Dinner Rolls
Homemade Cinnamon Rolls
Fruit Cobbler
Ice cream

Rocky's Italian Restaurant

Appetizers

Toasted Ravioli $3.65
Cheese Garlic Bread $2.75
Mozzarella Sticks $3.50
Peel and Eat Shrimp $4.95
Zucchini $3.50

Entrees

All entrees served with baked fresh daily bread and salad

Stuffed Pastas

Canneloni **$8.50**
Large pasta tubes stuffed with meat and cheese topped with a rich tomato sauce and parmesan cheese

Tortellini **$7.95**
Cheese tortellini and peas served in a delicate cream sauce

Lasagna **$7.50**
Layers of cheese, meat sauce, and pasta baked to perfection

Stuffed Shells **$7.75**
Delicate pasta shells filled with a rich creamy blend of three cheeses

Ravioli **$8.75**
Tender pasta stuffed with savory beef and herbs

Pastas

Linguine with Meatballs, Italian Sausage, or Meat Sauce **$6.75**
Thin flat noodles smothered in tomato sauce with Rocky's own meatballs, Italian sausage, or meat sauce

Fettucine Alfredo **$7.50**
Butter, cream, cheese, and a blend of spices creates this classic Italian masterpiece

Spaghetti Carbonara **$8.50**
Prosciutto ham, sausage, and cheese combined with spaghetti

Seafood

Seafood Fettucine **$8.75**
Shrimp and seafood blended in a rich cream sauce over fettucine

Shrimp Scampi **$10.25**
Shrimp sauteed in the classic garlic and butter sauce

Linguine with Clam Sauce **$8.75**
Thin, flat spaghetti-like noodles smothered with clams and your choice of red or white sauce

Chicken

Entrees served with pasta

Chicken San Marino **$8.95**
Thinly sliced chicken breast covered with prosciutto ham and mozzarella cheese baked to golden perfection

Chicken Marsala **$9.50**
A pair of hand breaded chicken breasts sauteed in olive oil and marsala wine, then topped with prosciutto ham

Chicken Parmesan **$8.95**
All white chicken breasts baked with tomato sauce and cheese

Chicken Picata **$8.75**
Chicken Breasts sauteed with capers and lemon juice in olive oil

Beef and Veal

Entrees served with pasta

K.C. Strip Steak **$10.50**
10 oz. prime KC strip steak charbroiled to your liking

Veal Marsala **$11.95**
Lightly breaded veal sauteed in a rich marsala wine sauce then topped with prosciutto ham

Veal Picata **$11.25**
Tender veal sauteed with capers and lemon juice in olive oil.

Veal Parmesan **$11.75**
Thinly sliced veal lightly breaded and baked in tomato sauce and cheese

Desserts

Cheesecake **$2.50**

Spumoni **$1.95**

French Vanilla Ice Cream **$1.75**

Please ask your server about our selection of house and Italian wines, and draft, domestic, imported bottled beer

Lunch Menu

Salads

Rocky's Special Salad **$3.95**
Fresh crisp California iceberg and romaine lettuce with artichoke hearts and Italian red onions tossed with a blend of imported olive oil, red wine vinegar and grated parmesan cheese

Garden Salad **$2.45**

Low-cal Primavera Chicken Salad **$2.95**

Tortellini Salad **$4.25**

Pastas

Served with baked fresh daily bread and salad

Spaghetti with Tomato Sauce $3.50
Spaghetti with Meatballs, Italian Sausage, or Meat Sauce $4.50
Lasagna $5.25
Cheese Ravioli with Meat Sauce $5.25
Tortellini with Cream Sauce $5.25
Chicken Fettucine $5.50
Fettucine Alfredo $4.75

Sandwiches

Meatball Sandwich $3.25
Italian Sausage Sandwich $3.25
Italian Steak Sandwich $3.75
Hamburger $2.75
Hot Pastrami with Pepper Cheese Sandwich $3.95
Hamburger with Cheese $3.00
Grilled Chicken $3.50
Italian Grilled Chicken $3.50

Rose O'Neill Friendship House

ROSE O'NEILL TEA ROOM
The Friendship House

Daily Buffet **$7.35**
Featuring: Carved Meat, Country Fried Chicken,Various Meat Entrees, Full Soup and Salad Bar, Beverage and Desserts

Child's Buffet **$4.00**
Ages 6–13 with accompanying adult

Soup and Sald Bar **$5.00**
Includes soup of the day, tossed green salad, various vegetables and fruit salads, fresh fruit, hot vegetables, potatoes, homemade breads, beverages, and desserts

Child's Soup and Salad Bar Only **$3.00**
Ages 6–13 with adult

Full Dinner Menu for Your Dining Pleasure Available after 4:00 p.m., the following dinners all come with fresh tossed dinner salad, choice of one baked potato, mashed potato, rice, french fries and homemade bread and butter.

Country Fried Chicken Dinner (3 pieces) **$6.75**
Please allow 20 minutes for cooking

Grilled Breast of Chicken **$5.95**
Lean boneless-skinless breast of chicken with honey Dijon sauce

Country Ham Steak Dinner **$6.95**
Generous cut of the best ham you ever ate, served with pineapple slices

Farm Fresh Pork Chops **$6.95**
Two center cut pork chops grilled to perfection served with fried apples

Roast Beef Dinner **$6.95**
Tender lean beef served with brown gravy or au jus

Chopped Sirloin (10 oz. bacon wrapped) **$6.95**
Served with mushroom Bordelaise sauce

Country Fried Steak **$6.25**
Lean cubed steak served with country creamy gravy

Two Boneless Catfish Fillets **$7.25**
Breaded and deep fried, served with tartar sauce and hushpuppies

Hot Turkey Dinner **$6.75**
Tender lean turkey served with turkey gravy

Chicken Stir Fry **$5.95**
Stir fried chicken and fresh vegetables in a light sauce served on a bed of rice

Small's Restaurant

Appetizers

Shorty's World Famous Onion Loaf $3.99
Sliced onions lightly breaded then deep fried to a golden brown in the shape of a loaf. Shorty slings a bunch of tabasco and ketchup on his and recommends you do the same

Boiled Shrimp $7.99

Sexy Sadie's Hot Nachos $5.79

Buffalo Wings $5.49

Guacamole Dip & Chips $4.99

Salsa & Chips $2.99

Shorty's Macho Nachos $6.99

Bacon & Cheese Potato Skins $5.99

Fried Mozzarella Sticks $5.99

Chicken Finger Snack $6.99

Soups and Salads by Sadie

Famous U.S. Senate Bean Soup .... crock $2.99

Dinner Salad $2.99

Sadie's Southern Salad $6.99

Grilled Chicken & Fresh Spinach Salad $7.59

Gonzales' Famous Taco Salad ... $6.99

Shorty's Famous Hamburgers

All of the sandwiches are served with French fries

Juicy Burger $5.69

Juicy Cheeseburger $5.89

Bacon Cheeseburger $5.99

Mushroom Cheeseburger $5.99

Fresh Shorty's Pond

Catfish Platter $8.99
Catfish fillets served with fries and slaw

Shrimp and Salad $9.99
Tender, gulf boiled shrimp with red sauce for dippin' and a big ol' dinner salad

Ribs, Steaks, and Platters

World Famous St. Louis Ribs .. $12.99
These ribs are so darn tender that they almost fall off the bone. Shorty serves 'em up in a big way with fries, slaw, baked beans, Cheddar cheese biscuit, and his own world-famous BBQ sauce

BBQ Brisket Dinner $11.99
A large helpin' of tender brisket smothered in BBQ sauce served with french fries, coleslaw, baked beans, and a steam Cheddar cheese biscuit

Chicken Fried Steak $8.99
Smothered in country gravy, served with fries, Cheddar cheese biscuit, and slaw

Chicken Finger Platter $8.99
Strips of chicken breast that's batter dipped, hand-breaded, and fried to a golden brown, served with crisp french fries, country gravy and coleslaw

Combination Platters $13.99
Pick any two: ribs, brisket, catfish, chicken fingers

Prime Rib $13.99
10 oz. USDA Choice prime rib. Comes with a salad, baked potato and yummy Cheddar cheese biscuit

The One Pounder $17.99
16 oz. prime rib

Shorty's Sizzlin' Steaks:

Sizzlin' Strip (12 oz.) $14.99
Sirloin Steak $12.99
Porterhouse $16.99
16 oz. USDA Choice steak

Italian Chicken Breast Platter ... $8.99
A 6 oz. marinated chicken breast charbroiled and served with a dinner salad

Grilled Chicken and Fresh Spinach Salad $7.59
Tender grilled chicken breast, and lots of other goodies; it's the mother lode of salads

Shrimps and Salad $9.99
Tender Gulf boiled shrimp with red sauce for dippin' and a big ol' dinner salad

Combination Platters $13.99
Pick any two of the following items: ribs, brisket, catfish, chicken fingers, and we'll pile 'em up high on a big platter with lots of baked beans, french fries, coleslaw, and a Cheddar cheese biscuit

From the Fountain

Thick Shakes and Malts $2.99
Ice Cream Sundaes $2.99
Cobbler of the Day $2.99
Pies and Cakes
Ask your server to show ya the big tray

Spaghettata

Salads

Spaghettata's soup, salad, and breadsticks $5.99
Seafood Stuffed Tomato $6.95
Antipasto Salad $6.95
Caesar Salad $4.95
beef and chicken $6.95
fresh Albacore tuna $7.95
Greek Salad $7.95
Peasant Salad $5.95
Herbed Scallop Salad $7.95

Pasta

Spaghetti $4.95
marinara $5.95
meat sauce $5.95
meatball $5.95
Italian sausage $5.95
Linguine with Clam Sauce $5.95
Clams, seasoned sauce (red or white) over linguine
Ravioli $5.95
Meat or cheese
Fettucine Alfredo $5.95
Rich butter, special creams
Pasta Primavera $5.95
Seasonal fresh vegetables, linguine pasta, alfredo sauce
Beef and red sauce $7.95
Chicken and alfredo sauce $7.95
Baked Mostaccioli $5.95
Served deep-dish, marinara or meat sauce topped with cheese
Lasagna $5.95
Meat, romano, mozzarella, and ricotta cheese
Vegetarian Lasagna $5.95
Special Taste of Sicily $11.95
Sausage, meatballs cooked together in a rich sauce with green peppers, onions and mushrooms, served over pasta

Sandwiches

Steak Sandwich $6.95
Roast Beef Sandwich $6.95
With lettuce, onions, tomato and cheddar cheese
Philly Steak Sandwich $6.95
Italian Meatball $5.95
Italian Sausage $5.95
Italian Hoagie $5.95
Chicken Breast $5.95
Chicken Parmigiana $5.95
Tuna Steak Sandwich $7.95

Baked Specialties

Mostaccioli **$8.95**
Served deep-dish with marinara or meat sauce topped with cheese

Lasagna **$9.95**
Meat, romano, mozzarella, ricotta cheese with sauce

Vegetarian Lasagna **$9.95**

Manicotti **$9.95**
Pasta tubes with three cheeses and marinara sauce

Spaghettata prides itself in making all dishes to order. We serve no deep fried foods. The chicken is all boneless and skinless. The meats and seafood are of the highest quality available. Our produce is delivered fresh daily. Olive oil is a major ingredient in our cooking

Unlimited refills of soup or salad and breadsticks, of course!

Steaks & Seafood

All entrees include soup or salad, our special garlic breadsticks and seasoned vegetables. Your choice of rice pilaf, baked or roasted potatoes or a side of pasta. Not responsible for well done steaks

New York Steak 10 oz. **$15.95**

New York Black Pepper Steak . **$16.95**

Porterhouse 16 oz. **$17.95**

Steak Pizzaiola **$15.95**
Filet mignon cooked in red sauce with mushrooms, peppers, onions, and capers

Steak and Lobster **$24.95**

10 oz. Sirloin **$15.95**

Albacore Tuna Steak **$13.95**

Mahi Mahi **$13.95**

Swordfish **$13.95**

Salmon **$13.95**
Served with Italian salsa

Chicken

All entrees include soup or salad, freshly baked garlic breadsticks and a side of pasta. All chicken is a sauteed boneless breast

Chicken Parmigiana **$11.95**
Red sauce, melted cheese

Chicken Cacciatore **$10.95**
Olive oil, white wine, green pepper, mushrooms, onions, and fresh tomatoes

Chicken Angelo, Our Specialty **$11.95**
Mushrooms, black olives, artichoke hearts and alfredo sauce

Chicken Marsala **$10.95**
Butter, sweet marsala wine and sliced mushrooms

Chicken Milanese **$10.95**
Lightly breaded, sauteed in butter with a lemon garnish

Chicken Vesuvio **$13.95**
Roasted half chicken, Italian sausage, roasted potatoes, sweet onions and peas

Italian Seafood

All dishes are sauteed

Shrimp Scampi **$14.95**
Garlic, white wine and lemon

Shrimp Linguine **$13.95**
Garlic, snow peas, scallions and tomatoes tossed with linguine pasta

Seafod Diablo **$16.95**
Shrimp, crab, scallops, mussels and peppers cooked in a marinara sauce served over linguine, "hot" or "mild"

Our Chef's Own Creation

Lobster Cardinale **$19.95**
Lobster, crab, shrimp and scallops sauteed in rosetta sauce (a light pink sauce) served over linguine

Veal

All dishes are sauteed

Veal Parmigiana **$15.95**
Red sauce, melted cheese

Veal Marsala **$14.95**
Butter, sweet marsala wine and sliced mushrooms

For Special Bambinos

For 10 and under

Spaghetti **$3.95**
Choice of marinara sauce, meat sauce, or meatballs

Lasagna **$3.95**

Cheese Ravioli **$3.95**

Your server will show you our fabulous dessert selections

Comprehensive wine list

Sugar Hill Farms Restaurant and Bakery

Breakfast

Skillet Breakfast **$4.95**
2 eggs any style, choice of smoked bacon, smoked country ham, or sausage patties, served with fried potato medley and toast

Eggs Benedict **$6.50**

Rib Eye Steak and Eggs **$6.95**

Homemade Corned Beef Hash .. **$5.25**
Served with 2 eggs and toast

Biscuits and Gravy **$4.25**
Served with sausage and fried potato medley

Stack: 2 large pancakes **$3.50**

Belgium Waffle **$3.50**

Pecan Waffle **$4.50**

Side Orders

Toast and Jelly **$1.50**

Cold Cereal **$1.95**

Oatmeal **$1.95**

Grits **$1.25**

Bacon, Ham, or Sausage **$1.95**

Lunch

11 a.m. til 4 p.m

Soups and Salads

Soup du Jour
cup **$1.75**
bowl **$2.95**

Sugar Hill Vegetable Soup
cup **$1.75**
bowl **$2.95**

Chef Salad **$5.95**
A medley of fresh vegetables, turkey, ham, Swiss and American cheese, choice of dressing

House Salad **$5.95**
Bed of lettuce, julienne chicken breast, mandarin oranges, and our homemade sesame dressing

Stuffed Tomato **$4.95**
Stuffed with our delicious chicken walnut salad or tuna salad

Farmer's choice **$5.95**
A scoop of chicken salad and a scoop of egg salad, served on a bed of lettuce

Hamburgers Sugar Hill Style

all served with french fries

Hamburger **$4.50**

Cheeseburger **$4.95**

Bacon Cheesburger **$5.50**

Children's Menu

beverage included

Sugar Hill Burger **$3.95**

Pasta of the Day **$3.95**

Grilled Cheese **$3.95**

Splendid Sandwiches and Hot Lunches, prepared fresh daily— ask your server

Dinner

Appetizers prepared fresh daily by our chef. Ask your server

Entrees

Entrees served with soup or salad, choice of saffron rice, mashed or baked potato & fresh bakery roll

Prime Rib **$11.95**
Generous portion served with au jus

Pot Roast "Specialty of the House" **$9.95**
Choice roast, cooked ever so slowly in beef stock and vegetables, served every day from noon til it's gone, with vegetable, mashed potatoes and gravy, soup or salad and our own bakery bread.

Chicken Fried Steak **$8.95**
Country-fried steak topped with creamy country gravy

Stir-Fry Chicken **$8.95**
Chicken breast, medley of fresh vegetables, blended and served on a bed of saffron rice with our own sweet and sour sauce

Chicken Piccata **$9.95**
Lightly sauteed chicken breast topped with lemon beurre-blanc sauce with capers

Pasta of the Day **$8.95**
Ask your server

Catch of the Day .... **market price**

On the Light Side

House Salad **$5.95**
Bed of lettuce, julienne chicken breast, mandarin oranges and our homemade sesame dressing

Chef Salad **$5.95**
Medley of fresh vegetables, turkey, ham, and cheese

Fruit Plate (in season) **$5.95**
Colorful array of fresh fruit from our farm

Burgers, Sugar-Hill Style .... **$4.50–$5.50**

Desserts

Your server will present a tray of delicate pastries created in our bakery, fresh daily

Choose your favorite **$2.75**

Tran's Oriental Restaurant

Family Dinners

For two or more

$8.49 Sampler Per Person
Soup: Won Ton or Egg Drop
Appetizers: Crab Rangoon and Egg Roll
Entrees: Sweet and Sour Pork, Cashew Chicken, Green Pepper Steak and Fried Rice or Steamed Rice
4 or 5 Persons: Add Chow Mein
6 or More Persons: Add Almond Chicken

$9.49 Combo Per Person
Soup: Won Ton or Egg Roll
Appetizers: Crab Rangoon and Egg Roll
Entrees: Teriyaki Beef, Sweet and Sour Pork, Cashew Chicken, Puffed Shrimp and Fried Rice or Steamed Rice
4 or 5 Persons: Add Almond Chicken
6 or More Persons: Add Green Pepper Steak

Luncheon Specials

Served from 11 a.m. to 3 p.m.

Special Combination Plates

Served with 1/2 egg roll, 2 fried won tons, and fried rice.

Cashew Chicken $3.69
Sweet and Sour Chicken $3.69

Combination (half of each) $3.79
Half sweet and sour chicken and half cashew chicken

Dinners

Served with steamed rice, hot tea, and fortune cookie

Combination Chicken $5.29
Half cashew chicken and half sweet and sour chicken

Kung Pao Chicken $5.95
Chicken with peanuts in hot spicy sauce

Cashew Chicken $4.99
Deep fried diced chicken served in an oriental sauce, topped with cashews and green onions

Green Pepper Steak $6.95
Tenderloin beef served with green peppers and onions

Hawaiian Chicken $5.29
Chicken Breast served with oriental vegetables and Hawaiian pineapple

Sweet and Sour Chicken $4.99
Boneless chicken deep fried with vegetables in a sweet and sour sauce

Beef Teriyaki $6.99
Sliced tenderloin marinated with onions, peppers and mushrooms in a teriyaki sauce

Chicken Teriyaki $5.79
Sliced chicken breast, onions, mushrooms, and green peppers, served in a sweetened teriyaki sauce

Ginger Beef $6.99
Ginger seasoned thinly sliced beef tenderloin served with oriental vegetables

Kung Pao Beef **$6.99**
Beef with peanuts in hot spicy sauce

Beef and Cabbage **$6.29**
Sliced beef, wok fried with cabbage and oriental vegetables in hot pepper sauce

Pan Fried Noodles **$5.29**
Steamed noodles prepared with choice of chicken or pork, then fried

Almond Chicken **$5.29**
Diced chicken breast with celery, bamboo shoots, water chestnuts and onions

Curry Chicken **$5.29**
Diced chicken breast wok fried with oriental vegetables in a curry sauce

Moo Goo Gai Pan **$5.29**
Boneless chicken wok fried with oriental vegetables in a thin sauce

Sweet and Sour Pork **$5.29**
Deep fried pork cubes served with vegetables in a sweet and sour sauce

Beef and Snow Peas **$6.99**
Sliced beef and tender pea pods wok fried with onions and oriental vegetables

Beef with Broccoli **$6.79**
Slivers of beef and broccoli sauteed in a brown sauce.

Chicken with Broccoli **$5.25**

Seafood Dinners

Served with steamed rice, hot tea, and fortune cookie

Crab Meat and Chicken **$6.99**
Crab meat, chicken and Chinese vegetables

Kung Shrimp **$6.99**
Shrimp with vegetables and peanuts in hot and spicy sauce

Sweet and Sour Shrimp **$7.29**
Fried shrimp with vegetables, served in a sweet and sour sauce.

Shrimp and Crab Meat **$7.49**
Crab meat, shrimp and oriental vegetables in oriental sauce

Shrimp and Chicken **$6.99**
Diced chicken breast and shrimp, stir fried with vegetables in an oriental sauce

Shrimp and Crab Meat in Lobster Sauce **$7.49**
Shrimp, crab meat and oriental vegetables in lobster sauce

Garlic Shrimp **$6.99**
Shrimp in a hot and spicy tomato sauce

Curry Shrimp **$6.99**
Diced shrimp wok fried with oriental vegetables in a curry sauce.

Shrimp and Scallops **$7.69**
Shrimp and scallops cooked with oriental vegetables

Seafood Combination **$8.29**

Combination of seafood sauteed with an assortment of fresh Chinese vegetables

Trotter's Breakfast Bar

Breakfast Bar $4.49
children 10–3 .... $2.50
children under 3 .... $1.00

Fresh Baked Cinnamon Rolls
Ozark Eggs
Homestyle Potatoes
Sausages
Hashbrowns
Waffles and Pancakes
Yogurt
Danish and Donuts
Homemade Biscuits and Gravy
Brisket Hash
Scrambled Eggs
Bacon
French Toast
Bagels and Cream Cheese
Fresh Fruits
Cereals

Build Your Own Omelet $3.25
Choose any 2 ingredients
Add 25¢ for each additional ingredient
Served with toast and hashbrowns

Green Pepper
Mushrooms
Ham
Swiss Cheese
Shrimp
Cream Cheese
Ripe Olives
Bacon
Turkey
Cheddar Cheese
Sour Cream
Salsa

2 Eggs Any Style $3.25
Served with hashbrowns, bacon or sausage, and toast

Biscuit and Sausage Gravy $3.75
Served with hashbrowns

Ozark Eggs $3.75
2 poached eggs stacked over sausage and our own potato pancake, topped with cheese sauce

Steak Special $5.95
5–6 oz. top sirloin served with 2 eggs and hashbrowns

Ham Steak Special $5.95
5–6 oz. ham steak served with 2 eggs and hashbrowns

Choice of 3 Pancakes, 3 French Toasts, or 1 Belgian Waffle with Bacon, Link Sausage, or Sausage Patties $3.25

Uncle Joe's Bar-B-Que

All dinners served with soup, salad bar, hot roll, and your choice of one side dish: beans, corn, fries, baked potato

Pork Ribs

1/3 slab **$10.75**
1/2 slab **$12.85**
full slab **$21.25**

Chicken

1/4 white **$7.35**
1/4 dark **$6.75**
1/2 chicken **$9.65**
Flame-Broiled Breast **$7.45**

Sliced Dinners **$10.95**
beef, pork, or ham

Combination Dinners

beef, pork, and ham **$12.80**
beef, pork, ham, and ribs **$14.95**

Super Sandwiches

Served with your choice of one side dish: beans, corn, fries, baked potato

Bar-B-Q Beef, Pork, Ham or Combination:

1/4 lb. **$5.50**
1/2 lb. **$6.50**
Flame-Broiled Burgers
1/3 lb. single **$4.25**
2/3 lb. double **$5.65**
Sausage Link **$5.90**
Roast Turkey **$5.90**
Ham-N-Cheese **$5.90**
Char-Broiled Chicken Breast **$5.90**
BLT **$4.65**
Pork Tenderloin **$4.75**
Hot Dog **$3.15**

Side Orders

Soup & Salad Bar
Side Salad
Bar-B-Q Beans
French Fries
Corn on the Cob
Baked Potato
Fried Mushrooms, Cheese Balls, Onion Rings or Jalapeno Poppers

Child's Menu

For children under 12 years, dinners have smaller portions of meat and include, salad bar and one side dish.

Beef, Pork or Ham
Fried Chicken
Mini Burger
Mini Bar-B-Q
Grilled Cheese

Uptown Cafe

Lunch Menu

Uptown Steakburger $3.50
"World Famous Recipe"-grade-A-choice steak, ground fresh daily. 2 patties (1/4 lb.) cooked on a greaseless griddle

Blue Plate Special $5.25
Hot brisket of beef sandwich with mashed potatoes and gravy

Sandwiches

You may request our homemade cranberry-pecan chutney or cole slaw with your sandwich selection

Smoked Turkey $4.50
Piled high on a kaiser roll with Swiss cheese and our own cranberry-pecan chutney

Fried Chicken $4.75
With lettuce and tomato

White Albacore Tuna Salad $4.25
On a croissant, with lettuce and tomato

Bacon, Lettuce & Tomato $4.25
On lightly toasted, mild sourdough bread

Classic Club $4.25
Tender smoked turkey, crisp bacon, lettuce and tomato on lightly toasted bread

Grilled Three Cheese $3.50
The perfect blend! Smoked honey-glazed ham add $1.00

Dinner Menu

All dinners served with: fresh-baked rolls, garden salad, vegetable of the day, plus our special Uptown corn

Baked Chicken $8.95
Half chicken, with light cream gravy, served with baked potato

Country Fried Steak $9.25
Fried to order, served with mashed potatoes and gravy

Baked Filet of Catfish $8.95
Served with 100% natural rice pilaf

Brisket of Beef $9.75
USDA Choice brisket, slowly cooked for tenderness and flavor, with mashed potatoes and gravy

Prime Rib $12.50
10 oz. portion au jus or with horseradish sauce, served with baked potato

Children's Menu

(12 and under)

Choice of Steakburger, Grilled Cheese, Chicken Tenders, or Junior Corn Dogs $1.85

Includes small drink, french fries, and a mini-sundae or creme-filled snack cake

Soda Fountain

Made the old-fashioned way with hand-dipped, top quality ice cream

Malts and Shakes, Ice Cream Sodas, Phosphates, Ice Cream Floats, Banana Split, Hot Fudge Brownie, Uptown Apple-Nut Pie, Yogurt

Breakfast Buffet

Your choice $3.99

children 12 and under $1.85

Brimming with all your breakfast favorites, plus fresh-baked breads, flavorful fruits and an array of delicious dishes

Wayne's Gravel Bar Restaurant

Lunch

Our burgers are our claim to fame. We use only 100% fresh ground beef, ground to our specifications right here in Branson. They are served with lettuce, tomato, pickles, onions, and fries. Be sure to try our special house relish.

Hamburger **$3.25**
  children's **$2.50**
Giant Hamburger **$4.25**
  children's **$2.80**
Cheeseburger **$3.55**
Giant Cheeseburger **$4.85**
  Swiss or monterey jack .... 30¢ extra
Blue Cheeseburger **$5.00**
Pattie Melt **$4.25**
Santa Fe Burger **$4.25**
French Dip **$6.00**
  Thinly sliced prime rib served on a toasted hoagie bun with swiss cheese, our homemade au jus, fries, and a pickle spear

Catfish **$5.50**
Pork Tenderloin **$5.25**
Reuben **$5.25**
  Thinly sliced corned beef, sauerkraut, swiss and thousand island dressing on grilled rye with fries
BLT **$4.25**
Club **$6.00**
Turkey on a Croissant **$6.00**
Pecan Chicken Salad
  on a Croissant **$6.00**
Grilled Chicken Breast **$5.50**
Coney **$3.75**
  Jumbo hot dog with our homemade chili, grated cheese, and onions

Soup and Salad

Large Mouth Chef Salad **$5.75**
Small Mouth Chef Salad **$3.00**
Spinach Salad **$4.75**
Seafood Salad **$6.50**
Stuffed Tomato with Pecan
  Chicken Salad **$5.25**

Clam Chowder
  bowl **$3.00**
  cup **$1.50**
Soup of the Day
  bowl **$2.25**
  cup **$1.15**

Entrees

Broasted Chicken

¼ **lb.** **$6.00**

½ **lb.** **$8.25**

Lightly floured and seasoned, then cooked under pressure to retain all the natural juices, served with broasted potatoes and coleslaw

Chicken Livers **$5.50**

Served with broasted potatoes and coleslaw

Catfish and Fries **$6.25**

Lightly breaded fillet, deep fried and served with french fries, coleslaw, and tartar sauce

Hamburger Steak **$6.25**

½ lb. fresh ground beef, grilled and served with grilled onions and peppers

Chili Burrito **$3.50**

Crispy fried beef and bean burrito covered with our homemade chili and grated cheddar

TMS **$4.75**

The ultimate chili burrito with lettuce, tomato, and onion, sour cream and jalapenos on the side

7

Twenty-six Celebrity Theaters—And We've Been to Every One of Them

A Ranking of Each—From Outstanding to Poor

You know why you're here. Though Branson has entertainment ranging from fishing to bungee-jumping, from outdoor pageants to historical theme parks, from magic shows to go-carts, water slides, and helicopter rides, it is another more compelling lure that attracts the crowds: upwards of two dozen large celebrity theaters whose total seat capacity now rivals that of the Broadway stage.

One of those playhouses—the Grand Palace—packs in more than 4,000 people each night on most days of the year. Another—the Shoji Tabuchi Theater—has chandeliers, dazzling reception areas, and marble-walled restrooms with gold-handled faucets, rivaling the splendor of a Metropolitan Opera. Most of them, nowadays, fill their stages with streaks of rainbow-hued lasers, dozens of computer-operated floodlights, multiple curtains, dance troupes and choirs, big bands. Others deliberately adopt the plainer, farmlike, and less formal settings of a Grand Ole Opry. All but one of them present well-known country performers, or groups of performers, and country music; nostalgic music of the '40s and '50s, performed by once-popular TV stars of the '50s, '60s, and early '70s; or Broadway and Off-Broadway musicals—currently, two of them—of uplifting American themes and history. One theater presents illusionists, in a high-tech magic show.

How do you choose from among them (and from a dozen other lesser shows ranging from Yakov Smirnoff to Anita Bryant)? How do you bring order out of chaos, certainty out of doubt, and five or six definite selections for your few days in Branson (you can theoretically see even more, as many as three shows a day, if you eliminate all other activities except meals)?

That, presumably, is where I come in. I've seen the shows of Branson, taken copious notes on them, and reached conclusions that may or may not give you guidance, depending on your own, very personal reactions to my tastes. If you sense that my own mindset is different from yours, you may even benefit by doing the exact opposite of what I recommend—and thus have a marvelous time at the theaters of Branson!

Individual reviews of 26 shows of Branson—both critical and admiring reviews—are what make up the bulk of this chapter. But to prepare you for them, it's important, I think, to first discuss some common characteristics that most Branson theaters and productions share, and that affect your enjoyment of different shows in both positive and negative ways.

Branson's Theater Culture

A musical theater in Branson is about as different from musical theaters in other parts of the country as a Kabuki drama in Tokyo is different from a chamber music recital in Cambridge, Massachusetts. Apart from their controversial aspects of religion and politics (see chapter 4, "Is There Anything *Not* to Like About Branson?"), most of Branson's celebrity theaters share other common themes, and unless you understand them in advance, you may be put off by them.

Audience Participation

Though it's country music that Branson is associated with, it's personal audience contact that defines these shows as characteristically Branson.

It works several ways. Invariably, bus tour groups in the audience are recognized from the stage by name. Even in the *Will Rogers Follies*, a show with a continuous story line, Pat Boone at one point stands on stage out of character to announce their identities. The precise custom is for the star or emcee to name each of the tours and one by one have the tour members cheer themselves. After the bus tours have all been named, individual travelers are coaxed to cheer when their state is mentioned. This gets competitive in a frothy

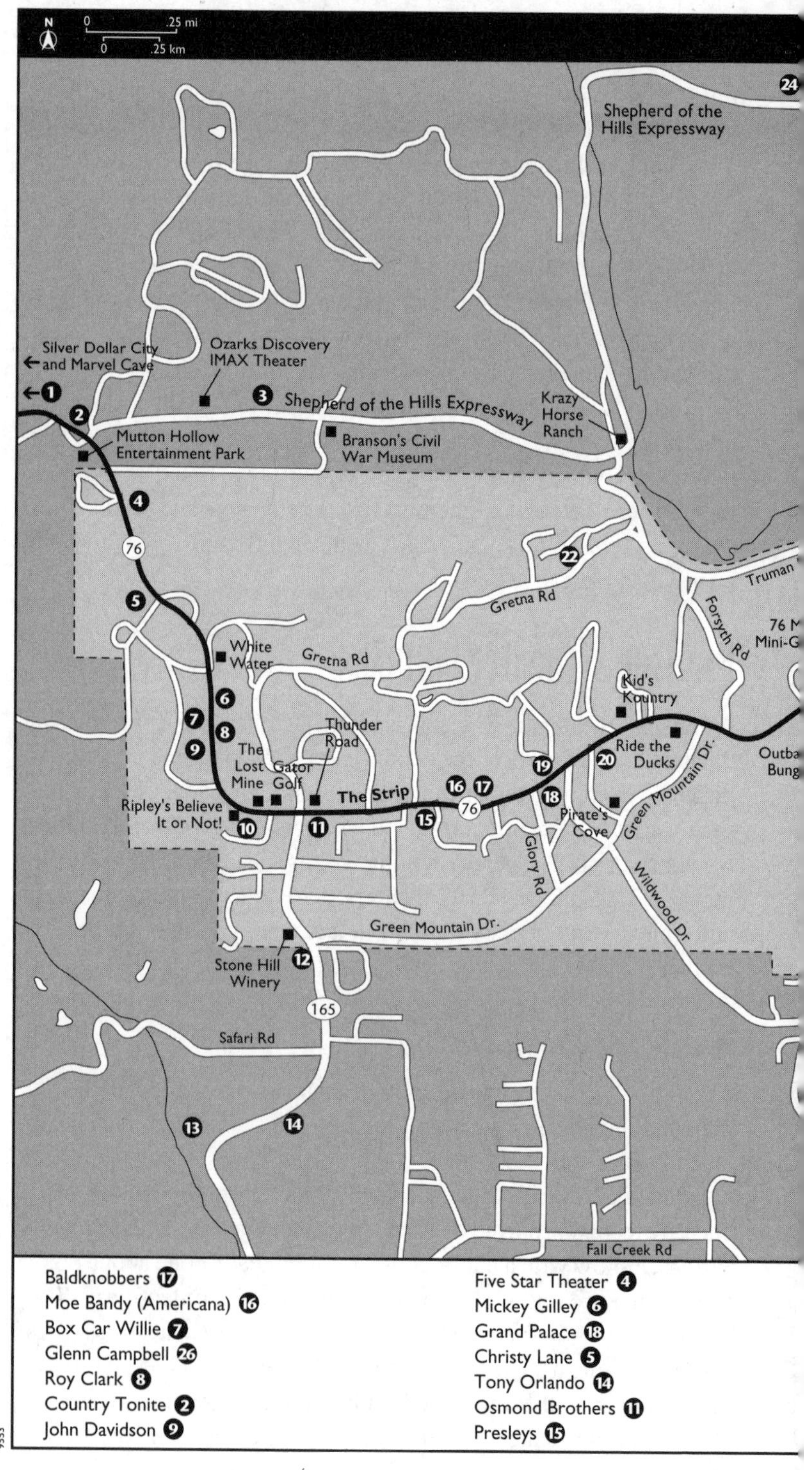
N
0 .25 mi
0 .25 km
Shepherd of the Hills Expressway
Silver Dollar City and Marvel Cave
Ozarks Discovery IMAX Theater
Shepherd of the Hills Expressway
Krazy Horse Ranch
Mutton Hollow Entertainment Park
Branson's Civil War Museum
76
Truman
Gretna Rd
Forsyth Rd
76 M
Mini-G
White Water
Gretna Rd
Kid's Kountry
Thunder Road
The Lost Mine
Gator Golf
Ride the Ducks
Green Mountain Dr.
Outba
Bung
The Strip
Ripley's Believe It or Not!
Pirate's Cove
Glory Rd
Wildwood Dr
Green Mountain Dr.
Stone Hill Winery
165
Safari Rd
Fall Creek Rd
Baldknobbers 17
Moe Bandy (Americana) 16
Box Car Willie 7
Glenn Campbell 26
Roy Clark 8
Country Tonite 2
John Davidson 9
Five Star Theater 4
Mickey Gilley 6
Grand Palace 18
Christy Lane 5
Tony Orlando 14
Osmond Brothers 11
Presleys 15

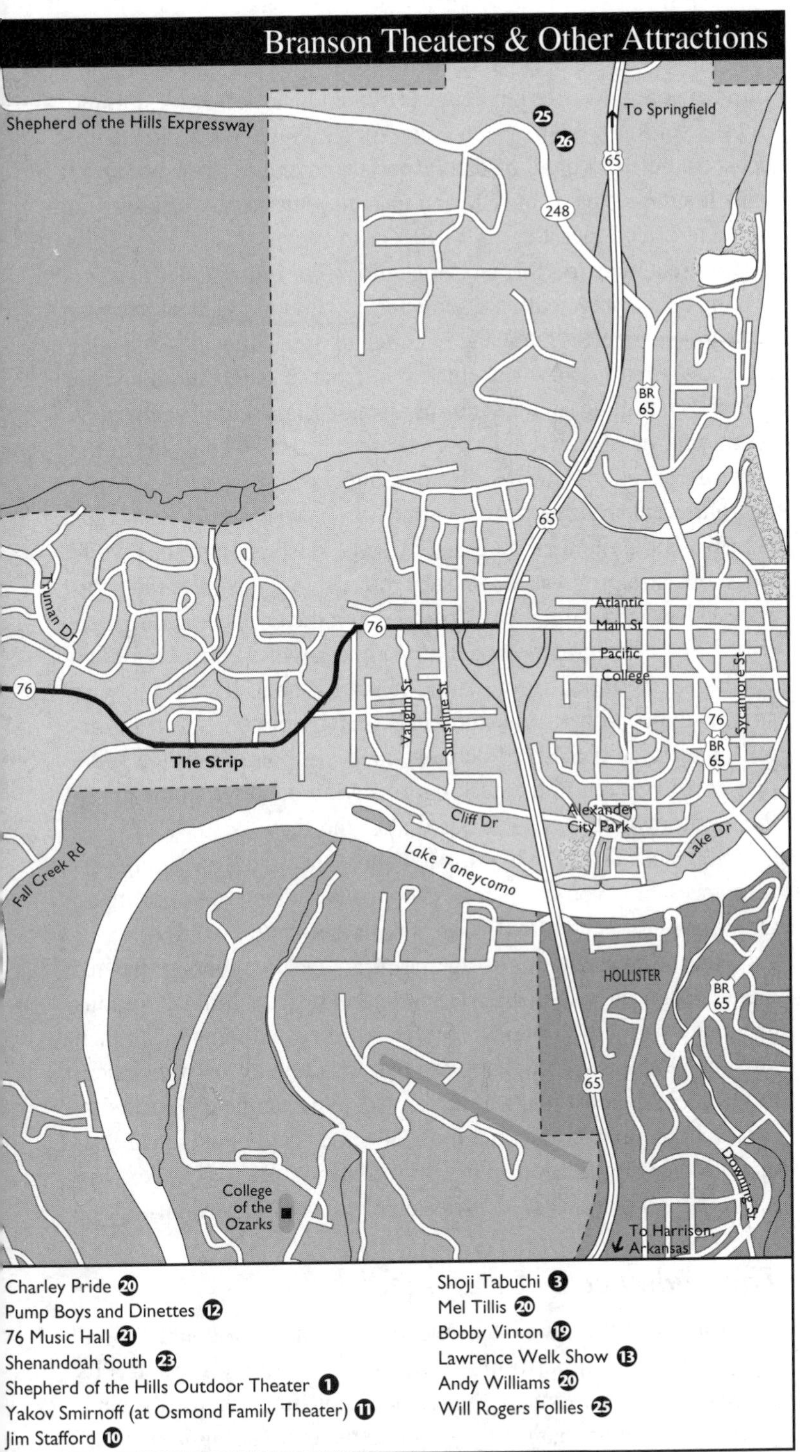
Branson Theaters & Other Attractions
Shepherd of the Hills Expressway
To Springfield
65
248
BR 65
Truman Dr
76
Atlantic
Main St
Pacific
College
Vaughn St
Sunshine St
Sycamore St
The Strip
Cliff Dr
Alexander City Park
Lake Dr
Lake Taneycomo
Fall Creek Rd
HOLLISTER
Downing St
College of the Ozarks
To Harrison, Arkansas
Charley Pride 20
Pump Boys and Dinettes 12
76 Music Hall 21
Shenandoah South 23
Shepherd of the Hills Outdoor Theater 1
Yakov Smirnoff (at Osmond Family Theater) 11
Jim Stafford 10
Shoji Tabuchi 3
Mel Tillis 20
Bobby Vinton 19
Lawrence Welk Show 13
Andy Williams 20
Will Rogers Follies 25

way, with star performer or emcee challenging the various states to make the bigger noise—a kind of "color war," as in a children's summer camp. And the challenge is tremendously effective; I found myself yelling hoorah! when New York was named. Branson appeals to the child in all of us that resists having to grow up. Or at least it supplies us, if only for an instant, with the joy of a second moment of childhood.

A great many performers sign autographs during intermission, mixing below stage with the audience and inviting visitors to come forward, shake hands, engage in chitchat. Mel Tillis does this after his show, inviting guests to line up in front of one of his souvenir stands. The autographing routine evokes high school memories, reminding us of how we preferred other phases of our life to the maturity or retirement we've settled into.

Different from performers almost everywhere else, Branson's entertainers invite their audiences to take flash photographs while the show is in progress. From start to finish, members of the audience will periodically move up and down the aisles, flashing their cubes. Some performers, like Bobby Vinton, will even pose on stage when visitors are up front getting ready to shoot. It's as if they're saying thank you to the audience that is making them multi-millionaires. Jim Stafford actually makes a point from the stage that he will be out in the parking lot saying goodbye to the group tour visitors at each of their buses after the show.

Some performers will drop down into the orchestra during performances, hug women visitors, chat up the audience on a live mike. Others will descend into the aisles with their entire band.

Nearly every show, at some point, invites members of the audience to go on stage. Tony Orlando has his son Jon ask various groups to name the funniest member of their entourage. Jon then tells the people selected that since they're so funny, he wants them to tell their funniest jokes to the crowd. This can be embarrassing for the hometown comic, but most of those brought onto stage put up with the stunt as good sports. It's all informal, and if not exactly impromptu, nonetheless it carries an element of uncertainty.

The Audience as Consumers

At least partly (you have to believe), this audience contact is intended to help sell performers' merchandise. Every show has its concession stands, some of them placed not simply in the theater's lobby, but right up against the stage, to the extreme right or left of it. The curtain comes down after the first act, and suddenly—at

Baldknobbers, where you'd expect it, but also at witty Jim Stafford's theater and elegant Shoji Tabuchi's, to name just two—lights come up on giant souvenir stands in front of the first row, within the auditorium itself. (If there is another theater city in the world that permits this kind of commercialism to mix directly with the art and fantasies of music and drama, I don't know it.) Some Branson performers—not the top ones, but those just below that level, or a top name's supporting performers—actually go out into the lobby during intermission to sell merchandise.

Most performers, in their theater's lobby, maintain a veritable department store–like spread of their signature paraphernalia. You can get everything from nightshirts reading "I slept with Mel Tillis's nightshirt" to the performers' records, tapes, CDs, autographed pictures, print biographies. Some shows make the most blatant pitches for merchandise, showing their t-shirts off from the stage, telling the audience exactly where the concession stands are, and reminding visitors that they will pass lobby stands on the way to the men's and ladies' rooms. Prices are hawked, discounts announced.

The country music shows seem to be the most audacious about this. Audiences seem to accept these pitches as if they were the equivalent of commercials on TV. Here, it's the stars, or their announcers, pitching the stars' own merchandise. So the pitch isn't as alienating, as intrusive, as it is advertising-agency inspired. It's as if to say that these stars—already, by intermission time, established as the audience's friends—need to sell this stuff to look after themselves and their poor families, as if buying some of it were part of the quid pro quo that allows the price of tickets to be kept reasonably low. The merchandise pitches actually seem to be a part of the bonding between star performer and audience.

Theater as Nostalgia

Except for peformances by visiting guest stars, as at the Grand Palace, the Branson productions are not meant to showcase new country music hits, or contemporary trends in country music, or younger performers coming up. This is not a theater of experimentation or of ideas. What is being presented is more like a retrospective, and the theater world of Branson is akin to a museum of the best in country music. One comes here to commune with the past, and especially with the most glorious moments of the performers' past lives (all of them being established stars of the past). And it is all immensely entertaining—like going to a film called *Here's Entertainment* that consists of clips from 20 different MGM musicals of the past. You, the audience, sink into reveries, relive your own happiest moments, savor the favorites that first put you "on" to country music or (in some cases) to the music of the '40s and '50s. By contrast, you go to Nashville to hear the younger, current stars, and witness their efforts to deal with contemporary themes, or modern social relationships, in country music.

Theater as Escape

In essence, Branson's shows are the theater of escapism—and are meant to be pure entertainment. Typically, they feature song, dance, comedy, virtuoso instrument solos, flag-waving, and gospel—a mixture of whatever sells—but with the common theme of escape from the outside world, a classic function of *some* forms of theater. Lost innocence is a thread running through all the shows, something about the waywardness of once-virtuous America. Not that we ever were that one-dimensional—reading *The Shepherd of the Hills*, one comes up against lawlessness and quick violence that were as much a part of pioneer life as were goodness and neighborliness. Branson theater embraces a largely one-sided innocence, and can be highly selective about what we're meant to forget while absorbed in theater's magic.

Branson thus far has been an escape into yesteryear America. Its shows invoke the lost heritage: safe America, sane America. No urban crime, no inner-city violence, no kids at risk, no homeless, no working women without child care, no underprivileged minorities. One senses a wish that the rest of that "other America" would just stay away. Nor is reference made to Branson's own problems other than traffic: no mention of the grossly commercial Strip, the violation of ecological sanity, the paving over of the Lord's domain, the creation of a fast-emerging set of urban problems in Branson itself. In recent statewide elections, more than half the communities in Missouri that considered *local* riverboat gambling voted for it, and rumors abound about gambling someday coming to Branson.

And thus the performances inside Branson's theaters are a type of make-believe, of denial, a fervent wish—if nothing else—for respite from the truths we otherwise face each day on our streets and on TV. Those productions are entertaining even to the most jaded, cynical visitor, and are a reason for Branson's unprecedented rapid growth into a vast entertainment center.

How We'll Rate Them

And now the shows themselves. Just so you'll have an immediate indication of my own personal preferences, I've selected a symbol to reflect those opinions. Three guitars (🎸🎸🎸) denote the shows I consider to be *outstanding*. Two guitars (🎸🎸) are for those *above average*. One guitar (🎸) is for the *average* shows. And no guitars indicates those shows that I regard as *poor*. I'd love to know whether you concur or disagree with those individual ratings, and would appreciate receiving your letters on the subject sent to Arthur Frommer, 1841 Broadway, New York, NY 10023; we'll print excerpts from them in the next edition of this book.

Jim Stafford

Jim Stafford Theater
3444 West Highway 76,
phone 800/677-8533 or 417/335-8080

🎸🎸🎸 He is like a cross between Victor Borge and Garrison Keillor, but with a little of David Letterman thrown in, a brilliant and sophisticated comic and social commentator, but with an Ozark twang. Though he dresses like a hillbilly and acts like an innocent rube, his wit is searing, and he dazzles you with insights on an amazing range of human foibles and American lifestyles. Stafford is about as good as Branson gets—and then some.

Stafford grew into adulthood in the '60s, playing music with Kent LaVoie of The Band and Gram Parsons of The Byrds (he is adept at guitar, fiddle, piano, banjo, Hammond organ, and harmonica, and plays them throughout his nightly Branson performance in tandem with other skilled musicians). He had his own show on ABC by 1975, hosted 56 episodes of "Nashville on the Road," more than two dozen appearances on the "Tonight Show." He was a regular performer and chief writer and producer for the Smothers Brothers, and over the years has worked with Joan Rivers, Tina Turner, Sammy Davis, Jr., and Bruce Springsteen—not exactly "hick" acts. With a background that worldly, and a nationwide exposure, how was he able to achieve the transition back to the hills of southwest Missouri?

He did it by refusing to talk down to his audiences in the course of his hillbilly monologues; the intelligence is always there; the subject matter is as up-to-date as that of any national comedian on the most powerful TV network. "Our children," he pointed out in one of the shows I recently saw, "are now able to play Nintendo games on a computer terminal capable of reproducing 986 shades of color and 112 tones of sound. We used to call that 'going outdoors.'" And yet he presents those bons mots (which I have paraphrased from memory) in a distinctive—but not exaggerated—Ozark accent, and only subtly costumed with largish shoes, loud socks, and a too-tight jacket.

He is also a likable person, genuinely unassuming and modest, with an obvious love for his Missouri audiences. His jokes are gentle, never hurtful. And yet, just as you, the audience, begin to relax in his presence, he displays an unexpected taste for the impish and mischievous, drawing on his subconscious for stunts that can only be regarded as surreal. After a medley of country favorites, a futuristic blimp suddenly soars over the audience, to the theme music of *E.T.* In a darkened theater, after a set of guitar-picking, he shines flashlights from the stage and then lets those points of light move off the stage to bob over the heads of his audience. He talks about the need for human kindness, and then reveals how much he'd like to strangle his pet chihuahua. Stafford makes his audience pay attention to everything he does.

And then, just after he's done one of those cerebral routines, playing with his audiences' minds, he reverts to the most outrageous slapstick, moving to high-energy music, lapsing into jokes that focus on marital spats, and cavorting about with talented yodelers and sing-along guys. He'll get into stuff about kids, and lightning bugs, the wonder of life.

I'm not delighted with 100% of his show; I wish he'd dispense with the vulgar appeals for purchases of various in-theater products by the audience. And yet, when he outrageously pitches his t-shirts and the rest of the concession stuff just before intermission—mind you, he has just brought his 2-year-old son, Sheaffer, on stage, and then Shaeffer's mom, has just sung songs as syrupy as pancakes about parental love and of kids' love for aging parents—you feel impelled to buy something just to help out this wonderful family. Why must Branson performers lower themselves, and the stature of Branson, in this manner?

Nevertheless, for the two and a half hours you're in the Jim Stafford Theater, you forget, childlike, that anything outside the darkened showplace matters. Stafford, better than anyone else in Branson, combines humor, friendliness, storytelling, music, pacing, contrast, lighting, and show business intelligence.

Performances daily (except for periodic one-week vacations) and year-around, at 2pm (on Sunday, Tuesday, and Thursday) and 8pm. Ticket prices: $17.50 for adults, $7.50 for children 7 to 12, with children 6 and under admitted free.

Charley Pride

The Charley Pride Theater
755 Gretna Road,
phone 417/336-2292

It is a quiet, low-key commentary that Charley Pride presents—his stories, his histories of country music, his asides. But when he launches into the songs for which he is famous, electric energy fills the theater, people sway with the beat, tap their feet uncontrollably, feel the excitement of his superb musicality and the thrill of the great tradition of country music. There seems less of the inane audience participation here than at other shows, a bit more dignity, a greater concentration on music, music, music.

When the Branson Chamber of Commerce recently chose a song to play on their telephone answering machine—something for callers to listen to while they're on hold, music classically country, irresistible, making you want to book the next plane to Branson—they chose Charley Pride's rendition of "Kiss an Angel Good Morning." The choice reminds me that though other Branson performers may be superb musicians, Charley Pride also has a superb voice of pure country flavor, with a broad twang, and accents of the hills. He is the 80th official member of the Grand Ole Opry—you can imagine the struggles that brought him to that status—and he has more gold records, platinum albums, gold albums, Grammy Awards, and such, than any other performer in town.

He remains a superstar of country, and his show is one of the few that largely sticks to the matter at hand: music. At one point in the second act of his current production, he simply sits on stage surrounded by a semicircle of his backup performers, and reminisces about the history and highlights of music played in Nashville and New Orleans, slipping seamlessly into song at times to illustrate his points. His classic numbers—"Mountain of Love," "Kiss an Angel," "Crystal Chandelier," "You're So Good When You're Bad," "Heartaches by the Number"—all get played in the course of the show, and send his fans, like me, into rapture.

It's interesting to note that Charley Pride has, so far as I know, never included themes or styles specifically relating to African Americans in his music, which may be one of the explanations for his ability to attract large audiences in Branson, or even to play there. Whatever, he is a major new attraction of the city—debuting in 1994—and could, possibly, perhaps pave the way to a broader selection of performers than is now the case in Branson.

Performances by Charley Pride are Wednesday through Saturday at 2pm and 8pm, mid-April through mid-December; all other days, Don Williams or another performer substitutes for him. Ticket prices: $19.50 per adult, $5 per child under 12.

The Presleys

Presleys' Jubilee Theater
2920 West Highway 76,
phone 417/334-4874

The show that was the first to appear on West Highway 76 some 28 years ago has grown tired, stale, lifeless, and routine. At times, the 17-member cast in their formal red-fringed tuxes and red or red-and-black evening gowns seem like department store mannequins, so impassive are their expressions and stance (they sometimes whisper to one another while others perform). As they are introduced to you throughout the evening, you get the distinct impression that the qualification for many of them is not their talent, but their membership in the Presley family. At one point, a 12-year-old is trotted out to play the piano, not because he displays any particular distinction at it, but again because he's family (John Presley). Would even the most tawdry TV producer do such a thing?

More like an amateur hour than a lively variety show (which it is trying to be), the acts are frequently played out, incongruously, against a seeming background of sophistication and elegance, like smoke created by dry ice covering the stage. Then, out of nowhere, comes the hillbilly archetype, Herkimer Presley, with two blackened front teeth and tubby overalls. When he fails to set off a firestorm, two other comics join him—at least one, undoubtedly, a Presley—and tasteless farmyard humor of the most ancient vintage ensues. Often, the 2,000-strong audience sits glassy-eyed, stunned and mute in response. Unlike Baldknobbers, whose overall presentation is cornpone, the alternation of country routines and seeming elegance is jarring.

This isn't to say there aren't moments. At one point, singers Lori Locke and Paula Wilhite bring down the house with a duet of "Does He Love You." The number has soul, conviction, doubt, pain—country at its best. But it's an oasis in an arid desert. Usually, the women performers are used simply to beat time, their faces pasted with inane smiles, while the men do the real thing, gamely sawing away at their instruments. There's none of the imaginative staging of a Jim Stafford, no stand-out personality like Roy Clark. The blocking is essentially symmetrical, the presentation predictable: comedy, gospel, country, bluegrass, banjos, guitars, fiddles, bass.

The Presleys need to rethink this one, liven it up. As they await the completion of their new, 1.6-million-square-foot Heartland America mega-complex, they ought to return to the basics of show business; they ought to simply improve what goes on behind the footlights.

Performances are Wednesdays through Saturdays at both 2pm and 8pm, mid-April through mid-November. Ticket prices are $19.95 for adults and $10 per child under 12.

Mel Tillis

Mel Tillis Theater
2527 Highway 248,
phone 417/335-6635

An above-average show by a veteran performer and a talented showman whose presentation is subdued, and with little flair. Yet he achieves a remarkable communion with his audience, makes them feel warm, happy, and content, perhaps because he works a personal handicap evoking sympathy—he is a stutterer—into his act. (But he never stutters while singing.) His pacing is somewhat like that of the late Jack Benny. You sense what's coming. An unexpected pause occurs, and the audience is immediately primed for what happens next. In an instant, your reactions go from uh-oh, to oh, yeah, to here it comes, to hang on a second, that wasn't the pause before the punch line, to it's bound to happen in a moment, to bang! If all art is a matter of presenting contrasts, then he turns comedy routines into a high art. And all the while he sings so smoothly, so beautifully, with all the heart of a great country performer, that you walk out in love with life again.

Mel's theater is brand new, more than 2,000 seats in an immense playhouse, with a department store's worth of merchandise off the lobby and a curtain big enough to cover a fleet of dirigibles. There's a 20-piece band, a world premiere's worth of stage lights. This is big band production all the way, but it never overshadows Mel (who sometimes shares the spotlight with a female duo he calls The Stutterettes, a designation that is pure Mel). He doesn't dance. He plays no instrument on stage, though there's a guitar propped to the side as if he might. Rather, he tells wonderful stories about growing up in Pahokee, real funny stories about everyday life in a town where the roads weren't paved and everybody used outhouses. When one woman installed a bathroom, her neighbors all declared they'd never have "one of those things" in their house!

Mel also recounts the history of country music, reaching back to Red Foley's early days on radio in Springfield, Missouri, where Mel got one of his early breaks some 40 years ago. You get to focus on him more than on most Branson performers because he's pretty much the entire act. So are Andy Williams and Bobby Vinton, but they're not country, and Mel is.

From the first night he opened, even though the theater wasn't a hundred percent, and even though it's on the north side of town where nobody else has been before, the huge house has been packed. It's likely to remain so. A single irritating element is his announcer, who comes on stage at the start of the show and pitches tapes, videos, merchandise, Mel's restaurant and lounge, the Jimmy Travis morning show. Too much! Lay off! We've already paid to get in. Give us a break.

Performances daily except Monday from April through mid-December, at 2pm and 8pm; ticket prices: $18.50 for adults, $5 for children.

The VanBurch & Wellford Show

Five Star Theater
3701 West Highway 76,
phone 417/336-6220

Another of the noncountry music shows of Branson setting a trend that is sure to be joined by others. This one's an elaborate magic act combined with juggling, comedy, and dancing, full of flash and sizzle. The headliners are illusionist Kirby VanBurch, who specializes in magical encounters with great live cats—leopards, tigers, lions—and comic and juggler Philip Wellford. It's all extremely well-paced, with VanBurch and Wellford generally alternating sets. Each frequently segues directly to the other, although some breaks are punctuated by the highly rhythmic routines of 12 male and female dancers, whose numbers include motorcycle stunts in zoot suits, accompanied by recorded music (somehow the recorded sound works here, in the way that it doesn't work in the *Will Rogers Follies;* see below). An ingenious bit of staging and pacing permits Wellford, on several occasions, to come on stage through one of VanBurch's illusions—popping unexpectedly, for instance, from a box into which some tiger or lion has just disappeared. The audience catches its breath.

Wellford is equally impressive as a juggler and monologuist. He does one routine that is sheer magic (and he's not the magician!). That's when, dispensing with the juggler's routine steel balls and Indian clubs, he tells the story of Adam and Eve while juggling an apple, a fabric snake, a doll of God, and various pieces of fruit from the trees of Eden—all the time changing bits of costume and character as he wisecracks his way through Genesis. Wellford, too, has the audience holding its breath. The Creation act won Wellford an Emmy in 1985, when he did it on "Comedy Tonight" with Whoopi Goldberg.

As I recall, this is one of the few shows that doesn't hawk merchandise from the stage or call out the names of bus tours. For that, our gratitude.

Performances daily except Tuesday from early March through mid-December, at 2pm and 8pm; ticket prices: $19 for adults, $13 for children.

Roy Clark

Roy Clark's Celebrity Theater
3431 West Highway 76,
phone 417/334-0076

Roy Clark is the essence of a country music star. He won a nationwide banjo championship when he was 16 years old; garnered every other country music award you can name; traveled for years and years and over tens of thousands of miles in a sit-up-overnight bus to appear before his adoring audiences in small towns all across America; represented the country music industry in appearances overseas; and emceed the popular TV program, "Hee Haw," again for years. And then he became the first really major country star to sense the potential of Branson and set down roots here.

Clark doesn't hawk merchandise. His theater is no rhinestone and colored-glass palace, but a simple structure of painted cinderblock. He is all music, nonstop music. He plays banjo, guitar, and fiddle, and plays them remarkably well, in the classic country fashion of banjo-picking, guitar licks, and frenzied hoedown-style fiddling. There is no dancing and no separate comedy acts in his show (maybe a few gags—but mostly winks, double entendres). He gives his band members big space for solos. They are all solid country music professionals, of both talent and drive. They play like there's no tomorrow, but tomorrow they'll be back.

And yet mixed with a style of classic country performance is an occasional change of pace, in which Clark comes across as a scamp, an imp. He does a version of "Thank God and Greyhound You're Gone," and he's got his audience smiling, grinning, laughing—applauding—with him. When he plays to the cameras popping in the aisles, he doesn't slow down. He barely poses, tipping his guitar toward them, smiling extra hard, and keeps on running. And just when you think you've heard every number in his repertoire, he astonishes by ending the night with a violin rendition of "Malagueña"—that's one you won't hear often in Branson!—sounding for all the world like a concert violinist. Roy Clark, as is often claimed, may be "over the hill," but he's climbing the next. He obviously doesn't plan to stop growing, and his show is one of the standouts in town.

Performances daily except Sunday at 7pm and 10pm, from April to just before Thanksgiving. Ticket prices: $17 for adults, $5 for children.

Moe Bandy

The Americana Theater
2195 West Highway 76,
phone 417/335-8176

Endlessly, again and again, he yells out "Yee-Haw," and his audience of senior citizens yells back "Yee-Haw." Even more interminably, through an entire long number, he sings "We got a mo-jo working," and the audience shouts back "We got a mo-jo working." "I like to hear people yell," he confides.

This is the single most puerile show in Branson, pandering to the lowest possible tastes. It carries the practice of audience participation to absurd lengths; yet even when the last untalented volunteer is banished from the stage, the show remains sophomoric. Moe Bandy—a stubby, little guy with beard, in black jeans and spangled black Ike jacket—is not entirely without ability. He sings, fiddles, and plays the guitar, and sometimes, almost accidentally, proves infectious in his appeal. Yet no one of wit or intelligence has produced his show, or varied its pacing, or added a single original production number; and most of the long first act consists simply of Moe standing in front of his large band and doing numbers so hoary with age, so cornball and mindless, so constantly rapid and rushed—like a rodeo competition (he is a former rodeo rider)—that you'll yearn for the intermission curtain.

At one point, his bandleader comes onto the stage dressed offensively as an old woman, a decrepit, stout, elderly woman, and performs several tasteless slapstick routines. On other occasions, the band yells derisively at Moe and puts him down. In a low point of the program, two women in the cast drag a portly man from the audience, place him between them, and proceed to yodel their way through "Good Ole Boys."

Before the show begins, an emcee from Australia warms up the audience with statements like, "As a recent immigrant, I say this is the greatest country in the world," and tells a joke about flag-burners. Then, after pitching the sale of merchandise in the lobby, he announces that the theme of the Moe Bandy show is patriotism.

And sure enough, toward the end of the opening act, Moe appears dressed in the Stars and Stripes, and everyone on stage—including a cornpone violinist—launches into "America the Beautiful," and then "The Star Spangled Banner," as the audience stands.

It may be, as his press releases proclaim, that Bandy has had a distinguished career and many hit records, was named the most promising male vocalist of country music in 1975 (after a career shaped by appearances and bookings during the time of the Vietnam War), and assisted former President Bush in his first presidential election campaign. He badly needs to put his talents into the hands of a producer who will not talk down to the public, as his present show does.

Performances at 2pm and 7pm, Monday through Saturday (except that matinees are not presented on Mondays), from March through December; partial schedule only, usually on weekends, in November and December. Ticket prices are $16.50 for adults, free for children 12 and under (probably because children won't take well to this show, in my opinion). Highway 165 and also Gretna Road will bring you to the Strip fairly close to the Americana Theater, avoiding the need to go long distances on the Strip.

Barbara Mandrell, Louise Mandrell, Kenny Rogers, and Others

The Grand Palace
2700 West Highway 76,
phone 417/33-GRAND or 800/5-PALACE

The pinnacle (in terms of spectacle and staging) among Branson's music shows are the productions in this 4,000-seat behemoth looking like an oversized, antebellum southern mansion on a rise overlooking the Strip. It's the largest in town. The theater's eminence is such that the Radio City Music Hall Rockettes have begun annual appearances here between Thanksgiving and Christmas.

Varying performers, not always of a country music ilk, appear throughout the year at the Grand Palace, usually for a month or two, sometimes only on a Sunday evening ("Super Sunday"). The month-long (and longer) performers include Kenny Rogers, who co-owns the Grand Palace with the Silver Dollar City organization; Barbara Mandrell (the biggest draw); and her sister, Louise Mandrell, who appears in a $1-million production called "Love My Country," a patriotic salute to the military and review of American musical eras. "Super Sunday" performers have included Tanya Tucker, Anne Murray, Neil Sedaka, Captain and Tenille, John Anderson, and Lorrie Morgan.

"We do the spectacles," an executive of the huge playhouse once stated. The theater has one of the largest permanently installed laser systems in America, together with indoor fireworks displays ignited on stage, and high above the audience, various harness-and-trapeze operations that enable performers to parachute from balcony to stage or to be lowered from 30 feet above the stage, all in such incredible space that a 2,100-square-foot American flag can be fully displayed against the upstage wall of the theater.

When Louise Mandrell appears in "Love My Country" (it may or may not be presented again in 1995), she has 14 costume changes, including one reincarnation as Carmen Miranda in a dress with a 40-foot train and 500 yards of ruffles. Fittingly enough, "Love My Country" was directed by an MGM musicals executive, who was called out of retirement to duplicate those famous film effects of the '30s. The subliminal message of "Love My Country," as it is of other military/patriotic production numbers in numerous other Branson shows: We are better than anyone else, our military engagements have always been right, we have no major problems in this nation, and if only those reform-minded politicians would leave us alone, we'd do fine. To mega-millionaires like the Mandrells, such sentiments may come easily.

Barbara Mandrell is excellent in her own appearances, in glorious costumes of white silk, emerging magically from a tube of smoke. Mind you, her music—and that of many other Grand Palace performers—is no longer pure country; it has a modern touch, is reminiscent of more contemporary musical styles, is not delivered with a broad twang or with weepy lamentations. She also does nostalgia. In her show, "Steppin' Out," she does such country numbers as "Crackers," "Good Old Days," and "Ten Pound Hammer," but then switches, without missing a beat, to "It Had to Be You" and "Dancing Cheek to Cheek." The ubiquitous, Branson-style, gospel medley—"Jesus Loves Me," "Jesus Loves the Little Children," "To God Be the Glory," and "Keep On Movin'"—is a climax of the second act.

The Grand Palace's goal, sometimes candidly admitted, is to be visited at least once by every visitor to Branson. Although I don't consider its shows to be the single stellar performances available to you in Branson, they are plenty good, and worth your consideration.

High-performance shows, as they're called here, are presented nightly at 8pm from May through mid-December, with 3pm matinees on most dates from June through August. Ticket prices vary according to performer: $15, $22, and $26 per adult for Kenny Rogers or Barbara Mandrell, $9, $11, or $13 for children 4 to 11; $12, $19, and $23 per adult for Louise Mandrell, $5, $9, and $10 per child; and for Super Sundays, limited engagements, and Christmas shows: $18, $23, and $28 per adult, $9, $11, and $13 per child. A back entrance from Green Mountain Drive avoids the Strip.

The Will Rogers Follies, Starring Pat Boone

The Will Rogers Theater
U.S. Highway 65 at State Highway 248, phone 800/994-9455 or 417/336-1333

This is Branson's first big Broadway musical, its first brush with the big time, the same *Will Rogers Follies* that won the 1991 Drama Desk Award, the 1991 New York Drama Critics Circle Award for best musical of the year, and six Tony Awards, including the one for Best Musical. Its star is none other than Pat Boone, of the fifteen 20th Century Fox movies (*State Fair*, *April Love*, *Journey to the Center of the Earth*, among them) and the long-running TV show on the ABC network. It is a Ziegfeld-style revue (for a long time, the late Will Rogers was featured in the Ziegfeld Follies), with gorgeous showgirls in the classic tradition, costumed to bring every male fantasy about women a-quiver. There is good-quality chorus line dancing that keeps the house roused even when these long-legged beauties seat themselves in the course of the routine. They perch on chairs, working their fingers, wrists, elbows, and feet in unison, and synchronously swiveling their heads.

And yet it's a strange show as presented here, oddly two-dimensional. The mechanics keep intruding; something intervenes that hints at the whole thing being machine-driven. From glittery headdress to high heels, the spectacle fails to come alive. Why?

You quickly realize it has to do with the absence of live music. The songs are canned, played from records, a disk, or a tape. In a money-saving challenge to the musicians' union hurled down by Lee Iacocca (a chief investor in the Branson production), the show uses no live musicians. Thus, there's no spontaneity. And of all shows, a show about Will Rogers cries for spontaneity, ad libs, inspiration. For all you know, maybe Pat Boone works a few asides into his memorized lines. But you become acutely aware that the whole production is on a timer. Everything is controlled. The slightest miscue and all the sequencing would fall apart. It's by the numbers. Instead of awakening us, dazzling us, making us come alive, we the audience become an automaton-like part of the rote cast.

It's a painful disappointment. You can't sit in a theater—even one as pretty as this, with a million dollars' worth of Will Rogers art, artifacts, and memorabilia—and not feel yourself defiled by the mechanical essence of the production.

Mind you, the show looks good and even sounds good. But it's the equivalent of hothouse tomatoes and artificial insemination. Most of us can still tell the real thing (and prefer it). You get Will Rogers's shrugs, head-scratchings, and cornpone. You also get, special for Branson, a sanitized Will Rogers vocabulary (the words *hell* and *damn* have been taken out of the Broadway script). But you don't get more. If he were still around, Will Rogers would be the first to walk out on this one. "Get a life," he'd probably mutter.

Twice-a-day performances, at 2pm and 7pm, Tuesday through Sunday from April through October (maybe longer), but Tuesday matinees are played by understudy Kent Sheridan and not Pat Boone. Ticket prices are $19.66 for adults, $9.83 for children 4 to 12. Children 3 and under are free on-the-lap.

Box Car Willie

The Box Car Willie Theater
3454 West Highway 76,
phone 800/942-4626 or 417/334-2500

Good, honest, unpretentious, country music, a lot of it, with only the slightest audience participation to mar the show, presented in a relatively plain theater by an experienced veteran who's seen it all and yet remains obviously in love with the traditions of country, and is determined to remain a professional and not a crowd panderer. Even the men in the lobby selling t-shirts and CDs seem like old country types, sometimes shabbily dressed, and making no concession to modern society in their mannerisms or speech.

Born in Texas, the son of a low-income railroad man, the performer now known as Box Car Willie (he no longer uses his real name) grew up familiar with the railroads and with the homeless tramps who rode the boxcars of their freight-carrying trains. After service with the Air Force for 22 years, he entered the world of country music by dressing in overalls and a shapeless blue jacket, a tattered hat covered with fly-fishing hooks, his lapels laden with various display pins, his face unshaven, and often with a scraggly red beard. His instrument is the guitar, just as it was for the scores of boxcar hobos he had known. He was discovered singing "Daddie Was a Railroad Man" and "Box Car Willie" by a British talent agent in Nashville in 1978, played all over Europe for years (and occasionally still does), and came to Branson in 1986 to open the Box Car Willie Theater. He is a member (#60) of the Grand Ole Opry (Charley Pride is #80), and has won just about every country music award you can name.

From a plain stage, backed up by the Texas Trainmen band, he does one musical number after another. He starts the show with "I Love the Sound of a Whistle," goes on to an enchanting Hank Williams medley ("Cold, Cold Heart," "Your Cheating Heart," "Lovesick Blues"), performs some of the most exciting country songs ever written, both of them, appropriately, on railroad themes ("Wabash Cannonball," "Wreck of the Old 97"), continues with "Mule Train," and sprinkles in several of the hit numbers written by him: "Hobo Heaven," "Winds of Yesterday," "Hobo's Meditation," "From a Rolls to the Rails." When the time comes for the compulsory Branson gospel number, he keeps it short and subdued, and limits the segment to one brief song ("Ain't Gonna Sin No More"), performed without the pompous piety and carefully reverent facial expressions affected by other Branson performers. Interspersed among his own numbers are the solos of a steel guitar man, a harmonica player, David on piano, Chuck on lead guitar, Patty Davidson in a ventriloquist act. But mainly there is "Box Car Willie," and I, for one, am in country seventh heaven listening to his songs.

Performances are mid-April through mid-December, on a tricky basis: Sunday at 2pm only, Monday at 8pm only, Tuesday at 2pm *and 8pm, Wednesday and Thursday at 8pm, closed on Friday, Saturday at 2pm and 8pm. Ticket prices are $17.50 for adults, $7.50 for children 12 and under.*

Tony Orlando

Tony Orlando's Yellow Ribbon Theater
3220 Falls Parkway off Highway 165,
phone 417/335-8669

This is by far the most sentimental of the Branson shows. Tony Orlando may be a kid from the slums of New York's Hell's Kitchen, but here he's an affluent, celebrated, national entertainer who fits right at home in Branson, despite the fact that his music isn't remotely country.

Orlando was brought up on the streets of New York, had his first success there at the age of 16 when he released two hit records ("Halfway to Paradise" and "Bless You"), and moved to Los Angeles where he had an immensely successful singing group and a popular TV show that ran on CBS for four seasons. He then experienced a career lull, but came back strongly when he returned to New York's Broadway and played P. T. Barnum in the hit musical *Barnum.*

Today, he combines an urban style with country sentiment. He leaps around both on stage and off, he "socks it to 'em." He's endlessly going on patriotically. He calls his 2,000-seat performance hall Tony Orlando's Yellow Ribbon Theater for his longtime connection with the song "Tie a Yellow Ribbon 'Round the Old Oak Tree," which became a national anthem, and the yellow ribbon, of course, an icon of hope and homecoming.

Tony periodically plunges from the stage into the audience as if on an A-team assault, but of course it's an assault of affection, of bonding. It's as if Orlando wants these Branson audiences to know that, Hey! he's here for good. No more Manhattan! No more crime-ridden streets. Southwest Missouri is the promised land. "I love ya! I love ya!" He sweats, he punches the air, he embraces the women. The guy is irrepressible. He's adored.

The band, whose members have been performing with Tony for 20 years, comes on explosively; they've got an ultra-loud style down to the last dynamite cap. The phenomenal drummer—and he is that—thumps, dings, gongs, and rattles his way through dazzling solos. Then comes Tony, a generous performer who gives his all.

He goes through his most popular numbers: "Stand by Me," "He Don't Love You," "Candida," "Gypsy Rose," "Knock Three Times."

The defining moments of Tony's show are the booming, big, patriotic veterans' salute that closes the first act, and then the entire second act, which is a gooey, sentimental, and autobiographical sketch called "Jukebox Dreams" acted out by Tony and troupe (including his son, Jon). It tells the story of how five city guys known as The Five Gents overcome all odds to sweep to top honors in a '50s-style, amateur doo-wop, rock 'n' roll competition. They achieve all this encouraged by Tony's muse, a guiding angel called Mr. Dreams, and after years of disappointment, putting aside their desperate financial needs and overcoming even the doubts of their long-suffering spouses. In the course of a long dream sequence in this show-within-a-show, Chubby Checkers, Elvis, the Everly Brothers, and Bill Haley appear on stage in enormous, carnival-like, papier-mâché heads to inspire the young, ambitious Tony to keep trying.

Most revealing in this entire sequence is the relationship of Tony to Donna Falterman, who plays his wife. So in love, they are. Yet in the suffocating intensity of Tony's sentiment, there's not the slightest trace of physical affection, as if his wife were the goddess in his life, not his mate, or as if Tony had decided his audience was unable to handle sex. More than anything you're likely to see in Branson, this husband/wife sequence portrays Branson as artificial and beyond the real world, escapist, innocent, and ultimately stultifying. To me, the post-show highway traffic jams become welcome relief.

Performances are from March through mid-December, every day of the week except Thursday, with two shows a day (at 2pm and 8pm) except no 2pm show on Friday. Ticket prices: $19 for adults, $7 for children 4 to 12, children under 4 free.

The Memory Makers

76 Music Hall
1807 West Highway 76,
phone 417/335-2484

THE 76 MUSIC HALL
76 MALL

This is the biggest and the only evening performance of the five different shows presented daily (at 8am, 10am, 1:30pm, 4pm, and

8pm) at the 76 Music Hall, in the 76 Shopping Mall complex, directly across the highway from the Outback Bungee Jump. It takes place in one of the smaller venues seating around 500 people. Essentially, the show reviews the history of country music (and some other popular music) from the early '40s into the '90s. But the history is done Branson-style. When the band gets to the era of the '60s, they play not Dylan, but "Itsy Bitsy Teeny Weeny Yellow Polka Dot Bikini." When the emcee works through the decades, and asks what the audience remembers most about the '60s, someone calls out Vietnam, another the Beatles, another Woodstock, but no one calls out feminism or women's lib, or the Civil Rights Movement. You get the feeling that the latter subjects would not be well received.

The level of professionalism is about three notches below that of the celebrity theaters named after a particular star; the lighting is only a bit better than rudimentary; the same with the staging; and performers really don't match the ones you've seen elsewhere in the bigger theaters. Pacing, variety, and that essential contrast that keeps audiences engaged and rooting for you are all lacking.

The show also ranges from doo-wop to gospel, finishing off with a patriotic flourish that combines religiosity with flag-waving. A visitor leaving the theater comments that, "Those were songs I hadn't heard in a long time." "Yeah," says another, "they keep reminding me I'm getting old." "Well," says still another, "I always say it's better than the alternative."

You may want to pass this one by.

Performances are from an early (for Branson) mid-February through mid-December, Monday through Saturday at 8pm. Ticket prices: $13 for adults generally, only $12 for seniors 60 or over, free for children 12 and under.

Glen Campbell

Glen Campbell's Goodtime Theater
U.S. Highway 65 at State Highway 248,
phone 417/336-1220

Glen Campbell
GOODTIME THEATRE

and almost . He arrives on the Branson stage as a former superstar of such fame and notoriety that you feel excited as you drive to the theater to see his show. He performed the theme music for *Midnight Cowboy,* the wonderful "Wichita Lineman,"

"Galveston," "Gentle on My Mind," "By the Time I Get to Phoenix," "A Lady Like You," and nearly three dozen other hits. He achieved, by the late 1960s, the difficult crossover from country music to pop-country, a more contemporary musical style appealing to national tastes (it got him a national TV show), and he delivers his songs in a beautifully mellow voice with skillful musicality and phrasing. The audience remembers each number—especially "Gentle on My Mind"—from its very opening notes, and applauds before he has scarcely opened his mouth.

And yet there is something too relaxed about Glen Campbell, too laid-back and lethargic, that deprives this show of the tense, nervous energy that any great evening in the theater must have. It is as if he is walking through his performance, anxious to return to the golf links or, in a few weeks more, to a palatial home outside Phoenix, Arizona. Though his own solos are pleasant and nostalgic, the rest of the production contains but a single moment of real distinction: a superb ventriloquist named Jim Barber; it is otherwise underproduced, lacking both decent ensemble numbers of wit or art and a strong supporting cast. The opening dance number is awkwardly choreographed. His daughter, who is featured in the show, would clearly not be if she were not his daughter.

Campbell virtually admits his fading fame when he sings "He's Building a Mansion," composed by a friend in very recent times. It tells of modern-day recording magnates turning down an old star, of TV roles for which the star is now too old, of all sorts of modern media for which he is no longer deemed acceptable. So what does he do, in both the song and life? He goes to Branson, where he can still make a fortune—and get the last laugh. "He's building a mansion," he sings, "right here in Branson"—and the audience cheers the triumphant, if somewhat vulgar, boast.

Glen Campbell's Goodtime Theater is named after his "Goodtime Hour" on TV in the early '70s; it is one of the newest and most tasteful playhouses in Branson (1994), in the town's newest theater area, near the Will Rogers Follies Theater that you see from Highway 65 as you first drive into town. Look, especially, for its lobby murals of the Ozarks. I agonized over a rating for Campbell, but eventually concluded that he simply wasn't doing enough, at least at the performance that I last saw. Maybe it was an off night.

Performances are from mid-April through mid-December, daily except Monday, as follows: Tuesday, Wednesday, Thursday, and

Saturday at 3pm and 8pm, Friday and Sunday at 8pm only. Ticket prices are $18 for adults, $9 for children 4 to 12, children under 4 (on the lap), free. Throughout the season, in scattered periods, the Oak Ridge Boys substitute for Campbell for a total of about six weeks.

Johnny Cash (on occasion), Ronnie Millsap (on occasion), Others

Shenandoah South Theater
199 Shepherd of the Hills Expressway, near Highway 248,
phone 417/336-3986

We give no rating because of the uncertainty as to who will be appearing on stage in 1995.

Opened in 1993 as the Wayne Newton Theater starring the Las Vegas entertainer of that name, it reopened in 1994 as Shenandoah South following disputes with Newton that led to his leaving Branson. Throughout that second year, stars like Johnny Cash, Ronnie Millsap, Eddie Arnold (and shows like the Ice Capades) had short runs, much in the fashion that the Grand Palace features changing performers and acts. As we go to press with this edition, policies haven't been set for 1995, and you're advised to call the above number in advance of your arrival in Branson, to learn who will be playing here at the time of your stay.

Performances are, generally, from May to mid-December, daily except Monday, at both 3pm and 8pm. Ticket prices vary widely from performer to performer, and range from $12 to $24 for adults, from $6 to $12 for children.

Bobby Vinton

Bobby Vinton Blue Velvet Theater
2701 West Highway 76,
phone 800/US BOBBY or 417/334-2500

He was a star vocalist of the rock era. And his name is associated with many of the big hits of that time: "Roses Are Red," "Mr. Lonely," "There I Said It Again," "Blue Velvet," "Melody of Love," "Blue on Blue." In 1993, and to the surprise of many, he brought that reputation and those pop melodies to Branson, where he joined Andy Williams in cracking the country music barrier. With no country music at all, no association with the Ozarks, not a single joke about outhouses or cows—in fact, with hardly any jokes at all—he established a theater that appears to be successful.

Acknowledging that achievement, I remain unimpressed by his current show, which relies almost solely on nostalgia. It's a frail support for an entire evening of entertainment. It often requires desperate measures, as when the performer brings his elderly mother on stage to do a soft-shoe version of "Doodley Doo," surely a Branson low. Then Vinton lets the audience know, "Anyway, this is my mom. You're gonna see her in the gift shop." Two of his daughters also appear.

Heavy audience participation, lots of sing-alongs, loads of trademarked shouts ("Ho-ho!") that Vinton likes to elicit from the audience. Except for numbers by the "big band" (more on this in a moment), the aging teen-throb is on stage for nearly the full two hours. He sings, he prances, and periodically urges the audience to repeat their "Ho-ho!" Gamely, they do so, again and again, especially at the end of a number. "Ho-ho!" In a demonstration of his virtuosity, he plays a half-dozen instruments in the course of a show, and tears the place up with a march up and down the aisles. Then, once more, "Ho-ho!" He not only encourages picture-taking, he even tries to fix a guest's camera that doesn't work. It's all rather studied and patronizing in my view, but some Branson audiences like that kind of thing.

Vinton shares billing with a so-called Glenn Miller Orchestra, one of several apparently licensed by the late bandleader's estate. When they come on stage and play a classically swinging version of "St. Louis Blues," the audience goes wild. They remain enthusiastic as the band performs many of the other Glenn Miller standards—"In the Mood," "Moonlight Serenade," "Chattanooga Choo Choo"—all done as the original band would, down to the identical riffs, note by note, that Miller created when he performed more than 50 years ago. Nostalgia carries the day; the clock is turned back; all is right with the world. As the first act ends, there's a rousing "God Bless America." And the crowd files out to buy their souvenirs in a sumptuous lobby with Renaissance-style frescoes on the ceiling.

Performances are daily from April 7 to December 16, except Monday, and twice a day, at 2pm and 7pm. Ticket prices are $19 for adults, $9 for children 12 and under.

Shoji Tabuchi

Shoji Tabuchi Theater
3260 Shepherd of the Hills Expressway,
phone 417/334-7469

SHOJI! The Shoji Tabuchi Show!

This is the most lavish—and probably the most heavily booked—of all the Branson shows, a glittering, glamorous production in a stunning, art deco, 2,000-seat theater that vies with the Grand Palace for sheer luxury and appearance. Yet its star has never recorded, let alone written, a major hit, and is unknown to the overwhelming bulk of the American population outside of Branson and its vicinity. His story is one of the most improbable in all the history of country music.

As an accomplished, young, amateur classical violinist in Japan, Shoji attended a Roy Acuff concert in Tokyo—and he was a goner, an instant convert to country. He borrowed the equivalent of several hundred dollars from his mother, flew to San Francisco, created a group called the Osaka Oakies, bounced about from one gig to another through years of privation and preparation, finally ended up in Branson as a performer on someone else's show, and got such raves that he was able to raise the money for this theater, the most successful in Branson. You can hardly get through by phone to book a seat.

His success is based on genuine talent as a violinist, and a charming, gracious, unaffected personality. He constantly makes jokes about himself. He complains that many Branson performers are unwilling to go fishing with him because, while their backs are turned, he supposedly eats the bait. He is a proud father, and boasts about how well his 14-year-old daughter, Christina—who appears twice a day on stage with him—is doing in school.

The show, produced by his wife Dorothy, is punctuated by remarkable laser effects and lighting, large production numbers of dancers and singers, Broadway-level scenery, and one particularly impressive opening sequence in which daughter Christina floats over the audience and onto the stage on a magic carpet, like one out of the Arabian Nights, but on invisible supports. Later, she is again harnessed, Peter Pan–style, and goes swooping about once more. There is a huge, religious, gospel number, mainly presented by Christina in prim, white dress, but with Shoji smiling proudly at her side, and there is the patriotism number to end all patriotism numbers, at the conclusion of the show.

But it is Shoji, and his skills at both country fiddling and contemporary violin, that make up the heart of the show. He plays "Rocky Mountain Breakdown," "Orange Blossom Special," and every bluegrass standard. He displays his virtuosity through a broad country repertoire, and then, in a later section of his act, carries the audience through the full range of postwar American music. He performs brilliantly and affectingly, and his performance is the one *must see* in Branson.

Is it, therefore, churlish of me to complain about the racial casting of his grand show? At one point, he does a large-scale Caribbean number, and talks about the training on steel drums that Shoji and his band received from a Caribbean native, whom they brought over to Branson for that purpose, but apparently they did not ask him to stay. Shoji's show does not have a black performer in it, and he and a host of white musicians play those steel drums. In a production that deals sympathetically with every major form, era, and movement of American music, a form of African American music gets knocked. It's telling, when he reaches the present in his history of music and announces, "And now we come to rap music." The audience audibly groans. Shoji messes up his hair and costume a bit, and launches into a stream of grunts and grinds that gets the audience laughing along with him. Earlier, in his Caribbean sequence, he walks down the simulated gangplank of a cruise ship and a black native, played by a white, holds out his arm for a handout. Both Shoji and the audience laugh.

The entire show bespeaks fairy tale, immeasurably helped by the improbability of a Japanese fiddler with a Beatles haircut in Liberace-style sartorial glitter. In a part of the world that might resist the idea of an Asian male married to a Caucasian woman, Shoji seems doubly adored for this, as if the great American heartland in its love for his showmanship is also able to embrace the aberration he represents. Especially if, in his own attitudes on stage, he poses no threat to other conservative values. After cracking the color barrier to an extent that no one else has, and becoming immensely rich in the process, Shoji has apparently decided to bring no one else of color along in his show. I find that sad.

Performances are from mid-March through December, daily except Saturday and Sunday in summer, daily except Sunday all other times, at 3pm and 8pm. No performances during the first two weeks in November, in order to permit rehearsals for the new Christmas show. Ticket prices are $22 per adult, $21 for seniors, $14 for children 12 and under.

Baldknobbers Hillbilly Jamboree Show

Baldknobbers Theater
2835 West Highway 76,
phone 417/334-4528

The show that started it all. Some claim it's the best pure-country music show in Branson. I look on it as a historical relic, in a category unto itself; it's unfair to assign it a rating, because its function is not to achieve top levels of entertainment, but to preserve a way of life, a bygone form of presentation. And yet it's wonderful fun. The audience is sometimes raucous, always heavy with families and children, and people eat popcorn in their seats. Souvenir stands adorn each side of the stage, just opposite the front row of seats. At intermission time, as many as seven or eight performers sit at the footlights, their feet dangling over the stage, signing autographs.

This is pure country, with no concessions to the modern age. Performers talk in broad, broad drawls; they pronounce Louisiana like "Loo-za-nah," Missouri like "Miz-ooh-rah"; they yodel on occasion; and don't require that every act bring down the house or consist of supertalents. Often, the show's two clowns cavort about on stage while someone else is singing his heart out at the mike. It's all like a mini Grand Ole Opry, in a plain and care-worn theater that's the essence of the Ozarks.

The show dates from the mid-'50s, when the four Mabe brothers started performing their country routines on a part-time basis, while holding down other jobs, later appearing as part of the original casts at both Silver Dollar City and The Shepherd of the Hills

Theater. They took their name, Baldknobbers, from a vigilante group that terrorized these Ozark hills in the last century. By now, the title had lost its dread and simply sounded funny, and the Mabes were onto the idea of earning a living by making folks laugh.

In a performing odyssey of difficult improvisation and hard times, the Mabes started downtown in Branson on the second floor of the city hall. They used folding chairs for the audience; sometimes played homemade instruments; and their marketing consisted of their wives walking around in country dresses and carrying signs to advertise the show to Lake Taneycomo fisherfolk. Once visitors began appearing in numbers, the Mabes moved to an old skating rink that accommodated 600, and that became Branson's first theater. Later they moved to West Highway 76 (the Strip), not far from where the Presleys had already opened (see earlier in this chapter). Today, the Baldknobbers Theater is only part of the Mabe family enterprises, which also include a heavily patronized motel and restaurant.

Only brothers Jim and Bill have stuck with the routine—and what a routine it is! Cornball and country all the way. It's got washboard-toting Droopy Drawers and rubber-faced Stub Meadows, the show's two favorite hillbillies, whose humor is nothing if it ain't broad—and they'll tell you "broad" while ogling the females who dress in skintights.

Baldknobbers music ranges from woeful country blues, to fiddling freak-outs, to Elvis imitators, to four-part male harmony. When third-generation Joy Bilyeu does "Cleopatra, Queen of Denial," you've heard country "hurting" you wouldn't want to experience firsthand. Gags and slapstick alternate with the tunes, as do purty gals and curly-haired, mustached cowboys. No big production numbers, no dancing to speak of, just music and comedy. Mike Ito, who has fiddled with the Baldknobbers since the early '80s, stars in the bluegrass solos. Obviously, the show has its share of gospel and hymns, and wraps up with a big flag-waving version of the "Battle Hymn of the Republic."

The only jarring note of the evening is an angry rendition of a song about flag-burners, surely the nonissue of the '90s, from which both the Supreme Court and the rest of the nation have long since moved on. Dropping their cornpone attitudes, becoming hard-eyed and vengeful, the young men of the ensemble sing: "Buddy, you've burned your flag, Burning a flag is a crime," and so on. The song reminds you of the penchant toward violence that lies buried in the gentlest of people hereabouts, and is a grim, unsettling note that really should be dropped.

Performances from the first of March until the second Saturday in December, daily at 8pm, except Sunday; there are no matinees. Ticket prices: $14.50 for adults, $6 for children 11 and under.

Andy Williams

Andy Williams Moon River Theater
2500 West Highway 76,
phone 417/334-4500

He enters dramatically from the back of the theater, walking down the aisle to thunderous applause, and everyone gasps at how well-preserved he is. Gaunt face without an ounce of fat or jowls, brilliantly white teeth, silver hair, smart tux, red handkerchief. And his tenor voice! In his 64th year, it is as good as ever, seemingly unchanged, as is his ability to hold a concluding note for what seems an eternity, and the steady falsetto of which he is capable at the end of his rendition of "Love Story."

He is, as if to improve matters, humility itself. He pokes fun at himself, jokes about his age, but also lets drop that he owns this magnificent theatre himself, and is also the landlord for the nearby restaurant, McGuffey's, which he invites you to visit for an after-theater snack. His was the first of the non-Ozark shows to open in Branson, in 1992, and it quickly became a hit.

Andy Williams may move a little stiffly on stage—he does no comedy, no dance—but his voice surmounts all. He's on stage virtually the entire two hours of his show, often performed without intermission. A national treasure who evokes a more innocent age, he relaxes and reassures, which is what the Branson audiences have come for, this sense of "Moon River" flowing unchanged through American life. You hear all of his classics—"Moon River," "The Days of Wine and Roses," "The Shadow of Your Smile," "Can't Get Used to Losing You," "Your Cheating Heart"—in his trademark-style delivery that won him the longest possible list of Emmy, Grammy, and Golden Globe nominations and awards. He brings tears when he sings "September Song" against a movie cast on the screen behind him of all the now-dead stars who appeared with him on television (some may find the sequence a bit morbid).

It is a quality show in a superbly restful (and art-filled) theater of more than 2,000 seats, with state-of-the-art lighting, sound, dancers, backup singers. Williams's band is among Branson's best, 11 musicians (4 are women), including a dynamite drummer, but no blacks, and no blacks either among an entire gospel choir of 20 members (the Moon River Theater Choir). Even Aretha Franklin's trademark "Respect," done by three female singers, is performed lily white.

If Williams is formally attired to open the show, he comes back for his second half informal in sweater, though to be sure, the pants are impeccably creased. Audiences love him. He reminds them of his midwestern upbringing, graciously poses for photos taken by audience members crouching in the aisles, announces the bus tours as if he were some junior emcee. Williams may be a national treasure, but now he belongs to Branson.

Performances are from early April to December 17, daily except Sunday, with two shows a day (3pm and 7pm) on most days, but with matinees eliminated on varying days that follow no set pattern throughout the year; call. Ticket prices: $21 for adults, $20 for seniors, $8 for children 12 and under.

Pump Boys and Dinettes

Pump Boys and Dinettes Theater
On Highway 165, a half-mile south of West Highway 76,
phone 800/743-2-FUN or 417/336-4319

A delightful production of the long-running Broadway show on life in a gas station and garage adjoining a diner in the Ozarks. It's a charming, touching, slice-of-humanity musical with talented performers (some from the Broadway cast), authentic country music and dancing, the dialects of southwestern Missouri ("pie" is pronounced "pah"), and witty, sophisticated lyrics—the latter, something you don't often encounter in Branson. Mind you, it isn't a big and splashy show, which is perhaps why it's put on in a dinner theater (the audience sits at tables, and has lunch or dinner immediately preceding the performance).

There are only six performers—four men and two women—and the story starts slow, needing time to win you over. But win you it does, and not simply with well-performed melodies (on guitar, piano, harmonica, and bass) and good voices, but with a great many wise comments on life itself that can sometimes bring tears. Everyone here is at one with their environment and culture, happy in their milieu: the "pump boys" take days and days to repair the cars that sit disabled on hydraulic lifts; they sing about the virtues of "Taking It Slow." When their fishing licenses arrive for the season, they instantly close the garage ("We're Goin' Fish'n") and one cancels the date he had made to take one of the "dinettes" and her two children to the softball game.

All these decisions are taken in an exultant, full-voiced quartet of male voices, while the girls next door beat a clanging accompaniment on pots and pans. But the jilted dinette responds with a hard-pounding Aretha Franklin–type song ("Be Good or Be Gone") and the garage attendant changes his ways. When a runaway cow eats all 37 marijuana plants on a nearby farm, the local sheriff confiscates the cow, but allows as to how he'll return it after the election.

Because the musical originated on the New York stage, there are moments when the pure country sound of most numbers slips into Broadway-style melodies and sock-it-to-them presentations, which to me is a refreshing change of pace from constant country. And because of the origin of the musical, there is no religious message and no awkward, blatant, patriotic number. Rather, a pride in America emerges subtly from the characters and the plot, which is the way talented theater people convey that message. I think you'll walk out of the theater in a glow.

Performances are year-around except for two weeks after Christmas, twice a day, but only four and five days a week, Wednesday through Saturday from mid-January to mid-April, Tuesday through Saturday from mid-April to mid-June, Wednesday through Sunday from mid-June through late August, Tuesday through Saturday from September through most of December. Those performances go on at 12:45pm (following lunch at 11:30am) and 7:30pm (following dinner at 6pm), and each meal and show can be separately purchased. Lunch is $9 for adults, $5 for children; the luncheon show is $15 for adults, $7.50 for children under 14. Dinner is $12.25 for adults, $6.25 for children; the dinner show (sans meal) is $15 for adults, $7.50 for children.

Country Tonite

Country Tonite Theater
3815 West Highway 76 at the Intersection with Shepherd of the Hills Expressway,
phone 800/950-9797 or 417/334-2422

Transferred to Branson after a run of more than two years in Las Vegas, this is a surprisingly entertaining and popular musical variety show, mainly because it breaks with all the Branson formulas. There are no "name" stars, which means there are no endless monologues or reminiscences, no long audience participation acts or invitations to come on stage to meet the great man, no interruptions of the show to read the names of tour groups in the audience (and thus demonstrate how democratic is the star).

We hear instead the repertoire of Patsy Cline, Hank Williams, and Reba McIntire. There is music, music, music, one number following fast upon another, in a boisterous, exuberant, and well-paced show that touches all the bases of country. We witness an act of heart-pounding, lightning-like clog dancing, featuring a national champion of the art; a fierce contest with the "devil" to determine the best fiddler around; a 12-year-old singer (Kimberly Caldwell) from the heart of Dixie, whose voice is the very essence of country; a cowboy rope dancer and a full dozen tap dancers giving their all; a national banjo champion (Cody Kilbey); an eight-piece orchestra jumping and swaying. It's a vision of what Branson could be, making Baldknobbers and Presleys look cheap and contrived.

When the obligatory gospel segment comes on performed by an all-white cast ("Amazing Grace," "Will the Circle Be Unbroken"), it's at least presented seamlessly, without a sudden change of mood or portentous lighting. A single, particularly jarring note, which I suspect was tacked onto this Las Vegas production for its presentation in Branson: an ending that includes a sudden burst of cannon and machine gun fire against martial music, as the flag is carried out and everyone stands. Up until then, Country Tonite has concentrated simply on the legacy of music for which so many more people could be persuaded to visit Branson. We can at least be grateful that earlier audience participation has been totally dispensed with.

Peformances are twice daily at 3pm and 8pm, except Sunday, March through December. Admission prices are $17.50 for adults, $8.75 for children 4 to 11, free for children under 4. Children will especially like the several talented child performers who appear in several featured numbers.

Cristy Lane

Cristy Lane Theater
3600 West Highway 76,
phone 417/335-5111

Cristy Lane

The importance of the song, "One Day at a Time," as performed by Cristy Lane, was something I had not known prior to my first trip to Branson, nor had I heard of Cristy Lane. (Have you?) It was therefore with growing curiosity that I waited to see and hear Ms. Lane, through an interminable, $1\frac{1}{2}$-hour first act in which she never once appears. Throughout that time, a mild-mannered, self-effacing emcee (her husband) in gray hair and mustache makes reference in respectful, indeed awe-struck, terms, like announcing a Second Coming, that she will eventually be on stage, but only after we have first heard (1) a British fiddler who allegedly has a graduate degree in the violin, (2) a giant young man in white silk costume who sings "Pretty Woman," later shaking and gyrating in an Elvis routine, and (3) a "living legend," white-bearded comedian Foster Brooks (more on him later). Has everyone enjoyed the show so far, asks the emcee?

Finally, post-intermission, Cristy Lane shows up. "Did you enjoy Foster Brooks as much as I did?" she asks. She is a trim, middle-aged woman in glittery blue dress, carrying herself with solemnity, like the icon she has been portrayed as. Her delivery is flat, studied, and done from a script, and studded with such 1930s instructions to the band as "Play it, Brady," or "Take it away, Ken." Every gesture is staged. She does an assortment of numbers: "Sweet Dreams of You," "I Fall to Pieces," hymns. And finally, after the longest evening of my life, she ends the show with "One Day at a Time, Sweet Jesus," which is no sooner finished when the emcee advises the audience to keep their ticket stubs so that they can pay only $10 for another and different show. "How nice to see you in God's country," he ends.

In the meantime, what has been Foster Brooks's contribution to this pious production? It has been, among other things, a string of jokes about the drooping breasts of aging women, of which one of the mildest is about a grandmother who fires a gun at a spot two inches below her left breast and blows off her left kneecap. The audience roars. At another point he tells of a woman returning home from a workshop in women's lib, announcing that she will no longer prepare dinner for her husband. "If you don't," he responds, "you will not see me for the next three days." And sure enough, she does not "see" him for the next three days because he has closed and blackened both of her eyes with two punches to the face. The audience again roars. In a city that gets excited about the use of the word *hell* or *damn* on stage, this right-wing imitation of George Burns creates an entire act based heavily on jokes denigrating women, wives, and people of Polish descent (that gets in there, too), in leering raunchy fashion.

The Cristy Lane show is performed year-round, daily except Thursday, at 7pm, for an admission charge of $20. There are no matinees.

John Davidson

John Davidson Theater
3446 West Highway 76, in the heart of the Strip (next door to the Jim Stafford Theater), phone 417/334-0773

He beams, he shines, he glows, his pearly white teeth blind you with their brilliance, his spangled blue suit reflects the light, his face exudes goodness. He bounces about, he leaps and cavorts, he exhausts you with his energy. When he grasps the hand of a woman in the audience, he doesn't simply kiss it—he starts gnawing on it, sucks and licks it, while her husband seated alongside grows more nervous by the minute. No other Branson performer puts out more effort (he appears on stage—singing, dancing, leaping, and reciting—from beginning to end), and 10 minutes after he has started he is drenched in sweat.

And the funny thing is, it works. This former emcee of "Hollywood Squares," without what I regard as a distinctive musical talent, literally overcomes his audience with his energy, and leaves them applauding for more. He does musical medleys that build and build, and are composed of such irresistible songs that eventually they weave a spell in the theater. One of them is a touching recitative about a man taking his wife to a party for the first time in years; "Could I have this dance for the rest of my life?" he ends, and cheap tears fall from every face in the theater. It is clear that in addition to his energy, he has utilized the skills of brilliant contemporary music directors and producers, and he pays tribute to them in the course of the show.

The music is noncountry and wouldn't be out of place in a Chicago nightclub; the material is relatively sophisticated for Branson and wholly unlike the hackneyed routines and dumb humor that infect so many other Branson shows. There is an imaginative use of multimedia that sometimes surrounds the performer with video images of his past, his family, various themes of American life. And he does an interesting and gently amusing quarter-hour on his upbringing as the son of a Baptist minister, joining three band members in a rousing quartet, "My Father Was a Preacher."

To his father, who loved the songs of Al Jolson, he dedicates an Al Jolson imitation and medley of the hits that Jolson used to perform in blackface ("Swanee," "You Made Me Love You," "Rock-a-Bye Your Baby," several others); it is obvious that the 52-year-old Davidson is sensitive to racial matters (the photos of a black astronaut and Martin Luther King briefly flash upon a backdrop screen), but not to such an extent that he would have the courage (in Branson) to hire a black musician for his band. And then he spoils the goodness that he has both exuded and preached throughout the show, this minister's son, by stepping before an intermission curtain and pitching the sale of a geography card game that he created to teach youngsters about the world. He has donated copies to schools, he tells us, and has seen children's knowledge of geography improve, but the game is of course on sale to the audience in the lobby, and wouldn't they like to buy it?

Performances are from March through December, twice daily at the unusual hours (for a celebrity performer) of 10am and 2pm, with no evening show, Monday through Friday. The admission is $17.50 for adults, $8 for children.

The Lawrence Welk Show

Welk's Champagne Theater
1984 State Highway 165,
phone 800/505-9355 or 417/337-7469

This is a big show, lavishly mounted in an opulent, new theater. Its purpose: to re-create the atmosphere, style, and content of the former Lawrence Welk television hour that was already a journey into nostalgia when it was presented during the famed bandleader's lifetime many years ago. Since Lawrence Welk himself is no longer alive, the producers have resuscitated several of his starring acts: the Lennon Sisters, pianist Jo Ann Castle, singer Mary Lou Metzger, tap dancer Arthur Duncan, and a 22-piece big band with three violins, mellow trombones, and a number of the actual musicians who once played for him; on occasion (but certainly not always), their tempo is so slow that you wonder how they stay awake.

It is all presented in tuxedos, against white net curtains, crystal chandeliers, white Lawrence Welk bandstands, periodically with the entire stage cast in a rosy glow. Most performers come out with broad smiles pasted on their faces, which they keep, unvaryingly, rigidly, throughout their time on stage. They are the essence of American goodness, innocence, cleanliness, adherence to majority values. There's a tango act, a Pennsylvania polka (natch), a hoedown, a young woman descending on a swing from high above the stage and singing "When You Wish Upon a Star," then "Singing in the Rain" is performed on a darkened stage by dancers wearing fluorescent hats, shoes, and umbrellas, a simulated Fred Astaire and Ginger Rogers "Top Hat" and "Stepping Out," and numerous other wholesome numbers. A largely elderly audience sits wreathed in memories, fantasizing about the past, and even the most cynical youngster finds the evening to be so campy as to constitute sheer delight.

The show comes alive with the appearance of the four Lennon Sisters, with their perfect coordination and harmony, doing a version of "The Boogie-Woogie Bugle Boy" that reminds us of the Andrews Sisters at their very best. They swing into "Falling Leaves," "You Made Me Love You," "My Favorite Things," sometimes done a capella, and establish a level that no one else matches until the appearance of honky-tonk piano player Jo Ann Castle in the second act. She, too, is a marvel, bringing thunderous sound from a piano, as if she had 20 fingers. It's a pity that at the end of her act she treats her audience like children. She plays "Somewhere My Love" from *Dr. Zhivago* with such exaggerated gestures and contorted grimaces as to insult the entire tradition of recital music.

The show of course contains the compulsory religious segment, the compulsory patriotism segment. Like the eerily similar flag-waving numbers that ended "The Dance of the Red Guards" ballet in Mao Tse Tung's China, like the exhortations on stage to Communist victory in Stalin's old Soviet Union, the patriotism and religious sequences come on abruptly, mechanically, without reference to any preceding logic; one wonders—and it would be interesting to ask—why the same weren't performed on the actual Lawrence Welk TV program to a national audience.

Nevertheless, there are small indications of mental growth in the Welk program that perhaps create hope for the future. One is the featured appearance of tap dancer Arthur Duncan, a black, who pokes gentle fun at his color (but is careful never to mention faults of the white race). More significant is the appearance of a normal, ordinary, young black man in the troupe of dancers, surely a Branson first. Someone at the Welk organization has obviously attempted to challenge the color bar in Branson, and it will be interesting to see whether they stick to their guns.

Performances are from mid-March through mid-December, daily except Tuesday, at 2pm and 8pm, for $18 per adult, free for children under 6. An ultra-early breakfast show by the Lennon Brothers is presented in the Stage Door Canteen restaurant of the theater building, daily except Wednesday at 8am, every day of the week in October, for admission of $16 per adult, $10 for children 7 to 12, free for children 6 and under.

The Osmond Brothers

Osmond Family Theater
3216 West Highway 76
(near the intersection of Highway 165),
phone 417/336-6100

At one point of this silly, senseless show, the Osmonds invite members of the audience with cameras to line up at the foot of the stage, and then go on stage, one by one, to have their photos taken with the Osmonds by an usher to whom they have handed the camera. Often, as many as 30 people accept the invitation, and the process of taking these photos—in the very midst of the show—uses up 10 to 12 minutes. All that time, while posing, the Osmonds sing "When I Fall in Love" in barbershop quartet fashion, over and over and over and over again.

At another point, the silvery haired father of the Osmonds, at least in his late 70s, and not a professional or outstanding singer, comes on stage to do an awkwardly presented number with his sons. Still earlier, they have had the audience engage in shouting contests and other inanities, and every few moments throughout the show, brother Wayne tells jokes so amateur and juvenile as to be embarrassing. "Why do cows wear bells? Because their horns don't work." "I dreamt I was a wigwam, and then I dreamt I was a teepee. You're too tense (two tents)." He roars and slaps his knee at his own jokes, blows bubbles at the audience, and persists at these high school routines throughout the show, as if what works for Baldknobbers when performed by Ozark clowns will save the Osmonds' show from deadliness.

How else do the brothers fill up the two hours of their performance? They do a loud and cacophonous medley of country and jazz, displaying no musical talents beyond the ordinary. They prove to the audience that they can play a number of instruments, and move from saxophone to drums to accordion to fiddle and banjo; the drummer brother is quite good. They do other songs, none particularly well. I found myself asking, Why are we here?

They have, in the show, not one but two big patriotic sequences, both coming out of the blue at the end of each act: the first act finale, with "Dixie," "The Battle Hymn of the Republic," and flag-bearing young women marching down the aisles as everyone stands. It's done because—one of the brothers explains—Elvis told them always to have an American song to round things off, and he was right—the short moment of fervor saves the most dispiriting first act you could possibly imagine. I again thought of Samuel Johnson's admonition about patriotism being the last refuge of scoundrels. Later, at the end of the second act, the patriotism number is, in effect, presented for a second and equally lengthy time.

Were it not for their name, no self-respecting theater in America would book these middle-aged gentlemen; more talented barbershop quartets are available in every city. They have no unique musical approach, no special sound, no classic songs still associated with their lives by the public. Whatever talent they had as kids is no longer in evidence. The toll that time takes! And, in fact, the show picks up considerably in the second act when the Osmonds' children—the second generation of Osmonds—come on stage to do several song and dance numbers (to the squeals of a few teen-aged girls in the audience), and these youngsters prove quite entertaining, which tells you something about the Osmonds' fame; it is based on youthful cuteness and precocity.

I've pointed out in an earlier chapter that just before their repetition of a patriotism spectacle in the second act, the Osmonds line up on stage for an equally prominent religious song spectacle of outright, unabashed, sectarian, proselytizing virtually shouted to the audience and backed by giant watercolor portraits of Jesus beamed upon the stage. Wouldn't the Osmonds be truer to themselves if they were to do so in one day a week of free performances in a church? As the Osmonds loudly sing out their religious beliefs with such obvious zeal, I can't help thinking that they are accepting ticket income for delivering that message.

Performances are from late March to mid-December, but in 1995, Rich Little will be substituting until the end of May, with the Osmonds starting again in June. The schedule is daily except Sunday and Wednesday at both 2pm and 8pm. Admission price is $17.50 per adult, $6 per child 12 and under.

Yakov Smirnoff

Appearing in the Osmond Family Theater
3216 West Highway 76
(near the intersection of Highway 165),
phone 800/33-NO-KGB

Suffering from repression and poverty, he and his family emigrated from Russia to the United States some 15 years ago, where he proceeded to do several well-received turns as a comedian on TV ("Major Dad"), in films *(Moscow on the Hudson),* and on the night-club stage, commenting—among other things—on the foibles and failures of the Soviet system.

But now that the Cold War is over, and those matters seem less relevant, what subject matter does he use for his act? How does he replace his former surefire topics?

He does so by engaging, among other things, in vicious, thuggish attacks on a sitting president of the United States. "I believe people from Arkansas are very smart," he says, at one point of his Branson show. "You had one guy you wanted to get rid of—and you did! And you got rid of *her,* too!" Earlier he has implied in the show that President Clinton should be "spanked." Though he now lives in the United States, he sounds like the very commissars from whom he escaped.

His one-man show—he simply stands on stage for two acts and delivers a continuous monologue, sometimes aided by movie clips cast upon a screen—consists of otherwise innocuous one-liners about his difficulties with English, his misunderstandings of what Americans said to him during his first several months here, his relationship with his father-in-law, the fact that Russians say "yup" when they refer to sex (a joke he repeats on several occasions), and other pallid topics. Many of the anecdotes are not really true stories, or meant to be taken as such, and therein lies the curious lack of appeal of his present act.

The best of comedy routines relate to actual life situations and remind us of what we have personally experienced or instinctively understand; they are social commentaries, if you will, which deal with true people or events, and are not simply contrived plays on words or made-up situations. When Smirnoff tells us that he thought "baby powder" referred to pulverized babies, he may draw a smile, but no real, heartfelt response.

After 40 minutes on stage, he calls an intermission, and the audience is served a box lunch or dinner in their seats (thick and chunky potato soup, a Russian *pirojee*—dumpling—of chicken and mushrooms with cottage cheese, a *Bobka* dessert, and apple cider). In about 15 minutes, he returns to the stage and invites audience members to tell their own jokes, then answers questions from the audience. A few more contrived jibes about funny situations that never happened, and he closes by singing an ode to the Statue of Liberty while shaking hands with audience members, thanking them for his newfound liberty, an affecting moment. But the show is otherwise totally unimportant, and with its harsh political comments leaves a bad taste.

The Yakov Smirnoff show is presented from April through mid-December, twice daily (except on Sunday and Wednesday) at the unusual times of 11am and 5pm. Ticket prices, which include a box *lunch or dinner served in your seat, are $17 for adults, $12 for children 12 and under.*

Mickey Gilley

Mickey Gilley Theater
3455 West Highway 76,
phone 800/334-1936 or 417/334-3210

A precurtain video on a large screen at the front of the auditorium tells you how great he is, how he had so many hit records in the past, and ran the world's "number one honky-tonk cafe" in Texas, and how "a handful of dollars led him to country music." Then the curtain parts to reveal him standing dramatically before a big band, in well-tailored tuxedo and with humongous diamond rings on each hand. It's all downhill from that moment on.

I have a hard time understanding the appeal of Mickey Gilley. His on-stage personality is colorless and to me not particularly attractive, his current-day singing is undistinguished, his repartee dull ("I'm gonna do lots of the number one singles I've done"); his show is utterly standard and without a single original moment, and although I have to accept his claim to have made dozens of hit records, I see no evidence of that in the show itself, whose music is mainly forgettable.

One gets the impression that he is as much interested in his next-door restaurant venture (Gilley's Texas Cafe) as in the show, which portrays very little evidence of having been worked on by talented producers. It consists in the main of Gilley standing in front of an orchestra for interminable periods and talking about his cousins, Jerry Lee Lewis and the disgraced Reverend Jimmy Swaggart, occasionally switching to a song ("Talk to Me," "Put Your Dreams Away") while the band plays loudly as if to drown him out. Occasionally, a long-haired blond (Peggy Carton), of standard talents, walks out to contribute a song of her own. About the best thing in the show is a steel guitarist, who talks back and forth to Gilley, and tells long jokes about traffic in Branson and the operation of toilets in the theater (displaying a toilet cover); he is actually pretty funny.

The entire, long first act is exactly as I have described it. Gilley—who is no Frank Sinatra—carries the first half of the show aided by only a single other act. Is he trying to save money? The more varied second act gets a bit better, and that, plus the steel guitarist, and the comfortable theater warrant an "average" rating for the show.

Performances are from mid-April to mid-December, usually at 2pm and 8pm, daily except Friday, but from Thursday through Sunday only in November and December. Tickets are $17 for adults, $8.50 for children 12 and under.

The Shepherd of the Hills Outdoor Theater

West Highway 76, two miles west of the Strip,
phone 417/334-4191

Until now, we've been visiting shows within Branson's city limits; we've described all the big ones, and will save a half-dozen more of the smaller or morning variety for next year's edition. But before you leave Branson, there's an evening pageant that history-minded readers will want to schedule for a last evening—and *pageant* is the only adequate term for it. At one point, on a 50-yard-wide stage consisting of the unpaved, earthen, main street of a re-created, turn-of-the-century Ozark village called Mutton Hollow, an entire large herd of actual sheep comes running before the audience. At other times, giant Clydesdale horses thunder past, as do Ozark-style cowboys galloping full speed on straining ponies, large horse-pulled carriages going all out, and an honest-to-goodness 1907 car.

Here is the colorful visual enactment, two hours long, of Harold Bell Wright's 1907 novel, *The Shepherd of the Hills,* presented at a spot 2 miles beyond the end of the Strip, but still alongside West Highway 76. Its 2,000-seat amphitheater setting is at the very spot where the actual models for two of the protagonists of Wright's novel—Mr. and Mrs. J. K. Ross, the Uncle Matt and Aunt Mollie of the story—had their cabin, later moved to a nearby site. And just a few hundred yards away, marked by an observation tower (see our sightseeing chapter, later on), is Inspiration Point, the hill on which Harold Bell Wright pitched his tent and slept and gazed onto the hills for inspiration as he wrote *The Shepherd of the Hills.* To romantics and dreamers, this is a holy site; but even to less impressionable tourists it's still an important location, and an entertaining place for learning more about the early history of the Branson area.

The Story Itself, Highly Compressed

Under the stars, in an awesome setting, you'll learn about the highly educated, mournful, city stranger who mysteriously appears in these Ozark hills, fleeing from a private tragedy, and becomes a shepherd of both sheep and souls. You'll witness the daily life of the Ozark people, the love story of Sammy (Samantha) Lane and the uneducated but noble Young Matt, who are eventually betrothed despite Sammy's engagement to another Ozark boy (Ollie) who had been sent to the city to be brought up by rich relatives. You'll meet evil Wash Gibbs, head of an underground group of Baldknobbers who terrorized this area both in the book and in real life. You'll witness his comeuppance, and then, in the strangest twist of all, you'll learn that the shepherd's lost son is still alive, living in a cave near Mutton Hollow. There he grieves for a young Ozark woman (daughter of Uncle Matt and Aunt Mollie) betrayed by him, left with child, and caused to pine away, dying, after he—the young city boy—had painted her picture (and thus made his fortune as an artist in New York City). The repentant young son of the shepherd dies, but is first forgiven by Uncle Matt in a supreme act of charity.

What You Won't See

Obviously, no two-hour pageant can capture all the plot twists, characterizations, and nuances of a major novel, and what you are seeing here bears only a slight resemblance to the actual book. For one thing, the character of Ollie is made slapstick beyond all justification; he was not so ridiculous a city slicker, and Sammy (Samantha) Lane had a difficult time deciding to reject his offer of marriage and thus lose the chance to improve her own lot and help her father financially. Very little is told in the outdoor play of the patient instruction the shepherd gave to Sammy in the ethics of an honorable life, of Sammy's growth and wisdom. Nor does one have the chance to ponder the dignified and noble aspects of the life these Ozark hill people lived and that so captivated Harold Bell Wright. The drought that wiped them out financially, the failure of their bank, their tenuous ability to hold on to their land are only briefly depicted in the play. We learn very little about the origin of the Baldknobbers, a group of local vigilantes that turned corrupt. We see little of the struggle of Jim Lane, Sammy's father, once a Baldknobber, now anxious to lead a moral life. And we see very little of Sammy's grief when her father is killed in a raid on their cabin.

Why You Should Go

Finally, there is an absolutely inexcusable prelude of slapstick Ozark humor (hillbillies smelling their socks and armpits, that kind of thing) that the current producers of the pageant have devised to warm up the audience; the dignified Harold Bell Wright would have been outraged.

But all that being said, *The Shepherd of the Hills* pageant—and the book itself—are important to the enjoyment of Branson by thoughtful tourists, and you really ought to set aside an evening for the play. It is well-performed, the action is colorful, and most important, the setting is the glorious vista of Mutton Hollow (the present Branson) before it was paved over.

The Breakfast Shows

Finally, consider the breakfast shows of Branson that go on at 8, 9, and 10am, as remarkable as that may seem. They are all presented in someone else's theater, maximizing the use of real estate and staff, and to every outward appearance seem successful and reasonably well booked, despite having no nationally famed stars associated with them. Twelve such shows were offered in 1994, and the surprise decision of headliner John Davidson to join them (he will appear at 10am in his own theater starting in 1995) may quicken a trend to this sort of half-awake presentation.

Except for Davidson's, the breakfast shows are country without glitz or big talents, theater without production numbers or scenery. Some find them more authentic than the showier afternoon or evening versions, but they all try to duplicate the same elements that make for success in the Branson productions performed at normal hours: hoary old jokes (like Buck Trent's "I was downtown last week and ran into Dolly Parton; she was across the street"); and right-wing political comments (like two highly antagonistic comments by Trent [Mr. Banjo] about Hillary Clinton, and *Jennifer in the Morning*'s repeated references to the country's having been better off in the past); various doses of religion.

If you'd like to take in a morning show or two, you can catch the *Buck Trent Show* at the Pump Boys and Dinettes Theater (9am, $18 for breakfast and the show) and *Jennifer in the Morning* at the Roy Clark Theater (10am, $12 and $5 for tickets, adults and children, respectively, show only). The talented, bubbly Jennifer, in particular, pulls out all the stops, from clog-dancing to pure country to rock 'n' roll, but spoils it all by virtually commanding a grandfather whom she has selected from the audience to tell her how much better it was in the good old days. I was hoping the venerable gentleman would respond, "No, the elderly often lived in poverty in the good old days before Social Security and Medicare."

Branson's Theaters—A Reprise

What can be done to improve the theaters of Branson? As someone who has now seen more Branson performances than perhaps any other human being, I feel entitled to proffer some gratuitous advice.

As you've now seen from the above summaries, the theaters here are not meant to experiment or to convey new ideas; they are museums for the best of a certain kind of country or more recent American music (of the '40s and '50s). Since there's a hunger for that kind of performance art, Branson theaters can enjoy an ever greater success, in my view, if they maximize the time devoted to presenting those musical numbers, by eliminating the silly audience participation, the dumb monologues and asides, the right-wing political messages, and the hypocritical patriotism and pieties by some persons entitled to claim neither attribute.

Many Americans believe that selling religion for a ticket price is inappropriate, as is getting rich from religion. If these barriers to greater public acceptance of Branson are removed, and apparent policies of all-white casting reversed, then in my opinion Branson can reach out to a far larger and more sophisticated audience than presently patronizes it, and become the national attraction it so obviously hopes to be.

How to See Three, Four, or Even Five Shows a Day in Branson

For three shows a day, simply go to a morning show (of which there are many), a matinee, and an evening performance.

For four shows a day, go to the 8am performance of the Lennon Brothers at the Lawrence Welk Theater, the 10am performance of John Davidson, then a matinee performance, and an evening performance.

For five shows a day, follow the schedule set forth above for four shows a day, but be sure your matinee is at 2pm, and then take in the 5pm show of Yakov Smirnoff (disliked by me), before attending an 8pm evening performance.

8

Daytime Attractions, from Silly to Sublime

Twenty-one of Them

For some visitors to Branson, the idea of engaging in outdoor, daylight activities seems faintly treasonous, or at least unfair to the theaters. The country music and other shows get started as early as 8am (The Lennon Brothers at the Lawrence Welk complex), 8:30am (*The Tom & Jaynee Show* at the Mutton Hollow Entertainment Park), and 9am (Buck Trent's Breakfast Theater is one), resume at 10am (*Jennifer in the Morning* at the Roy Clark Theater, Jimmy Travis's *Morning Mania* at the Mel Tillis Theater), 11am (Yakov Smirnoff at The Osmond Family Theater), and 1:30pm (*Down Home Country* at the 76 Music Hall), and most of the major performers kick off their matinees at 2pm and 3pm. It's therefore possible to spend the entire day in a darkened theater, in a day-long orgy of country music and comics.

But not advisable. For a sensible change of pace, or to alternate sensations and restore your energy (like eating sherbet between the courses of a fine meal), it's wiser to schedule part of the day for outdoor entertainment, for which Branson has two outstanding opportunities (Silver Dollar City and Table Rock Lake), and about eighteen reasonably enticing ones. We're going to describe each one.

Silver Dollar City

Marvel Cave
From Branson go west on Highway 76 to Indian Point Road

The area's single major daytime attraction, Silver Dollar City is only a fraction of the size of a Disney theme park, but it compares quite respectably in the quality of the education it provides to young people. The theme is the Ozarks around the turn of the century. The subject matter is pursued through period Ozark cabins, churches, water mills, crude machines, living implements, and the like, brought to this site from their original locations and restored to working order. The people explaining it all are dedicated Ozark residents proud of their culture and unendingly courteous to the visitor.

Throughout the grounds, skilled craftspeople actually create their authentic products as you watch, before placing them on sale (we've named some of these remarkable artisans and recommended them in our shopping chapter, later on). There are, of course, amusements, too—rides and country music shows, both indoors and out—and restaurants, cafes, and stands for snacks and drinks (sarsaparilla is a popular item). But mainly it is the world of the Ozarks that is on display, in one of the finest regional theme parks of America.

Before Silver Dollar City, there was (and still is) a remarkable cave on these very grounds. It had been discovered by the Osage Indians in the 1500s. Over the years, others tripped upon its entrance, but not until archaeologist William Henry Lynch bought the cave in 1884 was it eventually opened to tourists. Lynch and later his daughters exploited the cave's guano deposits and led intrepid visitors through its dark chambers by mule. Then, in 1949, two modestly incomed residents of Chicago, Hugo and Mary Herschend, seeking a retirement business, took a long-term lease on the cave and its surrounding property. Using such limited resources as they possessed, they began improving access to the cave and promoting greater visitation. After Hugo's death, Mary and her two sons installed a cog railway to make it easier for visitors to come up from a nearby cafe. By 1957, the cave was attracting 50,000 visitors a year.

In 1960, to drum up further business for the cave, and with nothing else in mind, the Herschends re-created an old-time Ozark Mountain Village next door, a hamlet complete with blacksmith forge, general store, ice cream parlor, doll shop, and stage coach ride. Two authentic restorations were also included (and survive today): one of a 110-year-old log church, and the other a traditional homestead. They called the village Silver Dollar City and gave change in silver dollars so that, as visitors spent them around the countryside and back home, word would spread about the attraction.

The village caught on, and even began to overshadow Marvel Cave. Area craftspeople were drawn to the site because of the large crowds willing to buy products representative of the village atmosphere and its early times. Musicians came to play, including a group of local fellows who preferred making music to their day jobs, and who, because of a catchy name rather than for any connection with its notoriety, began calling themselves the Baldknobbers.

Long before the eruption of country music theaters on the Strip, Silver Dollar City began attracting visitors to the Branson area; and indeed, Silver Dollar City laid the groundwork for the immense touristic destination that Branson later became. Today, the Silver Dollar City organization not only operates the theme park and cave, but also the Grand Palace Theater in town, the adjoining Grand Village, White Water Park, and the new *Branson Belle* showboat on Table Rock Lake. Silver Dollar's owners, the Herschend brothers, are among the leading citizens in town, and deserve much of the credit, but also bear much of the continuing responsibility, for Branson and what it stands for.

A Typical Day at Silver Dollar City

If you get here on a Sunday, as I usually do, you'll find the theme park already packed by 9:30am. The yeasty smell of freshly cooked sourdough bread (of which half-slice samples are usually handed out) pervades the open courtyard where you enter. Nearby, at rustic Mollie's Mill, a huge, buffet-style, country breakfast—grits and all—is being served to ravenous guests. Elsewhere, people are making funnel cakes and fudge.

In between are the performing craftspeople—the artisans who practice their Ozark skills at making ironware, blowing glass, weaving reed baskets, spinning wool, carving baseball bats and mantels such as you'd hang over a fireplace (a particularly good buy). Most of them are with beards or bonnets; they wear overalls; some top 6 feet in height, and look like heroic characters from a Harold Bell Wright novel. There's a wonderful old-timey flavor to their wooden stalls and handmade signs. It's quickly apparent that foods and crafts are staples at Silver Dollar City, maybe even more popular than the rides, the exhibits, and the cave that started it all.

But not more so than music, which is played everywhere. At a steeply banked amphitheater (Echo Hollow), the top 100 country songs are performed nightly, and there's no extra charge to stay into the evening to attend that show. Nearby, live indoor performances of a condensed Broadway musical–type drama called *Listen to the River* take place in the new 1,000-seat opera house. Other groups are fiddling and picking (banjos) all around you—music is being played at all times, in places starkly named as Saloons, Dockside Theaters, Gazebos, Riverfront Playhouses, and more.

It's not long before you realize that one of the pleasures of Silver Dollar City is the absence of Mickey Mouse and dressed-up characters—what a relief *that* is!

The Cave

There's no added admission to Marvel Cave, the genesis of Silver Dollar City, at the side of the property—and you quickly descend to the Cathedral Room more than 200 feet below the earth's surface, where blind cave salamanders and gray bats are two endangered species living in the cave (they keep a fair distance from visitors). The giant vaulted space offers a magnificent view of the bright world we inhabit at the surface of the earth as you look up to the narrow aperture through which you've entered. Stunning.

Tours of the cave began in 1894. Visitors went down wooden ladders, with lanterns and special-issue coveralls with reinforced bottoms and knees. Some of the ancient ladders have been kept, and 9 miles of cave passages have been found, although only a half-mile is used for touring. The most amazing part of the visit is the cog railroad that at the end pulls you back in wire-enclosed cars up an incline of about 30 degrees. The train has a 38-ton capacity, but a typical full load, you're assured, doesn't exceed 12 tons. An estimated 20 to 30 percent of all visitors to Silver Dollar City go into the cave.

The Rides and Other Attractions

Visitors to Silver Dollar City have many rides to choose from, including the Wilderness Waterboggan, the Frisco Silver Dollar Line narrow gauge railroad (guaranteed to be held up by bandits), the Thunderation roller coaster, and rubber boats (guaranteed to get you wet) on the Lost River of the Ozarks. Other top attractions include countless other rides; a waterfall that you can walk behind; Tom Sawyer's landing; a steam-powered duplicating lathe from 1920 still at work using a steam engine that, new in 1885, cost $124 when bought from the Sears Roebuck Catalog. (In the same catalog you could have bought a complete house for $600.)

Sunday here also offers the pleasure of services held in the Wilderness Church. Nearby are racks of quilts hung in front of an 1843 cabin built by a pioneering Ozark family. Outside under the slanty eave, a group of musicians are fiddling and working out their Ozark harmonies. It's easy to feel at home here.

Silver Dollar City is open daily except Monday and Tuesday from April 10 to May 20; seven days a week from May 21 to October 30 (from 9am to 7pm until August 21, then until 6pm); and Wednesday through Sunday, except for Thanksgiving, from November 9 to December 23. Admission is $23 for adults, $22 for seniors 55 and older, $14 for children 4 to 11.

The Drive Back to Branson from Silver Dollar City

Driving back toward Branson from Silver Dollar City, you come to the Shepherd of the Hills Homestead and Theater, which I've described in Chapter 7 on evening theatergoing. For now, you'll want to know that a tall, elevator-serviced observation tower adjoining the Shepherd Theater (open 8am to 7pm daily, $4 for adults, $2 for children, but admission to the tower is included free in admission to the Shepherd of the Hills Homestead) offers panoramic views of the entire area, including Branson, from both open and enclosed decks. And you can see down below how several of the country buildings that figure in Harold Bell Wright's book have been relocated and reassembled at the site. All around on this glass-enclosed uppermost level are quotations from Harold Bell Wright's book.

Still closer toward Branson is the Hennings State Forest with an overlook of forest, glade, creek topography, and trails. *Glade* here, as you soon learn, refers to an open rocky habitat. Here, too, you can see the so-called White River *balds* (from the term *Baldknobbers,* and the geographical designation *Dewey Bald,* which figured so prominently in Harold Bell Wright's book).

Glades are open, rocky, and usually very dry. Posted legends describe how shallow soils and bare rock discourage growth of trees, exposing the glade to climatic extremes year-round. Grasses are the most common glade plants, but wildflowers grow here too, including yellow cornflower, wild blue indigo, Indian paintbrush, Missouri primrose, pale purple cornflower, prairie dock, and beautiful rose verbena. Many of the grasses and wildflowers growing in these glades are also found on prairies and in deserts.

As you drive the final stretch into Branson, you find the last magnificent and undisturbed views into the hills and hollows. A broad vista opens upon entering Taney County, just past Shepherd of the Hills Theater (after Inspiration Tower), but after just a few more bends, the theaters, shops, motels, and appurtenances of Branson hove into sight. Coming from the country to this, you are not thrilled. And yet, strangely, you feel resigned to having a good time.

Riding the Ducks

West Highway 76 (see map)
phone 417/334-5350

Now in their 23rd year of operation, the "Ducks" of Branson are a fleet of clunky, amphibious trucks that seem awkward as they roll along highways, but become graceful "ships" when they enter the water—in this case, the waters of Table Rock Dam. They leave from their depot on the Strip (near the turnoff for Green Mountain Drive, and next to McDonalds West) every few minutes throughout the day, with about 30 passengers apiece, and then drive up an exceedingly steep hill and then down again on their way to the banks of the lake, several miles away.

En route, they pass through a "graveyard" of World War II amphibian vehicles (from which they derive), motorized personnel carriers, tanks, jeeps, and the like—presumably to show you still other weird and innovative vehicles that, like the Ducks, had to be developed to serve various wartime needs. Once out of the vehicle graveyard, you go scooting down a dirt road to the side of the water, and plop! you're in Table Rock Lake, observing all its maritime sights exactly as you would have from the decks of a real boat.

You go cruising around for 20 minutes (the entire trip from start to finish is 70 minutes long), entertained by the joke-filled commentary and broad Ozark accent of your driver-captain, then return to base. Price of the 70-minute excursion, round-trip: $9.98 for adults, $5.95 for children 4 to 11, free for children 3 and under. Some folks find the ride-and-cruise enchanting; others regard it as a waste of $9.98; others say they could have done without the World War II vehicle graveyard. I come out somewhere in between. Certainly, it's a curious, quirky, sightseeing activity, but one you could have lived without—especially if you're planning to see the lake by car, driving over Table Rock Dam, in any event.

"Ride the Ducks" takes place daily except in the month of January (when they don't operate at all), from 8:30am to 4:30pm, at intervals of 15 to 20 minutes, and can be contacted at P.O. Box 1837, Branson, MO 65615.

The Branson Scenic Railway

Downtown Branson
phone 417/334-6110
or 800/2-TRAIN-2

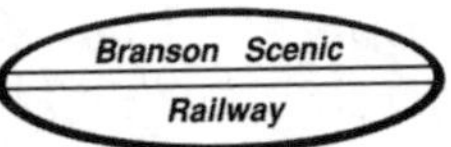

For railroad buffs and/or scenery lovers and/or tourists wishing to glimpse the majesty of the Ozark hills, this is a railroad train of silvery-gray, domed observation cars that leaves periodically from the otherwise-no-longer-in-use railway depot at the foot of Main Street in downtown Branson (about five blocks east of Highway 65). The trains make a 40-minute round-trip into and through valleys of the area, and on high, elevated trestles over sharp ravines, through some of the heaviest forests you will ever encounter and other charming scenes of country life.

They depart daily except Tuesday from January through October, and on weekends (either Thursday or Friday through Sunday) in November and December, at 8:30am, 11am, 2pm, and 4:30pm. And they keep to those schedules through thick and thin; I recently saw off friends traveling on a departure for which they were the only passengers, and yet the train pulled out on time and as if nothing was amiss. Ticket prices: $17.50 for adults, $16.50 for seniors, $9.75 for children.

White Water Park

The Strip
phone 417/334-7487
or 417/336-7100

Here, now, is one of those classic water theme parks full of slides, shoots, nozzles, sprays, and just plain swimming pools. From the tops of immensely high water chutes that curve and coil on the downward ride, you climb aboard an oversized, red inner tube and hurl yourself down on the water-filled slide, at considerable speed. Children of all ages do it. There's a Caribbean Plunge, a Paradise Plunge (207 feet long), a Tropical Twister, a Typhoon Tunnel, a Hurricane Rapids, for the thrill-seeker; a Paradise River, Splash Island and Surfquake (with 4-foot waves) for calmer sorts. Lifeguards and free life jackets keep everyone safe. White Water is right on the Strip.

White Water is open from 10am to 6pm from May 14 to September 5, and for two hours more—until 8pm—in the summer months. One-day admissions are $15.50 for "adults" 12 to 54, $11 for children 4 to 11, $5.50 for seniors and very young children.

Hollister

A tiny Missouri town of 2,600 people, designed to look like an English country village with Tudor facades, lots of "Ye Olde's" in the signs of lodgings and antique shops, and all the rest. A virtual sister city to Branson, it's diagonally across Lake Taneycomo from downtown Branson, no more than a 10-minute drive, and should be given at least an hour or so of your Branson-area vacation. You simply head south on Business Highway 65 or Highway 65, cross their respective bridges, then turn off onto historic Downing Street, the main thoroughfare, which is now on the National Register of Historic Sites.

Hollister was an important railroad junction and tourist destination long before Branson; a prominent turn-of-the-century resident, W. H. Johnson, had the dream of making it into a worldwide attraction by creating rows of Elizabethan structures along what was then to be called Downing Street, centerpiece of an Olde

English Village. Grape carnivals were promoted here by the Missouri-Pacific Railroad to attract visitors to the Ozarks, and Hollister—in a burst of creative building—became the first town in Taney County to have an iron bridge (going over Turkey Creek to the rear of Downing Street), a movie theater, a steam-heated hotel, electric lights, and an actual paved street.

Today, Hollister continues to promote itself touristically, and offers quaint shopping and dining opportunities, but seems to be overwhelmed in that effort by the greater success of Branson. *Sic transit gloria mundi.* A visit to Hollister can be combined with one to the College of the Ozarks and its Ralph Foster Museum; and from Hollister, one gets fairly easily to Table Rock Dam and Table Rock Fish Hatchery

Reeds Spring

An even tinier Ozark town (population 411) is also found near Branson, one without the architectural flair or consistency of Hollister, but charming in its own right, and with period buildings. It's been revived by several rather sophisticated entrepreneurs, populated mainly by artists and artisans (potters, painters, weavers, and the like), and now sports an art gallery managed by Jeannett Bair (New Coast Gallery & Cafe Expresso), a local bar with old San Francisco Haight-Ashbury-style posters and psychedelic art (Fernando's Hideaway), shops of standard American art, clock-work and carvers, The Old Barn (for Ozark gifts), the Sawdust Doll (for unique dolls, highly regarded), a Hungry Hunter Restaurant, a Mennonite women's restaurant serving sandwiches and salads (all under $5), flea markets, and outlets for sugar-cured hams and Ozark baskets along the road.

Don't miss the expansive estate of the former mayor of Reeds Spring built into a hillside just across from Sawdust Doll; its high-lights are American eagle motifs, attractive gardens, terracing, and sculpted birds. Altogether a charming town, fun to browse. You reach Reeds Spring by simply continuing west on West Highway 76, past Shepherd of the Hills Homestead and Theater, and past the terrible commercial eruption represented by the town called West Branson (whole areas paved over, like in the inner city of a declin-ing American metropolis); Reeds Spring is about 2 miles farther on, on State Highway 13.

The Ralph Foster Museum

College of the Ozarks
phone 417/334-6411

Though some of its exhibits have nothing to do with the Ozarks (stuffed polar bears, African birds, a 1931 Rolls-Royce), this three-story museum on the campus of the College of the Ozarks (across Lake Taneycomo from downtown Branson) is nevertheless the closest thing the region has to a serious collection of its major natural and historic artifacts. They range from the actual car filmed in the "Beverly Hillbillies" TV hit of the 1960s (a cutdown version of a 1921 Oldsmobile), to a 19th-century log cabin dismantled from its location several miles away and moved here, to sketches of the classic Kewpie Dolls created in 1908 by Ozark resident Rose O'Neill, to paintings of the area, and documents of its history.

I find the total impression charming and am especially taken by its Ozark Mountain Music Pioneers Hall of Fame, its old Andy Williams shows on video, its sobering photos of Country Music Boulevard from just a few years ago. The residents smile when they call this the "Smithsonian of the Ozarks," but they may not be kidding. You'll want to visit for the articles and relics relating to Branson, its wonderful displays of primitive Americana (ploughs and quilts, stone corn-grinding machinery), but probably not for the other general collections donated over the years by various local contributors.

The museum was given its major funding and collections by Ozarks radio magnate, Ralph Foster, who dreamed of a country music radio station that could reach every "deer lick, rabbit warren, and hawg waller" in the area; one of the two stations he founded is called KWTO, after "Keep Watching The Ozarks."

Hours are 9am to 4pm, daily except Sunday, and admission is $5 for adults, $4 for seniors, free to high-schoolers and children.

Branson's Civil War Museum

Shepherd of the Hills Expressway
Phone 417/334-1861

About 200 yards from the Shoji Tabuchi Theater and next door to the ultra-cheap Ozark Mountain Buffet, this is a serious, subdued presentation of Civil War artifacts, including both Union and Confederate uniforms, arms, old newspapers, historic photographs, the clothing of women of that time, the kits and camping equipment of both officers and line soldiers. All of it is authentic and original, in a quiet establishment that makes no effort to emulate the show business glitz down the street.

Be sure to have an attendant point out the museum's two most significant items: the frock coat of Confederate General Joseph Shelby of Missouri, and the uniform of Union Major General Benjamin Butler. The exhibits, surprisingly enough, are all from one private collection, that of the individual who owns the museum.

Hours of operation are 9am to 6pm Monday through Saturday, 1pm to 6pm Sunday, and admission is $4.25 for people 13 to 55, $3.75 for seniors, $2.50 for children 7 to 12.

Horseback Riding at the Krazy Horse Ranch

Surprisingly enough, Branson still has a giant (1,500 acres) working ranch (Krazy Horse Ranch & Railroad Park) less than a quarter-mile from its city limits, whose entrance is on Shepherd of the Hills Expressway, downhill from the Shenandoah Theater at the bottom of the canyon, where you'll quickly spot the western-style sign and ranch buildings. It's equipped with numerous riding horses, a large staff of capable riders and instructors, stagecoaches, and the Civil War train that was featured in the film, *The Blue & The Grey* (the train is in its early stages of operation, and will eventually be supplied with a track enabling it to make longer runs than at present). Various riding formulas are offered: a one-hour ride for both adults and children 5 years and up, $12.50 (younger children can share a parent's saddle for half price); a two-hour breakfast ride to a chuckwagon cookout area where participants receive a full ranch breakfast, $25; a three-hour dinner ride (ending with steaks, baked potatoes, cobblers, ice cream, iced tea, and more) to a more remote cookout area for $30 (with older folks able to substitute the stagecoach for a horse). For detailed information, phone 417/334-5068 or 417/334-5080.

Showboat Branson Belle

Table Rock Lake
phone 800/282-2489 ext. 2

Brand new for 1995 is a large and authentic, four-deck-high, 1,000-seat paddle-wheel riverboat built by Kenny Rogers and the Silver Dollar City organization to make several two-hour cruises daily on Table Rock Lake. It's about the only new boat of its kind in America that was not designed for casino gambling, and the advance literature for it, issued by Rogers and Silver Dollar City, continually repeats their pledge that no gambling of any sort will ever take place upon it.

Rather, the *Branson Belle* is designed as a showboat. There will be breakfast, luncheon, and dinner cruises always involving a meal on board served to passengers seated in a theater ballroom; passengers will dine as they watch a reenactment of the life of a turn-of-the-century White River family; and at other times will stroll the decks of a ship that's the equivalent in height of an 11-story building, and almost the length of a football field. Because the *Branson Belle* will sail for the first time in April 1995, shortly after this edition of our guidebook has gone to press, there's no way to review it, or know its prices and exact hours of operation, at this time. But it will be a major addition to the Branson scene, bringing a seagoing experience—akin to that of a cruise ship—to the landlocked Ozark town.

What's already known is that the season for the boat will be April through December, and that it will depart from White River Landing on Table Rock Lake, about 8 miles from the center of the Strip. From West Highway 76, passengers will drive along State Highway 165 south, then pass over Table Rock Dam, passing the Dewey Short Visitor Center for the dam, as well, and there they'll see signs for the turnoff to the dock for *Branson Belle.* If you'd care to make advance reservations, or contact the organization for any other purpose, you can write to Showboat *Branson Belle,* c/o Silver Dollar City, HCR 1, Box 791, Branson, MO 65616-9602.

Cruising the Polynesian Princess on Table Rock Lake

HC1, Box 770
Branson, MO 65615
phone 417/334-4191

Another sleek, new, sightseeing and dinner boat built as recently as 1994, this one operates a 1½-hour sightseeing cruise on Table Rock Lake at 10am daily from May 1 to October 30, and then does a 1½-hour dinner cruise (Polynesian entrees and desserts, much like a Hawaiian luau, and rather upscale, plus Polynesian entertainment) at both 5pm and 8pm daily from May 1 to October 30; friends from Branson who have sailed upon it are enthusiastic about the quality of the food. The departure dock is at Gage's Long Creek Marina on Table Rock Lake near Branson, reached by taking Highway 65 south to Highway 86, and turning west on 86 to reach the marina. Rates for the sightseeing cruise: $10 for adults, $9 for children 4 to 12. Rates for the dinner cruise: $23 for adults, $21 for children. And incidentally, the same Gage's Marina, about 7 miles south of Branson, is an excellent source of rental boats of every sort for your own recreational use on Table Rock Lake. It has 18-, 21-, and 24-foot Sun Trackers, Bass Trackers, Ski Boats, and more, and will provide rental information to people phoning 417/334-4860.

The Sammy Lane Pirate Cruise

The Sammy Lane Boat Line
280 N. Lake Drive
phone 417/334-3015

The reference, as we've pointed out before, is to Samantha (Sammy) Lane, heroine of Harold Bell Wright's *The Shepherd of the Hills,* and the boat bearing her name and operating that 70-minute scenic ride (on which participants are attacked by pirates, guaranteed) leaves from a dock near the foot of Main Street in downtown Branson. The "river" you'll see there is Lake Taneycomo (turn left along it, to reach the dock), which became a lake when its two ends were dammed, though it still looks more like a river. The trip has been operated for many years, to become a tradition in Branson, and the children who join it are permitted to help the captain steer the boat, save the ship from a fiery pirate, meet slow-witted Elmer (that ubiquitous Ozarks clown), and visit the Boston Ridge Gold Mine. But plenty of adults without children also sign on.

Departures are daily from April 23 to October 16, daily until September 5, then daily except Wednesday until October 16, and boats depart nearly every hour from 9:30am to dusk. Prices: $6.95 for adults, $4.50 for children 3 to 12, $6.50 for seniors 60 or older, free for children under 3.

Lake Queen Cruise

280 N. Lake Drive
phone 417/334-3015

An alternative cruise on Lake Taneycomo is offered on the larger (140 passengers), two-deck-high, paddle-steamer, the *Lake Queen,* seven days a week in season; and tickets are sold from the same dock that services the *Sammy Lane* cruise. The breakfast cruise ($12.95) is at 9am (featuring eggs, bacon, sausages, biscuits with gravy, hash browns, fruit, muffins, juice, and coffee)—reserve the day before, by 7pm; sightseeing cruises ($6.95) are at 11am, 12:30pm, 2pm, and 3:30pm; and the dinner cruise ($16.95) is at 5pm (beef, ham, chicken, or fish, rice pilaf, garden salad, vegetable, dinner rolls, tea, coffee, and hot cobbler for dessert)—reserve the day before, by 2pm; the dinner cruise comes back to dock in more than enough time to make an 8pm show. Generally, the *Lake Queen* seems to me to attract an older audience than the parents-with-children who go on *Sammy Lane*'s.

Ripley's Believe It or Not!® Branson Museum

West Highway 76
phone 417/337-5460

Ripley's Believe It or Not!®

The world's largest ball of string (6 tons). An actual shrunken head. A 30-foot stretch limousine with a heart-shaped Jacuzzi in the trunk. An 8-foot model of an aircraft carrier made from matchsticks. A car of the future, with wings and propeller. Except for the exhibits associated with (and contributed by) Branson's own country music celebrities, you've seen it all before, in Ripley Museums scattered around the nation. It's 14,000 square feet of exhibits, in a fanciful building looking as if it has just cracked in half from an earthquake, and it is open daily throughout the year from 9am to 10pm, for an admission charge of $8.95 for adults, $5.95 for children 4 to 12. Location: directly on the Strip, West Highway 76, one block west of Highway 165 and Gretna Road.

The Stone Hill Winery

Highway 165, two blocks south of West Highway 72
phone 417/334-1897

An enjoyable hour of instruction in wine making, including a free wine tasting at the end (children get grape juice). It's sponsored by Stone Hill Wines, whose award-winning reds, whites, blushes, champagnes, and spumantes are distributed only in Missouri, Kansas, and Illinois, but have a big following here. Stone Hill is headquartered in the historic, well-preserved town of Herman, Missouri, about 1½ hours from St. Louis, and also has its vineyards and fermenting operations near Herman. (It has been there since 1847, when immigrants from the German Rhineland began the operation.)

Here in Branson, they do bottle the slightly carbonated Stone Hill spumantes, but do nothing else other than present this tour, which is totally free of charge, and conducted every 15 minutes from 8:30am to dusk (Sunday from noon to 6pm), throughout the year. You're shown a movie on wine-making, hear an entertaining (and quite informative) lecture, then proceed to the tasting room where you can drink a reasonable amount of Stone Hill wines.

The Ozarks Discovery IMAX Theater

Shepherd of the Hills Expressway
phone 417/335-4832

And now we're taking you indoors again for a worthwhile change of pace, to a large structure seating 530 people and housing a six-story-high motion picture screen. On it are cast films similar to the ones (like *Flight*) you'll see in the Smithsonian Institution in Washington, D.C.: giant, all-enveloping images of natural wonders, scientific phenomena or events of world importance. The films are shown hourly from 8:30am to 9:30pm from March to May 31, and August 29 to December 31; and from 8:30am to 11:30pm from June 1 to August 28.

All but four of the showings are of the theater's classic, *The Grand Canyon and Its Neighbors*. One other, a two-hour showing at 7:30pm, is of *Titanica,* relating the history of that maritime tragedy, and the subsequent filming of the ship at the bottom of the North Atlantic. At three other showing times, the film is *Speed: Man's Quest to Go Faster,* depicting advances in transport from the bicycle to the Blue Angels (an aerial flying team). I've seen *Titanica* and found it quite absorbing. Tickets to *Grand Canyon* or *Speed* are $8 for adults, $4.75 for children 3 to 12. Tickets for *Titanica* are costlier (because it's a two-hour film): $12 for adults, $6 for children, discounts at all times for seniors or AARP members. The IMAX is located on Shepherd of the Hills Expressway, just a short distance from West Highway 76.

Mutton Hollow Entertainment Park

Shepherd of the Hills Expressway
phone 417/334-4947 or 800/531-7893

A somewhat smaller version of Silver Dollar City, located much closer to town, off the junction of West Highway 76 and Shepherd of the Hills Expressway. It's open 9am to 5pm daily and is meant for a three- to four-hour visit of shows, shopping, and dining. There are both breakfast and dinner shows of country music (breakfast guests enter at 8am, ahead of normal opening hours and are entertained by "Tom & Jaynee" starting at 8:30am), other outdoor country shows, 30 specialty shops, craftspeople demonstrating their skills, flower gardens, and a "county fair" for children, with Ferris wheels, merry-go-rounds, a miniature train, and other rides.

Periodically throughout the year, various ethnic festivals are scheduled for the park (like a German/Polka Festival for September/October in the year just past), and both the music (polkas, in that case) and food (bratwurst and wienerschnitzel) follow the theme of the month. Admission to the park is $9.95 for adults (much less than at Silver Dollar City), $3.95 for children 4 to 11, and additional charges of $7.95 for adults and $3.95 for children are assessed for having breakfast at the breakfast show.

Talking Rocks

Branson West
No phone

The other great cave of the Branson area, and second only in popularity to Marvel Cave on the grounds of Silver Dollar City, this one is quite a bit smaller than Marvel Cave, but also—in my hesitant view—more attractive inside, with numerous stalactites and stalagmites resulting from eons of "dripping;" it is also somewhat less worn and abused from the footsteps of visitors than is Marvel Cave. Anyway, lovers of spelunking will love it, even though they pay an admission fee: $7.95 for adults, $4.95 for children 5 to 12, free for children under 5. Talking Rocks is on a 411-acre site, near the town called Branson West. Simply drive out on West Highway 76, and turn left on State Highway 13, where you'll soon see the signs. The cave is open daily throughout the year, except for December 15 to January 15, from 9:30am to 5pm.

Indian Point/The College

I have also enjoyed driving over to the Indian Point peninsula that juts into Table Rock Lake, mainly to see the rustic lodges in lakeside settings that a great many wise and experienced visitors choose in preference to hotels and motels in the built-up areas of Branson. Here also is the Indian Point marina (phone 417/338-2891) with boats and jet skis for rent. You drive out on West Highway 76, and just beyond Inspiration Point (the tower of the Shepherd of the Hills complex), you'll see the turnoff point for the verdant, forested Indian Point, with its many log cabins, bungalows, and modern condos with balconies overlooking the lake. Most of the resorts here—especially Eagle View Cottages, Trail's End Resort, and Indian Point Lodge—will be happy to let you inspect their properties, maybe in the hopes of an eventual future stay by you.

Returning to downtown Branson, and then proceeding across Lake Taneycomo to the campus of College of the Ozarks, I also find it pleasant to visit the several structures of that institution (a chapel, a restored Ozark grist mill, an actual dairy farm with

Holstein herds, a library, and a learning center for art shows and lectures); its students, in addition to having academic qualifications, are accepted primarily for reasons of financial need, and then given campus jobs or jobs with campus industries to earn their tuition, room and board for the four years of undergraduate study that lead to a B.A. or B.S. This is an interesting, self-conducted tour made independently of a separate visit to the school's Ralph Foster Museum, described earlier in this chapter.

Attractions Just for Children

Five different go-cart tracks, called *Tracks*, are located up and down the Strip, at locations determined by phoning 417/334-1612. The same Tracks operate bumper boats. An alternative location for go-carts, but also bumper cars, batting cages, game room, and virtual reality devices, is at *Thunder Road*, phone 417/334-5905. Bungee jumps are also at the aforementioned Thunder Road, but more prominently at *Outback Bungee* at 1924 West Highway 76 (the Strip), phone 417/336-JUMP.

Mini-golf courses and rides for children 2 to 8 are at both *Candy World*, 3425 West Highway 76, and *Kids Kountry*, 2435 West Highway 76; the latter operates a small Ferris wheel and train, as well. Other mini-golf courses are at *Gator Golf* at 3335 West Highway 76, *Kids Kountry* at 2435 West Highway 76, and *Lost Mine* at 2515 West Highway 76. The *76 Mall Complex* has an indoor mini-golf course for rainy days. And finally, Adventure Golf, a rather difficult mini-golf course for both adults and children, is available at *Pirate's Cove*, 2901 Green Mountain Drive, a bit east of Route 165, phone 417/336-6606. You putt your way through mountain caves, over footbridges, and under waterfalls, on two 18-hole courses designed for everyone. Rate for playing one 18-hole course (requiring a bit more skill than the other): $6; for the easier course $5.50; for playing both $10. Pirate's Cove is open seven days a week from 9am to either 10pm or 11pm, depending on the season, and is clearly my favorite among the mini-golf courses, but only for visitors over, say, 11 or 12 years of age.

9

The Shops, Stores, and Malls of Branson

What's Outstanding, What's Inexpensive

For the casual tourist to Branson, the really special shopping opportunities—the unique ones, the kind you won't find at home—are (1) Engler's Block, at 1335 West Highway 76, a mile away from downtown Branson, at a point just before the crowded Strip begins; and (2) the arts and crafts stores of Silver Dollar City, about 9 miles from the outskirts of Branson. Apart from those, you'll find several large manufacturers' discount outlet centers indistinguishable from dozens you've seen elsewhere (but it's relaxing to spend the pretheater hours at one of them, searching for a bargain or two); a rather elegant upscale shopping complex called the Grand Village, alongside the giant Grand Palace Theater on the Strip (it features home furnishings, CDs, records and books, handsome and fashionable clothing); a downscale crafts center; a whole bevy of cheaper and rather standard shopping malls; a large Wal-Mart; and my own particular favorite, Dick's Five and Dime, in downtown Branson, the authentic re-creation of a 10-cent-store of the 1930s.

We'll visit them in order of preference.

Engler's Block

Engler's Block (1335 West Highway 76) is the collective name for some 30 arts-and-crafts stores, all of them opening into each other, in a labyrinthine single building that seems to be several smaller buildings (but isn't) on a section of West Highway 76, about a mile from downtown Branson, just before the Strip begins; you park your car and enter from the bottom side (toward downtown Branson).

It began as the woodworking shop of master carver, Peter Engler, who had earlier won fame as an on-site Ozarks woodcarver at Silver Dollar City. He was so successful there that he soon opened his own shop at this location, and then, over the years, progressively rented out 30 adjoining spaces (all connected to one another by large doors or arches) to other artisans. Today, although Engler's remarkable wood sculptures dominate the complex, his own products are matched in quality by numerous other crafts on display, ranging from country fudge cooked before your eyes, to unique Christmas ornaments, to Ozarks-made-and-designed home furnishings, to glassware blown from the molten material within the store, to lace, to full-scale Cigar Store Indians (offensive wooden sculptures of an expressionless Native American holding a packet of cigars—a medium- to large-sized example costs from $1,000 to $2,000, but cheaper smaller versions are also on sale).

Of particular distinction is a bookstore here specializing in regional publications and tomes, including the Works Progress Administration–produced guidebooks to American locations published during the Depression of the 1930s, the latter being collectors' items. Engler's Block is a remarkable institution with homemade products you won't find elsewhere, and it's a worthy sightseeing attraction, as well. Wayne's Gravel Bar Restaurant is in the back (and described in our restaurant chapter). Note that most shops here do *not* accept American Express credit cards. Engler's Block is open seven days a week, free of admission charge; call 335-2200 for current hours.

The Performing Craftsmen of Silver Dollar City

In an earlier chapter on Branson's daytime attractions, I described the important turn-of-the-century theme park of Branson called Silver Dollar City, on the outskirts of Branson, dedicated to reviving the culture of the Ozarks. Scattered about Silver Dollar City are cabins and other structures occupied by artisans and craftspeople whose handmade products are on display and for sale at reasonable prices (though each is a one-of-a-kind item).

What's most distinctive about these shops is that their proprietors and salespeople are the actual creators of the products, and each is on hand throughout the day, actually creating the wares that will eventually leave his or her lathe, carving knife, potter's wheel, or glass-blowing pipe to be placed on tables for sale. Like those of the similar "performing craftsmen" (some are women) of Engler's Block, the products here are of such quality that the area becomes a museum as well as a store, inviting sightseers' attention.

When you do pass by, look for the following particular artists who all belong to the Society of Demonstrating Craftsmen of Silver Dollar City, and whose work has been the subject of a recent special exhibition at the well-regarded Springfield (Missouri) Art Museum: Jim Adam (a former executive of the Ford Motor Company, he's now become a maker of wooden toys at Silver Dollar City, and grins delightedly when you ask him about his change of profession); Doug Andrews (award-winning master toymaker here); Terry Bloodworth (for 16 years, an accomplished master glassblower); Warren Cook (woodworker), Dan Deckard (a sculptor in glass); Karen Horn Deeds (a decorative artist of toys); Ray Johnson (a bladesmith, maker of knives, in an ancient technique known as Damascus); Joyce Huth (who demonstrates the art of candlemaking); Steve Miller (a blacksmith who learned his trade from his father and grandfather; he makes ironware for fireplaces and gates); Todd Nelson (master potter, but in porcelain as well as stoneware); George Stiverson (floral and other designs on glass); and Bill Thompson (a leatherworker). All told, there are 100 resident craftspeople at Silver Dollar City, in 44 separate shops. I've reported on them at such length so that you may have an adequate picture of the high caliber of the retailing activities here.

Silver Dollar City is open daily except Monday and Tuesday from April 10 to May 20, seven days a week from May 21 to October 30 (from 9am to 7pm until August 21, then until 6pm); and Wednesday through Sunday, except for Thanksgiving, from November 9 to December 23. Admission is $23 for adults, $22 for seniors 55 and older, $14 for children 4 to 11.

Branson's Other Shopping Opportunities

Though our two opening selections are of particular merit, the shops of Branson possess several other standouts.

The Grand Village

2800 West Highway 76, next door (although across a street) from the Grand Palace Theater, phone 417/336-SHOP, open seven days a week from 9am to 8pm.

Owned by the Silver Dollar City organization, this is a rather upscale shopping center in a delightful simulated village setting of 28 shops in nine buildings clustered about a cobblestoned central square that could have been lifted from Charleston, South Carolina; there are peaked roofs and dormers, high-quality facades, and a Village Cafe for cakes and pastries, an amusing Hard Luck Diner for full-scale meals. Products are not handcrafted, but rather a well-selected stock of women's and men's clothing, home decorating items, resort and Western wear, novelties, and a large, comprehensive selection of books, at my own favorite shop. Prices are reasonable for high-quality goods. You'll enjoy strolling about the complex, even if you're not in a shopping mood. The Grand Village is directly on the Strip, across a side street from the same organization's Grand Palace Theater.

Factory Merchants Outlet Mall

On Gretna Road five minutes from the Strip, phone 417/335-6686 for the main office. Open 10am to 6pm daily in January and February, from 9am to 9pm on Monday to Saturday in March through October, from 9am to 6pm on Sunday in that period; and from 9am to 8pm on Monday to Saturday in November and December, 9am to 6pm on Sunday.

Currently Branson's largest discount shopping mall of this type, consisting of 80 independent manufacturers' outlets in a sprawling and rather undistinguished (and strictly utilitarian, which lends to its appeal), two-story, arcaded building under an orange-red roof. It will be given a hard battle by the new Tanger factory outlet opening in 1995. Some sample names of its member shops will give you the flavor: Farberware, London Fog, Van Heusen, Corning Revere, The Book Warehouse, Banister Shoe, Hush Puppies, Evan-Picone Fashion, L'Eggs/Haines/Bali, Oshkosh B'Gosh, Socks Galore, Toys Unlimited.

Like a dozen others you've seen, offering bargain rates on familiar brand-name merchandise; its merchandise is generally, and with some exceptions, better than what you'll find in the Branson Mall directly on the Strip, although the latter has a large Wal-Mart that generally beats everyone on price (for the less distinguished brands). As we've noted above, Factory Merchants Outlet will soon face major competition (by mid-1995 at the latest) from the sprawling, new Tanger discount complex, with its own entrance road running directly off the Strip; that access road is directly across the street (West Highway 76) from the Andy Williams Theater, and adjacent to Peppercorn's Restaurant. Phone 800/4-TANGER for more information.

Coffelt County Crossroads

Highway 165, just a short distance from the Strip (100 yards farther on from the Pump Boys and Dinettes Theater, on the right as you drive away from the Strip).

And then there's my own cherished source for buying cheap, corny, Ozarks-style gifts for friends back home when I'm tired of the more dignified, upscale crafts centers of Branson. A self-described "Flea Market and Crafts Village," the Coffelt County Crossroads is nothing but two lines of wooden huts, sheds, and tables under canvas on either side of a dirt road jutting off from Highway 165. Yet this unpretentious (to put it mildly) poor man's "mall" has become such a minor sightseeing attraction of the area that touring motorcoaches now include it as a stop.

Almost everything is handmade by people from the area; they produce "down-home" items. Mainly you buy handcrafted wooden jokes: porch signs that read "Home of One Nice Person and One Old Grouch," amusing wooden mobiles, plaques, magazine bins, birdhouses, lawn decorations, $4 cedar boxes, simulated gravestones ($12.95) that say, "Here lies the last dog that pooped on my lawn"; but also homemade country quilts at rock-bottom prices, "bandanna coolers," "pony beads." And don't miss the flea market in a big wooden barn with items you'll never see outside the Ozarks: second-hand fiddles, ploughs, old metal signs for chewing tobacco. The Grand Village, it ain't.

Dick's 5 & 10

103 W. Main Street, in downtown Branson, phone 334-2410, open daily throughout the year, 8:30am to 8:30pm, but opens a half-hour later on Sunday, and closes evenings in January and February.

A real-life, honest-to-goodness "dime store" of the 1920s and '30s, which has occupied this location since around 1920 (although under the name of Ben Franklin's General Store until 1961, when Dick Hartley bought the building and turned it into a five-and-dime). If you've ever experienced, or seen pictures of, those classic American variety stores in the days before the advent of Wal-Mart, you'll rub your eyes in disbelief as you enter the cluttered, compact, merchandise-crammed interior of Dick's, and turn back the clock to gentler days (the loudspeaker was playing Perry Como's "I'm Just a Prisoner of Love" when I last looked in).

Merchandise is an inventive selection, ranging from yellowing photos of old-time baseball stars ($2) to straw hats ($1.97) to hummingbird feeders ($3.99), hairnets (29¢), and bandannas ($1). There are tapes of Roy Clark, Glen Campbell, and Charley Pride for $6.99 apiece (cheapest in town), jars of Ozark honey and sorghum for $2.99, the *Old Farmer's Almanac* for $3.95. Don't fail to stop by; and when you do, you'll also enjoy browsing among dozens of other small independently owned stores and shops in downtown Branson.

Other Downtown Shops

A dozen other quirky shops of downtown Branson and the Lake Taneycomo waterfront, most along Main and Commercial Streets, whose intersection is the very center of town.

Though Dick's 5 & 10 is the highlight, 50 other downtown shops vie for attention with merchandise that often can't be found in the modern malls. I've described my own favorite dozen below.

Yours, Mine and Ours Pawn (119 E. Main Street, 417/335-2500) is the shop to which guitarists bring their high-quality musical instruments when their shows bomb; along the wall are stunning guitars averaging $125 for the acoustic variety, $175 to $200 for the electric kind, a poignant reminder that not everyone scores big in the Branson musical world. Workaday guitars for beginners (and fiddles, banjos, and dulcimers, too) sell for much less at **Mountain Music Shop** (109 N. 2nd Street, just before the intersection of West Highway 76 and Business Highway 65, and thus near the Main Street traffic light, 417/334-0515); several hundred factory seconds start at $49 for guitars of every sort, $99 for violins (with their cases and bows), $129 for mandolins. Mountain Music's proprietors claim they'll teach anyone to play the dulcimer in five minutes.

Paperback Exchange (114 E. Main Street, 417/334-8735, closed Saturday) sells used paperback books from 50¢ to $3.50, but for an average of only $2; Branson residents bring their old paperbacks here for exchange, and get credits against the purchase of another paperback. **Encore** (203 S. Commercial Street, 417/336-2059) sells "preowned" (i.e., secondhand) clothing, sometimes of celebrities, it claims. **The Body Hanging Shop** (111 E. Main Street, 417/337-5517) sells everything that you simply "throw on": shawls, scarves, capes, and cloaks, for both men and women.

The Fudge Shop (106 S. Business Highway 65, near the stoplight) sells the candies it has made in its own front window. **Christmas & More** (122 S. Business Highway 65, a half-block from Branson's traffic light, 417/334-1039) stocks small gifts and Christmas ornaments all year-round, a convenient time-saver. **Copywrights of Branson** (104 N. Commercial Street, 417/335-COPY) will reproduce your favorite photo on t-shirts, coffee mugs, aprons, and tote bags. And finally, four convenient flea markets offer a wide assortment of oddities sold to them by Bransonites; these are **Bits & Pieces** (204 N. Business Highway 65, 417/334-4564), **Flea Bag** (106 E. Main Street, 417/334-5242), **Caldwell's** (114 E. Main Street, 417/334-5051), and **Finders Keepers** (204 N. Commercial Street, 417/334-3248).

Unless otherwise mentioned above, most Branson shops are open seven days a week, at least from mid-March to mid-December.

10

The ABCs of Life in Branson

Important Miscellanies for All Your Needs

Often, on your trip to Branson, you'll need information that doesn't fit into the subject matter of our earlier chapters. This chapter attempts to remedy that problem by collecting and alphabetizing a large number of miscellaneous Branson services, and then presenting them to you in concise form.

Airport Limos: *See* ***Taxis.***

All-Night Pharmacies: Branson Drug *(101 East Main Street, in downtown Branson, phone 334-3187), stays open and has a pharmacist on duty "late nights" (as they explain it), and on Sunday, but not all night. No other pharmacy does, either; but the emergency room of* **Skaggs Community Hospital** *on North Business Highway 65 (phone 335-7000) will gladly handle your emergency needs for pharmaceuticals at any hour of the night. In daytime hours, the city's chief pharmacy is that earlier-mentioned Branson Drug (also called Branson Rite-Aid) at the corner of Main Street and Commercial Street, across from a major, but privately operated, Tourist Information office.*

Ambulances: *Call* ***911*** *in a dire emergency; otherwise call 334-1441.*

ATM Machines: *They're at the banks in downtown Branson, on Main Street, and on Commercial (where Capital Bank of Southwest Missouri is found, taking Cirrus and Plus System cards) and South Commercial Streets. There's one just outside the Consumers Supermarket at the Mall on West Highway 76 (where Wal-Mart is located). And more at other locations.*

Automobile Repairs: *Try* **John's Automotive** *on Highway 165, across from the Treasure Resort, phone 334-4931. For 24-hour towing, contact* **Big D's Auto Clinic,** *on East Highway 76, phone 334-5619 or 334-6317.*

Babysitters: *There is no organized central service for finding an evening babysitter, and most parents simply ask the front desk of their hotel to recommend an employee who might be willing to take on the task. The daytime child-care service listed below is not a source for evening babysitters, unfortunately.*

Barber Shops and Beauty Parlors: *Though one or two of the larger hotels maintain them, you'll pay normal prices by going instead to* **Chick's Barber Shop** *at 112 East Main Street in downtown Branson ($6 for a haircut) or to* **Hairitage** *(for women) next door at 110 East Main Street in downtown Branson ($12 for a wash and set). Both are patronized by local residents and seem thoroughly professional.*

Branson Information: *We've tried to fill this book with everything you'll need to know, but if there's something you need and still can't find, call the information service of the* **Branson/Lakes Area Chamber of Commerce**, *417/334-4136 or 1-900/884-BRANSON (the latter costing $1.50 a minute). As you'd expect, the first listed number is often busy.*

Child Care (or Day Care): **Play Pals Child Care Service** *in Branson, phone 336-2233; comes well recommended.*

Dentists: *Try the* **Branson Dental Center** *at 101 Skaggs Road, phone 334-6120, or 336-8478, but open only Monday through Thursday,*

7:30am to 5:30pm (its answering service will give you instructions for receiving help in a dental emergency); or try **Dr. Art Weigel** *at 114 West Adams, phone 334-7170 (same-day denture repairs, among many other services).*

Doctors: Branson Mediquick *is a walk-in medical clinic open seven days a week from 9am to 9pm, and staffed by Dr. Gordon Patterson, Dr. Roy Lee, and Dr. Allen Jackson, all M.D.s; they require no advance appointment, and deal with every malady and need from minor injuries to acute illness. They will also administer lab testing and X-rays on site. The location is a modern office building called Corporate View on Highway 165, across from Pointe Royal and the new Lawrence Welk Champagne Theater. Phone 337-5000. All major credit cards accepted.*

Gift Wrapping and Shipment: Ozark Postal Express*, 1316 West Highway 76, phone 335-4306.*

Health Club: *To keep up whatever regimen of exercise you've set for yourself, keep in mind that* **Club Roark** *(405 North Business 65, Branson 65616, phone 334-8090) has Stairmasters, Nordic Tracks, a Nautilus, free weights, occasional aerobics classes, a heated pool for "aquacise," a personal trainer and massage therapist on staff.*

Highway Emergencies: *Call the* **Missouri Highway Patrol** *at 800/525-5555, or, from the 417 area, call 895-6800.*

Hospital: Skaggs Community Hospital*, on North Business Highway 65 (phone 335-7000), is a modern facility with specialists in nearly two dozen medical fields, and a staff of nearly 500 people. Although the hospital offers traditional emergency services for traumatic accidents and serious sudden illness, it also operates a Minor Emergency Clinic for lesser problems; open noon to 10pm, seven days a week. You contact the Minor Emergency facility by entering the main Emergency Department at Business Highway 65 and Skaggs Road, where you'll see an admitting desk staffed by a nurse. Cost for a simple visit is $49, with laboratory, radiology, pharmacy, or supply fees added to the basic charge.*

Late-Night Dining: *Emerging from a show at 10:30pm, or thereabouts, it's awfully hard to find a meal; therefore, treasure the large steakhouse known as* ***B. T. Bones*** *on Shepherd of the Hills Expressway, about 2 miles down from Shoji Tabuchi's Theater (open until 1am, with last service at 12:30am), the* ***McGuffey's Restaurant*** *next to the Andy Williams Moon River Theater on the Strip (open until 1:30am every night of the week other than Sunday, when it closes at midnight), and* ***The Farmhouse*** *at 119 West Main Street in downtown Branson (open until midnight). I haven't mentioned McGuffey's Diner (see our restaurant chapter) on Violyn Drive because of uncertainty as to its months of operation.*

Laundromats (Coin-Operated): *Most motels have them. For guests staying in those that don't, there's* ***Koin-O-Matic Laundromat*** *at 1145 West Highway 76, in the Branson Heights Shopping Center, open seven days a week, phone 334-2507. You simply drop off your laundry; the attendant washes, dries, and folds everything, at a charge of $5.25 for the first load, $9.50 for the first two.*

Real Estate Brokers *(for buying homes in the Branson area): I'm impressed by the large photograph collections of homes for sale maintained by two downtown realtors:* ***Round the Clock Realty*** *at 107 East Main Street (most homes under $100,000), phone 334-1980; and* ***Table Rock Realty****, 100 S. Commercial Street, phone 334-3138.*

Reservations for Theater Tickets/Rooms: *There's a ton of them, so-called theater brokers and tour companies selling Branson packages. Keep in mind that you can always make your own direct calls to the theaters/hotels, and read a credit card number over the phone to secure your space. Still, if you'd like assistance, consider calling:* ***Ozark Country Vacations*** *at 417/335-2332;* ***Dee Tours to Branson****, 800/800-1882;* ***Country Connection Reservations****, 800/613-6800;* ***Ozark Prime Time Tours & Reservations****, 800/475-2519;* ***BransonTix*** *(apparently theater tickets only), 800/888-TIXS or 417/334-8497;* ***Branson Ticket and Travel****, 800/432-4202;* ***Fountain Head Tours****, 800/334-2723 or 417/335-2323;* ***Day by Day Tours*** *(owners of the Days Inn and Howard Johnson hotels in Branson), 800/871-9494;* ***SelecTix****, 800/947-3747 or 417/335-3132.*

RV Campsites: *Branson has a vast industry of organized RV campgrounds accommodating up to 11,000 people and requiring—ideally—a separate guidebook to describe them. One found, surprisingly enough, two blocks from the very heart of downtown Branson, alongside Lake Taneycomo, is the 325-unit* **Branson City Campground** *at 300 South St. Limas Drive, phone 417/334-2915 or 334-8857. The campground closest to Silver Dollar City:* **Indian Point's Deer Run**, *HCR 1, Box 1168-B, Branson, MO 65616 (phone 800/908-DEER), with 140 campsites and 50-amp full hookups; they operate a shuttle service to the music shows for a nominal charge. A particularly scenic campground close to the Shepherd of the Hills amphitheater and farm:* **Old Shepherd's Campground**, *West Highway 76, P.O. Box 97, Branson, MO 65616 (phone 800/544-6765 or 417/334-7692). A campground within walking distance of Cristy Lane's Theater, Box Car Willie, Jim Stafford, and John Davidson:* **Branson Shenanigans**, *3575 Keeter Street, Branson, MO 65616 (phone 800/338-PARK or 417/334-1920). And a campground off Highway 165 on the way to Table Rock Dam, but still close to the theaters:* **Chastain's RV Park**, *Route 8, Box 270, Branson, MO 65616 (phone 417/334-4414), the latter open year-round. All of those we've listed tend to charge from $15 to $18 a night for a full, 30-amp electric and water hookup.*

Taxis: *I've had good luck with* **Branson Cab Company** *at 334-5678, which charged a flat $65 for the one-way ride from an on-the-Strip hotel to the airport in Springfield, and arrived punctually for a 7:15am pickup. Alternatively, try* **Show-Me Shuttle Service** *at 800/795-7555 or 863-9111, which can sometimes do the same for less by combining other passengers with yourself. Obviously, most visitors will drive between Branson and Springfield in their own cars or rental cars.*

11

A Side Trip to Eureka Springs

Another Capital of Ozark Tourism, Across the Border in Arkansas

When residents of Branson need a rest or a change of scene, they often go to Eureka Springs, Arkansas, 50 miles away. It's a good choice. A city that cascades down the sides of steep hills, Eureka Springs is one of the most dramatic small towns in America—and one of the most charming, to boot, a place for reveries and relaxation. It has been called the "Switzerland of the Ozarks," the "Stairstep Town," but it is more than a place that simply goes up and down. It is one of the most perfectly preserved, turn-of-the-century locations in America, and therefore awesome in its Victorian elegance, with its pastel colors and gingerbread adornments.

Eureka Springs got that way because it died economically in the time just before World War I, and therefore missed the industrialization and frantic modernization that befell so many other more prosperous U.S. cities in the ensuing years. (It reminds one of Bruges, that Belgian metropolis that died economically in the 15th century, slumbered for several centuries to come, and therefore missed the Industrial Revolution, remaining in its magnificent medieval state.)

Prior to World War I, the renowned natural mineral springs of Eureka Springs had made the town into one of the most prominent spas of America, and luxurious pullman trains arrived at its station each day, bringing well-to-do health-seekers from other parts of the country. They came here to "take the waters" and thus cure or ward off a list of ailments ranging from arthritis to psoriasis to diabetes and cancer.

Magnificent Victorian hotels arose to house them. Glorious Victorian homes were built—many of expensive limestone—for tourists and patients who had decided to live permanently in Eureka Springs. When water cures lost their credibility in the face of other medical advances in the immediate prewar years, Eureka Springs died. And it was just as well: Wastes from a growing population had so polluted the springs that municipal authorities had decided to shut down many of them, in any event.

The Revival of Eureka Springs

In the years between the two World Wars, a Chicagoan named Marge Lyon wrote a series of admiring articles about Eureka Springs for the *Chicago Tribune,* and began attracting some interest to these rural parts. In 1947, an Ozark folk festival began here—well before country music theaters first began popularizing Branson—and attracted still others.

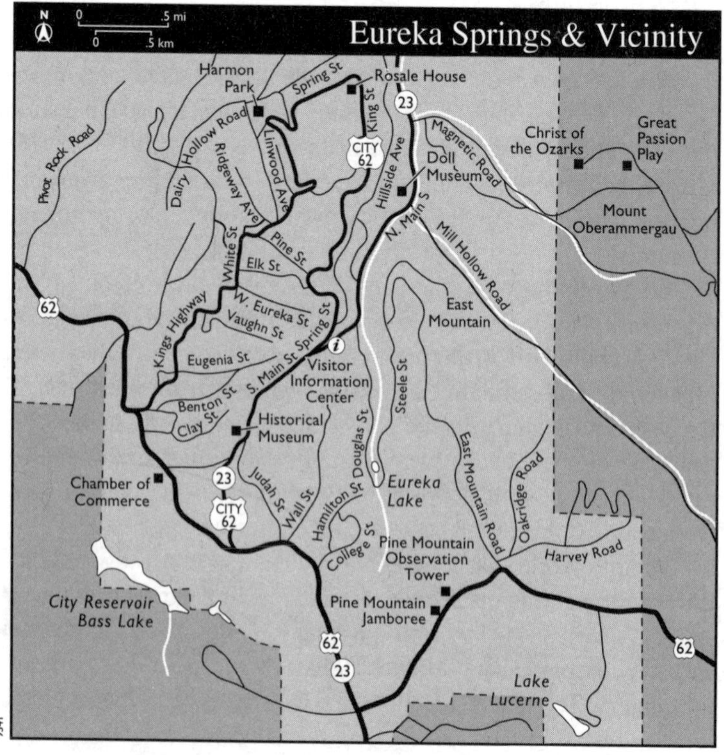

But it was the discovery of Eureka Springs by two diverse elements in the 1960s—one a social movement, the other an infamous, wealthy hatemonger—that caused the full revival of Eureka Springs. The movement was that of the so-called hippies; the individual was the late Gerald L. K. Smith, who decided to create a passion play on the outskirts of town. We'll provide you with a short biography of Smith later in this chapter.

The hippies found Eureka Springs while criss-crossing America; what attracted them was both aesthetics and economics. The town sat there, barely functioning, its hundreds of Victorian houses run-down and sometimes boarded up, all up and down the hillsides, its scores of business buildings in the same state in the twisty downtown. The houses were at that time inhabited by people too poor to invest in anything that might have made the town come alive again. The hippies, of course, didn't need a whole lot of money to live on. They liked the absence of commerce and industry. Land and buildings were available cheap. They started buying. The bush telegraph worked fine. More came. Downtown got resurrected hippie-style.

Smith's motivations are more difficult to discern. From California, where he published his violently bigoted newspaper, *The Cross and the Flag,* he somehow heard of Eureka Springs, moved here in 1964, and soon proceeded to build, with his own funds, *The Christ of the Ozarks,* a seven-story-high statue of Jesus Christ with outstretched arms, atop a 1,500-foot-high hill called Magnetic Mountain, visible both day and night from 10 miles away. Later it became clear that the statue was but the prelude to a giant amphitheater in which a passion play of Christ's last week on earth would be performed nightly. The play opened in 1968, was an immediate success, and attracted still another audience, about as different from the hippies as it is possible to get.

The two groups inhabited different parts of Eureka Springs, dividing the town into two radically different sections whose separation remains evident and important today. While downtown Eureka was becoming a hippie enclave in a haze of marijuana smoke, Highway 62 on a high ridge overlooking the city was being developed with motels to accommodate visitors to the passion play. People attending Smith's pageant weren't so much vacationing as they were observing a religious obligation. They didn't require much by way of overnighting. The motels they stayed in were plain, to put it mildly, and "plain" set the standard for Highway 62.

Two Different Styles

While the Highway 62 merchants were putting up these plain motels, the old-town hippies were opening bed-and-breakfasts. The B&B style, naturally, was handcrafted, full of detail, and idiosyncratic. It involved restoring the gingerbread trim of Victorian facades and ornamenting other features of them. Soon, the B&B entrepreneurs, the former hippies, began opening crafts shops. They sold art and earrings, began operating restaurants that offered pâtés or onion soup as the opening course.

For a time, people up on Highway 62 began improving their properties. While building larger and larger motels, and opening fast-food restaurants, they briefly initiated their own look, a pseudo-Swiss style of which you can still see imaginative traces. Mostly, the Swiss approach shows up near the western end of Highway 62 closest to the old town, where it set off controversy among old-town people who felt that the look wasn't authentically Ozarkian. But the same critics began to worry more recently about the eastern end of Highway 62, which was starting to resemble the Strip in Branson, Missouri.

True, that Highway 62 segment doesn't have Branson's 32 theaters. Only three so far. It doesn't have Branson's 180 motels. Only about 60 at last count. It doesn't have Branson's big discount shopping malls. So far, only a few little places that still pretend to sell Ozark crafts more than bargain Guccis. It doesn't yet even remotely resemble Branson's West Highway 76.

And yet, you are starting to see blacktopping at the side of Highway 62, where more care might have been taken to mask parking areas from the roadside. You are starting to see the kind of neon-dazzle, Me-First motel signs put up to make sure they're bigger than the signs put up by the last guy who opened. The forest that used to edge the road everywhere has been cut back—clear-cut in some cases. The cover of green that once made this roadside so attractive has become window dressing, trim, a perfunctory attempt to emulate the appearance of downtown.

Chamber of Commerce members, who own the highway motels, deny that Eureka Springs is at all in danger of becoming like Branson; downtown preservationists argue that the same economic imperatives that turned Branson into Branson—the ceaseless building of new motels, the cut-throat competition between them, the lack of aesthetic zoning and other regulations—are stealthily at work in Eureka Springs.

Each business group—the old town entrepreneurs and the highway developers—caters to a distinctly different kind of tourist. Up on the highway are mostly the passion playgoers, a generally older, more conservative, retired crowd. They look for inexpensive rooms, and find them on the highway, in the range of $40 to $60 a night, even in the high summer season. Competition keeps the rates down. These visitors stay a night or two. They go to the passion play, which runs from late April to late October, and catch a country music show (Eureka Springs has three of them). They ride the tourist trolley through the old town, buy a funnel cake or fudge, maybe a t-shirt or other souvenir. They can eat inexpensively at Bubba's Barbecue, Myrtie Mae's, or Sheridan's Ozark Buffet. For many of these visitors, the old town is simply a sightseeing attraction—a Victorian theme park (which is what most of the highway-oriented Chamber of Commerce officials would like to see the old town become).

By contrast, tourists to the old town tend to stay in bed-and-breakfasts. Eureka has dozens now, easily more than 50. (No one knows exactly how many because people are currently converting old houses from residential use to lodgings for transients on an almost monthly basis.) These visitors typically spend $100 a night in summer. They also ride the trolley around the loop, but tend to walk the loop also, and spend more in the shops. More than the passion playgoers, they buy art and authentic crafts. They eat in the better restaurants, of which there are several. Their composition is so different that the commercial interests serving them are in a near-constant state of opposition to the owners of the highway motels serving the passion play; it's an interesting part of the touristic experience to discuss these conflicts with the merchants and other residents you encounter in the course of your visit.

Eureka Springs Today

For the time being at least the old town holds its own against the covetous glances of the highway developers, who would love to route more and more tour buses through it, institute local-option gambling, or perhaps cap the number of B&Bs and cause some to shut down. It has more than 150 shops selling handcrafted items ranging from colorful quilts to corn-husk dolls to wood carvings and country clothing; the entire downtown area is now listed on the National Register of Historic Places. Everywhere are tiny gardens, outdoor band shells in larger parks, multiple museums of every collectible you can name (but also an important historical museum, with pictures of the old town in its heyday, and relics of its early inhabitants), a church where you enter through the bell tower, whimsical Victorian homes with their turrets and casements and funny gables sticking out in every odd direction. There are art galleries and fudge shops, fine restaurants and sidewalk cafes, a large botanical garden, and a restored railroad station from which excursion trains depart. And there are remarkable lodgings, if somewhat expensive ones by Ozark standards.

Overnight in Eureka Springs

My own stays have been at historic hotels and B&Bs of the old town, in preference to the motels of Highway 62, where the latter are slowly, slowly developing into a junior Branson. The old town resists conforming.

The Five, Grandly Historic Hotels of Eureka Springs

Few cities of this small size can boast such distinguished, antique properties. That they've been saved is due, in part, to the hippies of the '50s and '60s who respected Eureka's smaller heritage architecture and could afford its restoration but not its replacement. As these modest downtown efforts began attracting visitors who also valued heritage, the old hotels eventually attracted investors who began rehabilitating them and customers who appreciated their historic appeal.

Crescent Hotel

Prospect Street, Eureka Springs, AR 72632, phone 501/253-9766

Rates: Considerably cheaper than most other of the grand properties; rooms with one double bed are priced from a low-season $29 to a high-season $62, with king-bedded rooms renting from $49 to $80, respectively. AE, D, MC, V.

It dates from 1886 and the coming of the railroad: a grand heap of limestone block with a high-ceilinged lobby of old-fashioned, bold columns and upholstered seating, the walls with old newspapers describing a time when the Crescent was (extravagantly) said to be the most luxurious hotel in America.

Today its four floors offer 68 large rooms and suites, all carpeted, each with at least one upholstered chair, and furnished with Victorian reproductions. Each of the rooms is different, with a range of twin beds to king; some have balconies overlooking either the gardens to the front of the hotel or the broad view across the hills and hollows to *The Christ of the Ozarks* statue in the distance. Most bathrooms have tub showers.

The hotel's restaurant is a grand, old, high-ceilinged room where dinner entrees that include catfish, trout, ribs, chicken, pasta, pork chops, and steak are priced from $7 to $14. The hotel is best booked for its grounds and grand views; the rooms, though of a middling character, are still good value.

Palace Hotel and Bath House
135 Spring Street, Eureka Springs, AR 72632
phone 501/253-7474

Rates: From $103 to $121, double, year-round. AE, D, MC, V.

After the Grand Central (described below), this is the best of the restored grand properties. With its French-style dome, its canopied limestone facade, and its wonderfully high, antique neon sign out front like a misplaced movie set in between the old town's commercial and residential districts, it becomes all the more charming because of its anomalous setting. The lobby is a Victorian mix of high ceilings and bulky, highly textured wood paneling. Its eight suites on two floors are exceptionally large, furnished with beautiful antique king beds, upholstered pieces, ceiling fans, and mauve and chintz fabrics. Baths have been done in a mix of tiles and pedestal sinks, each with a Jacuzzi-style tub for two. Wet bars and refrigerators are included in each unit, and a turndown service is provided in the evenings, a free continental breakfast brought to guest suites each morning.

The mood is altogether European more than upscale frontier American, more relaxed than pretentious, and more authentically high style than, for example, the far less expensive Crescent. Downstairs, in the basement, there's a complete spa dating from the origins of the property when Eureka was known as "America's medicine teepee." The bath house, as it's called, includes eucalyptus steam taken in the same giant wood barrels that travelers to Eureka enjoyed at the turn of the century.

New Orleans Hotel
63 Spring Street, Eureka Springs, AR 72632,
phone 800/243-8630 or 501/253-8630

Rates: Year-round rates of $50 for a small double room, $69 Sunday to Thursday for queen- and king-bedded rooms, $80 to $100 on weekends and holidays; $5 per room increase in October; discounts usually available in late fall, winter, and early spring. AE, D, MC, V.

The New Orleans, second oldest (1892) of Eureka's grand historic "five," rates for quality in the middle of the grand hotels; it offers 22 fairly spacious rooms and suites on four stories, and declares its period with an antique children's barber chair in a front window and an antique register at the check-in desk. The high-ceilinged lobby could only have been designed well in the past.

Rooms on the three floors are done in period furnishings with at least one authentic antique in each room, the rest reproductions; the larger rooms come with a small fridge stocked with soft drinks; all rooms are carpeted and have self-making coffee units; and 19 of the rooms have Jacuzzis for two and showers (the three small double rooms are with stall shower only). No elevator.

Basin Park Hotel
12 Spring Street, Eureka Springs, AR 72632,
phone 800/643-4972 or 501/253-7837

Rates: Smaller rooms rent from $29 in low season, from $50 high; suites from $49 to $85, highest-priced suite from $99 to $125. Free parking. AE, D, DC, MC, V.

Architecturally the most imposing of the city's antique hotels, though its rooms don't quite live up to the promise of the exterior. The building, constructed in 1905 of local stone, rises eight elevator-served stories at the entry to Spring Street's most interesting section of shops. Each of its upper floors provides a "bridge walk" to the hillside behind it, offering a ground-floor entrance on each level—something once noted in Ripley's "Believe It or Not." Basic rooms are small, furnished with an occasional antique and otherwise inexpensive and reproduction furniture. Baths are mostly tub-showers (stall showers in the smaller rooms), though suites have Jacuzzis for two. Of the several antique hotels, the Basin Park is most frequently used by tour bus groups, and its interior is the least impressive of any.

Grand Central Hotel
37 N. Main Street, Eureka Springs, AR 72632, phone 800/344-6050 or 501/253-6756

Rates: $95 to $125 for two; two-bedroom/living room suites $155 for four. November through March rates considerably discounted. No elevator. AE, D, MC, V.

The oldest of Eureka's hotels (1883), it was designed as a retreat for railroad executives and their families, and is located close to the railroad station that's still in use for Eureka's excursion train. Though the plain red-brick facade hardly suggests the elegance inside—one wall has a stenciled "Aristos Flour" sign on it—the Grand Central is actually the grandest of Eureka's Victorian restorations.

All 14 guest suites are unusually large, with high ceilings and ceiling fans, period wallpapers, king beds, lavish reproductions of Victorian antiques, kitchenettes with dishwashers, whirpool tubs in bathrooms. They put you in mind of the better B&B restorations done with panache and fine detailing—they are homelike to those of the manor-born. Most suites are with imported English antiques; one has a five-piece, Hepplewhite-style armoire 8 feet long and 8 feet tall, a dresser, and a wash stand. Best of all, you enjoy one of the best views of downtown Eureka Springs at night, looking for all the world like a stage set. You can hardly imagine it's real and that you're here.

Eureka Springs' Most Gracious B&Bs

A Eureka Springs hotel clerk once told me that people come here "full of the world," then step into an old-city accommodation and "leave the world." Later, she said, they hate to return home because here "they've been allowed to dream." Nowhere can you experience that atmosphere better than in the gracious, period setting of a Eureka Springs bed-and-breakfast. Though they're far more costly than a motel, they leave you with memories.

Heart of the Hills

5 Summit Street, Eureka Springs, AR 72632, phone 800/253-7468 or 501/253-7468

Rates: One of Eureka's best buys at rates for a double room of between $69 and $89, including desserts provided nightly to each room, and full gourmet breakfast for two, served on the rear deck overlooking the woods or in the small dining rooms. The cottage rents for $109. MC, V.

An exquisitely shingled, bracketed pair of houses that together provide visitors with three guest rooms and a private cottage. With their steep gables, stained-glass windows, turquoise trimming, overhung porches with wicker furniture and neat shutters, a cream-and-gold sign with outlined heart, the house is fairy-tale perfect, one of the architectural wonders that makes touring the scenic loop of old Eureka the most agreeable way to spend time in this historic town.

Inside are such decorative pleasures as a hall tree that once belonged to a great grandmother of owner Jan Jacobs Weber. Her great uncle appears in a cameo portrait in sailor suit with boyish curls. A bouquet of artificial flowers ornaments a brass queen bed that is beribboned and full of frills. Elsewhere, a spindled staircase curves up to a loft where a pink-framed bed is backed by pink curtains. All around are books and puzzles and pieces of art of the sea—and hearts in every possible material and in great profusion. Each unit has its own sentimental decor, its own private bath, and is set with fresh flowers on arrival. The setting, which I've described in only partial fashion, is enchanting.

Primrose Place

39 Steele Street, Eureka Springs, AR 72632, phone 501/253-9818

Rates: $77 a night for "Princess Di's Suite," $89 for "Fergie's Flat," $150 for the "Gypsy Hideaway." Credit cards not accepted.

The two cottages for visitors in this hillside lodging are located alongside a lovely, old c. 1882, pink clapboard house with white trim that drops down a sharp slope. If the rose bouquets on the porch are false, next door in the terraced hillside garden are petunias, tulips, and other greenery, with pretty fountains. Also next door is the Little Eureka Antiques shop (a Second-Empire, grandly mansarded and dormered little structure) and the Carrie A. Nation House known as Hatcher Hall. A perfect setting, on a quiet street.

The Princess Di cottage has a handwoven floral rug in the entry room, which is a bedroom with a double Eastlake bed, a frilly pastiche with lots of primroses, lacy curtains over shades over windows, bric-a-brac on the walls, marbletop tables. The second room has a single twin bed, sofa, chairs, TV, and Victorian art. To the rear, perched high on the slope, is a charming breakfast room with fridge, stove, microwave, and coffeemaker. And, of course, pictures of Princess Di are strewn here and there to complete the fairy tale-like touch. Downstairs, the separate cottage called Fergie's Flat is equally detailed, equally picture-book-beribboned, blushed in roses and bits of fancy theoretically suited to a member of the royal family. A third suite, the Gypsy's Hideaway, with canopied king bed, wood-burning fireplace, VCR and stereo, Jacuzzi for two, and private porch, is even more luxurious.

Tweedy Cottage
16 Washington Street, Eureka Springs, AR 72632, phone 501/253-5435

Rates: Year-round from $79 to $125, depending on unit. All credit cards accepted.

A softly colored, modestly gray (but with peach-and-white trim), Cape Cod shingled and rustic house. It is on the scenic loop of Eureka Springs, and adds to the scene with eccentric asymmetry in its twin-peaked roofs and big porch. Inside, the house also asserts its character with impressive interior arches, some curved, some flat, some inset with stained glass. The house dates from 1883, and many Eurekans have taken piano and organ lessons here when it was owned by the music-teaching Tweedy family.

Of the five suites, Col. King's Suite is a bit formal, with old world prints, antiques, and fine decorator furnishings. It has a bay window that neatly accommodates the three-piece cane headboard of the room's bed. But the bathroom, with Jacuzzi tub and heat lamp, is totally modern. Other suites display a variety of Victorian antiques and details: footed tubs with beautiful old brass and porcelain fixtures, double vanities, wallpapers in green and white stripes and a matching canopy over the beds, white lace, pink carpets, wicker furniture, and a Metropolitan Museum of Art floral poster. In some of the rooms, innkeepers Lillian Freeman and Pamela

Williams have displayed sentimental memories of their families. One suite shows the framed Mother's Day card from Lillian's mother and father to Lillian's maternal grandmother.

The downstairs spaces, shared by everyone, are full of Victorian and Eastlake pleasures including an Eastlake fireplace, lots of sofas, and great bursts of artificial flowers. Here and there: the original wavy glass of the 19th-century house. Evening desserts are presented free to guests, and can be eaten on a deck for snacking or reading found high up, in back, in a forest. A full sit-down breakfast is served either in the breakfast room or on that same deck.

Sunnyside Cottage

5 Ridgeway Street, Eureka Springs, AR 72632,
phone 800/554-9499 or 501/253-6638

Rates: $80 to $125 per double room per night, year-round. No credit cards except as deposit.

A dashingly Tyrolean Victorian from 1893, with elaborate bracketing, fishtail shingling, and grand bays, and with entries at two levels because it backs onto a sharp hillside. It has been listed on the National Register of Historic Places since 1966. Of the six guest rooms, one is a honeymoon suite with a red, heart-shaped double Jacuzzi and wicker furniture, all ensconced behind an interior wall of limestone and furnished (yes, we're talking about the bathroom) in wicker. An adjoining "frontier" living room features Alaskan skins and hides, including those of a baleen whale and several wolves. Another bedroom features a bedroom suite from roughly the time of Abraham Lincoln. Another is late Victorian, with elaborate moldings and lots of lace curtains. Still another is all woody and cedar-framed, and comes with lovely knotty-cedar desk and panelings.

The woodsy dining room sits in a large bay with interior transom windows in stained glass. Breakfast is served here daily at 9am (all guests are served together) and typically consists of fruit, quiche, maybe grits and gravy, maybe waffles, sometimes cinnamon rolls. (Guests requesting an earlier breakfast receive a somewhat more limited selection.) And finally, this wonderful discovery-of-a-house has stained-glass panels in the entry door, beautiful interior pillars between the two sections of the living room, and very high and steep carpeted stairs leading to a turreted room with observation windows.

Ellis House and Trail's End
1 Wheeler Street (end of Wall Street), Eureka Springs, AR 72632, phone 501/253-8218

Rates: From $100 to $130 for a double room, year-round. You can request a discount, January through March, or during occasionally slow midweek periods. No smoking indoors. AE, MC, V.

A stunning Tudor home built in 1933 by the owner of an antique shop, then bought and made into a bed-and-breakfast in 1970 by Eureka banker John Cross, partly to display his collection of local art and antiques; if you can afford the price, it is the choice place to stay while in Eureka. Nowhere else enjoys such a magnificent view, one that causes your imagination to swirl. From this high hilltop, you see all of Eureka, its town hotels, its silver domes, its yellow or blue clapboard homes, its vertical brick buildings on the town's slopes, precarious as history among the forgetful—though in warm seasons largely obscured by the dense foliage. Multiple views claim your attention whether outside on the grounds or inside the house.

At breakfast (a fully cooked meal served on a former monastery table that shows the indentations where the monks rested their arms as they prayed), the glorious Palladian window off the dining room carries your thoughts across far hills. After entering across oak floors and past a library with local scenes in original art, you have a choice of five bedrooms, each with its own bath, four with Jacuzzis, one bath not inside its room but dedicated to it.

Guest rooms are spacious, done with antiques, and with unusual features. One has a tassle valence done by the wardrobe maker for the Maid of Cotton. Olive's attic suite is one of those with a splendid view of the old town. It also features a bathtub in the bedroom. Suite Doris has a carved Pennsylvania Dutch-styled dresser and handsome watercolors of the town. Most important, the attitudes of the staff make you feel more like a houseguest than a B&B customer.

Dairy Hollow House
515 Spring Street, Eureka Springs, AR 72632, phone 501/253-7444

Rates: Double rooms (actually, suites) for $125 to $155, year-round; $20 a night surcharge for holiday dates and throughout October. Required minimum stay of two nights on weekends, three nights over holiday dates.

Six suites furnished with such imagination that you feel enlivened upon first seeing them; you become a child again. When I recently stayed in the Summer Meadows Suite, I had a fireplace, skylight, and a bed fully recessed on a raised platform with curtains that completely closed it off. I almost felt like giggling "Can't see me!" On an earlier visit, I had slept in Spring Gardens, full of wicker furniture, a buttery yellow canopy bed, charming quilt, and a stuffed cow leaning against a soft buffer of bed pillows. The Tulip Room has a potbelly stove, rich pine plank paneling, cheerful red trim, lots of windows. The Rose Room, with its Victorian furnishings, has an antique clawfoot tub, a skylight, fireplace, and a view upon a forest all white with dogwoods, a tulip garden, a bubbling outdoor hot tub.

In a separate cottage, the Iris Room in the Farmhouse in the Hollow (a hidden-away, cherished, revived farmhouse) has a fireplace, a window seat, and again a garden view. And as a delightful dividend, each of the suites contains a remarkable collection of books (most recently, works by John Sayles, Susan Sontag, Cormac McCarthy's *All the Pretty Horses*, and selected prose, poetry, and children's books of co-innkeeper Crescent Dragonwagon, a much-published writer and teacher of writing). Dragonwagon and Ned Shank are the creators of this B&B masterwork.

Do open all the closets; they will reveal mounds of extra blankets, towels, and pillows. Baths are supplied with scalding hot water (so be careful) that flows like a flash flood, and with various kits containing every sort of toiletry.

Breakfast each morning is brought to you in a large straw basket beneath an oversized plaid napkin; you can make all kinds of special requests with the expectation of having them mostly fulfilled (like for freshly smoked catfish). A gift shop contains Crescent's own books and those of her mother, Dorothy Zolotow, along with herb tea samplers, country-packed foods, a corner of items for kittens. The great pleasure of Dairy Hollow House is that as an adult, you will appreciate this moment for feeling young again, and like a child, you are provided for with the care of adults who love you. The value is here, even if the rates are high; you are, after all, in suites.

A Less Expensive Motel Room

And finally, there are those many, many Eureka Springs motels on Highway 62 leading to the passion play. Though many are the essence of ordinary, or worse, a few are distinctive and can be recommended.

Tradewinds Motel
77 Highway 62 (also known as Kings Highway), next door to the official tourist information center, phone 800/242-1615 or 501/253-9774

Rates: From a low-season "low" of $24 per double room to a high-season "high" of $52, depending on supply and demand. AE, D, MC, V.

An excellent choice, this 17-unit lodging with detached and semi-detached units on the west side of the highway around town. These are not merely old-fashioned but charming, with screened porches overhung by high oak trees and flowering shrubs. Though they are close to the highway, they are quiet at night, and offer shag carpets, double beds, large baffled hanging racks, veneer paneling, tub-showers, direct-dial phone, cable TV, swimming pool, and picnic area—but unfortunately, only a single reading lamp. Free morning coffee in the lobby, a lovely forest just in back.

Eureka Matterhorn Towers
98 Highway 62 (Kings Highway), directly across from the Eureka Chamber of Commerce, where the trackless trolley stops, phone 800/426-0838 or 501/253-9602

Rates: The basic high-season ranges from $59.50 to $67 for a double room, the higher price for busy weekends. October rates are $10 to $15 higher, and mid-August to early September (except for the Labor Day weekend) rates decrease to between $50 and $65. Off-season (November through the third week in April), rates are $48 and $53, and the price throughout the year always includes continental breakfast and free morning newspaper. The few suites can go up to $107 to $114. AE, MC, V.

An exceptionally attractive lodging of 35 rooms and suites on the highway as the highway heads west beyond the main entrance to the old town. It reflects the Swiss architectural theming that for a time was in vogue in Eureka. Although Victorian purists revile the style as kitsch, I think it comes across tastefully, and with character, in this three- and four-story structure. The motel's sharply eaved exterior and pseudo bell tower are surrounded by attractive flower gardens, lawn, and flowing water.

The lobby and reception area, with fireplace and oil paintings, is a warm, glowing space, richly furnished in upholstered pieces, but not at all showy. Rooms are motel-like, but better. They are also larger than most motel rooms and include two fine upholstered armchairs, one with footrest. Typically, rooms have two double beds, two lamps, rustic (but not overly so) furniture, tile baths, real closets with doors, and full-length mirrors.

Fine Dining in Eureka Springs

Eureka has a great many high-quality restaurants, the best of which rate with those in far larger towns. You will find carefully marinated meats, subtle fish-stock sauces for your seafood plates, vegetarian fare on occasion, a growing reliance on organic produce, good wine selections, beautiful settings. And prices are considerably lower than in the bigger cities.

The restaurants that follow are, in my opinion, the best in town. Most are in the old town, a couple on the west side of Highway 62 around the town. Note, though, that none of the dining rooms in the grand old hotels are included; they're fairly ordinary.

We list restaurants in ascending order of cost, starting with our lowest-priced selections and proceeding upward from there. The symbols AE (for American Express), V (for Visa), MC (for Mastercard), DC (Diners Club) and D (for Discover) indicate the credit cards accepted by each establishment. The star symbol indicates that the restaurant is a special value in its price category.

Oasis
53-C Spring Street, "down the staircase,"
no phone

Open: Every day of the year from 10am to 3pm for lunch only. No credit cards.

An inexpensive, mainly Mexican restaurant in a hard-to-find hole-in-the-wall on one of Eureka's ladder-like connections between the lower town and the upper one. The lunchtime crowd is mostly locals who favor this casual, comfy, hippie-styled foodery that features Ark-Mex dishes. Only 11 tables in two woodsy rooms (think of these as two immense closets with a tiny open kitchen), their walls richly full of posters, from Matisse to the Eureka Blues Festival.

The place feels like it has been done on a shoestring, with prices to match (hardly any large platter over $5). Sign announces: "We'll cook fresh ginger into any dish, 50¢ extra—or garlic." Dishes are otherwise written on a green board with colored chalk. Lots of huevos rancheros (tofu choice available, $4), burritos ($2.65 to $3.25 to $4.25 for most), soft tacos made of corn tortillas filled with cheese, lettuce, tomato, onion, and salsa ($1.50 apiece), enchilada plates with cheese, chicken, eggplant, seafood ($4.25 to $4.74), salads. Bagels, too, and nondairy specials. Help-yourself coffee and tea: 65¢. No smoking at all.

DeVito's Restaurant

5 Center Street,
phone 501/253-6807

Open: Lunch and dinner daily except Wednesday. Closed January until Valentine's Day. Reservations accepted. Beer and wine. AE, D, MC, V.

Eureka's finest Italian restaurant, yet moderate in price, and tucked just off Main Street in a deep probe of the historic district. Intimate, with 10 tables in two sections up front, another five or six out back in the newly glass-enclosed, hot house–like porch with ficus tree and hanging baskets, overlooking a forest. Highly personalized mood. Restaurant is a hub for locals, of whom many try to work here because of owner James DeVito's civic-minded devotion to the old town. This Arkansas native (believe it or not, from Dogpatch in Newton County) and his wife, Susan, live above the restaurant. James may be the next Eureka Springs mayor. In his first try several years ago, he lost by only 14 votes out of a thousand cast.

The DeVitos serve traditional Italian specialties made with the freshest ingredients. Two excellent trout preparations are the trout Italiano (fileted, sautéed in olive oil, capers, sweet red peppers, and garlic, with a lemon zest herb spice topping, $14.95) and the boneless rainbow trout prepared with mushrooms, spices, and herbs, $12.95. A favorite of some: a vegetarian pasta plate redolent with fresh garlic and herbs and topped with seared grilled vegetables, $10.95. Phenomenal. Also outstanding: fettuccine DeVito prepared with sautéed, pimento-stuffed olives, fresh pressed garlic, cream

Parmesan cheese over fettuccine noodles, $10.95. Large angel-hair spaghetti plates with various sauces are much cheaper ($6.95 to $7.95 for most), and most chicken or veal entrees—big, filling plates—are $11.95 to $14.95.

Ermilio's Italian Home Cooking
26 White Street,
phone 501/253-8806

Open: Lunch and dinner daily except Thursday, and no lunch on Sunday. Closed Christmas. Reservations accepted. Beer and wine. MC, V.

Another popular, 60-seat restaurant on the upper portion of the scenic loop through the old town of Eureka Springs. Owner-chef Paul Wilson grew up in Eureka and then, after attending hotel and restaurant school and working 12 years for Westin Hotels, came back to Eureka to open Ermilio's in the early '90s. It's dressier now than when it opened, with floral drapes, black accents, checked-and-striped tablecloths—and a prominent new cappuccino machine.

Guests enjoy the old house setting and multiple choices from a big menu. Ermilio's offers the same appetizers, salads—even sandwiches—at both lunch and dinner, and at the same prices. Pastas, too, all but for the clam sauce version, are on both menus, but for pastas the prices differ between lunch and dinner, generally $2.50 to $3 less at midday.

Chef Paul offers eight different pastas at dinner, all for only $7.50 to $9.95 a plate, including a ricotta-filled ravioli and a ricotta-filled tricolored tortellini; each is garnished with Parmesan cheese and served with salad, fresh baked bread, and roasted garlic (though at lunch only with grilled garlic toast), and I find their $7.50 to $9.95 price something of value, especially considering that you can have them served with a variety of ingenious sauces (of which the two most popular are a basic garlic and olive oil version simply garnished with parsley; and a sauce primavera done with assorted fresh vegetables sautéed in garlic, virgin olive oil, and seasonings. Also served, but only at dinner, are a variety of more standard items: an 8-ounce filet, pan-seared in olive oil with red wine and tarragon sauce ($16.95, highest item by far on the menu), and such items as pork chops ($13.50), shrimp dishes ($12.95 to $13.50), and sole ($11.95) or grilled chicken breast ($11.95). There's a Tuesday and Friday eggplant Parmesan special, and a Wednesday and Saturday lasagna. Plus the usual Italian desserts priced at a top of $4 for the tiramisù, but only $2 for a refreshing, creamy, cool concoction of ice cream, a spumoni.

Cottage Inn
Highway 62 West,
phone 501/253-5282

Open: Daily except Monday for lunch and dinner, brunch only on Sunday 9am to 2pm. Reservations accepted. Full bar. MC. V.

Beneath big shady oaks just west of old Eureka at the edge of country is Linda Hager's wonderfully colorful, arty, bright, flower-filled, and fresh-feeling restaurant of eclectic, undefinable dishes. About 100 seats in several rooms, wood floors, big windows. What she does is offer imaginative preparations of foods chosen more for their individual appeal than for devotion to a particular ethnic cuisine.

Entrees (which all come with the filling accompaniments listed below, at no extra charge) include a mixed grill (shrimp, chicken breast, loin lamb chop served with pasta and vegetable), $14.95; shrimp à la grecque, $13.95; chicken Romano (breast of chicken breaded, with fresh Parmesan cheese, sautéed in olive oil on capellini pasta with marinara sauce and vegetable) for only $10.95; cheese tortellini ($8.95). There's a luxurious filet dijonnaise ($16.95), grilled mahi mahi ($13.95), seafood newburg ($12.95), roast loin of pork ($11.95). Priced at those moderate levels, and accompanied by soup or salad and homemade bread, some choices with vegetables, those plates are values. Totally à la carte choices include a pasta primavera ($6.95), grilled chicken Caesar salad ($7.95), and crab Louie ($7.95). Desserts, made fresh daily, are $3.50.

Plaza Restaurant
55 Main Street,
phone 501/253-8866

Open: Lunch and dinner daily. Closed Thanksgiving. Reservations accepted. Full bar. AE, D, DC, MC, V.

One of Eureka Springs' best, and the place for continental dining, the Plaza was converted in 1980 from a gas station to fine dining, but its origins still show in a winning way. Two enclosed dining rooms downstairs were once the drive-up station and the office behind, the two rooms separated by an attractive slanting wall partially converted to a wine rack. The look today is open beam, rustic—but designer rustic. From the front room you can look through multi-paned sash windows onto the little town outside, where weathered roofs over the years have acquired idiosyncratic slants—same as the restaurant's window frames have their own carefree angles. The effect altogether captures the free spirit of the old town.

Guests dine on filet mignons served with herbed rice, vegetable of the day, and French breads, $16.95; beef Wellington with the same side dishes, $19.95; grilled Pacific mahi mahi filet, again with the same side dishes, only $12.95; shrimp scampi so accompanied, $15.95; sautéed boneless pork tenderloin with accompaniments and a Pinot Noir sauce, $10.95. Cuisine tends toward the French, both nouvelle and traditional. Big wine list. Other entrees in the low- to mid-teens. About 60 seats in the two rooms, the same upstairs on the open deck under a canopy.

Dairy Hollow House
515 Spring Street,
phone 800/562-8650 or 501/253-7444

Open: Thursday to Monday from April through September, nightly in October, closed otherwise. Reservations advised. Beer and wine. AE, D, DC, MC, V. Note: two seatings on Saturday night in April through October, 5:30pm and 8pm.

★ Devoted to cuisine as imaginative as its guest lodgings, this is Eureka's top-rated culinary extravagance, a bit pricey by Arkansas standards. Three-course $25.95 prix fixe dinners are served Monday, Thursday, Friday, and Sunday, and a $36 six-course dinner is served at 5:30pm and 8pm on Saturday evenings, in the bright, airy, and festive, 45-seat, country dining room with spindle-backed chairs and a potpourri of Ozark crafts.

Country is what it is. Chairs are a light oak with denim and mattress ticking cushions. Tables are neatly set with white cloths and peach napkins, sparkling crystal, real silver. Service plates are blue-and-white collectibles with paintings of the gazebo at the Crescent Spring Hotel.

And the food? Entrees typically include recipes from the many cookbooks of owner Crescent Dragonwagon, always with vegetarian entree choices and a kitchen ever willing to cater to special diets. Among book-featured specialties available one night or another: potage Barcelona (Spanish-style spinach and split pea soup); breads made from scratch, and served with blue ribbon–winning inn-made preserves.

Entrees from the books and otherwise include a game hen Casablanca stuffed with oranges, olives, bay leaves, and dates, served with a cinnamon couscous; wine-braised "carpetbagger" pork chops stuffed with local smoked ham, bacon, shiitake mushrooms and herbs (and more); catfish Catalan, locally raised and prepared in a wine-and-herb-enriched sundried tomato sauce; and a mushroom stroganoff for the vegetarians in a rich sauce of vegetable stock and sour cream, finished with fresh-ground black pepper and nutmeg.

Desserts typically include three to five choices (à la carte on the three-course dinners), typically including some chocolate sin, inn-made sorbet, and a plate inspired by the season's freshest fruits. All are part of your three-course, $26 prix fixe dinner, which ascends to $35 only on Saturday night. For those who care about such things, the proprietors are FOBs (Friends of Bill); Bill and Hillary have more than once stayed at the inn, and supped on its remarkable food.

Cottage Inn

Our "Bistro Menu" includes a choice of soup du jour or green salad vinaigrette with all entrees. Served with homemade bread.

Dinner Menu

Entrees

Filet Mignon au Poivre $16.95
Choice filet mignon patted with cracked peppercorns cooked to order with sauteed onions. Served with pasta and vegetable

Filet Dijonnaise $16.95
Thinly sliced choice filet sauteed and served with a sauce of mushrooms, red wine, Dijon mustard, tarragon, and cream

Mixed Grill $14.95
Shrimp, chicken breast & loin lamb chop served with pasta and vegetable

Shrimp á la Grecque $13.95
Shrimp, artichoke hearts, tomatoes sauteed in olive oil and tossed with cappellini pasta, feta cheese, lemon, and garlic

Grilled Lamb Chops $14.95
Brace of loin lamb chops seasoned with mild herbs and grilled to order. Served with pasta and vegetable

Chicken Romano $10.95
Chicken breast breaded with fresh parmesan cheese, sauteed in olive oil on cappellini pasta with marinara sauce and vegetable

Cheese Tortellini .... $ 8.95
Pasta filled with ricotta cheese topped with tomato garden sauce

Grilled Lobster $19.95
Succulent 8 oz. lobster tail served with drawn butter

Grilled Mahi Mahi $13.95
Grilled ocean white fish topped with herbed butter

Seafood Newburg $12.95
Shrimp, scallops, and crabmeat in cream sauce flovored with Pernod and served in delicate crepes

Roast Loin of Pork $11.95
Medaillions of tender pork served with creole mustard sauce

À la Carte

Soup du Jour .... bowl $3.95, cup $2.95
Grilled Chicken Caesar Salad ... $7.95
Greek Salad ... large $6.95, small $4.95
Cottage Inn Pâté $4.95
Pasta Primavera $6.95
Crab Louie $7.95
Garden Salad $2.95
Spanakopita $4.95

Desserts made fresh daily 50¢

A Springtime Dinner at Dairy Hollow, prix fixe $25.95

Salad of Tender Spinach,
with our own curried vinaigrette

1 of 2 soups of the night

Potage Barcelona: a Spanish-style spinach and split-pea soup

Pumpkin-Tomato Bisque (as featured on "Good Morning, America")

A basketful of homemade-from-scratch breads:
Our daily bread,
skillet-sizzled buttermilk cornbread with butter,
our own blue-ribbon-winning inn-made preserves

Choice of Entree

Game Hen Casablanca
A whole 22-ounce roast Cornish hen with a stuffing of oranges, olives, bay leaves, and dates, with a port-laced orange-and-honey glaze, served with cinnamon cous-cous

Wine-braised "Carpetbagger" Pork Chops
A thick, pocketed center-cut chop, stuffed with local smoked ham, bacon, and shiitake mushrooms and herbs, browned, then braised with onions in red wine

Beef Bistro Style (Add $3.95):
Tenderloin pan-sauteed steak with peppercorns, flamed in cognac, and finished with a pan sauce of beef stock, raisins, and a touch of dijon mustard and cream

Catfish Catalan
Our own locally raised catfish baked in a lusty wine-and-herb enriched tomato/sundried tomato sauce, with a crisp almond finish, Spanish country style

Mushrooms Stroganov
Sauteed domestic and shiitake mushrooms with onions, garlic, red and green peppers in a rich sauce of vegetable stock and our cream with plenty of fresh-ground black pepper and fresh nutmeg; served over rice

DeVito's of Eureka Springs

Appetizers

Toasted Ravioli **$3.95**
(7) cheese-stuffed pasta squares with our red sauce for dipping

Trout Fingers **$5.95**
Boneless strips of trout with a seasoned cornmeal coating served with smoky dill sauce

Calamari Rings **$4.95**
Tasty rings of squid with an Italian seasoned coating served with red sauce

Fried Cheese Sticks **$3.95**
(6) Mozzarella cheese sticks with an Italian season coating, served with red sauce

Antipasto Tray **$6.95**
Genoa salami, provolone cheese, olives, calamari, pepperoni, etc.

Fritto Misto **$4.95**
Zucchini slices, baby carrots, cheese-dipped broccoli florets, battered then fried, served with sauce for dipping

Pasta

Made with 100% durum semolina wheat

Our spaghetti sauce, meatballs, Italian sausage and bread are made by hand, using DeVito family recipes. Dinners are served with a mixed green salad and fresh bread

Spaghetti (angel hair)
- **with sauce** **$6.95**
- **extra sauce** **$1.50**
- **with meat sauce** **$7.95**
- **extra meatballs (2)** **$1.50**
- **with meatballs** **$7.95**
- **extra sausage** **$2.50**
- **with Italian sausage** **$8.50**
- **extra plate** **$3.00**

Ravioli Dinner **$10.95**
(5) Large handmade pasta squares stuffed with chicken, spinach, and two Italian cheeses

DeVito's Combo **$11.95**
Spaghetti and ravioli served with Italian sausage and meatball

Fettuccini DeVito **$10.95**
Fresh pressed garlic and pimento stuffed olives sauteed in virgin olive oil finished with cream and parmesan cheese, served over fettuccine noodles

Pasta Primavera **$9.95**
Broccoli, cauliflower, and carrots in creamy white sauce, served over fettuccini noodles

Grilled Primavera **$10.95**
Chargrilled broccoli florets, cauliflower florets, and baby carrots, sauteed with fresh garlic in virgin olive oil, served over fettuccini noodles

Shrimp Alfredo **$11.95**
Shrimp sauteed in butter with cream and parmesan cheese, served over fettuccini noodles

Seafood Fettuccini **$12.95**
Shrimp, crab, and broccoli in a creamy white sauce, served over fettuccini noodles

Shrimp Scampi **$13.95**
Jumbo shrimp sauteed in lemon butter, fresh pressed garlic, and white wine on a bed of pasta

Italian Dinners

Dinners are served with a mixed green salad, vegetable, fresh bread, and choice of baked potato or spaghetti

Chicken Parmesan **$11.95**
Parmesan-coated chicken breast filets topped with red sauce and mozzarella cheese

Chicken Bolognese **$13.95**
Sauteed chicken breast filets with prosciutto ham and provolone cheese broiled then topped with a marsala wine sauce

Veal Piccata **$14.95**
Veal slices sauteed in butter with lemon, capers, and white wine

Veal Bolognese **$15.95**
Sauteed veal with prosciutto ham and provolone cheese broiled then topped with a marsala wine sauce

Trout Italiano **$14.95**
Boneless butterflied trout sauteed in olive oil and garlic, topped with sauteed sweet peppers, capers, and lemon

Broiled Trout Parmesan **$12.95**
Boneless butterflied trout topped with a light white sauce and parmesan cheese

Trout Pataté **$12.95**
Boneless butterflied trout topped with garlic potatoes, broiled to a golden brown crunch

From the Grill

Chargilled over an open flame

Chargrilled Trout **$22.95**
Boneless butterflied trout with the chef's special seasoning

Lemon Trout **$11.95**
Boneless butterflied trout chargrilled with a lemon-herb seasoning

Chargrilled Chicken Breast **$10.95**
Boneless, skinless breast filets chargrilled with the chef's special seasoning

New York Strip **$13.95**
12 oz., USDA choice Angus

Filet Mignon **$14.95**
8 oz. USDA Choice Angus

Ermilio's Italian Home Cooking

Appetizers

Stuffed Mushrooms $4.75
Grilled Eggplant $4.50
Gorgonzola Bread Rounds......... $4.50
Pesto Bread Rounds $5.00
Roasted Peppers $5.00

Salads

House Salad $2.75
Vegetarian Chef Salad $4.95
Grilled Chicken Breast Salad $6.50

Homemade salad dressings: House (Italian vinaigrette), "Too blue for you" (thick and chunky blue cheese), Pesto (fresh basil and garlic vinaigrette)

Sandwiches

Sausage $5.25
Chicken Breast $6.25
Meatball $5.25

Ermilio's Sauces and Pastas

First choose your favorite sauce. . .

Mom's Homemade Meatballs with Meat Sauce **$8.50**
100% lean ground beef, hand-rolled and seasoned with Mom's favorite Italian herbs and spices; simmered in her rich, flavorful sauce. This is a family tradition!

Arlene's Chicken Sauce **$8.75**
A peasant-style (bone-in) skinless chicken breast baked in herbs, then simmered until tender in Arlene Ermilio's mild and tasty red chicken sauce

Italian Sausage **$8.50**
A link of sweet and spicy Italian sausage covered with Mom's red sauce. This is Uncle Sal's favorite!

Tomato Basil **$8.50**
Aunt Millie's own combination of fresh whole-leaf basil, ripe tomatoes, and a subtle blend of herbs. A light, tasty marinara

Pesto **$8.95**
A robust combination of basil, garlic, pine nuts, parmesan and romano cheeses blended in virgin olive oil. This is Aunt Jessie's favorite!

Primavera **$8.75**
Assorted fresh vegetables sauteed in garlic, virgin olive oil and our own medley of seasonings. Combined with vegetable broth, this is a light, healthy dish

Gorgonzola Cheese Sauce $8.95
Chunky, creamy sauce made with tangy aged Italian blue cheese softened in hot olive oil with garlic and a touch of cream

Garlic and Olive Oil $7.50
Plain and simple, garnished with parsley. Delicious on any pasta

Alfredo Sauce $8.95
King of cream sauces! Butter, heavy cream and parmesan cheese make the base for this rich northern Italian classic

Clam Sauce $9.95
A true Yankee clam sauce. Chopped clams simmered in a light, flavorful broth of olive oil, clam juice, garlic, and Aunt Mary's favorite seasonings

Now pick the perfect pasta (our pasta is made from 100% durum semolina wheat)

Spaghetti—traditional round pasta
Linguini—narrow, flat ribbons
Fettucini—wide, flat noodles
Spinach fettucini—a green variety noodle
Mostaccioli—large, ribbed macaroni tubes
Gnocchi—small potato pasta dumplings
Ravioli—ricotta-stuffed rounds (add $1.50 to price of any sauce)
Cheese-filled tortellini—tricolored ricotta-stuffed pasta rings ($8.95 with any sauce choice)

All pasta garnished with parmesan cheese and served with salad, fresh-baked bread, and roasted garlic

Half portions available for children 12 and under

The Oasis

The Original Ark-Mex Cuisine

Specialties

Mexican Pizza **$5.00**
Toasted flour tortilla topped with beans, cheese, onion, enchilada sauce, jalapenos, mushrooms, tomato, salad, sour cream & salsa

Frito Pies
Baked corn tortilla, layered with beans, cheese, chips, onions, jalapenos, mushrooms, tomato, and salad
vegetable **$4.75**
chicken **$5.75**

Chicken Melt **$5.00**
Sauteed chicken on toasted whole wheat bread, topped with Monterey Jack cheese served open-faced with chips and salad

Vegetable Fajita **$2.50**
Flour tortilla, tofu, spinach, cheese, and side salad

Nachos

Super Nachos **$5.00**
Cheese and Jalapeno **$3.30**
Bean, Cheese, Jalapeno **$3.95**
Spinach and Tomato **$4.25**
Add chicken **$1.25**

Food for Kids

Soft bean and Cheese Taco **$1.00**
Enchilada Plate **$2.50**
Cheese Melt **$1.00**
Chicken and Cheese Melt **$2.25**
Bean and Cheese Burrito **$1.75**
Cheese Nachos **$1.75**
Peanut Butter and Jelly **$1.00**

Enchilada Plates

Two enchiladas rolled to order. Served with refried beans, salad, chips, sour cream, and salsa. Create your own combo!

Cheese **$4.25**
Cheese and Onion **$4.25**
Cheese and Fresh Garlic **$4.25**
Cheese, Mushroom, and Onion **$4.50**
Seafood—available .... **market price**
Chicken **$4.75**
Chcken and Mushroom **$5.00**
Spinach and Mushroom **$4.75**
Cracked Wheat and Mushroom **$4.75**
Eggplant **$4.75**
Tofu **$4.75**

Soft Tacos

Corn tortilla filled with cheese, lettuce, tomato, onion, and salsa

Bean **$1.50**
Chicken **$1.85**
Chicken and Bean **$2.00**
Seafood—when available **$2.50**
Vegetable **$1.50**
Potato **$1.50**
Tofu **$1.50**

Our Famous Burritos

Served on a whole wheat flour tortilla, with sour cream and our fresh salsa

Jacquito
served with beans,
cheese, and salad **$3.25**
without salad **$2.75**

Cheese and Jalapeno **$2.65**

Chicken **$4.45**
sauteed chicken, beans, cheese, salad

Spinach and Mushroom **$4.25**

Word of Mouth Burrito **$4.25**
tofu, cracked wheat, spinach, mushrooms, with or without cheese

Cracked Wheat Deluxe **$4.25**
cracked wheat, beans, mushrooms, cheese and salad

Cheese and Tomato **$2.65**

Spring Street Burrito **$4.85**
sauteed chicken, beans, spinach, cheese, and salad

Cheese and Mushroom **$2.95**

Brunch

Served any time of day

The real deal! Deluxe
Huevos Rancheros **$5.00**
2 eggs on a flour tortilla, refried beans, cheese, jalapenos, lettuce, tomatoes, onions, sour cream and our fresh salsa

House Huevos Rancheros **$4.00**
1 egg on a corn tortilla, refried beans, cheese, jalapenos, lettuce, tomatoes, onions, sour cream, and salsa

Vegetable Huevos Rancheros **$4.00**
1 flour or corn tortilla, tofu, spinach, refried beans, jalapenos, lettuce, tomatoes, onions, and salsa

2 Egg and Cheese Burrito **$3.50**
with salad, sour cream, and salsa

2 Egg, Potatoes
and Cheese Burrito **$3.75**
with salad, sour cream, and salsa

Potato and Cheese Burrito
with salad, sour cream,
and salsa **$2.50**
without salad **$2.00**

2 eggs any style **$3.50**
with potato and toast

Omelet of the Day **$4.50**
with potato and toast

Breakfast Taco **$2.00**
1 egg, corn tortilla, lettuce, tomato, onion and salsa

Toasted Bagel
with butter **$1.25**
with cream cheese **$1.50**

New York Bagel **$1.75**
with cream cheese, tomato, and onion

Toast .... **75¢**

Non-dairy or special dietary needs prepared upon request

Plaza Restaurant

Hors d'oeuvres

Pate **$7.50**

Vol-au-Vent **$6.95**
French pastry shell filled with medley of crabmeat, shrimp and mushrooms

Shrimp Cocktail **$5.95**

Cheeseboard **$6.95**

Escargots **$6.95**

Baked French Brie Cheese **$6.95**

Pan-fried crab cakes **$6.95**

Soups and Salads

Soup du Jour
cup **$2.50**
bowl **$3.95**

French Onion Soup
cup **$2.50**
bowl **$3.95**

Salad **$1.95**

Caesar Salad **$3.95**

Caesar Salad with Grilled Breast of Chicken **$7.95**

Entrees

Filet Mignon **$16.95**
"The best steak in Arkansas" *Arkansas Times Magazine*
Choice beef tenderloin sauteed in olive oil and served with a fresh mushroom red-wine sauce

Beef Wellington **$19.95**
Our famous filet wrapped in a flaky pastry, served with a Burgundy sauce

Broiled 10 oz. Lobster Tail **$25.95**
Broiled lobster served with hot drawn butter and fresh lemon

Steamed Alaskan King Crab Legs and Claws **$23.95**
One full pound, served with drawn butter and fresh lemon

Sauteed Veal Tenderloin **$15.95**
With tarragon sherry cream sauce

Boneless roasted breast of duck **$15.95**
Served with orange Grand Marnier and fresh ginger sauce

Shrimp Scampi **$15.95**
Tender shrimp sauteed with fresh garlic and lemon

Grilled Pacific Mahi Mahi Filet **$12.95**
With drawn butter and fresh lemon

Sauteed Scallops **$16.95**
Large, tender scallops in ginger, lemon, and sherry sauce

Boneless Breast of Chicken $10.95
With mushroom, lemon, and vermouth sauce

Sauteed Boneless Pork Tenderloin $10.95
With pink peppercorn pinot noir sauce

Baked Orange Roughy $11.95
With fresh lemon butter

Linguini Pasta with Sauteed Fresh Vegetables $9.95

All our entrees are served with herbed rice, vegetable of the day, and our fresh-baked French breads

Full bar and wine list

Desserts

Creme Caramel $2.95

French Silk Pie $2.95

Fresh-made Cheesecake $3.25

On parties of 5 or more or separate checks, 15% gratuity will be included

SIGHTS, ATTRACTIONS, AND OTHER THINGS TO DO

Apart from strolling and shopping along the loop, which here is an activity of sheer delight; apart from visiting museums of the most idiosyncratic—and therefore fascinating—sort (bells, buttons, dolls, model trains, frogs, Bibles, and antiques) and legions of art galleries; and apart from taking a train excursion, going underground to a subterranean river, breathing the perfumed air of a major botanical garden—most visitors will be going to what's called *The Great Passion Play* at the giant, 4,000-seat amphitheater cut into a nearby mountainside. It draws close to 400,000 visitors each year to this portion of the Ozarks (including tour buses that couple the attraction with those of Branson), and has become the center of a major complex of other sights (a wood-carving gallery, a reproduction of Moses' Tabernacle in the Wilderness, replicas of Jesus' tomb, life-sized reproductions of the Last Supper and the Nativity, a Church in the Grove, the "New Holy Land," the Sacred Arts Center, Bible Museum, a 10-foot section of the Berlin Wall, gift shops, a 400-foot buffet restaurant—and last but not least, the Gerald L. K. Smith Memorial Chapel).

The Great Passion Play of Eureka Springs is said to be the most popular outdoor drama in America. It is a testament, among other things, to the commercial skills of its founder, Gerald L. K. Smith, whose heirs still control the play. Having amassed a fortune from the systematic propagation of hate, he either created this attraction by way of atoning for his sins, as some think, or to continue propagating his own violent views about Jews, as others think. To reach your own conclusions, you'll need to know something about him.

Gerald L. K. Smith was born in 1898, the son of a Wisconsin minister, and was himself ordained at the age of 18. After attending several colleges in Indiana, where he was a prominent member of the Ku Klux Klan, he was appointed minister of a church in Louisiana, but was soon forced from that position by his parishioners. After briefly flirting with William Dudley Pelley's Silver Shirt Movement, a paramilitary, Nazi-like organization whose members dressed in the regalia of storm troopers, Smith became the chief assistant to Huey Long, then the powerful governor of Louisiana.

After Long's assassination, he helped form and lead a political third party to participate in the presidential elections of 1936 "to duplicate," as he stated in a report appearing in the *New York Times* for September 22, 1935, "the feat of Adolph Hitler in Germany."

Smith became violently racist. Even I, a child in the 1930s, remember his fearful, blood-chilling taunts that were widely reported. He continually referred to the black population as a "child race," maintained a constant drumbeat of loud, shouted attacks on Jews, referred to "Jewish bolsheviks," claimed it was blasphemy to refer to Jesus as a Jew, began one of his columns with the words "Speaking of Jewish tyranny." In his weekly newspaper, *The Cross and the Flag*, in the period immediately after Pearl Harbor, Smith called the war against Hitler and Tojo "unnecessary," a conflict instigated by "power-mad internationalists operating under the direction of international Jewry."

In 1948, Smith accused General Dwight D. Eisenhower of being a Jew, and headed a "Stop-Ike-the-Kike" movement prior to the presidential primaries of that year. He renewed that effort in 1952, when Eisenhower won the Republican nomination for president, and also circulated charts at that time claiming that the late Franklin Roosevelt had been descended from Jews.

As Smith's tirades against blacks and Jews increased, his income soared, especially after he moved *The Cross and the Flag* to headquarters near his wealthy supporters in Los Angeles. (On July 22, 1966, p. 23, *Time* pointed out how Smith, ironically, had made "a career and a fortune" from bigotry.) And then, in 1964, he purchased Penn Castle (a massive Victorian mansion) in Eureka, made it his home, and announced he would build a seven-story statue of Jesus on the 1,500-foot-high Magnetic Mountain of Eureka Springs. The statue, he later admitted, was a prelude to an eventual outdoor theater for a passion play that might make Eureka Springs into "the Oberammergau of America" (referring to the village in Bavaria, Germany, where a notoriously anti-Semitic passion play had been performed during the Hitler era).

Alone among the local media, only the Little Rock, Arkansas, *Gazette* drew attention to the curious coincidence of the nation's leading anti-Semite deciding to create a passion play, which historically and for centuries had been used as a vehicle for anti-Semitism. "We were never surprised," it wrote (July 14, 1966), "by Mr. Smith's having the nerve to try it. We were surprised, frankly, by Eureka's falling for it, and suppose that, in the end, it was local boosterism that was largely responsible. It has occurred to us before that the local booster spirit in America is such that some Chambers of Commerce would jump at landing the annual reunion of Sepp Dietrich's old Waffen SS outfit if it meant a little something in the till."

For additional background on the life and works of the late Gerald L. K. Smith, you may want to consult *Demagogues in the Depression* by David H. Bennett (Rutgers University Press, New Brunswick, NJ, 1969; found in most large public libraries), *Gerald L. K. Smith: Minister of Hate,* by Glen Jeansonne (Yale University Press, New Haven, CT, 1988), "U.S. Journal" by Calvin Trillin, *The New Yorker* (July 26, 1969), "A Monument to Himself," *Time* (July 22, 1966), to all of which I am indebted for many of the references in this chapter. And for a defense of Smith by Smith's family and chief associate, see *Besieged Patriot: Autobiographical Episodes Exposing Communism, Traitorism and Zionism,* from the *Life of Gerald L. K. Smith,* edited by Elna Smith and Charles Robertson (Elna M. Smith Foundation, Eureka Springs, AR, 1978).

The Passion Play Today

I find it difficult to report with calm objectivity on Eureka Springs' *Great Passion Play* (P.O. Box 471, Eureka Springs, AR 72632-0471, phone 800/882-PLAY or 501/253-9200; D, MC, V), which continues to be controlled by Smith's family. And yet the play is, from all accounts, a superb spectacle, presented with great professionalism and impact. It has clearly become a part of the culture of the South and Midwest, and audiences—many of them with tears rolling down their faces—are obviously moved by this portrayal of Jesus' last days on earth. Most Americans will find it a worthy or important attraction. I would point out only that the National Conference of Catholic Bishops has set several guidelines for the presentation of passion plays in a way that avoids their becoming vehicles for anti-Semitism. According to some observers, the passion play presented by the late Gerald L. K. Smith and his family violates every one of those recommendations.

As for the practical details: The season runs from late April to late October, nightly except Monday and Thursday, and curtain time is 8:30pm until Labor Day, and thereafter at 7:30pm. The grounds themselves open at 8:30am, Sunday at 1pm, for visits to the many exhibits, displays, gift shops, and chapel. Seats to the two-hour play cost $10.50, $11.50, and $12.50, with children 4 to 11 admitted at half price; a buffet restaurant serves lunch from 11:30am to 2pm, and dinner from 4:30pm until a half hour before the play begins. Rainouts average only twice yearly. On stage, a complete, 400-foot-long street of ancient Jerusalem has been re-created, with real buildings, horses, donkeys, doves, sheep, and camels. And, of course, you find the 4,000-seat amphitheater by simply driving in the direction of the seven-story Christ of the Ozarks statue, which can be seen from almost anywhere in Eureka Springs.

Eureka's Country Music Shows

The other thing you do at night in Eureka Springs (apart from lingering over a fine meal) is attend a country music show, of which there are three major ones (by Eureka Springs standards, not to be compared with the massive and modern celebrity theaters of Branson). Eureka's country music shows started around the same time as *The Great Passion Play* in 1968, and are given a tiny bit of credit for reviving Eureka Springs.

By common acknowledgment of nearly everyone, the best of the shows is the first one to have opened, in the mid-'60s, the **Pine Mountain Jamboree** (Highway 62 East, Route 1, Box 283, Eureka Springs, AR 72632, phone 501/253-9156), consisting of a dozen performers in red jackets or all-black cowboy costumes who run the entire country gamut and repertoire, from traditional country, bluegrass, and gospel to pop and Cajun, with comedy thrown in. The Drennon family—father Dave, son, and son-in-law—lead the ensemble, in a show strongly similar to the Presleys and Baldknobbers in Branson (down to a comic with long tie, overalls, and funny felt hat); the Drennon women act as ushers and sell t-shirts in the lobby. The show plays nightly except Sunday from April through October, starting each night at 8pm, and tickets sell for $12 to adults, $5 to children 3 to 11.

Pine Mountain Jamboree was followed out on the highway, 13 years ago, by the **Ozark Mountain Hoe-Down** (Highway 62 East, Route 1, Box 457, Eureka Springs, AR 72632, phone 501/253-7725): nine musicians who are also, predictably, "Branson," and who perform in a barnlike theater of corrugated metal brightly illuminated by neon. Standouts of the show are the four-part harmony of the Kings River Boys and the comedy of a madcap janitor character called Tator "Chip" Patches. He's acrobatic and wild-eyed and cracks up the band as much as the audience. Showtime is 8pm daily except Tuesday, April through mid-November, with shows on weekends in off-season; and ticket prices are $12.50 for adults, an odd $5.34 for children 12 and under.

But my own personal favorite is the newest and poorest in facilities, a show that plays in the plainest, least pretentious, cinderblock hall of recent memory, in which the lighting is primitive, and the staging is nothing to write home about either. Yet one of the "tightest" music shows in either Branson or Eureka Springs is that of the **Swannee River Boys** appearing at the Gem of the Ozarks Theater (Highway 62 East, next door to McDonald's, phone 501/253-6011). (They may not know how to spell Suwannee, but this ain't Goo Goo Bar music). It's only their third season. But they've picked up a hard-driving country guitarist from down Maine who bites off his notes tough as a machine hammering nails in board. He's just a thin young kid in a big-brimmed cowboy hat, but he drives this band like a locomotive. His rushing style leads the Swannee River Boys' country standards with urgency. You're never sure at the intro of each whether the music is about to break through to Duane Allman or smooth out into modern, hip country à la Lyle Lovett. Sure the Boys do such flimsy preaching as "I Believe If It's Good Enough for Jesus It Oughta Be Good Enough for Uncle Sam." But they also let the kid take on one or two of his own folk ballads, and you won't hear the likes at any country show anyplace else in these Ozark music halls. Comedy in this show seems to interrupt the music, though the dunce-type female does get off a funny line when she tells about Scum Pond, Arkansas, where she's from, and where the biggest industry was a 400-pound Avon lady. Otherwise go for the music. Tops. Performances are at 8pm, Tuesday through Saturday, with another group appearing at 2pm and 8pm on Sunday and Monday, April through October. Ticket prices: $12.50 for adults, $11.50 for seniors 55 and older, $5.50 for children 7 to 16, nothing for children under 7.

Eureka's Other Main Attractions

Back in the daylight hours, you owe yourself a mind-cleansing interlude at the newly opened (since 1993) botanical gardens of Eureka Springs, whose access roads give you a superb vista of valley farms and their embracing hills, almost as much of a balm as the gardens themselves. (And there are all-you-can-eat catfish restaurants along these and neighboring roads that step their way down terraced hillsides to bridges across rushing streams.)

Eureka Springs Gardens

The gardens surround Blue Springs, which is northwest Arkansas' heaviest volume springs, a flow of 38 million gallons every 24 hours. Native Americans once regarded these waters as having healing powers, and when white settlers arrived, they immediately made them into a tourist attraction, with both a mill and a guest-accepting inn erected alongside. The exact location is a 33-acre site of year-round blooming plants and flowers, about 4 miles west of Eureka Springs off Highway 62, and then a mile and a half along Eureka Springs Garden Road (Route 2, Box 362, Eureka Springs, AR 72632, phone 501/253-9244, open year-round from 9am to 6pm; from 9am to 5pm in November through March, for an admission charge of $6.90 for adults, $4.25 for children 12 to 17, $2.13 for children 5 to 11).

Its focal point: a display of red-and-pink shrub roses in raised planters around the spring. More than 30,000 annuals and 8,000 perennials were planted in the first phase of the area's development, and an additional 15,000 bulbs began blooming in the spring of 1994. In 1995, the site will debut a Japanese garden and a separate garden for weddings. The flowers peak in their color from April through October, though the gardens can be visited and enjoyed throughout the year.

Other attractions here include a multimedia presentation entitled *The Way We Were,* which presents the early history of Eureka Springs (slides of historic photographs, artists' renderings, and contemporary images; showings take place hourly and last 20 minutes). Near the entrance: a hand-carved, native-limestone sculpture of President Bill Clinton standing near a garden of some of the favorite flowers of Hillary Rodham Clinton. Visitors stroll the gardens along a gently sloping, barrier-free boardwalk, intermittently using 107 stone and wooden benches. Typically, visitors spend up to an hour and a half there, and briefly step into a gift shop adjoining the entrance.

(Incidentally, the Museum of the Early 1900s is passed when you head back from here to town. It wasn't open when I last visited the gardens, but might be worth your visit.)

Thorncrown Chapel

An exceptionally graceful chapel of wood and glass in a forest just shy of halfway to Eureka Springs Gardens from downtown Eureka, on West Highway 62; the exact address is Route 6, Box 140, Eureka Springs, AR 72632, phone 501/253-7401. It rises in a grand lattice construction beneath giant eaves and suggests an abstract pastor of sheltering embrace; it conveys—to my eye—a peaceful, spiritual integrity. Although the chapel is approached from, unfortunately, a large paved parking area designed to accommodate tour buses, the site is at least free of commercial intrusion, such as troubles the grounds of *The Great Passion Play.*

The chapel's architect, E. Fay Jones of nearby Fayetteville, Arkansas, was awarded the American Institute of Architects Gold Medal for this work, in 1990. It is said to receive more than 2 million visitors a year, despite being open only from June through October, daily from 9am to 6pm. Admission is free, donation requested. After your visit, you might consider driving over to Lake Leatherwood just west of the chapel, which can be approached along a rough road 1.7 miles north off Highway 62; it, too, offers lovely views without commercial distractions.

The Eureka Springs and North Arkansas Railway

Leaving from a restored downtown depot (just north of where Main Street cuts off from Spring Street), six times a day from April through October, 10am to 4pm, the charming, old-fashioned, steam-engine train takes you through gently graded forest alongside an old country road, for about 4 miles out and then back, a popular, one-hour ride with live entertainment costing $8 for adults, $4 for children 4 to 11, free for children under 4. There's even a dining car serving lavish meals for $13.95 (including the ride, and not in addition to it) per adult, $7.95 for children up to 8. Phone 501/253-9623 for any further explanations or details.

... And That Wonderful Trolley

Here, now, is the best way to get around Eureka—not only through the historic district, but even around the upper town along Highway 62 to both east and west. The ride is convenient and scenic and recalls how Eurekans got around their streets a hundred years ago, though in those days the trolley ran on rails and was electrically driven (earlier, for eight years starting in 1891, it was pulled by a mule).

Today's trolley is diesel-powered, and for $1 carries passengers around a variety of routes that range west as far as the Razorback Observation Tower (100 feet high, with gift shop), but unfortunately shy of Thorncrown Chapel (you can walk to the chapel from the trolley stop in 15 minutes, but the last several hundred feet are up a hill). To the east the trolley goes 8 miles round-trip to *The Christ of the Ozarks* statue. The best scenic ride is along the 5-mile historic loop through the old town. The trolleys run on fixed schedules along each of their six routes and stop at some 80 sites frequently throughout the day. Most lodgings and restaurants are directly served by it. Fare is $1 for a single round-trip or $3.50 for a day's unlimited travel. Tickets are on sale at most lodgings, at many shops, at terminals at the Chamber of Commerce, and at the trolley depot in the historic district. Fares can also be paid upon boarding, but only with exact change.

But bear in mind: trolleys operate only from April through October, on the following schedules: April through May 26, from 9am to 5pm on weekdays, until 8 p.m. on Friday and Saturday. From May 27 to September 5, service is from 9am to 8pm every day. From September 6 through October, 9am to 5pm on weekdays, and 9am to 8pm on Friday and Saturday. Sunday service is offered only from May 27 through Labor Day.

Miscellanies of Eureka Springs

Like so many other tourist towns, Eureka Springs schedules a batch of *festivals* throughout the year, mostly to attract tourism during slow periods. One of the best of these annual events is the early June **Blues Festival**, which in 1994 featured John Mayall, among others. Contact either the Chamber of Commerce (800/6-EUREKA or 501/253-8737) or the Arkansas Department of Parks and Tourism (501/682-7777) for the dates and details of all of them.

Best of the *arts and crafts* outlets, in my experience, is the **Arkansas Craft Galleries** (33 Spring Street, phone 501/253-7072), displaying works by more than 300 members of the Arkansas Craft Guild. On sale are jewelry, leatherwork, needlework, pottery, quilts, toys, wood carvings, wood furniture, baskets, dolls, dried flowers, items of glass and iron. The guild schedules an especially important annual show and sale the third weekend in October at the Four Runners Inn, across from the entrance to *The Great Passion Play* (the trolley stops at the front door). Admission is free.

In addition to visiting historic bed-and-breakfast houses (all available for a quick peek), lovers of Victorian homes can visit several home showcases, most prominently: the **Rosalie House** at 282 Spring Street, phone 501/253-7377 (in the historic district) and the **Queen Anne Mansion** on Highway 62 West, phone 501/253-8825 (which was built in Carthage, Missouri, and then moved here). But far more numerous are the Victorian B&Bs. They're a treat, and you can ride the trolley to dozens, all on a single fare on any given day, or you can combine trolley rides with walks, as suits you.

Also not to be missed, and just at the entrance to the historic town, is the **Historical Museum** (95. S. Main Street, phone 501/253-9417), displaying a highly absorbing collection of Eureka memorabilia, from official documents and home furnishings to artifacts from the great bank robbery of 1922. **Harp's Grocery Store** (63 N. Main Street, phone 501/253-8717) dates from 1895, and is still open downtown. It's run today by old-timer Albert Harp, whose wife recently died after they'd been married some 70-plus years. There's still an old pot-bellied stove in the back. Harp sells bread, mixed beans, antique coin-banks, some sad-looking produce, and soft drinks. People love to come in, look around, and talk with him. **Hatchet Hall** was the last home of axe-wielding temperance leader Carrie Nation. It's on Steele Street, just next to Primrose Place (which is one of the B&Bs I've described in my discussion of Eureka Springs lodgings).

Cosmic Cavern (18 miles east of Eureka on Highway 21, north of Berryville, phone 501/749-2298) and **Onyx Cave** (3 miles east of Eureka on Highway 92, phone 501/253-9321) are the area's two outstanding cave attractions.

Parking in Eureka

This is a killer. One sign says that cars improperly parked will have their tires deflated. Another, warning about unauthorized parking, says "Guests Only. All others, $50 a minute." Another: "If you dare park, 0–10 minutes, $20; 11–20 minutes, $50; 21–60 minutes, $100." Park anywhere on a street where you're not supposed to, and you'll be instantly ticketed. But you can park for only $3 for 4 hours next to where the trolley parks downtown in the historic district; and from there, you can walk all around the main retailing area.

12

The Future of Branson

Can the Country Music Capital Maintain Its Current Pace?

Branson continues to grow. Its nearly 20,000 hotel and motel rooms are figured to reach 25,000 in a short while, comparing respectably to the 70,000-some-odd rooms that Las Vegas and Orlando each required 30 years to build.

New attractions. New and ever-larger shopping malls. Sprawling condominium developments and tracts of retirement homes. For some notion of the scope of developers' plans, you'll want to scan the descriptions of projects that have passed the planning stage and are already in construction or about to begin:

- ***Heartland America,*** combining 725 hotel rooms, a 450,000-square-foot shopping mall, six restaurants, a new 3,300-seat theater along with the existing, 2,000-seat Presley Jubilee Theater, an office complex, and a theme park that its promoters compare to one of Disney's. Hyped attractions include finds from the vault of Al Capone and treasures reportedly from the Bermuda Triangle.
- ***Sportopia,*** opening as part of the Branson Meadows complex of three new music theaters, several hotels and restaurants, 70 acres of condominiums, and Factory Stores of America retailing, will provide "virtual reality experiences," according to its planners, "for people who are really into sports." Forty million dollars is the cost of creating Sportopia, wholly apart from the impressive real estate it adjoins.

- ***Branson Hills,*** with 1,000 acres scheduled for development into homes for 4,500 people in addition to apartments and condominiums, at least two golf courses, and Branson Hills Factory Stores discount retailing. The area was annexed by tax-dollar-hungry Branson even before a first spade of dirt was turned, thus increasing the area size of the city by a fifth.
- ***Tanger Factory Outlets,*** largest of the nation's discount outlet chains. Its immense building is already easily seen from the Strip and will be fully completed by spring of 1995.
- ***Dolly Parton's Stampede,*** an immense new dinner theater backed by the famed country star, and consisting of a form of rodeo—scores of horses, dozens of cowboys—performed while you dine.

These are apart from the new motels and restaurants for which acres of concrete are being laid, even as I write this book.

Will a continued growth of visitors to Branson sustain these developments? Or will the tourist figures level off, even decline, leaving empty steel skeletons and bankrupt motels? Most observers of tourism remain optimistic, but I suggest that two concerns should occupy their attention. One is the possibility that large numbers of the public may react poorly to Branson's continued despoiling of its environment; the other is the equally strong chance that Branson will find it has overly limited its audience to members of a narrow theological and political outlook, a group incapable of providing the larger tourist numbers that Branson will now need.

Environmental Backlash

Apart from frantically building additional bypass roads all up and down the nearby hills, the officials of Branson do not appear to be taking any other really fundamental steps to channel and regulate the continued growth of Branson, in the hope of making it more aesthetic, more consistent with the area's heritage and appearance.

The ideology of Branson—which relies on market forces to solve all problems—would seem firmly opposed to any serious planning for the city's future. And thus, in their free-for-all to get rich, developers and tourism promoters continue, without hindrance, to scrape bare the Ozark hills that first attracted visitors, and to "clear-cut" immense spaces among the once-glorious forests that so enchanted *The Shepherd of the Hills.* As astonishing as it may seem, the county in which Branson is located imposes no impact fees upon developers to compensate for the damage or burdens they have created; the city of Branson charges them only for the building of sewers.

Has there been any vision at work? I asked an official. "Not really," he answered. "We're playing catch-up. It hasn't been a boom, it's been an explosion. We're still asking what 'visionary' means."

And yet vision, and a sensitive regard for the environment, are what an increasing number of modern American tourists require of the destinations that seek their patronage. They no longer find it acceptable to live in a sea of neon and t-shirt shops. For them, the preservation of environment, cultural heritage, and sensitive, sustainable growth are high on the vacation agenda; and they are no longer amused by the worst excesses of American tourism. As appealing and affordable as country entertainment may be to an older and sentiment-driven market of midwesterners, it's impossible for anyone alert to issues in the real world to come upon the Strip of Branson without exclaiming, "Oh my God!"

Political and Religious Backlash

And there is that other grave concern about Branson that other media—distinguished magazines reporting on Branson, distinguished Sunday evening television shows—have been so careful not to mention. In writing candidly about the ideological content of some Branson shows, we needn't even appeal to the tolerance that Americans have always shown for divergent religious and political views; we're talking about Branson's own self-interest.

If only for economic reasons, the future growth of Branson requires that some of its promoters cease being blindly insensitive to the feelings of large racial, religious, and political groups. There are not enough elderly fundamentalists in America to support the grandiose plans for Branson's expansion. The nation is a diverse one: It has Democrats as well as Republicans, liberals as well as conservatives; Jews, Muslims, and Confucians as well as Catholics and Protestants, blacks as well as whites. If Branson is to fill its ever-expanding hotel plant and theaters, it must cease taking an exclusionary path and practice the policies of inclusion. There is also morality behind such a change in course, but I am speaking only of economic interests here.

The Role of Tourists

We as tourists can help that large body of Branson residents who also believe in a policy of inclusion. Among other things, the joys of country music warrant that we come here and increase the diversity of Branson's visitors, lighten the atmosphere, and aid those policies of inclusion. We can, through our conversations, comments, contacts, and patronage of the more open Branson theaters, remind the city that there is a broader world out there, and one that can produce the large future audiences that Branson now needs.

The Appeal of Branson

Though it has serious negatives, Branson remains one of America's top attractions. It has something for everyone: country music and ballads of the '40s, charismatic performers in comfortable theaters, performances morning, noon, and night, low costs and classic Southern cuisine, and the distinctive culture of the Ozarks. Even the most sophisticated travelers—the kind that journey to view exotic people in faraway lands—will have an absorbing, fun-filled vacation here that will never cease to interest them at every moment. And if they like country music as well, they may find that those rhythms banish all other thoughts.

What a large and colorful mass of attractions awaits you! The nightly pageant of *The Shepherd of the Hills*. Silver Dollar City and its performing craftspeople. Jim Stafford and Shoji Tabuchi. Box Car Willie and Roy Clark. Baldknobbers and Barbara Mandrell. Barbecued ribs and country-fried steaks. Fishing and boating, music and more *music* five times a day. Those entertainments warrant your visit, and an ever-better Branson deserves our support.

Appendix: A Short History of Country Music

American country music, as we know it today, is generally believed to have developed as the result of a coming together of the musical traditions of two cultures: that of the Scotch-Irish immigrants to Appalachia in the 1700s, and that of the black slaves who lived and worked among them in the same period. Appalachia was then the western frontier of the United States, and many of the country's poorest and most desperate settlers—the Daniel Boones and others like him—traveled to its difficult hills and set down roots there. They brought with them songs from the old country about their difficult plight; at times, these seemed like lamentations, and were performed in a wailing manner, the voice swooping up and down upon a single musical phrase.

Alongside the Appalachian settlers were communities of black slaves, leading an even harsher life, whose own songs were played to the accompaniment of the banjo—an instrument whose origins are quite clearly traced to Africa. Though the two groups lived apart, they heard each other's music, and gradually fused them into a common form of melody and presentation, which became the folk music of the rural South, and was largely confined there until the advent of radio and records in the 1920s.

When fledgling radio stations in Texas, Georgia, and Tennessee began broadcasting "barn dances" with country songs in the mid-1920s, they scored an instant success, and recording companies rushed to manufacture records of the new music, of which the most successful were by a singer named Jimmie Rodgers. He is rightfully called "the father of country music." Almost simultaneously with his nationwide success, a "barn dance" program broadcast from a Nashville station changed its name to "The Grand Ole Opry," and grew dramatically in popularity over the next several years (Roy Acuff, Ernest Tubb, Eddie Arnold, Minnie Pearl, Uncle Dave Macon, Red Foley, and Chet Atkins were its early stars), bringing country to additional millions of radio sets, and changing a regional art into a music that was enjoyed nationwide.

The trend got its biggest push in June 1949, when a country singer named Hank Williams appeared on "The Grand Ole Opry" and created a sensation; some consider him to have been the greatest country singer ever. Like those before him, his themes were personal tragedy and sadness: unrequited love, loneliness and separation, poverty and hard times, jealousy and betrayal. They spoke to the inner emotions of America and catapulted country into an important position in American music.

The rest of the story will probably be known already to our readers. The 1950s saw the appearance of the Carter family, Hank Snow, Johnny Cash, Patsy Cline. In the '60s: Dolly Parton and Porter Wagoner, Loretta Lynn. In the '70s: Barbara Mandrell. And then a split. A portion of the country community began importing pop and other contemporary styles into their sound; they achieved a crossover, as the music journalists call it. Another group remained true to the original style—heavy country accents and twangs, the swooping notes, sobs in the voice. Essentially, and much simplified, the first group now operates out of Nashville and dominates both the radio and recording industries; the second group either performs in Branson, or roams the small towns of America by bus, presenting one-night stands.

As to that religious offshoot of country music known as gospel, it was a total creation of the African-American community; its origins are usually attributed to the black musician and composer Thomas A. Dorsey, the "father of gospel singing." It is all the more remarkable, therefore, that in Branson, gospel is presented solely by white performers and never by African Americans, and no Branson theater—to my knowledge—has ever used a black to present them, unless that performer is Charley Pride.

Index

Save $2.50

per ticket, for up to four members of your party,
on adult admission only, to the:

GRAND PALACE THEATER

On presentation of this coupon at the box office of the Grand Palace Theater, 2700 West Highway 76, Branson, Missouri, phone 417/334-7263 or 800/5-Palace. Discount may not be combined with any other discount offered by the Grand Palace Theater, and is not available for previously purchased tickets. Discount valid until December 31, 1996. AFGB95

Save $2

per ticket, for up to six members of your party,
on both adult and children's admission, to the:

ROY CLARK CELEBRITY THEATER

On presentation of this coupon at the box office of the Roy Clark Celebrity Theater, 3425 West Highway 76, Branson, Missouri, phone 417/334-0076. Discount may not be combined with any other discount offered by the Roy Clark Celebrity Theater. Discount valid until December 31, 1996.

Save $2

per ticket, for up to six members of your party,
on adult admission only, at the:

JIM STAFFORD THEATER

On presentation of this coupon at the box office of the Jim Stafford Theater, 3440 West Highway 76, Branson, Missouri, phone 417/335-8080. Discount may not be combined with any other discount offered by the Jim Stafford Theater. Discount valid until December 30, 1996.

ARTHUR FROMMER'S BRANSON

ARTHUR FROMMER'S BRANSON

ARTHUR FROMMER'S BRANSON

Save $2

per ticket, for up to six members of your party,
on adult admission only to the:

JOHN DAVIDSON THEATER

On presentation of this coupon at the box office of the John Davidson Theater, 3446 West Highway 76, Branson, Missouri, phone 417/334-0773. Discount may not be combined with any other discount offered by the John Davidson Theater. Discount valid until December 31, 1996.

Save $2

per ticket, for up to six members of your party,
on adult admission only, to the:

PUMP BOYS AND DINETTES THEATER

On presentation of this coupon at the box office of the Pump Boys and Dinettes Theater, Highway 165 (1/2 mile south of West Highway 76), Branson, Missouri, phone 417/336-4319. Discount may not be combined with any other discount offered by the Pump Boys and Dinettes Theater. Discount valid until December 31, 1996.

Save $2

per ticket, for up to six members of your party,
on both adult and children's admission, to the:

SHEPHERD OF THE HILLS OUTDOOR THEATER

On presentation of this coupon at the box office of the Shepherd of the Hills Outdoor Theater, 5586 West Highway 76, Branson Missouri, phone 417/334-4191. Discount may not be combined with any other discount offered by the Shepherd of the Hills Outdoor Theater. Discount valid until December 31, 1996.

ARTHUR FROMMER'S BRANSON

ARTHUR FROMMER'S BRANSON

ARTHUR FROMMER'S BRANSON

Save $2

per ticket, for up to six members of your party,
on both adult and children's admission, to the:

COUNTRY TONITE THEATER

On presentation of this coupon at the box office of the Country Tonite Theater, 3815 West Highway 76, Branson, Missouri, phone 417/334-2439. Discount may not be combined with any other discount offered by the Country Tonite Theater. Discount valid until December 31, 1996.

Save $1

per ticket, for up to six members of your party,
on adult admission only, to the:

CHARLEY PRIDE THEATER

On presentation of this coupon during the months of June, July, and August only, at the box office of the Charley Pride Theater, 755 Gretna Road, Branson, Missouri, phone 417/366-2292. Discount may not be combined with any other discount offered by the Charley Pride Theater. Discount valid until August 31, 1996.

Save $1

per ticket, for up to six members of your party,
on both adult and children's admission, to the:

BOX CAR WILLIE THEATER

On presentation of this coupon at the box office of the Box Car Willie Theater, 3454 West Highway 76, Branson, Missouri, phone 417/334-8696. Discount may not be combined with any other discount offered by the Box Car Willie Theater, and coupon must be presented prior to when the tickets in question are printed. Discount valid until December 31, 1996.

ARTHUR FROMMER'S BRANSON

ARTHUR FROMMER'S BRANSON

ARTHUR FROMMER'S BRANSON

Save $2.50

on each one-day regular admission, for up to six members of your party, to:

SILVER DOLLAR CITY

On presentation of this coupon at the Silver Dollar City ticket booth, West Highway 76 and Indian Point Road, Branson Missouri, phone 417/336-7100. Discount may not be combined with any other discount or offer by Silver Dollar City, and discount is $1.50 per person during "Old Time Country Christmas." Discount valid until December 31, 1996. AFGB95

Save $2

on each one-day regular admission, for up to six members of your party, to:

WHITE WATER

On presentation of this coupon at the White Water ticket booth, 3505 West Highway 76, Branson, Missouri, phone 417/336-7100. Discount may not be combined with any other discount or offer by White Water. Discount valid until September 6, 1996. AFGB95

Save $1.50

per person on the price of adult admission ($1 off children's admission) for up to six members of your party, at:

RIPLEY'S BELIEVE IT OR NOT!® MUSEUM

On presentation of this coupon at the box office ticket window of Ripley's Believe It or Not!® Museum, 3326 West Highway 76, Branson, Missouri, phone 417/337-5300. Discount may not be combined with any other discount or offer by Ripley's Believe It or Not!® Museum. Discount valid until December 31, 1996.

ARTHUR FROMMER'S BRANSON

ARTHUR FROMMER'S BRANSON

ARTHUR FROMMER'S BRANSON

Save $1

per person (for up to four persons in your party) off the ticket price of any departure occurring between noon and 4:30pm, of:

"RIDE THE DUCKS"

On presentation of this coupon at the "Ride the Ducks" ticket booth, West Highway 76, Branson, Missouri, phone 417/336-7100. Discount may not be combined with any other discount or offer by "Ride the Ducks." Discount valid until December 31, 1996.

Save $2

per person off the price of either a luncheon or dinner check totaling at least $10 per person, for up to six members of your party, at:

OUTBACK STEAK & OYSTER BAR

On presentation of this coupon to your waiter or cashier at Outback Steak and Oyster Bar, 1418 West Highway 76 in Branson. Discount may not be combined with any other discount offered by Outback Steak and Oyster Bar. Discount valid until December 31, 1996.

Save $1 or $2

(depending on time of day) per dinner entree, for up to six members of your party, at:

B.T. BONES STEAKHOUSE

On presentation of this coupon to your waiter or cashier at B.T. Bones Steakhouse, 2346 Shepherd of the Hills Expressway in Branson. Discount is $2 off the price of any dinner entree ordered prior to 4pm, and $1 after 4pm. Discount may not be combined with any other discount offered by B.T. Bones Steakhouse. Discount valid until December 31, 1996.

ARTHUR FROMMER'S BRANSON

ARTHUR FROMMER'S BRANSON

ARTHUR FROMMER'S BRANSON

Receive a FREE SUNDAE

at:

THE HARD LUCK DINER

in the Grand Village.

On your visit to the Grand Village on West Highway 76, adjoining the Grand Palace Theatre, present this coupon when you purchase a specialty item and receive a one-scoop sundae free. Coupon must be presented at time of purchase, and may not be combined with any other offer or discount. Coupon must be presented at time of purchase. Discount valid until December 31, 1996. AFGB95

Save 10%

on a:

TWILIGHT DINNER CRUISE ABOARD SHOWBOAT BRANSON BELLE

Present this coupon and save 10% on each twilight (8pm) dinner cruise. Discount limited to six members of your party. Reservations recommended (call 800/417-7770). Coupon must be presented at time of purchase, and may not be combined with any other offer or discount. Valid May through December, until December 31, 1996. AFGB95

Save 20%

on any purchase over $20 at:

THE GRAND VILLAGE

On your visit to the Grand Village on West Highway 76, adjoining the Grand Palace Theatre, present this coupon at any shop (excluding eateries) and save 20% on any purchase over $20. Coupon must be presented at time of purchase, and may not be combined with any other offer or discount. Discount valid until December 31, 1996. AFGB95

ARTHUR FROMMER'S BRANSON

ARTHUR FROMMER'S BRANSON

ARTHUR FROMMER'S BRANSON

ARTHUR FROMMER'S BRANSON

ARTHUR FROMMER'S BRANSON

ARTHUR FROMMER'S BRANSON

Save 10%

off any purchase of $50 or more, at the:

SPRINGMAID/WAMSUTTA FACTORY STORE

(in the Tanger Factory Outlet Center)

On presentation of this coupon to the Springmaid/Wamsutta store in the Tanger Factory Outlet Center, 300 Tanger Boulevard (off West Highway 76), Branson. Discount does not apply to sale merchandise, and may not be combined with another coupon or discount offer. Limit of one coupon per customer. Discount valid until December 31, 1996.

Save $10 or $20

at the

JONATHAN LOGAN SHOP

(in Factory Merchants Outlet Mall, Branson)

This coupon, when presented at the Jonathan Logan Shop in Factory Merchants Outlet Mall, Branson, will entitle the bearer to a discount of $10 off any purchase in the amount of $50 or more, and a discount of $20 off any purchase in the amount of $100 or more. Discount is available to only one person per coupon, and may not be combined with any other discount(s) offered by Jonathan Logan. Valid until December 31, 1996.

Save 10%

on

AMERICAN TOURISTER LUGGAGE AND PRODUCTS

(in Factory Merchants Outlet Mall, Branson)

When presented at the American Tourister shop in the Factory Merchants Mall of Branson, Missouri, at 1000 Pat Nash Drive, this coupon will entitle the bearer to receive a discount of 10% on the purchase of any regularly priced merchandise. Coupon must be presented at time of purchase, and may not be combined with any other offer of discount. Valid until December 31, 1996.

ARTHUR FROMMER'S BRANSON

ARTHUR FROMMER'S BRANSON

ARTHUR FROMMER'S BRANSON

Save 10%

on

CASUAL CORNER MERCHANDISE

(at Factory Merchants Outlet Mall in Branson)

When presented at the Casual Corner shop in the Factory Merchants Mall at 1000 Pat Nash Drive, this coupon will entitle the bearer to receive a discount of 10% on the purchase of Casual Corner's merchandise. Coupon must be presented at time of purchase, and may not be combined with any other offer, discount or coupon, nor on special promotions, super-savers, price breaks or previous purchase. Valid until December 31, 1996.

Save 15%

off the room charge for you and your party (not to exceed six persons), at the:

WELK RESORT CENTER

On presentation of this coupon at the reception desk of the Welk Resort, 1984 State Highway 165, Branson, phone 417/336-3575. Discount may not be combined with any other discount offered by the Welk Resort Hotel. Discount valid until December 31, 1996.

ARTHUR FROMMER'S BRANSON

ARTHUR FROMMER'S BRANSON